JERRY B. JENKINS

MULTNOMAH BOOKS SISTERS, OREGON

This book is a work of fiction. With the exception of recognized historical figures, the characters in this novel are fictional. Any resemblance to actual persons, living or dead, is purely coincidental.

ROOKIE

published by Multnomah Books
a part of the Questar publishing family

and published in association with the literary agency of Alive Communications, Inc., 1465 Kelly Johnson Boulevard, Suite 320, Colorado Springs, Colorado 80920

Edited by Rodney L. Morris
Cover design by Kevin Keller
Cover illustration by Martin French
Lettering by Tim Clark

International Standard Book Number: 1-57673-045-X

Printed in the United States of America.

For information:
Questar Publishers, Inc.
Post Office Box 1720
Sisters, Oregon 97759

Library of Congress Cataloging-in-Publication Data
Jenkins, Jerry B. Rookie/by Jerry B. Jenkins.
p.cm. ISBN 1-57673-045-X (alk. paper) I. Title.
PS3560.E485R6 1008b 06-50946
813'.054--dc21 CIP

97 98 99 00 01 02 03 04 05 06 — 10 9 8 7 6 5 4 3 2 1

To R.W. and M.H.

with gratitude for your confidence.

1

WHAT MADE ELGIN WOODELL A LEGEND is not the stuff of magic or fantasy. There were other reasons that within four years he filled every stadium in the National League whenever the Cubs came to town, but the love of his mother played a major role.

"You're not gonna go barefoot in Chicago," Miriam Woodell told her pale ten-year-old on the Trailways bus from Hattiesburg. "And you're not gonna say 'not gonna' up there neither."

"Either, Momma," he said, turning from the window to face her. "You mean either."

She pursed her lips. "Thank you, Mr. Know-It-All."

Miriam's red hair hung heavy and dark from sweat as she shook her head, but she was not really upset. It was she who had taught him to read when he was four. She'd watched him devour baseball books and school texts ever since. Elgin scampered over his mother into the aisle and dug an aluminum bat out of his bag overhead, as the driver glanced casually at him in the mirror.

"There's no room..." Miriam began.

He climbed over her again to sit by the window. "I just want to hold it. Daddy told me—"

Miriam's freckles realigned with the narrowing of her mouth. "If you're gonna play with that thing, you can go sit by yourself."

Her son let the bat slide between his knees. "You shouldn't have said that, Momma. You know I'd rather sit with you than even feel a bat."

It was the highest compliment Miriam could hear from him. She fought a smile and hugged her son. She wasn't much bigger than Elgin, but when she held him she felt a strength borne of ownership and responsibility.

"Elgin," she said simply, "just don't—"

"I know," he said, closing his eyes. His moist arms were cool against hers. "Don't talk about Daddy."

Miriam and Elgin lugged four suitcases from the bus station to a transient hotel on a littered Chicago street. It was all she could afford. In her purse was nine hundred and ten dollars in cash. She had squirreled it away over seven months on a meager salary. The sale of their house trailer had been break-even. Miriam Woodell's net worth was in that purse.

By the end of the day, Miriam and her son had settled into a two-room flat on the sixth floor of a building she thought smelled like the rescue mission in Hattiesburg.

"Even this," she told Elgin, "is better than livin where people know your business."

Elgin sat silent. There were things he missed already. Screen doors. Room to move. Buddies.

"If I never see another IRS form as long as I live, it'll be too soon," his mother told him. "I hated that job with a passion."

"But you were good at it, weren't you?"

She snorted and nodded, setting a plate of red beans and rice before him. "All those months I don't believe I saw more'n two, three adjusted gross incomes lower'n mine."

It was clear to Elgin she didn't want to talk about that job. She had her wish. She was out of it, away from it, away from Hattiesburg. If only she could explain it; he didn't understand why they had to move. She'd tried to tell him enough times, and he had learned to quit pestering her. But still he wondered.

The next day his mother found a job in the accounting department of a distributing company four and a half miles away by bus. "You could act a little more excited," she told him. "This *is* food and rent."

But he had his own news. He had discovered a game close enough to baseball to hold him until his mother could find a real league she could afford. "They call it fastpitch," Elgin said. "You stand on one side of the street with a building behind you, and the pitcher stands in the street with a tennis ball that has the fuzz off it. The strike zone is chalked on the bricks behind you and the pitcher tries to strike you out before you get a hit. You make singles, doubles, triples, and homers by how high your hit goes on the front of the building across the street."

"How did you do?"

He smiled. "Haven't hit a foul yet. But I will. A couple of Puerto Ricans can really fire."

Three days later, Elgin came home crying. "A kid stole my bat. And we can't get it back cause he's not from around here, and he won't come back."

"Can't you use someone else's bat?"

"All they have are broom handles with black tape. But I was just starting to hit with my bat. I'll never hit anything with a broomstick! Anyway—"

"I know," she said. "Your daddy gave you that bat." His mother opened her arms and gathered him in. "Elgin, a broomstick is about all I can afford right now. Everything costs so much more up here."

"Daddy says I should hit with a wood bat anyway. Get a better feel of the ball."

Miriam stood quickly and stepped into the tiny kitchen area. "Money never meant much to your daddy. If he had his way, you'd have had a breakable bat whenever you needed one."

Elgin shook his head. "I don't want to hear about it all the time, Momma. I know. Okay? I know."

"You would've had a sister by now if it hadn't been for that man."

"I hate when you call Daddy 'that man.' He has a name."

"Yeah, and I don't want to hear it. Now he's also got a number."

She regretted that as soon as it came from her lips, but maybe now was the time. Elgin deserved to know. He brightened. "He's playing ball again?"

Miriam grunted. Just like Elgin to assume the best. "That's not what I meant." She reached into a cupboard and handed Elgin an index card bearing her own neat printing.

Neal Lofert Woodell
Lock Box 092349
Alabama State Penitentiary
Birmingham, Alabama

Miriam winced at the pain in Elgin's eyes.

"What for this time?"

She stalled, sitting next to her son. "Reckless homicide."

"What's that?"

"You know. Figure it out."

"Why do you always have to make everything like school? Homicide is like murder, right?"

"Um-hm. Drivin with no papers, drivin while drunk, hit an old man on a bike."

Elgin stared at the card. "Then he's not going to come see me? He said he would."

"When did he say that?"

"On my birthday last year and also the last time I talked to him on the phone. Just after Christmas."

"He was already in jail by then."

"He didn't tell me."

"Probably embarrassed."

Elgin nodded, his eyes filling. "Can I go see him?"

Miriam shook her head. "What do you want to see him for when he's only seen you once in more than a year?"

Elgin shrugged. "That's why."

⚾ ⚾ ⚾

The next morning, on her way to the bus, Miriam Woodell mailed a letter from her son to his father, a letter that had taken Elgin most of the evening to compose.

"I won't read it unless you say I can, El."

"It's okay. You can."

> Dear Daddy,
>
> How are you? I am fine. I didn't know you were in prison. I'll bet you're as sorry as I am. Momma says it could be lots of years. I hope not. I miss you and especially talking and playing baseball. Is there anyone there that can strike you out? I'd like to see them try!
>
> I'm switch-hitting like you taught me when I was little. My metal bat got stolen, so I'm going to get a wood one when I get enough money. I lost my batting helmet too. Sorry. Chicago is different, but we like it. At least I do. I can't go barefooted. I'm not looking forward to school, but Momma is. She doesn't like leaving me all day. I have to call her from the pay phone in the hall at the same time every day. Once I forgot and once I got my money stolen. I got whipped the first time and haven't forgotten since. I didn't get whipped for getting my money stolen, but Momma told me how to tell the manager so he could call her. She worries too much, but I'm not scared. I just play fastpitch all day. I'll tell you about it when I

see you. How much would it cost for me to come see you?

I love you and miss you, Daddy. I wish you would have told me what happened. It's bad, and I know you're sorry, so don't worry about me not loving you anymore or anything like that.

You still love me, don't you? Mom doesn't love you anymore because of that night, you know. I was mad at you too, but I knew you meant it when you cried. I'm never ever never going to drink beer or anything like that, Dad. It makes you do stuff you don't want to do, and it makes people quit loving you, but not me.

Love , Elgin

2

IT WAS SEPTEMBER BEFORE ELGIN BEGAN getting the broomstick on the tennis ball with regularity. He was in school most of the day, and fastpitch was not allowed during recess.

"Too many broken windows last year, I guess," he told his mother. "And I don't have that much time after school before dark."

Every day at about 3:40, Elgin was to call his mother from the pay phone in the hall. Usually, he was panting from the run home.

She gave him quick instructions on how to start supper. It would be simmering when she returned to the empty flat. Work kept her mind off her loneliness, but getting supper on the table wasn't enough to keep her from missing her son. He played fastpitch for two hours a few blocks away. Five minutes after his expected return time she would begin to worry, to think about heading to the street where he played. Her mind would fight the thought of losing him. She could not fathom that, would not entertain it. But she would not risk embarrassing him again. She had wandered over to watch him once, but the game ground to a halt until the others found out who the woman was. They teased him unmercifully. No adult spectators were allowed.

He always made it home safely, just before dark. Every day he told her that the next day would bring the letter he longed for. "Do you think Dad still loves me? Could he forget about me?"

"No," Miriam would insist. "I never knew anybody who could forget about you. I'm sure he loves you the best he knows how. He was never much good at that, you know, lovin anybody but himself."

For a year before she and her son moved to Chicago, Miriam had lived in a trailer park in Hattiesburg with haunting memories of her husband. Before he had moved away and then been sent to prison for what appeared the last time, Neal Woodell had raced stock cars on a dirt oval and hit .550 in a local semipro league.

She hadn't wanted much. Just a husband who kept a job and came home after work and didn't get drunk. Because when Neal Woodell got drunk, he got crazy. He had never turned his rage on his only son, but Miriam knew Elgin was terrified of him nonetheless. She was his protector, diverting his father's attention when a rage would come upon him, threatening to leave and take Elgin with her if Neal dared hurt their child. She wouldn't even let her husband spank him.

"I don't trust you," she'd tell him. "You could kill that boy and call it an accident."

One night her drunken husband fell to his knees before his pregnant wife after she made such a charge. "You can't hurt me more'n sayin I could ever hurt my own child, Miriam!" He wept and wept.

"You can hurt *me* and I shouldn't think you'd hurt *him?*" she challenged.

"He's my own flesh and blood! You're not!"

"I'm your wife!" Miriam was in her husband's face now, raging at him in a hiss just above a whisper.

"That was my mistake," Neal Woodell said. "We're only related by law."

She grimaced. "You can say that after all we've been through? Nights I've bailed you out, put you to bed, made excuses for you, forgiven you?"

"I had a momma," he said, rising. "I don't need another."

"I don't want to mother you," Miriam said, whining now. "I don't want to have to." Neal cursed his wife and called her ugly names. He punched her in the stomach, and as she lurched forward he drove his knee into her abdomen.

The pain dizzied her, and as she lay whimpering on the floor, she realized that little Elgin stood frozen in the doorway to his tiny bedroom, watching.

He had seen and heard it all. He wanted to charge his daddy, to kill him. But Neal had quickly come to his senses. "Oh, honey, sweetie, I'm sorry! I'm sorry! I'm sorry! Oh, forgive me! I'll kill myself if I've hurt you! Oh, God! Oh, please! Jesus, don't let anything be wrong with my baby!"

Elgin saw his mother fight for breath as she struggled to her knees. Neal reached for her shoulder, but she wrenched away. "Don't touch me," she said in a pitiful, small voice. "You will never touch me again."

While he cried, she called the police. "Yes, sir, I'm willin to press charges this time… No, I'm not gonna be changin my mind like last time."

Elgin's father sat at the kitchen table with his head in his hands, sobbing. "Forgive me, Mir, I swear I'm sorry. I'll never—"

"If anything happens to this child, Neal," she said, not looking at him, "I hope you die in prison."

⚾ ⚾ ⚾

Her husband spent nearly six months in the county jail. She indeed lost her female child, but prosecutors could not prove the beating had caused the miscarriage. It seemed to her that Elgin was as sad and almost as mad as she was, but he apparently believed his dad was sorry.

"That's what matters, right, Momma? If he's truly sorry, we have to forgive him, don't we?"

"I don't," she said. "Some day you'll learn to never believe a drunk, no matter what he says."

During Neal's nearly half year in jail, Miriam was informed that he had been hospitalized twice, suffering from delirium tremens. She never visited, wrote, or called. A sheriff served papers on her, requiring that she let her husband see his son. Even then, Elgin went with his Great-grandmother Lofert.

Elgin reported that Neal spent most of each visit holding his son, crying, and pleading with him to convince his mother that he was truly sorry.

"You can just tell him it's too late," Miriam told Elgin. "No, better yet, don't tell him anything. And don't promise him you'll pass along his messages either. He has no right to ask that of you."

When Neal was released, Miriam got an injunction against his coming to the trailer. (They had purchased it, used, eight years before in her name, because she had been the one with a source of income, meager as it was, for the small down payment.)

Miriam allowed Elgin to visit his father at a park close to town, while she or Grandma Lofert watched. There was no softening toward her husband, but it was during those weekly and sometimes twice weekly visits that she realized that at least something good was happening. Elgin was learning to play ball. Not only that, but he was learning the game from one of the best players she had ever seen.

Miriam had grown to hate her husband, but she would never be able to deny that he was a marvelous baseball player, a man born to the diamond, a man people loved to watch play.

Play was the perfect word for what Neal Woodell did on a baseball diamond. He was a center fielder, but he could play any position. He knew what to do, when to do it, and how to do it. He was fast, graceful, powerful, and smart. And most of all, he truly loved the game. If only he had loved her with as much sensitivity and abandon.

Even when it was just Elgin and his dad, playing catch, hitting fly balls, pitching, and batting, she watched in awe. She would not ever again love or accept or even want to talk to this man. But as he taught their son rules, strategy, technique, even style, she would not deprive herself the experience of watching him. If he noticed, if he tried to holler something to her—even some compliment on Elgin's progress—she stared back stonily, acknowledging nothing. He eventually quit trying to break down the wall between them and devoted his attention to his son.

"Aggressive, Elgin! Always look for the extra base, the advantage."

Elgin threw right-handed and batted left. His dad taught him to switch-hit. "See how you can see the ball better, El?"

When Elgin and his dad took a break and sat under a tree, Neal told his favorite stories—stories of childhood games, of incredible plays, of his four home runs in a rookie league doubleheader.

"If I'da stayed off the bottle, El," he told him more than once, "I'da been a big leaguer today."

"Is that true, Momma?" Elgin would ask her later.

"There's no doubt in my mind," she told him. She was impressed that a born liar had spoken the truth at all.

Miriam remembered him in a Pirate uniform, proudly posing for his spring training photos. He had started in the rookie league and ended in triple-A ball, but his scrapbook was full of pictures of him in the big-league uniform that every prospect was allowed to wear to spring training.

Neal Lofert Woodell had been a bona fide major league prospect. Now he was a sandlot player, a race-car driver who made twenty-five dollars a night Fridays and Saturdays, and barely enough more to live on by bagging groceries.

Miriam was aware that in Elgin's eyes, his dad was a giant. "I'm praying you'll forgive him, Momma."

"I know I'm bitter," she told her son, "and it tears me up. But I don't believe the man, and I don't think I can ever forgive him. I know I can't trust him. I can't stand the thought of him, and I don't even like you bein with him. You ever smell liquor on his breath, you get away, you hear?"

Elgin nodded. "I've never smelled liquor on his breath. I did ask him if he still drank."

"You asked him that?"

"Uh-huh."

"Good for you!"

"I told him he didn't have to tell me if he didn't want to."

"Oh, I'm sure he told you. I just wonder if he told you the truth."

"Yeah, he did."

"How do you know?"

"I just don't think he's a liar. He says he drinks beer after ball games to help him sleep, but he doesn't drive drunk. Anyway, he said they test the drivers at the racetrack now."

"He can't afford to lose that ride."

"That's what he said, Mom. He needs the money."

"What about weekends? He drinkin on weekends?"

Elgin nodded. "He says he drinks Saturday night after the races and all day Sunday."

Miriam had seen her husband in the grocery on Mondays, his eyes red and puffy, tiny slits against the sun that streamed through the plate glass.

On muggy summer evenings in Hattiesburg, Miriam had taken Elgin to the library where she taught herself the tax return filing business. For a year she couldn't get Elgin to read anything but baseball books: how-to's, biographies, histories, you name it. If it had to do with baseball, Elgin read it, including every baseball novel for children.

When he ran out of material for his reading level, she moved him up to adult baseball books. He expanded his vocabulary by checking with his mother on words he didn't recognize. She had been an honor roll student and had dreamed of college. When she didn't know a word, she made Elgin look it up and report back to her. Sometimes in her fatigue she felt impatient or frustrated with him, but she hid it. She wanted him to feel deeply loved.

"Momma," he would tell her, "there's no game like baseball. There's nothing like it. It has so many different things happening at the same time. It's a team sport but every play is also individual. You know what I mean?"

Talk of baseball made her think of her husband, but she worked at never shutting Elgin off. "No," she said. "What do you mean?"

"Like tennis and golf are individual sports, sports you play, like alone. I mean you're against everybody else, but it's just you and the ball and there's no team to help or hurt you."

"Yeah?"

"Yeah. And baseball is sort of totally a team sport, but when the ball is hit to you, it's an individual sport until you catch it. Then it's a team sport because you have to throw it to someone else. And when you're batting, it's all up to you. You have to get the sign, do what you're told, and get on base. But then it's a team sport because the next hitter has to do something or you die on base."

Miriam understood without really understanding. She knew what he was saying, but she couldn't see the beauty, the importance of it. That was all right, she decided. Someday she would see him play, and she would like that. It would be even better than watching Neal play.

"Do you like watching Dad play?"

She pressed her lips together. "Everybody likes watchin your father play, Elgin. He's gifted. But I don't like the man, so I guess I resent that he's that good at anything. Sometimes I wish he was as bad a ballplayer as he is a race driver."

Neal hardly ever won a race, but his sponsors kept him in because he was so daring. He was not so crazy that he ruined cars, but he was always on the brink of disaster, scraping the guardrails or tapping another car into the infield. He was a crowd favorite, a crazy man at the wheel. He seemed to love to drive fast without ever having mastered the sport. Two guys he drove against graduated to the NASCAR circuit, but Neal didn't have those ambitions. He drove for beer money and for fun. Baseball was his passion.

Elgin badgered his mother into taking him to his father's games, where he became an obnoxious fan. He combined play-by-play with coaching from the stands, trying to urge his dad's Zephyrs to victory. They would wind up the season even.

"Full count and two outs," Elgin would holler. "Runners will be going! Runners should be going! Runners are going, except for Shaw! There's the hit! C'mon, Shaw! Move with the pitch and you score on that play!"

After each game, Elgin would debrief with his father. "Outfield was too deep for their shortstop in the sixth, weren't they? I knew he was gonna drop one in."

Neal nodded.

"Would you have taken Crawford out so soon in the seventh, Dad? Why not let him walk the hitter to load the bases and give Mehlis a little more time in the bullpen? Mehlis wasn't ready. He got behind on the first guy and then had to come in with that candy pitch."

Elgin noticed the admiration in his father's eyes.

"You saw that too, huh? You also see that I've lost another step to first and that my throw has no pop anymore?"

"You've lost two steps but your arm is as good as ever. Ask Ernie."

Ernie was the Zephyr catcher who had taken a throw from Neal in the fourth to cut down a runner. Ernie had applied the tag and come up shaking the pain from his hand.

At the park in town, Neal hit Elgin harder and harder grounders and line drives. He pitched faster and faster until they had been forced to save their money and get Elgin a batting helmet.

The helmet gave Elgin a feeling he couldn't describe. His dad told him to open his stance, to make sure he was getting both eyes on the pitch. Now he could do that without worrying about getting beaned. It made his dad laugh, that open stance and the way he stuck his face right into the pitch before trying to drive it somewhere.

How he loved to hit!

3

MIRIAM WOODELL DIDN'T BELIEVE IN DIVORCE. Her family taught her that God hated it. She knew something about hate. It was such a concise, meaningful, appropriate word for what she felt for her husband.

She lived with the pain, the humiliation, the remorse for as long as she could stand it. Neal quit making attempts to get her to take him back, to allow him to return home. She had convinced him she was through with him forever, and apparently he was grateful that he still had at least some regular contact with his only son.

But a bad marriage—the separation of two people belonging to long-term, well-known families in Hattiesburg—was a topic of gossip, of scorn. Miriam saw it on the faces of everyone she came in contact with. She heard it in their voices. She saw it in their eyes. She was a failure, a pitiable woman. She was the wife of that violent drunk who washed out as a professional baseball player and was now just a good ol' boy, racin cars, baggin groceries, and playin a little ball on the side.

There was irony in Miriam's choice of a lawyer to handle her divorce. Billy Ray Thatcher was an old friend of Neal's family and had served for a time as his agent in contract negotiations. Neal had signed his first contract with the Pirates for a bonus he had not yet matched in twelve years of working elsewhere. It was a five-figure deal that let him live like a king, until the money ran out and his talent was booze-logged.

Billy Ray's claim to fame was that he had represented Bernie Pincham, an extremely tall black kid from an extremely poor rural family, a kid who had become a six-time NBA all-star and was now worth millions. The lawyer's commission on Pincham's salary and endorsement deals alone more than doubled his firm's gross receipts for several years. He had not only negotiated the dollars but had also shrewdly advised Bernie on investments.

Now retired, the local hero was worth many times what he had made playing the game. The Woodell family had projected the same for Neal.

Billy Ray Thatcher had done his best, but Neal had not heard him when he insisted that "everything, all of this—the bonus, the salary, the deals—hinges on what kind of a steward you are of your talent. If it doesn't happen on the field, it doesn't happen in the bank. The bonus is yours. You can pay your bills and put the rest away. You know as well as I do that the odds are one hundred to one against a rookie league player making a living as a big leaguer."

"I'll make it," Miriam recalled Neal insisting.

"I believe you very well could," Thatcher said. "But you want to be smart with this little nest egg. It looks like a lot to you now, and if we're careful with it, it can be a cushion for you if anything happens to your career."

"Do I get it in cash or like, what?"

Miriam saw Billy Ray Thatcher's eyes roll. "It comes to me in the form of a check, Neal. I recommend that you allow me to subtract my commission, pay your debts, put a quarter of it in a savings account, put a few thousand in your checking account, and invest the rest in some very safe, very conservative stocks."

"No way, José! Huh-uh! We agreed on your percentage. You take that and you give me the rest. And you can tell me one more thing: how to get a check that size cashed. I tried to cash a big check at the bank one time, and they said they needed a couple of days' notice."

"They would require a week's notice on a check of this size, Neal, but surely you don't really intend to—"

"You got my instructions and you're gettin your cut, so just let me know when I get the cash."

"I'd be doing you a disservice if I allowed you to—"

"You'll be fired if you don't. Now stick with me, Billy, because we're gonna make lots more money together."

Neal had left Thatcher's office that day without waiting for his wife. Billy Ray rose when she did and touched her elbow as he held the door for her. "Miriam, if he squanders that money, he'll ruin his career."

She was near tears and could only nod. She was the only one who knew his life was already in shambles. No one knew he beat her when he was drunk and that he was now drinking during the week for the first time. No one could advise him, tell him anything. She had quit mentioning even minor irritations. Husband and wife merely co-existed, she as his unsatisfied bed partner.

Miriam watched her husband slide from the frittering away of his signing bonus to the borrowing ahead on his small, minor-league paycheck, to the place where he began asking for his per diem meal money in advance.

The day after he was first warned by Pirate officials that his career was in jeopardy, he hit four home runs in a rookie league doubleheader. That, Miriam decided, was why they stuck with him as long as they did, that and his signing bonus. Neal rose to triple-A but soon dropped back to double-A and then A, and the Pirates told him they weren't going to make room for him with the eighteen-to-twenty-year-olds in the rookie league. Miriam was amazed that he could come back to Hattiesburg with his head high, admitting, *admitting* that it was drinking that had done him in. Finally, Miriam realized that the last thing Neal wanted anyone to think was that he hadn't had the talent to make the majors.

After years of beatings, drinking, lost jobs, and bankruptcy, what had attracted Miriam to Neal was now a vaporous memory. He had been the best-looking boy in high school, a three-sport star, homecoming king. He was Miriam's dream from the day she first tutored him in algebra. She had proved to be an albatross. He said he couldn't take his eyes off her red hair, her freckled face, her lithe body. His algebra grade went from an F to a D. She felt a failure.

He was charming and funny, but he was not bright. All physical. And now that alcohol had left him merely a better than average local jock, and her a struggling young mother with no more sympathy or tolerance, she called for an appointment with Billy Ray Thatcher.

"How long since you threw him out, Miriam?"

"More'n two years, plus his jail time."

"He sendin you any money?"

She snorted.

"Can I talk you out of it, tell you he's worth the effort, that you don't wanna be a divorced, single parent in this town?"

"I'm not going to be in this town much longer, Mr. Thatcher. Soon as I can get some money saved, I'm sellin that trailer, and Elgin and I are going to Chicago."

"Chicago? Why Chicago?"

"I had an aunt when I was little who moved to Chicago with her husband. She wrote the most beautiful letters about it. The culture and all." She sat with her hands folded, her eyes focused on the floor. Tears collected and tumbled. "I just want to get as far away from here and him as I can. My family knows what I'm doin, and they don't like me for it. Well, they can just hate me long distance."

Thatcher sat with his legs crossed, fingers entwined. "Can he accuse you of adultery?"

"No, sir," she said. "He accused me of a lot of stuff when he was drunk, but he knows better."

"And him? Could you use adultery as grounds?"

"I wouldn't even if I could, and I probably could. You know that girl at the grocery with the blond hair and—Mr. Thatcher, I don't want any more mess."

"He beat you, didn't he? Isn't that what he did time for?"

Miriam stiffened. "I don't want charges and countercharges. I don't want anything but to be out of this for as little money as possible."

"Miriam, you know I could never charge you."

"I didn't come to you for any free deal."

"I know that, but please, let me do this for you. I would be hurt if you insisted on trying to pay."

Miriam snatched a tissue from her purse and fought for composure. "Thank you, sir. I had no idea how much it might cost."

"Don't give it another thought. I'll throw a little stationery at Neal and follow through with the paperwork. It shouldn't take long."

"Stationery?"

"Yeah. I just send him a letter on my office letterhead and use lots of legal jargon that basically convinces him he has nothing to gain and everything to lose by contesting this divorce. Now what do you want from him? At least child support, right?"

Miriam shook her head. "He has nothing."

"You're too generous."

"But he really doesn't. If he gave up drinkin he'd have a little extra, but I really want to be done with him."

"Well, just the same, I'm going to get a list of his assets, see what he's got. You can decide then if there's anything you want."

Miriam started to respond, but she didn't want to fight anymore. She knew there could be nothing of her husband's she would want. Everything would remind her of the horror years. She didn't even want his money to help raise their child; she thought of Elgin as hers alone.

"What I'll do is, I'll tell him that half his assets and his income are rightfully yours, but that if he'll peaceably allow your divorce action to go through, maybe even paying court costs, we may be able to negotiate a more reasonable settlement."

"Like nothin from him?"

"We'll get to that if that's really what you want, but I don't wanna tell him that until I've persuaded him that it's in his best interests to cooperate."

The letter from Mr. Thatcher sent Neal Woodell into a spin. He was offended, and said so, that his former agent would take his wife's side against him. He pleaded for the chance to make the marriage work, threatened to sue for custody of his son, asked a local charity attorney to at least protect his visitation rights.

"I've talked to his representative," Thatcher told Miriam. "I believe you have no recourse on visitation, and you're right that he has little to offer in the way of finances or property. But I can tell from the language his lawyer is using that at least he knows they have no hope of fighting this. Here's a list of assets and debts."

Miriam hated even looking at the typed sheet, a sad litany of junk and obligations. She had no interest in his eight-year-old car. She wouldn't need that in Chicago, and she had already promised her beater to her little sister. It wasn't more than a hundred-dollar gift that came with no guarantees.

Neither was she interested in his Harley, which he had bought off a junk dealer and had never had the money to get into running condition. It sat tireless in a shed near the room where he stayed.

"So, he's still got that old pitchin machine," she said quietly, studying the document. "Wonder where he keeps that."

Thatcher studied his own copy. "At a community college in Mobile. Friend of his coaches baseball there and borrowed it. It's in storage, not being used, but it's probably still worth a thousand dollars, so it's listed."

"You got him that thing, didn't you?"

Thatcher leaned back in his chair with a satisfied smile. "I was rather proud of that," he said. "Got it thrown in, pardon the pun, with his signing bonus. It was probably worth several thousand at the time. Helped Neal a lot with hitting the fastball. At least for a while. He'd forgotten about it, though. I had to remind his lawyer that I knew he had it somewhere. It's of absolutely no worth to anybody except that ball team that borrowed it, probably, but I was just trying to make sure his list showed everything so we'd have some leverage on him."

Miriam's eyes narrowed and she looked out the window. "I want it," she said.

"The pitching machine? Whatever for?"

"For Elgin."

"Oh, honey, he's a lot of years from being able to use that. This isn't one of those toys they use in batting cages. That thing is a monster. Where would you put it?"

"Maybe that college coach would keep it stored for me."

"Maybe he would, but do you really want me to go after it? It's gonna look a little silly in the divorce action. And won't it remind you of Neal anyway?"

"I can live with that. I don't want money, not even child support. I just want him to admit the trailer is all mine, give me that pitchin thing, and let me have this divorce."

"I could get you more."

"I don't want anything more."

"Nothing?"

"Nothin. If he was rich, maybe I would. But the best thing I can do for Neal is to remember that he's got nothin and forget he ever had me."

⚾ ⚾ ⚾

When the divorce was final, Neal Woodell quietly left town. He left a lot of his junk next to her trailer and gave his Harley skeleton to the people he had lived with. He gave one hour's notice at the grocery, took his pay, and drove east into Alabama.

The looks, the tones of voice, the condemning eyes, none of it changed for Miriam with Neal's departure. She began plotting her own escape to Chicago. Without a word to Elgin, she slowly began paying her debts, starting with the small ones and working her way up. When she was square with all her creditors, she started salting away a little each month.

Elgin's father visited one more time and played catch with Elgin, not mentioning that he had moved away. Miriam heard nothing more of him until Mr. Thatcher drove out one night with the news. Neal Lofert Woodell's sorry life would be remaindered in the Alabama State Penitentiary. That news would get around soon enough, and Miriam had had more than her share of pity and scorn. It was time to move on before time passed her and her beloved son by.

⚾ ⚾ ⚾

Elgin didn't know whether to ask his mother if she knew more than she was telling him about the whereabouts of his daddy. All he knew was that he desperately missed the man who encouraged him, clapped him on the back, looked into his eyes and told him he was "gon be a great one someday."

As Elgin lay in his bed night after night, he wished his father back. He wanted his dad to live in the trailer, to be a husband to his mother, to make their family complete. Other kids had daddies. He wanted his.

4

When Elgin first began asking when he would see his dad again, Miriam stretched the truth. "I'm not sure exactly where he is," she said.

"Well, am I supposed to meet him at the park this week?"

"We won't know till he calls," Miriam said.

Eventually, of course, Elgin discovered that his father was no longer bagging groceries, no longer racing cars, and no longer even playing local baseball. "Has he moved, Momma?"

"I expect he has," she said. "You know I don't care."

"Well, *I* care! What am I supposed to do? I'm just starting to get good at baseball!"

"You can keep playin baseball."

"Yeah, but not with anybody who knows what he's doing! You know our teacher was trying to get everybody to throw off their right foot the other day? Right-handers! She was having right-handers step with their right foot and throw!"

"Is that wrong?"

"Is that wrong! Mom, look!"

He went through the motion. She smiled. "You look like I look when I try to throw," she said.

"That's just it! I got in trouble because I wouldn't do it. I told her if she thought that's the way you're supposed to throw, she was wrong."

"You said that?"

"Yes! Momma, you know I usually don't talk back, and I called her ma'am and everything, but there was no way I was gonna throw a ball stepping with my right foot."

⚾ ⚾ ⚾

Miriam was astounded at the prices of aluminum bats. The salesman told her that if she bought one she would be ahead in the long run because, "It will never break. Figure what you would pay for breakable wood bats over the next few years."

She told him how tall Elgin was and asked for a bat he wouldn't grow out of too quickly. The man went on about length and weight and thickness, and Miriam wished she had brought Elgin with her and forgotten about surprising him for his birthday that April. She wondered how different bats could be and hoped Elgin would like it.

He did and he didn't. He'd never had his own bat before, but he had always dreamed of a wood one. This one was a little too long, a little too heavy, and Miriam could see in Elgin's eyes that he didn't want to tell her the truth. She was desperate. He was her life. She lied.

"El, I want you to know that your dad sent me the money for that bat and had me pick it out for you. He probably could have done better himself, or maybe I could have with you there, but we wanted it to be a surprise."

Elgin's eyes shone. "Dad hates aluminum bats, but I guess he figured I'd break a wood one."

She nodded, hating herself. That night she wrote Neal, mentioning nothing of his predicament. "I told Elgin his birthday gift, a metal bat, was from you. If you talk to him, cover me. Neal, I would rather a man like you have no influence on my son, but I don't think he could handle never hearing from you again. Don't do that to him. Sincerely, Miriam."

A little more than a week later a card came for Elgin with a lock box number as the return address. Miriam removed the card from the envelope before handing it to her son.

Neal had dated the card the day before Elgin's birthday. It was a silly card with a cartoon ballplayer on it. The card said, "Today is special in every way, swing for the fences and Happy Birthday!"

On the back, Neal had written, "Hope this reaches you on time. Hope you liked the bat. Had to follow work to Alabama. I'll come see you when I can. Love, Dad (#16)."

"He put his old uniform number on here, Mom."

"Did he?" she said, trying to hide her lack of interest.

"I was starting to feel bad about not hearing from him."

"I don't blame you."

"I mean, it was my birthday! He never forgot my birthday. The card must have got lost in the mail."

"Must have."

For Christmas Miriam made Elgin a sweater but could afford only two rubber-coated baseballs. She told him they were from his father. But she forgot to inform Neal. He called the day after Christmas.

"Oh, I'm so glad you answered, Mir," he said. "I was afraid Elgin would answer and thank me for some gift and I wouldn't know what I got him. What did I get him?"

"He's right here, Neal. He wants to thank you for the two rubber-coated baseballs."

"Rubber-coated? Miriam!"

"Here he is."

"Dad?... Yeah!... Great! How are you?... Yeah, they were nice. I've already played catch, but it's been cold out. Hurt my arm a little... No, it's okay. When are you coming to see me?... Well, let me know when you get a vacation or something... Yeah, here's Mom."

She took the phone. "Good-bye, Neal."

"Wait a minute, Miriam. Just tell me why you went and bought—"

"Good-bye, Neal."

"Miriam!"

"Excuse me a minute, Neal."

She covered the mouthpiece and spoke to her son. "El, could you give me a minute?" He hurried to his little room, and Miriam feared she saw hope in his eyes. "I'm back, Neal."

"I wanna know—"

"Listen to me, Neal. I don't have to tell you anything. If you want to get Elgin somethin for his birthday or Christmas, then you better remember yourself and save your money and buy him somethin right. Who do you think you are, scoldin me for doin the best I can? I'm not givin you the credit for any gifts anymore, so you'd better plan ahead next time."

"I don't have any money, Mir! How'm I s'posed to do that?"

"Well, you should've thought of that a long time ago."

"Well, lemme just tell you this, Mir: If you think about gettin him a glove, and you don't hafta say it's from me, make sure it's a Wilson A-2000. Got it?"

"Where do you think I'm going to get the money for a ball glove? Do you have any idea what those run these days? The cheap ones are over fifty dollars!"

Neal laughed. "Fifty dollars! It'd be just like you to get him a vinyl glove. You're lookin at three times that for a good one."

"Well, you can forget that. He's usin your old glove."

"That's old, all right. And dry. And too big for him."

"Neal, I am through talking."

"My time's up anyway, Miriam. I'll call you sometime soon."

"Don't bother."

"Well, I can call the boy, can't I?"

"I wish you wouldn't. I haven't told him where you are."

"I'm getting out soon."

"Oh Neal, don't start playing games with me, and quit promising Elgin that you're comin to see him."

"I was framed, Miriam. I'm gonna get outa here soon, and I *will* come see him. I wanna talk to you, too."

"No."

"I'm telling you I was framed, well, not framed, but railroaded."

"You weren't driving with a suspended license?"

"Well, yeah, but I was goin to work and—"

"You weren't drunk?"

"I was officially under the influence, but only by a hundreth of a—"

"And so, what, someone pushed that man out in front of you?"

"It was dusk, Miriam, and I should have sued the family for lettin their dad ride that three-wheeler that late in the evening."

"He was on a three-wheeler?"

"And just pokin along! I couldn't stop. I honked and he panicked and stopped."

"He didn't swerve out in front of you?"

"No, but if he'd swerved the other way, I wouldn't have hit him when I slid onto the shoulder."

"Neal! You're never gonna get off from a charge like that!"

"You just watch!"

"I'd rather not." She hung up.

The next day she asked Billy Ray Thatcher to see if Neal had filed an appeal on his case. That evening Billy Ray phoned.

"He doesn't even have a lawyer, Miriam. And the case was so open and shut that there would be no hope. He was driving while his license was suspended. Witnesses saw him get thrown out of a bar for being too rowdy. They say he was alternately laughing and crying as he staggered to his car. A friend offered to drive him home and Neal took a wild swing at him. He laid rubber screeching out of the parking lot, then flew through radar at over sixty miles an hour in a thirty zone. The officer saw Neal's car weaving as he pulled out to pursue him, and just as he was turning on his flashing lights, he saw the accident. Neal appeared to have not even seen the old gentleman on the bike. It was lucky no one else was on the sidewalk."

"The sidewalk?"

"Neal drove off the road, between two trees, and up on the sidewalk where he hit the man. The old guy was hardly moving."

"Neal said something about the man being in his way."

Thatcher sighed. "Open and shut, Miriam. He's in there forever."

⚾ ⚾ ⚾

Miriam broke the news to Elgin that they would be moving to Chicago the next summer.

"But won't it be harder for Dad to find me and get there?"

"Might be," his mother said. "But that's his problem."

"It's my problem too, Momma. You gonna let me play in a league up there?"

"The summer after we get there."

"A league with uniforms and all?"

"I don't know what they have."

"I want to play in a league with real uniforms. I can't stand this playing with just a team T-shirt. I'm ready."

"I know you are. But we'll be gettin there too late to try to join one right away."

Elgin had not even started in the league with the T-shirt "uniforms." He had only watched. Though it was clear he was better than the oldest kids in that league, he was still too young to sign up. The next summer he would be eligible, but he would play in just five games before his mother scheduled the bus ride to Chicago.

Had he known how he would perform in those five games, he'd have fought harder against leaving.

5

HATTIESBURG'S CHILDREN'S BASEBALL PROGRAM had one league for nine- and ten-year-olds, one for eleven- and twelve-year-olds, and another for thirteen- and fourteen-year-olds. When Elgin timidly approached the registration tables, a woman shoved a sign-up sheet under his nose, and a man leaned over and surveyed the new player prospect from head to toe.

"I'm the official guesser," the man said.

"Sir?"

"Before you tell me your age, I guess. I'm within a year ninety percent of the time."

A husband and wife team at the cash box smiled tolerantly and nodded. "He's been especially good today."

Elgin was lankier and taller than most older boys, so when the man guessed thirteen—"Am I right, huh, am I right? Between twelve and fourteen without a doubt, huh?"—Elgin wasn't surprised. "I'm ten," he said.

The man roared.

"Well, we'll see what your mama puts down for date of birth, and if it comes out to ten, well, we're gonna hafta see what Matt wants to do about it."

"Who?" Elgin said.

"League rep. He can ask you for a birth certificate."

His mother looked up. "The boy is ten," she said. "And I didn't bring any papers. I'm sorry."

Matt was summoned, a huge fat man with an unlit cigar at the corner of his mouth. "Trouble?" he said.

"No trouble," Guesser said. "Just that this boy and his mama say he's ten."

The big man studied his mother more than Elgin. "Well, a pretty little lady like this says her son is ten, he's got to be ten. But ma'am, you must understand, we're gonna get challenged on this every time we turn around. You have papers on the boy somewhere, right?"

"Of course I do."

"Well, just have him bring a copy of his birth certificate to the tryouts."

"My dad is tall," Elgin said. "That's why I'm tall."

"We'll, if you're as good as you are tall, you're gonna need that birth certificate. If you're not, nobody will care much. We had a kid in our beginner's league that was a year older than everybody, but he was so bad—ha, ha!"

Neither Miriam nor Elgin smiled. "My dad is a good ballplayer," Elgin said.

"Really? Someone I should know?"

"Neal Woodell."

"No kiddin? That's your old man? He was some kinda player before, ah...he was some kinda player."

"Maybe he would like to coach a team for us," the man at the cash box said. "We're still looking for help for the—"

"Ah, no, Clarence," Big Matt interrupted. "He's, uh, not a local man. Now let's get this boy signed up and tell him where to report for tryouts."

Elgin hid his nervousness at the tryouts and quit telling other kids about his dad after the first three didn't recognize the name. He was eager to show his stuff. Baseball was as instinctive to him as breathing, and he couldn't wait to run and hit and throw and catch, to impress his mother as much as anyone. Boys of all shapes and sizes showed up, all seemingly having been dressed at the local sports store in the latest shoes, sweats, hats, and gloves. Elgin wore raggy sweats, one of his dad's old, too-large caps, and that floppy glove. On his feet were almost year-old sneakers worn smooth on the bottoms.

Three volunteers double-checked with the league reps to be sure of his age. Then they explained to parents how the tryout would be conducted.

"We'll run them for time, hit em a coupla grounders and flies, and give em three swings apiece. We grade em from zero to five or A for automatic. Each coach gets a certain number of nine-year-olds and a certain number of ten-year-olds on his team, and they bid on players of different levels of ability. We don't claim to be perfect, and we don't tell anyone what the ratings are. Don't call us; we'll call you."

The kids were lined up at home plate and asked to stand in the batter's box, one at a time, with a bat. They were to swing and drop the bat and run all the way around the bases, touching each one. They were timed from the plate to the plate.

Most of the kids swung, set the bat down, then ran. They ran in a huge circle, touching each base and ranging almost into right field on their way to second and into left on their way to third. Several slid into home. Most slowed and jumped on the plate with both feet.

When Elgin's turn came, he stepped quickly into the box. He stood in left-handed to give himself an edge toward first.

"When you're ready," said one of the two men with a stopwatch. "You a lefty or are you just tryin for an advantage?"

"Switch-hitter, sir."

"Sure you are. Which hand you throw with?"

"Right."

"Bat righty for this."

Elgin's face burned. He moved to the third base side of the plate, stepped and swung hard. He was moving before he dropped the bat, and within three strides was at top speed. The other hopefuls stared and punched each other. "Whoa, look at that kid!"

Elgin was hardly two feet out of the base paths all the way around, digging, charging, flying around the infield in what seemed the shortest distance possible. Everyone watched in silence as he got ahead of himself on the way to the plate and almost stumbled, then righted himself and sped across the plate.

"Man!"

"Wow!"

Elgin smiled self-consciously and stole a peek at his mother in the bleachers. She raised a fist and smiled.

The timers looked at their watches and then at each other. They showed each other the times they had clocked. "Can't be right," one said.

"The watch doesn't lie. He looked pretty quick."

"He didn't look this quick. I don't think a fourteen-year-old has run this time. I think maybe I was late punching in at the start."

"Me too? We were both off?"

"Could've been. He got out of the box fast."

The time recorder approached with a clipboard. "Time?"

"We're not sure."

"What do you mean?"

Both displayed their watch faces.

"You want me to write that down? Or should I just note that both clockers think they're funny? C'mon, what's the time? I expected him to have the fastest time, but faster even than the big kids, and by more than a second? Are we sure this kid's only eleven?"

"He's ten."

"Sure he is."

"Woodell!"

"Sir?"

"When you catch your breath, get back in line. We need to be sure of your time."

Elgin looked at his mother with a shrug, as if to say, "When I catch my breath?" He was hardly panting.

Twenty minutes later, when Elgin was up again, it seemed word had spread across all the diamonds. Kids and coaches from all three tryout areas watched the big ten-year-old who ran like no kid they had ever seen. Elgin was aware of all the attention, and if anything, it made him faster.

He swung harder, started earlier, flipped the bat a little higher for emphasis, and dug straight for first. He hit every base with his left foot and this time he did not stumble coming around third. His time was faster on both clocks. He had been one-point-six seconds ahead of the best-ever time for the nine- and ten-year-olds and a tenth of a second slower than the best fourteen-year-old that day.

Very few kids Elgin's age could catch a grounder or a pop-up without luck, and the coaches gave up trying to give instructions after the fifth or sixth kid. They had been shouting, "Head down, glove down, butt down!" for ground balls, but it was all the kids could do to force themselves to stay in the front of the ball.

When Elgin's turn came he was so smooth and precise that the ground ball right at him looked too easy.

"Take two more," the coach yelled, "and you guys watch!" The next was hit sharply to Elgin's left and would have skipped past him if he had not angled back and cut it off. He went down for the ball and came up throwing, right to the glove of the catcher. The next went to his right. Faster in that direction, he hustled so he wouldn't have to backhand it, kept his hands in front of him, fielded the ball low, and fired it home again.

Miriam walked right behind the rating coaches without being noticed. What she saw and heard confirmed her highest hopes.

"Woodell."

"Birth certificate."

"Automatic."

"Best I've seen."

During the hitting tryouts Miriam learned what her former husband and her son meant by candy pitches. Easy, slow, arching tosses were the only things these kids had a chance of hitting. Elgin came to the plate eleventh and, batting right-handed, took the first two offerings, one high, the other outside. No one else had taken a pitch. They were supposed to get three swings, and it was understood that they would swing at just about everything. Elgin looked irritated with the pitches.

"Swing at this no matter where it is!" the adult pitcher yelled.

He lofted a high outside pitch with a three- or four-foot arch on it. Elgin went into an exaggerated hitch, then drove the ball over everyone's heads, almost two hundred feet into right field.

Whistles and gasps burst from the boys. The pitcher looked insulted. "I'm going to throw harder," he said.

Elgin nodded as if he appreciated that.

The next pitch was a fastball, low and inside. Elgin stepped a little farther than usual and drove the ball right back up the middle, making the man jump out of the way. He lost his balance and fell. Most of the kids laughed, but Elgin didn't.

"Nice hit," the man said. "Get ready."

"Can I bat lefty?" Elgin asked.

"It's up to you, hotshot. But I'm throwin just as hard."

Elgin hardly ever hit right-handed. His father was a righty and always pitched to him that way, so Elgin usually hit left. He could hardly wait.

A couple of dozen boys ringed the infield. Only a few were even on the outfield grass, until Elgin hit the long one to right. Then everyone had backed up ten feet or so, but when he switched to hitting lefty, they moseyed back in. That was an unfortunate choice for a chubby ten-year-old with glasses low on his nose and his hat pulled down almost over his eyes.

The pitch was waist high and harder than the previous one. Elgin stepped and began that liquid swing of his. The ball rocketed off the bat, rising and spinning toward where the second baseman would normally play.

The resounding bat caused players on the other fields to turn in time to see kids scatter in every direction. Chubby ducked and turned his back, but the ball pursued him like a heat-seeking missile and hit him above the right biceps as he spun.

The ball caromed all the way to the fence while the boy went down in a squealing heap, hat and glasses flying. In seconds he was surrounded by coaches telling the players to back off. When the kids drifted away, Elgin remained. He still held his bat, fighting tears himself. The kid had gone from wailing to moaning, and an ugly welt was already rising under his shoulder.

"I'm sorry," Elgin said, as they tried to get the boy to stand.

"You don't need to apologize," the boy said in a high-pitched whisper. "I never seen any kid hit a ball like that. I just couldn't get outa the way."

"Well, I'm real sorry."

"You ought to be!" a man shouted, rushing to the injured boy.

"Now, Earl," one of the coaches began.

"Don't 'Now, Earl' me! You're just as much at fault, lettin this big kid try out with these young ones."

"He's ten, Earl."

"Ten, my rear end! If this kid plays in this league, my kid doesn't! Somebody's gonna get killed out here! Then what?"

"Dad," the injured boy whined, "at least find out if we're on the same team. I don't mind bein in the same league with him if I'm on his team."

Everyone laughed, but later, as Elgin left the field, the injured boy's father insisted on seeing a birth certificate and demanded that something be done.

As Miriam and her son were leaving, a man with a clipboard approached. "Ah, ma'am, would you have a few more minutes? I'd kinda like to see the boy throw a few."

"They didn't say anything about pitchin," she said.

"I know, and usually we don't worry about that until the teams are picked, but I know I'm going to get your son, so—"

"How do you know that?"

"Well, we've already flipped for first pick, and I've got it, and there's certainly no one else out here who could compete with Elvin for first pick."

"Elgin."

"Elgin?"

"His name's Elgin."

"I have down here Elvin Worrell."

"It's Elgin Woodell."

"Woodell? Really? Is he related to—"

"Yes, sir. Neal is Elgin's father."

"Well, now, that sure explains a lot, doesn't it?"

Does it ever, Miriam thought.

His mother turned to ask Elgin if he wanted to try out for pitcher, but he was already out of the car and standing at her elbow.

"Which team is yours?" Elgin asked. "Pirates or Braves?"

"How did you know it was one of those?" the coach said, smiling.

"Just hoping."

"You're going to be on the Braves, buddy. Just call me Coach Kevin. You want to throw a few?"

"Sure!"

"My son John is our catcher. Let me get him."

By the time they were set, word had spread that the ten-year-old phenom was going to show his stuff. Several dozen kids and parents crowded around. Elgin was nervous at first, but he was also excited. He threw easily and quickly, pitch after pitch right to the glove.

"Just let him know when you're ready to throw harder," Coach Kevin said.

"Isn't he going to wear a mask?"

"Not without a hitter in there. Just let er fly."

"My dad always wore a mask when he caught me, in case of a short hop or something."

"Just cut loose, Elgin," the coach said.

Elgin's next pitch was a strike, but it wasn't down the middle like the slower stuff had been. It came in like a laser, a pitch that would have sliced the corner of the plate. John moved late on the pitch and saw it tip the edge of his glove and whiz past. He looked as if he knew he should have caught the ball, so he sprinted after it as he would have done in a game. The pitch, however, was not so easily retrieved. It bounced twice and rolled more than a hundred feet.

John ran back with it and neither he nor his father said anything. Elgin wound and fired again, this time a pitch at John's ankles that sneaked under his glove and rolled as far as the previous one. John looked hard at Elgin and swore, then jogged after the ball. When he got back he threw the ball hard to Elgin.

"Sorry," Elgin said. "I thought it was an okay pitch."

"It was low," John grumbled.

"You don't have to apologize for pitching a ball," Kevin said. "That pitch was catchable, even if it wasn't in the strike zone. Right, John?"

John said nothing.

"Right, John?" his father demanded. The catcher shrugged.

"You got a curve ball, son?" the coach asked.

"My dad said I shouldn't throw a curve till I'm thirteen."

"You're bigger than a thirteen-year-old, but whatever—"

"I've got another fastball that I hold a little different that moves some."

"Moves how?"

"It'll look to rise as it comes across the plate. I'm not sure it really does, but I throw it harder and it looks like it comes up."

"You throw it harder than you threw the first two?"

"I try, yes sir."

"Hard riser, John! Be ready!"

"I'm ready," the coach's son grumbled.

Elgin gripped the ball across the seams and wound up slowly. Though he was big enough to look older than most ten-year-olds, he was still a lanky little kid and had to rely on mechanics more than on a great arm. He kicked high, swept around, and followed through with tremendous arm speed. It was a good thing John had been warned that the pitch would rise. He might have taken it right in the chest, just above where his glove had been.

At the last instant a pitch much faster than the first two seemed to climb, and John reacted by jerking his glove up. The ball smacked into the web and drove the glove into John's chest. He wound up on his seat in the dirt, causing some of the onlookers to laugh. The pitch appeared to have knocked him over, but he had merely been slightly out of position and surprised, and now he was not happy. He also looked scared.

"I'm not catchin this guy," he said, his eyes filling. "He's too wild."

"Wild?" his father said. "You just got knocked on your can by a strike. Give me that glove."

John tossed it to his father and skulked away to the car.

"Now, big boy," Kevin said, "put me on my butt."

Elgin couldn't. In fact, Kevin caught everything he threw. Elgin could tell this man had done some catching. Elgin also knew he had impressed his new coach.

"How does 1.2 million over two years sound?" Kevin said.

Elgin looked at him blankly. "What?"

"Just kiddin. Show up Monday at six for practice."

As they were leaving, Elgin heard Kevin ask another coach if he had ever seen a ten-year-old throw a pitch that actually moved in the strike zone.

6

THOUGH MOST OF THE KIDS WANTED to be on the Braves team because of the proximity of the big league Braves, they were a sorry bunch. Apparently Kevin had paid attention to hardly anyone at the tryout except Elgin, because he wound up with a band of typical nine- and ten-year-olds who couldn't catch lobs from the coaches, let alone hard throws from short by an unusual player.

Elgin and John were the only kids who could throw the ball over the plate, and though Elgin could catch John, John didn't want to catch Elgin. Both wanted to pitch and play short, but there was precious little other talent to speak of. The kid Elgin had hit with a line drive was wisely placed on the Braves to keep the father quiet, but that didn't satisfy everyone.

Elgin came home with his uniform T-shirt and cap, and displayed it for his mother. She exulted, but he said he still wished it was a "real uniform."

He was also upset that whenever he came up to the plate, no one would play the infield. They would laugh and run for cover or play deep in the outfield.

"Coach can't even make them stay in the infield."

"Well, I suppose you can hardly blame him if you're hitting the ball that hard."

"Well, I didn't know I was hitting that well until I saw the rest of these kids. Momma, this is like a league for babies. Half these guys can't even catch the ball. Nobody knows what a force out is. It's terrible. I said something to one of the kids about John and me being like Ruth and Gehrig, batting third and fourth, and the kid didn't even know who I was talking about. How can somebody play ball and not know who Ruth is?"

"Who is she?" his mother said, smiling.

"Oh, Mom! And Coach said he was going to hit me *fourth.* He said, 'How do you like that?' as if I was supposed to be thrilled."

"Weren't you?"

"No! Nobody hits their best hitter fourth. That's the place for your power hitter. Your best hitter hits third. And if your best hitter is also your power hitter, you hit him third and let your next best power hitter hit fourth."

"Why?"

"So your best hitter gets up in the first inning. It also gives him a better chance to come to the plate one more time during the game."

"Makes sense. Did you tell Coach Kevin that?"

"Yeah. I don't think he likes me telling him stuff though. He said, 'You play and I'll coach, okay?'"

The Braves were the visitors in their first game. Elgin was on deck with two outs when John hit a one-hopper to left field and was thrown out at second trying to stretch it. As Elgin tossed his helmet in the dugout and was getting his glove, he looked to his mother in the stands.

"See?" he mouthed.

Kevin gave him a hard look and motioned him over with his index finger.

"We'd better get something straight, superstar. You may know more baseball than me, but I don't want to hear it, all right? And I don't want you talkin to anyone during the games."

Elgin shrugged in agreement. He was near tears.

He threw about three-quarter speed so John could catch most of his pitches. The other team was out three up and three down on strikeouts, mostly on called strikes. Only one hitter swung twice and he was the only one to even tip a ball foul. Players ducked and stepped out as each pitch came.

Miriam heard a low rumble in the crowd.

"Unfair."

"Too big."

"Gonna hurt somebody."

"Like to see his birth certificate."

"This isn't right."

"How are beginners s'posed to hit this kid?"

The opposing pitcher was a right-hander who threw huge rainbow pitches, most over the catcher's head. When the count got to three-and-oh on Elgin, batting left-handed, he looked pleadingly at Kevin, coaching at third base. Miriam knew he was hoping against hope that he wouldn't get the take sign.

He got the signal to hit away, but could this pitcher bring one in close enough to reach? With a funny little motion, the pitcher let one fly that came in on the outside corner at the waist. Elgin knew he should drive the pitch to left field, but he couldn't hold up his swing enough and wound up pulling the ball between the first and second basemen.

Each dove away from the ball as it whistled past, bringing gasps from the parents. The right fielder waved a tentative glove in the direction of the ball as it skipped past him and bounced, breaking a piece off the top of the snow fence and rolling all the way to another diamond.

Elgin stood on second with a ground-rule double. Miriam clapped and sat beaming at his first ever official hit in a real game. But as she looked at him she saw the disappointment on his face. He couldn't be thrilled over hitting a double off a pitcher who could hardly get the ball to the plate.

One of the parents of the opposing team speculated that this was "an older kid using his little brother's birth certificate." Others started in again about how dangerous it was to have a player like Elgin Woodell on the field.

Miriam knew the first charge was false. She was finding it hard to disagree with the second.

⚾ ⚾ ⚾

No one on the Braves except Elgin and John could hit the ball with authority. The team lost the opener by the slaughter rule, 12–2 in four innings. Because everyone on the team, including the four kids on the bench, were required to hit in order, Elgin came to bat only one more time. He was walked on four ridiculously wild pitches.

He was stony all the way home, and when they arrived he was in an angry mood. He threw his glove on the ground and kicked it. He flung his bat so hard he had to crawl under the trailer to get it.

"Stinkin, lousy, stupid stinkin team!"

Miriam let him vent for a while, then waited to talk to him until he had flopped onto his bed.

"Your temper reminds me too much of your daddy," she said. "I pray you don't inherit all his traits."

"Daddy woulda been disgusted today," Elgin said. "Do you believe that team? We can't throw, hit, run the bases, nothin."

"The other team wasn't much better."

"They wouldn't have been able to hit me if I'd had a catcher who could catch me."

The defense was no better the next game, and the Braves were massacred once again. But what set that game apart was Elgin's hitting. As was feared, he hit a ground ball so hard at the second baseman that the boy merely closed his eyes and turned away. The ball hit his foot, glanced off his glove, brushed his forehead, and rolled to a stop between the infield and outfield. The boy went down, more scared than hurt.

Elgin never slowed, rounding first as the center fielder checked out the injured second baseman and the right fielder picked up the ball and froze. Elgin didn't even turn to look.

"Third! Third! Throw it, Robbie! Third!"

Right fielder Robbie finally threw the ball, which bounced and rolled to the third baseman just as Elgin steamed in. But he didn't slide, didn't stop, didn't look. He made his turn and raced for home. The third baseman bobbled the ball, then threw wild and Elgin scored easily.

"This isn't even fair," a parent complained. "He's going to hurt somebody."

The second baseman stayed in the game, rubbing his foot. But when Elgin came to bat for the second time, the first baseman backed up fifteen feet down the right field line and the second baseman ran over and stood at second.

Elgin looked at Coach Kevin with his eyebrows raised, as if to ask if he should push a bunt to the right side past the pitcher. He could probably run all the way around the bases again. Kevin shook his head. Elgin stepped in, and on a three-and-oh pitch launched a line drive through the hole at second that seemed to never get more than eight or nine feet off the ground. It landed about two hundred and twenty feet from the plate.

Elgin received polite applause even from the opposing fans, but Miriam noticed that a couple and another man left the bleachers, heading for the concession stand where the league officials hung out.

By the time Elgin was up again, leading off an inning, several men from the league board were watching. With nobody on and nobody out, the opposing pitcher began walking Elgin intentionally.

"Ho! Wait! Time out!" the league president hollered.

The umpire, a young man in his late teens, whirled to reprimand the fan who was trying to interfere and realized who he was looking at. "Time is out!" the ump yelled.

The president went to the opposing coach as Kevin followed. "Clarence, what do you mean by an intentional walk with nobody on? Come on! We came down here to see this boy hit, not to see bad sportsmanship."

"Bad sportsmanship? If we don't walk this kid, he's gonna take somebody's head off."

Some of the fans agreed and let it be known.

"Pitch to him," Kevin said, "and I may bunt him."

"Now don't be doin that either, Kev," the president said. He turned to the other coach. "Play your kids deep and let him hit. We'll decide if he's too big for this league."

With a count of two balls, Elgin got out in front of an inside pitch and hammered it foul down the first-base line, causing a half-dozen fans to scramble for cover. Everyone looked at the president. He seemed to be pretending not to have seen.

Elgin drove the next pitch as far as he had hit his first home run, but foul. The opposition was giggling nervously, dancing around in the field as if looking for a safe spot. The count went to three-and-two on a high, outside pitch, and Miriam could tell Elgin was worried that he might walk after all.

He fouled off a low, inside pitch on purpose, and then did the same on another that was low and outside. The next pitch almost hit him, but he fouled that off too. He wanted to show the league bosses what he could do, and he was going to hang in there until he got a hittable pitch.

And here it came. It rode slow and about chest high and would have nipped the outside corner. Elgin wanted to reach out and hit a homer to left, but he got too far under the ball and sent it towering into shallow left, the highest pop-up anyone had ever seen from a kid that young.

Elgin threw his bat away in disgust and sprinted to first, making the turn and almost reaching second before the ball finally came down in the midst of the left fielder, the center fielder, the shortstop, and the third baseman. The pitcher and the catcher stood watching from their positions, mouths agape. No one was covering third.

Elgin ran, and though he was the only one near the bag the center fielder threw the ball anyway. Of course, Elgin scored.

The league president slapped his palms to his thighs, rose, and left with a pronouncement.

"That ball wasn't gonna hurt nobody."

He left amid a wave of boos and complaints.

"You'd better stay and watch!"

But he didn't.

The Braves lost big again. In the next game Elgin played shortstop. He hoped John would have enough control to keep the ball inside and try to force the other team to hit to the left side of the infield.

He did and they did, but Elgin couldn't find the arm speed slow enough for his first baseman to handle the throws, yet fast enough to get the runners out.

"Mom," he said later, "there's nothing more fun than baseball, and nothing worse than playing it the way we're playing it."

Neither Miriam nor Elgin had said anything to anyone about moving from Hattiesburg after the fifth game. Miriam knew she should have, but it hadn't come up, and now it would be too difficult. What she didn't count on was Elgin's performance in his last two games. The Braves won only one, and Elgin walked several times, but in the fourth game, he was actually out once.

He hit another towering fly ball, not quite as high as his first, but a skyscraper nonetheless. Three fielders converged on it, and one—as surprised as everyone else—saw it land in his glove. Even Elgin had to smile.

Fortunately he had not hit anyone with a batted ball since injuring the second baseman, but he'd had several near misses, two on a pitcher who could have been seriously hurt. Two families made it clear that they would not allow their children to play any position but catcher when Elgin was at the plate.

By the end of the fifth game the hapless Braves were one and four, but Elgin was ten for eleven, all extra base hits, including four homers, plus a bunch of walks. In the last game he clubbed one past the ear of the pitcher that also nearly decapitated the center fielder.

"Are you havin fun now?" Miriam asked Elgin at the trailer.

"No. It's too easy. And our team is too weak."

The phone rang. It was the league president. "Mrs. Woodell, it would be very helpful to me if I could come visit with you this evening."

"This is not the best time. In fact, we're—"

"I would be only a few minutes. Not more than fifteen. I have good news for Elgin."

Miriam didn't know how to turn the man down, but she knew it would come out during the meeting that they were leaving.

"Ma'am," the man said a few minutes later, a sweaty glass of tea in his hand, "we're going to promote your son to the next level."

"Sir?"

"He's clearly too good for the level we have him at now, and we're making room for him on the Pirates of the eleven- and twelve-year-old league."

"Yes!" Elgin exulted. "The Pirates! And they have full uniforms, don't they?"

"Indeed they do, son. In fact, I've got one in the car."

"Sir," Miriam said, "I'm afraid I have some bad—"

"Just let me get that uniform, ma'am, and see how it looks on the boy."

"Yeah, Momma, let me at least try it on."

It was against her better judgment, and when Elgin emerged from his bedroom looking like a miniature version of her former husband at his first spring training, she could hardly breathe.

"The fact is," she said, her voice quavery, "we are leavin, movin from Hattiesburg this weekend. We're going to Chicago."

"Well, can't the boy stay with friends or family so he can finish out the season? It's hardly fair to—"

"The only person it's not fair to is Elgin. It won't make a bit of difference to the Braves, and the Pirates don't even know they have him yet, do they?"

"Well, their coach does, and he's going to be plenty upset when he hears this."

"I'm sorry."

"I can't stay with Grandma, Momma?"

Miriam gave him a look that shut him up. After he had taken off the uniform and the league president had left, Miriam scolded her son for crossing her in front of somebody.

"It was hard enough for me as it was," she said, bursting into tears.

Elgin apologized, and she realized he hadn't cried yet. "This is harder on me than it is on you, isn't it, El?"

He nodded. "I won't miss the Braves, but I didn't know about the Pirates. Playing with the bigger kids woulda been fun."

"But I can't leave you here, honey."

"I wouldn't want you to, Momma. I wouldn't want to be here without you, and I sure wouldn't want you in Chicago without me."

"You wouldn't?"

"Are you kidding? You'd get to watch two big league teams play whenever you wanted, and I'd be down here hitting home runs and pitching no-hitters you'd never see."

Three days later they headed north.

7

IF THERE WAS ONE THING that could be said for fastpitch, it was that Elgin could play it until the cold, late fall days when the sun set too early after school. Even then he played most of the day on Saturday and Sunday.

"I kept track," he told his mother after a non-stop, six-hour game with just two players on each team. "I had sixty-two hits today and thirteen homers."

"Not a bad day," she said. "Can't do that in Little League, can you?"

They had been to see several games in organized leagues, including the one Elgin would play in the next spring, when Miriam could afford it. The league played all its weekday games at night under the lights, and they had beautiful uniforms. The equipment and the field were not kept up the best, but the competition was far better than what Elgin had endured in Hattiesburg. He pestered his mother to take him whenever she could, and though she was exhausted from working all day, she often did. What fascinated Miriam most about these visits was the baseball mind of her son. He sat fidgeting, hollering, and pointing, and he commented on every play. Nearly everything reminded him of something he had seen on television or read somewhere. He gushed stories of baseball from the past and the present, and she wondered what else might be in that head of his.

"With guys on first and second, they're not even watching the guy at first. But unless they're afraid the pitcher or catcher will throw the ball away, the first baseman ought to duck in behind him either just before the pitch or just after so they can pick him off. They'd still have time to get the guy going to third. They're just handing him a huge lead this way. He's got as much chance to score on a single as the guy on second does."

Miriam had grown up with brothers. She knew how boys could be about sports they loved. But she had never seen anything like this. Not even

Neal had loved the game the way this boy did. It was too early to tell whether Elgin had Neal's ability, but if she could keep him off booze and anything else that might destroy him, his desire alone could take him far. If only Neal had loved baseball more than he loved the buzz of a six-pack.

Maybe it was her loneliness that kept Miriam from being bored by Elgin's constant baseball chatter. The only thing she grew weary of was tossing a sock ball to Elgin all the time. If she hadn't protested, he would have kept her throwing it for hours. Whenever there was a commercial or a break in the action on television, he would toss her the sock and run and dive on the couch. She had learned to lead him so he could catch the "ball" in the air and then flop onto the couch, as if saving a dramatic home run.

In the late evenings, when she was watching an old movie on television and he was supposed to be asleep, he would call out to her.

"Momma, can I come tell you just one thing?"

"Just one."

He would pad out with some bit of trivia she could hardly believe anyone could remember.

"Cool Papa Bell, from the Negro Leagues, could run around the bases only a second slower than Carl Lewis could run the same distance in a straight line. That's how fast I want to be." When he was finally asleep she would pace the tiny efficiency and long for someone to hold her. She was not unaware that her pale, red-haired beauty was noticed in Chicago. She knew she turned heads when she entered a room, and up north men were bold enough to comment on her looks. She had been asked out by three different men at her office. Two of them were married.

It was nice to be noticed and thought pretty. But she didn't feel available. She didn't feel free. She would have loved to have had an adult to converse with about something other than business or kids; that was something she hadn't had since the early days with Neal. They had had what she felt were halfway intelligent conversations at one time. But when the alcohol took the place of his career and he saw everything falling apart, he took it out on her. There was no adult conversation after that.

Her family had been little help. Her mother and grandmother reminded her that there had never been a divorce in their family, and that a real woman could hold a man, regardless. She knew she could have "held" Neal. There would have been nothing to that. He wanted a punching bag and a bed partner who would pay his way, pick up after him, and let him do what he wanted. She might have done all that except put up with the beatings. To a point, though the rest was not a fair trade, it was a trade.

But who knew when the anger would be directed at Elgin? And what good would she be to him or any future children if she were injured? To her remorse, she believed she had left one fight too late. And on those nights when she dreamed of a mature, soft-spoken, loving man merely holding her, hearing her, she could just as easily shift to a wrenching need to cuddle her baby girl in her arms.

Tears dripped in her lap as she sat curled up on the couch, watching TV but not really watching. She would fold her arms across her chest and imagine cradling a newborn, a helpless, pale, feathery girl with wisps of hair and a pink bow, huge blue eyes and a rose petal mouth. In her mind she enveloped the child without hurting her, protected her, made her feel warm and secure and loved.

When she imagined that sweet, unnamed child at her breast, the pain became too intense and her hands curled into fists and her nails dug into her palms. She wanted to scream, to wail, to, yes, cry like a baby. Sobs caught in her throat as she forced herself to remain silent. Elgin would never understand.

Miriam buried her face in her hands and wept, renewing her resolve. She would pour her grief, her loneliness, her passion, her motherly and wifely instincts into her surviving child. This was the reason she had fled Hattiesburg. She had hated the shame, but even more, she didn't want her son to live with it. To have a daddy in prison, to have the whole town know of your legacy of failure—no, she would not subject him to that.

She knew Elgin had wanted to stay, to play ball, to be around friends and family. He had come because she did. Miriam had tried to take the blame for leaving, making it sound as if it were her problem and that she hated to make him the victim. But if she had her way, he would not be a victim. She had already succeeded in getting him away from Hattiesburg, away from his daddy, away from bad influences and dead-end possibilities.

She didn't know what Chicago held for him, but she had been able to find work and a place to live. They were getting by, not falling into debt as had always been predicted for her. She knew Elgin wanted nothing more than to play baseball, and if he was anything like her brothers and his father, he wanted to make a career of it.

But she also knew the incredible odds against that. She didn't hope for a big league career for him, even if that's what he and every ballplaying kid his age wanted. What she wanted for him was an unlimited horizon. She based his privileges on his success at school.

"I don't expect you to do better than you can do; I just expect you to do as well as you can do. Then you can play and have lots of time for fun."

He had risen to the challenge as she knew he would. He was such a good reader, so inquisitive. And competitive. Within the first two weeks of school, he told her he knew who the girl was to beat for best grades.

"She's got me in arithmetic now," he said, "but not for long."

He had been right. By early spring he had the highest grades in the class, including arithmetic. Miriam allowed herself to entertain broadcasting as a potential career for him in spite of his shyness. With her first raise, which came six months after she arrived, she began putting aside money for college.

She had asked her boss what he recommended for financing college for a kid who was almost ten now.

"How do you feel about crime?" he had said.

Maybe Elgin could earn a scholarship. Did colleges offer baseball scholarships? If she was trying to get him into the big leagues, she would have stayed in a climate where he could play the year around. Chicago held other opportunities. Reading did not depend upon the weather. With his brain, his memory, his scholastic ability, the future was his.

They rarely talked about it, but she could see him anchoring a sports roundup show, maybe doing play-by-play or even color work for major events on a network. She knew there were many levels of broadcasting before that and lots of competition—everyone in the business looking for the same plum assignments—but that didn't have to deter Elgin any more than it had deterred her. Leaving Hattiesburg for Chicago in the face of uncertainty and criticism had been like taking off for Mars. But she had a feeling. She had to do what she had to do, and there were no problems too great.

She wanted a nicer place to live, would have loved to be able to afford the suburbs, but there was no way. Any extra money would go for sports equipment, sign-up fees, and the college fund. Everything would point toward Elgin's success. That was the greatest investment she could think of.

Could he be more than she dreamed? Could he do something for people that was far beyond what would bring him success and money in a profession he loved? Was it possible he could be a doctor, a lawyer, or a college professor? Who knew? It was delicious to think about all the options. Everything about Elgin spoke of the future, not of the past.

The past was gone, a painful, bitter memory that sneaked up on her late at night when she needed a baby in her arms or to be a baby in someone else's arms. In her mind, she would take Elgin's face in her hands and turn him toward the future, toward the rising, not the setting, sun. She wouldn't push; she would merely enable. She would steer, guide, help, provide. He had the tools, and so far he seemed to have the drive.

She would give him what she had never had: freedom. She didn't want him to be perfect. She knew he was not. For all the skills and talents and the wonderful mind, he could still be selfish, sometimes obnoxious, sometimes angry. Sensitivity and maturity would come with age. She desperately wanted to stay close enough to be assured of that. But she also knew the day was not far off when she would have to let him become what he wanted to be, not what she had mapped out for him.

She was amused one evening in the early spring, the day after they had signed him up for the local Little League tryouts, when he did a play-by-play of their sock tossing game.

"Woodell goes back, back. He may never get to this one!" He motioned to his mother to throw the sock ball. "He leaps!" She tossed it higher than ever, just missing the ceiling and heading for the faded drape above the couch. Elgin got a finger on the sock, causing it to tumble end-over-end. As he settled onto the couch, he reached up with both hands and gathered in the sock.

"He's got it!" he cried. "Elgin Woodell, youngest player in the history of baseball, saves the game for the Cubs! The ten-year-old center fielder climbed the vines for that one, tipped it, and came down with it!"

Miriam smiled and waved at him with an "Oh, go on!" gesture. That line of Elgin's was one she had never heard from her brothers. They had always imagined themselves as Braves, making the game-saving catch or the game-winning hit when they grew up.

This was something else that set Elgin apart from others in her life. They all waited and hoped to get the big promotion, to win the lottery, to get a break. But Elgin didn't dream about being a big leaguer when he grew up. He dreamed about being a big leaguer now.

8

MIRIAM TRIED VAINLY TO INTEREST ELGIN in football and basketball throughout the fall and winter, and while he enjoyed following the Bulls and Bears on television and in the sports pages, baseball remained his true love. Not even the rough and tumble brand of hockey exemplified by the Blackhawks lured him from his favorite, and only, sport.

He invented his own dice baseball game and badgered his mother into rolling for one of the teams a few hundred games more than she really had the patience for. She wondered how a boy his age could care so much about box scores and statistics. She had to admit, though, they were learning a lot from each other. It hadn't surprised her to discover that he had inherited her knack for math, and soon he was using fractions and percentages to teach her how to figure ERAs and batting averages and slugging percentages.

"It isn't just the numbers," he told her. "There's always the chance for a perfect game, or a no-hitter, or a shutout, or a blowout."

One night, after he had finished a series with a couple of his imaginary teams, he waxed philosophical and made her wonder whether she or her husband had ever possessed such depth. And if not, where had he gotten it? Was there some dormant gene from an ancestor from which Elgin had benefited?

"Baseball is, like, sort of balanced, I guess you'd say. You're supposed to suffer when you walk too many people, and usually you do. But sometimes you get out of jams when you shouldn't, and you see things fall apart with no one on and two outs. The best play of a game might not work. It's just like how we live."

It's just like how we live? Miriam repeated in her mind. Could he have been thinking of the difficult choices she had made—the divorce, the move, the leaving of her man-child until she got home from work? She wanted to pursue it, to ask him, to see if he would run with it, but he quickly moved back into the game.

"I saw a third baseman for the Astros charge a bunt, pick it up barehanded, and throw a strike to first, but the guy was safe. Earlier in the game, that same third baseman was out of position and lucked out. He backpedaled and caught a ball as he tripped over the bag, forcing one runner. As he's falling, he fires to first and they get a double play."

"Uh-huh," Miriam said, not quite following him.

"Do you see it, Momma? On a bad play, out of position, lucky, the guy makes a double play that takes his team out of a jam and keeps them in the game. Then, on the best play he made all year, the runner is safe and the game starts to turn. In the scorebook, his best play looks like his worst and his worst play looks like a five-to-three double play."

"So what's the moral of your story, El?"

He smiled. "The moral is, you talk to your mother about baseball stuff and you get to stay up later."

She chased him to bed. "There really is a moral to that story, though, isn't there?" she said as she tucked him in. "I think that if you do the right thing because it's the right thing, sometimes you win and sometimes you lose, but it evens out. You can do the right thing and fail, or you can do the wrong thing and get lucky. But you can never do the wrong thing on purpose and hope to get lucky very often. Isn't that just like life?"

He shrugged, but she could tell it wasn't because he wasn't interested in where she was heading.

"That lesson works in life as well as in baseball, El."

"Does it?"

"Don't you think so?"

⚾ ⚾ ⚾

Elgin didn't know what she wanted him to say, so he just scowled and concentrated on getting situated under the covers. She had pushed him too far. She was talking adult stuff now, and though she seemed to think he was following her, it was making him uncomfortable. He didn't want her to make such a big deal of it.

"I tried to do the right thing with your dad and nothin worked out. I tried to do the right thing by movin to Chicago. We won't know till spring if that was the right thing to do, at least for you."

"You mean if I get to play in a good enough league, we'll find out how good of a player I really can be?"

"El, I didn't come here just to find out what kind of a baseball player you would become."

"I know."

"No, you don't. You think I moved you here for that. If I only wanted to see how good you were, I would have kept you down there where you could play most of the year and where they would've moved you into a higher league."

"Will they do that here?"

"I don't know."

"They'd better."

"Why?"

"Cause I'm better than the kids my age here."

"Are you sure?"

Elgin nodded. "I wouldn't mind playing with the men in the softball league."

Miriam threw her head back and laughed. "Let's not get carried away."

⚾ ⚾ ⚾

Miriam was glad the conversation had found its way back to reality, to baseball, as their talks usually did. She felt guilty that she often tried to steer such a young boy into adult talk. She longed for the day when he would be old enough to understand. She didn't think he was far afield from what was going on in her mind and heart; she just didn't know how much he understood.

The Chicago winter had been depressing for them both. There were not the snow drifts and traffic jams the locals predicted and reminisced about, but it was bitter cold. Hot water was an inconsistent luxury. A hot-meal charity mistook their address for another and tried to deliver dinner one night. Miriam had explained that they were not needy, that their dinner was on the stove.

Elgin, however, was curious to know whether what they had to offer was better than the ravioli in the kitchen. Miriam dragged him from the door and explained the situation to him. They had a good laugh over it, then Miriam went to her bed and wept.

She didn't understand her own emotions. The sun setting so soon after Elgin's school let out depressed her. The sweetness of people delivering hot meals to shut-ins or the elderly touched her. But being mistaken for a charity case, probably because of the building she lived in, reached her soul.

Yes, she thought, we are needy. But she couldn't bring herself to accept handouts. They were not eligible and did not need the hot meal, but when a church group came by with warm winter coats, it took all her reserve to send them away with a polite thank-you.

She had had to experience them to believe the sub-zero temperatures, the wind-chill waits for the bus, the piercingly frigid walks from the bus to the transient hotel. She had taken to wearing several layers of clothing, but her porous cotton overcoat made her long for something down-filled.

She had sacrificed to buy Elgin a warm parka. She would not have been able to live with herself if he'd had to get to and from school and play outside without it. For herself, ear muffs, a hat, a scarf, and decent gloves augmented her flimsy coat. By spring, if it ever came, she would have not only her savings, her college fund, and her bills up to date, but she would also have enough to register Elgin in a real baseball league.

As the days grew longer, but seemingly no warmer, Elgin began playing fastpitch with his friends a few blocks away on weekends and for a little less than an hour on school days. He devoured the sports pages, which Mr. Bravura saved for him from the lobby.

Ricardo Bravura was a man in his late fifties, short with spindly legs and arms but a girth that belonged to a much larger man. His remaining wisps of hair were greasy and unkempt, and only occasionally did he keep his teeth in all day. He was not an intimidating man, but he maintained the policies of the absentee ownership of the hotel, which meant no breaks for anyone. He knew how to throw out the drunks who wanted to doze in the lobby. And he knew how to evict the tenants who didn't keep their rent paid in advance.

He was not there as a referee for the residents. It was up to them to keep out of each other's way. He might threaten people to keep them quiet, but once a renter got past Bravura's desk, he was on his own. Two maids changed the linens once every three days or with each new client, unless you rented by the month, which the Woodells did. Then you did your own housework.

It was plain to Miriam that the evidently harmless Mr. Bravura was enamored with her and might have been a devout lecher in his day. But now he was old and tired and contented himself to just notice and compliment nice-looking women when the mood struck him. He was solicitous to her to a fault, but he had never been inappropriate. She tried to exude an air that precluded that.

She appreciated that he was nice to Elgin. He let him use the office phone in emergencies, though Elgin was to use the pay phone whenever he had change. Best of all, Mr. Bravura finally caught on that Elgin was willing to tidy up the dingy lobby in exchange for the day's paper—specifically the sports section.

So every morning after the early risers had cleared out, Ricardo would dutifully cache the most unwrinkled sports section from those that had been left and save it for his young lobby attendant. Elgin could breeze through the suffocating darkness of greasy wood and cracking leather in just a few minutes, clearing and tossing the trash. Then he would glide past the cluttered, glassed-in cubicle with "Manager" stenciled on it. Without slowing, he would take the proffered *Tribune* or entire *Sun-Times,* promise to greet his "lovely mother," and retreat to the studio couch in their apartment.

There, with just enough time between breakfast and school, while his mother dressed for work, Elgin devoured the numbers that defined his world. All through the dark, cold days there had been scant mention of trades, deals, and winter meetings. But with February had come spring training.

"The scores mean nothing, Momma," he tried to explain. "The managers are experimenting, trying everyone, working on plays, pitches, situations. But the batting averages mean a lot. The veterans don't care if they're facing the Cy Young award winner or some guy who'll never play a regular season game in the big leagues. They're there to prove they still have it. They don't want a rookie proving it's his turn."

Miriam would listen with one ear as she steeled herself for the day. With every layer of clothing she reminded herself that this was worth it. This was why she had come to Chicago. Today it would be spring training box scores. Tomorrow it would be Little League. But someday, it would be broadcasting. Or something. Anything. Elgin Woodell would be something more than his daddy, more than anyone who had ever borne that name. She would make it possible, give him all the opportunities, and he would not squander it.

9

"HOW YOU DOING WITH YOUR FASTPITCH HITTING, El?" Miriam called, pulling on a boot.

"You won't believe it," he said. "You should come and watch sometime. I'm the best hitter every day, and I'm still the youngest."

She stopped and looked at him. "Are you serious?"

"Yes, ma'am. Hardly anybody can get me out twice in a row."

"You caught onto that pretty fast."

"It seemed like forever to me. Using a broom handle to hit a tennis ball, pitched from up close like that, seems like the hardest thing to do. But once you catch on, it's fun."

"When it starts getting lighter, I'll come watch. By the time I get off work now, it's already pitch black."

⚾ ⚾ ⚾

The day Miriam decided to make good on her promise to Elgin was also the day Charlie from marketing decided to make his latest move on her.

"At least let me walk you to the bus."

"I'm watching my son play ball on the near west side."

"Bad neighborhood," Charlie said. "Pretty woman like you ought not to—"

"I'll be perfectly fine," she said, not looking at him. "Thanks anyway."

"Any time," he said, as if he meant it.

Usually Miriam appreciated the attention. But not from Charlie. The white mark on his ring finger told of his fresh second divorce.

She knew the neighborhood was bad where Elgin played fastpitch. She lived close enough. When she got off the bus she thought about dropping her stuff off at the hotel, but the sun was setting fast and she didn't have the time or the energy to endure Mr. Bravura's eyes, or his fawning. He would offer to look after her things or even deliver them to her apartment, but that would cost her precious minutes of polite small talk. So Miriam kept trudging. The walk home with Elgin would be no ordeal. He was her existence.

Spring was around the corner, but no one had informed Chicago. Miriam was dressed almost as she had been for the dead of winter, though she wore walking shoes rather than boots and her scarf hung inside her coat, not wrapped around her neck and face. She wondered how pretty she looked now, the bulky garments hiding her petite figure, a floppy knit hat pulled over her flaming hair.

She sat on a stoop across the street from where the kids batted. There were three kids to a team today, and Elgin was waiting his turn to hit. He gave a small, shy wave, as if not wanting to draw attention to his mother. She smiled at him and remained in the shadows, though it was even colder there.

A black kid of about fourteen was pitching. He was wild, but he threw the bald tennis ball so hard Miriam wondered how anyone could see it, let alone get a stick on it. The bat was exactly what Elgin had said it was: a broomstick with electrical tape wrapped at one end for a handle. No wonder his palms were black every day.

The hitter stood in front of a wall, and if the pitch got past him and slammed into the chalk-drawn strike zone (which was the same for everyone, regardless of height), the pitcher called it a strike. That led to countless arguments, of course, but everyone wanted to keep playing, so compromises always ensued.

"Oh-and-two," the pitcher hollered as he began his wind-up. Miriam squinted, trying to pick up the flight of the ball. The hitter, a big white kid with long, dark curls, spun to get out of the way, but the ball hit him in the temple. It skied high above the pitcher and drifted back toward the buildings on Miriam's side of the street.

"He hit that?" one of the two fielders said as he settled under it.

"No!" the pitcher squealed, doubling over. "It hit him!"

Everyone was laughing, including the hitter, though it had to have stung. The pitcher hollered, "One-and-two," as he wound to fire again. This time he threw a lazy curve that started toward the hitter and broke to the outside. Curls started to bail out, then tried to stay in and swing. The ball curved away from him so far that he missed it with a weak swing and looked silly. The boys all laughed again, including the hitter.

"I burned you, man!" the pitcher said. "You shoulda seen yourself, man! Two down!"

"Okay, El-El, get in there. Big stick, heat against heat. Let's see what you got."

That was the first time Miriam had ever heard anyone call her son El-El. Was it a teasing name, as if he were a baby? She would have to ask him.

"You already know what he's got, man," Elgin's Puerto Rican teammate sang out. "He seven for nine against you already, and three homers."

The pitcher threw so hard that the ball bounced off the wall and back to him on one hop.

"Strike one!" he said.

Elgin had stepped into the pitch and opened his hips, but he had held his swing at the last instant. The pitch had been at about Elgin's eye level. He cocked his head and pursed his lips at the pitcher.

"It was in the zone," Darnell said in an apologetic falsetto.

"It was in the zone," Elgin mimicked, and Miriam was stunned. To make fun of a black person constituted the fixings for a fight where she came from. She watched in amazement as everyone laughed, including the pitcher. "Come on, Darnell, I'm not a seven-footer here!"

"That pitch was in the zone, wasn't it, boys?" Darnell said, turning to look at his fielders. They both nodded.

"O-and-one," Elgin sighed. "Now I dare you to bring that pitch down six inches."

Darnell went into his exaggerated wind-up, and again the fastball hurtled toward the wall. Elgin followed the pitch with his eyes, keeping his chin down and his head steady as he stepped and opened his hips. The ball came in at about chest level, and Elgin blasted it straight back at Darnell. The pitcher flinched and tried to move, but Miriam was sure he hadn't moved a muscle until the ball was well past him, though it had come within inches of his ear. One of the fielders shot out his glove and the ball slammed into it and ricocheted back to Darnell, where it hit him just below the knee and bounced harmlessly away.

The team in the field whooped and high-fived each other and ran in to hit. Elgin and his teammates shook their heads and grabbed their gloves. The ball had not reached the building across the street, so it wasn't a hit; it was as simple as that. Though Elgin had hit it as hard as Miriam had seen a tennis ball hit, he was out.

Elgin hit three more times before it became too dark. Once he lofted a high pop-up that was uncatchable but fell as an out in the street. The other two times he rifled doubles off the wall across the street. As they walked home he explained his new nickname.

"I don't really like it, so don't start calling me that. But they took the first syllable of my first name and the last syllable of my last name."

"Clever."

"But I don't like it."

"I heard you, El. I can still call you El, can't I? Aren't you cold?"

"I'm still sweating," he said, his parka slung over his shoulder.

"That's a good time to stay bundled up," she said. "That wind will chill you."

"C'mon, Momma. I'm no baby anymore."

She looked at him and realized he was right. He was no baby anymore. He was smaller than the kids he played fastpitch with, but for his age he was tall, lankier than ever.

"So, how'd I do?" he asked at home as they ate.

"How'd you do? You did fantastic! I don't understand how you can hit that ball."

"I don't either. I remember when I couldn't hit that thing to save my life. It would come in there and bang off the wall before I had time to think."

"So how do you do it?"

"I don't think."

"What do you mean?"

"I mean I really don't think about it. Daddy used to tell me to use my instincts rather than my mind. I didn't really know what he meant until now. I mean, Daddy pitched as hard as he could to me, but from—"

"Did he really?"

"I think so. He said he did, and I know I couldn't hit him."

"You hit him a lot, El."

"But not when he was pitching his fastest. Nobody could. At the end of each practice he'd throw me a dozen or so of his hardest pitches. I don't think I fouled off more than one or two ever."

"Did he throw faster than this Darnell?"

"Yeah, but this is a little tougher. A tennis ball is lighter and can move a lot more, and it comes in from so much closer. I finally realized I didn't have time to think. I could guess, but I couldn't really think about it."

"That doesn't make sense."

"Yes, it does. Big leaguers try to guess what pitch a guy will throw and about where he'll throw it. It gives them a little edge."

"Only if they're right."

"Exactly. But there's not enough time to think about where the pitcher's arm is and the spin of the ball. Daddy says that all goes into the hitter's computer."

"His brain."

"Right. But you just see that and react and hope for the best."

"Do you realize that baseball tryouts are next Saturday?" Miriam said.

"Momma, I know how many days and hours there are to go."

10

Miriam found herself one of hundreds of parents who showed up with their kids for the baseball tryouts the following Saturday. Elgin had not slept well. She had heard him up in the night several times.

"Sick?" she had asked him.

"No, ma'am."

"Nervous?"

"I don't think so. Excited, I guess."

They sat in bleachers, huddled in their coats, as kids continued to sign up and pay.

"This league goes from age eight to twelve, El. Lots of competition. The man told me they have a minor league and a major league. He said it's just as likely to see a twelve-year-old in the minors as it is to see an eight- or nine-year-old in the majors. It's all based on ability."

"But the minors are mostly the younger ones and the majors the older ones?"

She nodded. "Don't worry. I'm sure you'll be one of the younger ones in the majors."

Elgin leaned forward, elbows on his knees, and looked into his mother's eyes.

"You don't get it, do you, Momma?"

"Get what?"

"What I'm excited about. I can hardly wait to get out there and play some real baseball. You know there's nothing I'd rather do."

"I know. But don't pretend you're not just a little worried—"

"I'm not."

"Then why are you sittin here fidgetin?"

"You're gonna think I'm bragging."

"Well, I probably will. You've been gettin a little showy here lately."

"Then I'd better not tell you why I'm so excited."

"Go ahead."

"I don't want you thinking I'm too big for my britches, like you always say."

"Go ahead and tell me. If you can't tell me—"

"Momma, what I'm starting to really like about baseball is that I'm so good at it. I love for people to see me play. Nothing makes me feel better than for you to tell me I did good. And I love it when everybody stops and watches."

"That would make me so nervous I'd just fall apart," Miriam said.

"Not me," Elgin said. "I pretend not to notice, but I do. I thought it was great when I heard people in tryouts or at practices talk about me. But when we got into games and I did something that made people clap and cheer, well..."

He couldn't find the words. Miriam looked at him. "A little humility would do you some good, Elgin."

"Now, see, Momma, I told you you would think that. But I'm not bragging. I'm just trying to be honest. I don't know how I got so good, except Daddy was good and he taught me everything. I'm fast and I'm tall and I've got a good arm. But I don't think that's that important."

"What is important then?"

"I just love the game so much. You know I love the game."

"Do I ever! You love it more than anybody ought to. I mean, you see things in this game your daddy never saw, and that's the truth."

"It's a beautiful game, Momma."

"I know. I didn't always know, but you're teachin me, and more than your dad did."

"Really?"

"Honest. I can't get into all those statistics you love and everything, but the little things you notice, the strategy you come up with, well—maybe you oughta be a coach someday."

"You mean after I've played twenty years in the big leagues?"

She smacked him on the shoulder. "Mr. Humble," she said. And she hugged him. She felt him stiffen and pull away and realized he was getting past the age where he would let her do that in public.

The eight- and nine-year-olds were on the field, baseballs flying everywhere, hardly anyone catching or throwing with any accuracy. When the ten- through twelve-year-olds were summoned to an adjacent football field,

Elgin jumped up and began to run. He skidded to a stop, raced back, shed his coat, and took off again, this time forgetting his glove. He whirled to retrieve it and Miriam tossed it to him. She surprised him and he missed it.

"Hope you get an ovation for that!" she said. "If you can't catch a big old floppy glove thrown by an old woman—"

"You don't look that old to me," a young father said from behind her.

Miriam hated herself for turning to look.

"Good morning," the man said.

He was younger than she, no wedding band.

"Good morning," she said, turning back to watch the tryout.

"My son is just starting," he said. "Your boy?"

"Second year," she said, turning only enough so he could hear her. "He's almost eleven."

"Go on! I'm talking about the one who was just here."

"So am I," she said, her hands in her pockets, one fingering a copy of Elgin's birth certificate. Would it always be this way?

"That boy's eleven?"

"Almost," she said, trying to mask her sarcasm. "Almost eleven is ten."

"Well, it sure is, isn't it?" he said, scooting down to her row. She looked the other way, frustrated and disappointed. She wasn't this lonely. And she wanted to watch Elgin play. The field where he was trying out was to her left, and when the man noticed she was looking that way, he moved to that side of her. Now she was angry and would not look at him. She answered him in the least cordial ways she could think of, short of rudeness.

The man kept trying to get her to watch his Robin.

Robin! Who would name a boy Robin? Does he have a brother named Batman?

"What's your boy's name?"

"Elgin."

"Elgin! Now there's a name for you! I don't think I've ever heard of a person named Elgin before. I mean, there's Elgin Watches, and the city of Elgin. Oh, course there was the basketball player, Elgin Baylor, but I think that's the only other one I've heard of."

"Really?" she said, as if she did not care.

"Yeah. How bout you?"

"Me?"

"You heard of any other Elgins, or is he named after somebody?"

"He's named after one of my husband's great uncles."

She hadn't meant to refer to Neal as her husband; she really hadn't. She was glad for the slip though, because she heard the life die in the voice of this new "friend."

"Do you have an unusual name too?"

"No, sir. I'm Mrs. Neal Woodell."

"What does your husband do?"

"He's a professional race car driver."

"Have I heard of him?"

"How would I know that?"

"What did you say his name was?"

"Kyle Petty."

"You're putting me on!"

"Yes, I am. Now, do you mind? I just want to watch my son."

"Well, sorry! I just wanted to make sure you didn't really see yourself as an old woman, like you said to the boy there. Elgin. I mean, someone as lovely as you..."

Miriam stood and moved five rows down to the front where she stared straight at Elgin. She was relieved to hear the man behind her get up and move back to where he had come from.

⚾ ⚾ ⚾

On the field Elgin and the others his age had been instructed to find a partner and warm up. He had hooked up with a kid who couldn't throw or catch. Elgin had to toss the ball easily so the boy could grab it. And Elgin had to chase just about every one of the throws the boy made. Fortunately, a coach noticed and paired Elgin off with a better player. But even he stepped out of the way and took Elgin's crisp throws out to the side, away from his body.

They had the boys run a lap around the goal posts. Elgin far outdistanced everyone.

"You get to hit first," a coach called to him. "Pick out a bat."

Elgin stood in the makeshift on-deck circle while a teenager strapped on the catcher's gear and an adult warmed up from the pitcher's rubber.

"All right," the man said. "Step in there and take six cuts. Hey! You're only eleven now, right?"

"Ten," Elgin said.

"Ten!"

"Well, officially eleven. Almost eleven."

The pitcher looked at another coach and shook his head. Then he stepped and threw. The ball was a foot over Elgin's head. The next one was outside. The next low.

"I'm still getting loose," the man said. "But let's not be too picky in there."

Elgin shrugged. The next pitch was inside and high, but hittable. Elgin ripped it to right field on a line, about 200 feet.

"That woulda been a homer in this league," the pitcher said, grunting as he released another.

It was a fat pitch, a little faster than the last. Elgin hit it in the same spot, maybe twenty feet farther. The pitcher spun to watch it go. "I must not be as loose as I thought," he said.

He went into an exaggerated wind-up and Elgin knew his best, fastest pitch was coming. He crushed it, driving it high and deep to center, at least two hundred and fifty feet.

The pitcher had turned his back on Elgin to watch the flight of the ball. He faced that direction until all the balls had been tossed back. He cradled six in his big glove and turned back around. "All right, son, listen up. I want you to take six more swings. I'm gonna throw you my best stuff, sliders, curves, changes, fastballs. As soon as you've swung, I'm comin with the next one, so be prepared. Ready?"

Elgin dug in and stole a glance at his mother in the stands. He had to search for an extra second, because she had moved. She raised a fist to him, and he turned back to face the first of six quick pitches.

Elgin fouled the first pitch straight back, then hit the next five solidly, every one a line drive to the outfield. Two were to left, one to center, two to right, including one longer than the shot to center had been. Elgin noticed, and he knew his mother would have too, that people had stopped to watch.

Elgin liked getting extra swings, but he was embarrassed because the other kids were waiting to hit when the coach asked him to stay in there. He had already taken three more swings than they had planned for, and now they were bringing in another pitcher, an older teenager, a friend of the catcher.

"Can you hit breaking balls?" the coach asked as the new pitcher warmed up.

"Well," Elgin said, "you said you were going to throw me some. Did you?"

"Are you trying to be smart?"

"No, sir. I just never had anybody throw me anything but straight pitches except my daddy, and I don't remember what breakin balls looked like."

"Well, the last three I threw you were half-decent sliders for one of my vintage. I pitched at Purdue and was in the White Sox organization for a couple of years."

"Did you ever know my dad? He was with the Pirates in the minors. Neal Woodell?"

The man shook his head. "Don't think I ever ran across him. He probably came along later." He turned to the pitcher. "You ready, James?"

"Yeah!"

"Now, son, this guy's a lefty, so be careful not to bail out."

"I never bail out. I switch."

"You switch! Now ain't that somethin! Go ahead, then. If you can hit this guy like you hit me, we're gonna hafta have a look at that birth certificate."

"My mother has it."

"And is she here?"

"Yes, sir."

"Where you from, boy?"

"Hattiesburg, Mississippi."

"You play ball down there?"

"Not much. A few games before we moved last year."

"I sure coulda used you then."

"Can't you use me now?"

"Oh, I believe we'll find a spot for you, son. Yes, sir, I believe we will. Right now we're just trying to figure out where."

Elgin moved to the other side of the plate and stood about ten feet away, watching Jim, a tall, powerfully built left-hander, throw his last two warm-up pitches. Elgin finally felt fear. This guy threw hard enough to hurt somebody. Maybe he *would* be bailing out.

"Get in there, Woodell," the coach hollered.

The first pitch popped the glove before Elgin could react, except that his lead foot had uncontrollably stepped toward third base. "Strike one!" the coach yelled. "Right down the pipe! Where you goin?"

The next pitch was inside, and though Elgin looked determined not to step in the bucket, he almost fell down trying to get out of the way. But the pitch was not really close to him. It merely caught the inside corner.

"Strike two! You were a flash in the pan, son. You were hitting off a broken down old pitcher. C'mon, show me what you got!"

The young pitcher came straight over the top and the ball appeared to be spinning vertically. It dropped through the strike zone and Elgin swung and missed. The coach laughed. The pitcher smiled. The catcher spoke.

"Would you like to see that one again?"

"Yes, sir."

"Do you trust me?"

"I have no choice."

"I'm callin for the same pitch. Trust me."

Sure enough, the motion was the same. Elgin reacted instinctively and shot the ball right back at the pitcher. He caught it but it spun him around. Elgin stepped out of the box, shaking his top hand.

"That's a heavy ball," the coach said. "The harder it's thrown, the heavier it feels on the bat. Did you feel the resistance when you hit it? Feel like it was drivin your bat back at you?"

Elgin nodded.

"Okay, listen, Elgin. Jim here is the ace of the local American Legion team. He's already been scouted by the pros. Has a promising future. I've seen him pitch three games where nobody got that much bat on one of his pitches. Was that luck, a fluke?"

"I don't know. I don't think so."

"Try three more."

"What's he throwing this time?" Elgin asked the catcher.

"Huh-uh. I'm already gonna hafta answer for tipping you off on that one. You're on your own now, buddy."

The next pitch was a sinking fastball, down and in. Elgin got around late and hit it directly to where a second baseman would have been. The bat was solid on the ball. Jim pumped another fastball, this one with more on it, and Elgin couldn't catch up with it. Swing and a miss. Elgin stepped out and pretended to be getting a better grip.

"Do me a favor," he said softly. "Call for the same pitch."

The catcher did, and Elgin drove the ball deep to the opposite field. Jim stood on the rubber, eyebrows raised. The coach asked someone else to take over the tryout and told Elgin to bring his mother to the registration table in the hallway of the school.

"This is your *mother?*" said the man who introduced himself as Mr. Morrison. "Maybe you are as young as you say. Ma'am, do you have proof of the boy's age?"

She produced the copied document.

"Uh-huh. Ma'am, we have a little problem, which could be an opportunity for your boy if you approve of it."

"A problem?"

"Well, yes. One of my jobs as league commissioner, in fact my most important job, is to ensure the safety of everybody on the field. We spare no expense for the best helmets, and we hire the best umpires—who also look out for the boys. From time to time I have to make difficult decisions about individual players, and I've made one about your son as it relates to the safety of other kids in this program. I confess this is the first time I have outlawed a boy under twelve, and I'm still finding it hard to believe this boy is only nearly eleven, but—"

"What more proof do you need?"

"Oh, I'm taking your word for it, ma'am. I don't see any reason why you would want to lie to us. But I need to tell you from the perspective of a parent, a commissioner, and as one who pitched to this boy, he does not belong at this level of baseball."

"But he's only—"

"I know. And we go up to twelve, and we have some twelve-year-olds who might give him a run for his money. You know, we have a boy in our program, well, he'll be in the thirteen- to fifteen-year-old league this year, but he got his picture in *Sports Illustrated* last year when he hit five straight homers."

"In one game?" Elgin said.

"Well, no, in two games, but it was five straight. And son, not one of those homers was hit as hard as three balls I saw you hit today. Mrs. Woodell, I'm going to have to ask you to let me try him out for the next level. He'll be eleven by the time the season starts. I know that doesn't seem to make much difference, but—"

Miriam glanced at Elgin. He looked so excited he could hardly stand it.

"I don't know," she said. "If those kids are as big as the ones who pitched and caught today..."

Mr. Morrison laughed. "Oh, no, ma'am. Those are both eighteen-year-old American Legion players. He won't be facing anything like that."

"Well, I don't want him pitchin or catchin or playin the infield with kids too much older and bigger than he is."

"I understand," Mr. Morrison said. "I just need your written permission to try him out at that level and see where he lands."

"You mean I might not make a team?" Elgin asked, suddenly ashen.

"That's the bad news," Mr. Morrison said. "And I want to be straight up with you. I've already made the decision to keep you out of the younger league. I'm not gonna change my mind about that. But I'm not the commish of the higher league, and I can't make them take you. They might be afraid to, or you just might not be good enough. Personally, I think you're better than average for a kid starting out in that league, so you shouldn't have any trouble. But you need to know that you just might find yourself in no man's land."

"Sir?"

"You might find that you're too big and strong and accomplished for our league, but not ready for theirs."

"Then what happens?"

"Then you sit out a year and we look at you again."

Miriam looked at Elgin and squeezed his knee. "That might be for the best, El," she whispered.

"Are you kidding, Momma? I'd die! You know how long I've been looking forward to this! I need better competition."

"But thirteen- through fifteen-year-olds? Elgin, I don't know."

"At least let me try out, Momma. Please!"

"I don't guess there'd be any harm in takin a look at you on the field with those kids. When do they try out?"

"This afternoon, ma'am. But let me put you in touch with that league commissioner first. There's no sense makin any promises before I get a chance to talk to him."

The four of them met in a classroom away from the registration table. Mr. Richter, the older league's top man, was tall and bald. He held a red cap in his hand as he greeted Miriam and Elgin.

"You have another son who wants to try out for our league?" he asked.

Miriam looked pleadingly to Mr. Morrison. "No, Carl," Morrison said, "this here is the boy."

"Fine. What's the problem?"

"Well, he won't be eleven till the season starts."

"Eleven? Have you seen the—"

"Yes, I've seen the birth certificate "

"What happens if he gets hurt in the tryouts?"

"If you saw him hit, you wouldn't worry about it. His mother won't let him pitch, catch, or play the infield anyway."

"Well, neither would I. But what's the sense of having a younger kid on a team if he's going to ride the bench? How about we have a look at him, and if he doesn't make it, you take him back?"

"I've already explained to them, Carl, that this boy will not be playing at our level."

"You afraid of him? Afraid you won't get him on your team and he'll show you up?"

Morrison looked at Richter with a pursed, tolerant smile. "Carl, if I'm afraid of anything, it's that I'll get him, and he'll kill somebody with a line drive in the first inning of the first game."

11

BY THE FIRST PRACTICE OF THE TIGERS, the thirteen- to fifteen-year-old team Elgin was assigned to, he had had his eleventh birthday. The kids who had graduated to this level by turning thirteen looked young and inexperienced and wide-eyed. Elgin was the talk of the team, and of the league. He was the reason so many other kids and coaches from the league showed up to watch the Tigers practice.

The pitcher stood fifty-four feet from the plate, nine feet farther than Elgin was used to. He would find that only an advantage. He would have to get used to the new distance between the bases, seventy-five feet rather than sixty. He was no longer the fastest runner on his team. He was about fourth, and the only thirteen-year-old faster was Barry Krass, the one who had made *Sports Illustrated* by pounding out five consecutive homers.

Miriam was especially intrigued by the Krass boy, because Elgin was largely silent about him. It was a new experience for Elgin to be outrun by someone only a few years older than he, and Miriam watched for signs of jealousy. Elgin was clearly going to be a star, but it did not appear he would lead this team in hitting, running, throwing, or anything. He had found a level where he could compete equally, but he would apparently not dominate.

"There's a lot of pressure on the boy," his new coach, Maury Rollins, told Miriam. "I don't believe he's got the arm to pitch at this level, which means he can't catch either cause you need a strong gun to second base. The infield's too big for his arm, and he's too small to play first base. I put him in the outfield as you requested, which he admitted he's not too excited about. But he knows the game so he didn't argue with me."

"You noticed that?"

"Yes, ma'am. I could almost make him an assistant coach. I'm seriously thinking about having him coach one of the bases for me. He told me that if he was the manager and this was the American League, he'd make himself the designated hitter. I told him he'll have to wait a few years to make the American League! Ha! Anyway, I think he might have himself underrated as an outfielder. He's got better than average speed for a thirteen-year-old, and we both know how old he is. He gets to the ball well, senses it off the bat, hits the right cutoff man—not with a huge throw, but he gets it there—and I think he'll make a fine left fielder. I'll probably hit him in the lower third of the batting order."

Miriam pursed her lips. "I don't guess he'll like that."

"Oh, probably not, but there's five or six hitters on this club who deserve to hit ahead of him. Krass is one. He'll be the only player under fourteen hitting ahead of Elgin. Have you seen that boy hit?"

"I've only heard about him. Is he fixin to hit today?"

"He's in the hole," Maury Rollins said. "Stick around."

Miriam watched from the stands as the boys took batting practice. Elgin was in left field, but she detected no disappointment, no lethargy. He loved the game and he loved playing, so even though he might rather be in a more strategic or active position, he wasn't letting it show.

Because it was batting practice, one of the assistant coaches was throwing three-quarter speed, and the kids were teeing off. That sent a lot of fly balls and line drives into left, and Elgin seemed to be having great fun chasing them down.

From what Miriam could tell, and from what she had heard, the Krass boy would be difficult to dislike, even if he was better than Elgin. He was polite and good-natured, and though he didn't seem as obsessed with the game as Elgin, he clearly enjoyed it. He created a stir when it was his turn to hit. He was the most famous player the league had ever seen, based on the *Sports Illustrated* mention alone. Two local and one network television stations had come to the first game after his five homers. He didn't disappoint, going three for four but saving his lone homer for the last inning, after they had packed up and left.

The home run fence was 250 feet down the lines and 280 to center. Krass was a right-hander, so Elgin played him to pull. Of the fifteen balls he hit, Miriam counted six that would have been homers on the smaller field. He hit none over this fence, but once chased Elgin to the warning track. Elgin lost the ball in the sun and saw it bounce over the fence. Miriam could tell he was angry. He kept looking behind him and resetting himself, as if he'd love to have the chance to have that play over.

Krass hit nearly as well as the older boys, but they had a little more pop, most putting one or two over the fence, the big first baseman sending one over the center-field wall. Krass went out to play second after he hit, and when it was Elgin's turn, he stepped in left-handed against the right-hand coach.

Miriam sensed everyone watching carefully, and she could see that Elgin was nervous. She wanted to talk to him, to tell him to just relax and work on his swing and not try to impress anyone.

Apparently that was his plan too, because as the first pitch came, he swung easily and was way late. He'd been studying the coach's pitching for half an hour and thought he had his speed down. But with the tension of the situation, the coach threw harder to Elgin. He was ready for the next pitch and lashed a screamer at Barry Krass's feet. All he could do was skip out of the way. Miriam heard the low whistles of approval from the crowd and wanted to see Elgin hit one over the fence. Just one. One more than Krass.

Listen to yourself! she thought. Now who's jealous and competitive?

Elgin was fooled on a couple of more pitches, missing one and fouling one off. But on ten straight he drove line drives into center and right. On the second to last pitch he bounced one over the left field fence. Miriam wondered if he had done it on purpose, to show that he could hit as far as Krass but to the opposite field.

"Exactly," he told her later.

"Are you serious?"

He nodded. "I'm glad you noticed."

She smiled. "You little scoundrel."

"Tell me you didn't love it, Momma."

"I loved it. That Krass boy sure seems nice though."

"Oh, he is! We have a good team even without me. We've got trouble though."

"Trouble?"

"Last year's left fielder. His dad's not too happy. He hit ninth all year anyway, but this year he probably won't play much."

"Because of you."

"Right. His dad said something to Mr. Rollins about a little kid pushing a fifteen-year-old out of the starting lineup. Mr. Rollins told him no decision has been made yet, but that he was sure both of us would play a lot."

"But that didn't satisfy him?"

"He said he was going to take it to the board."

"Oh, great."

"I'm not going to worry about it, Momma. What can they do? They won't let me play with kids my age, so I tried out and made this team. If I'm the best left fielder, that's where I should play, right?"

Miriam shrugged.

"Am I wrong, Momma?"

"Course not. But how would you feel if you were that boy?"

"I'd feel like I got my butt whipped by a kid."

"Elgin, don't talk like that!"

"Well, that's how I'd feel, and I'd start working on my game till I won my job back, or some job anyway."

"Don't be gettin conceited on me."

"I'm not! You asked me and I told you."

"Well, I don't mind tellin you, young man, that if the shoe was on the other foot, I wouldn't like it one bit."

In his first game of the season, Elgin batted seventh behind Barry Krass. The Tigers won 7–1. Krass was oh-for-two with a walk, a strikeout and a ground out. Elgin was two-for-three with a double to right center, a single to left, and a deep fly to left. He stole a base, was caught stealing once, and was errorless in the field. After the game, Miriam saw the father of last year's left fielder standing toe to toe with Coach Rollins.

"You say what you want, Maury, but you're gonna find a place for my kid to play, or—"

"Ralph, he pinch-hit in the last inning and struck out!"

"That's cause his timing is off cause he's not gettin enough action!"

"Where am I supposed to put him? You still think he's better than my new left fielder?"

"I didn't say that. I'm just sayin he's a veteran with a lot of experience and he ought to be starting."

"When he beats somebody out or somebody gets hurt, I'll put him in, but until then, I'll coach and you watch, okay?"

"You haven't heard the end of this, Maury."

"No kidding!"

⚾ ⚾ ⚾

Elgin was high on the walk to the bus. When Miriam took a left instead of a right, he stopped and looked at her.

"What're you doing?"

"Oh, I thought you deserved a cheeseburger for each of your hits today."

"Really? We can afford it?"

"No, but I put a little aside for this."

"Yeah!"

Several kids in various uniforms of teams in the area sat with their friends and families in the fast food place.

"I can't do this every game," Miriam cautioned.

"I know, Momma. I can hardly believe we're doing it now."

"I know it's been hard on you, El. We've never had much."

"It's all right."

"No, it isn't. I wish you could have a bat bag and your own bat again, a newer glove, wristbands, all that."

"I wish I could go to a movie once in a while."

"*That* we really can't afford. Honestly, Elgin, I don't know how suburban people do it. Those kids are always at movies, buy the latest CDs, wear expensive gym shoes, and dress in style."

Elgin sat staring out the window after he had finished eating. There were long lines at the cash register and people looking for places to sit, but it was as if he wanted to savor the moment.

"Those kids don't work, though, Ma, and they aren't very good ballplayers. Even the ones who are in shape don't know not to throw behind the runner. They never take the extra base, they throw too many times on a rundown, or they run a man to the next base instead of back to his old one."

"You don't mind not havin all that stuff then?"

"Sometimes I do. I don't like people knowing where we live, and my baseball shoes are too small. My clothes never look like much, so I'm glad I've got a uniform. On game days I look like everyone else."

"But how about when kids play their music or talk about the movies they've seen?"

"Yeah, sometimes I wish I could see what everybody else is seeing, but I know we can't afford it." Elgin slid to the end of the booth but stopped before he stood to leave. "There's something I want more than any of that stuff, though."

"What's that?"
"A letter from Daddy."

12

BY THE END OF THE REGULAR SEASON, when it had come time to choose the all-star team that would travel to other cities for various tournaments, Elgin Woodell had had a remarkable year.

He did not dominate the league. And he was not the best player or even the best hitter on his team. But his average was nearly .500, second on his team only to the leading hitter in the league. A couple of players from other teams finished second and third. As an eleven-year-old Elgin had finished fourth in hitting in a league for thirteen- to fifteen-year-olds.

He had played every inning of every game and had made just two errors, one on a misjudged fly ball and one on an overthrow of home from in front of the foul pole down the left field line. Though it was charged as an error, it was the play of the game, no one believing a kid that age and size could throw a baseball that far. And it had been only a foot above the catcher's leaping reach. The throw, even the opponents admitted, had the runner beat. Elgin had moved up in the batting order, initially to second, and finally to lead off, where he had an incredible on-base percentage. He hardly ever struck out, and Miriam's recollection of the season was that every time she turned around, Elgin was spraying a single or double into the gap. He faced only a few left-handed pitchers and was nine for twelve from the right side of the plate.

Barry Krass had shown well for his age. He finished hitting in the eighth spot in the lineup, starting at second base, and hitting just over .250. He would not make the traveling team.

Best of all, from Miriam's and Elgin's points of view, there had been little controversy. Ralph had taken his son out of the program because the league refused to force his coach to start him, and neither would they put him on another team. But no one was saying that Elgin hit the ball so hard that their sons were in danger. He wasn't hitting home runs left and right the way he would have in the younger league. And he wasn't pitching, so no one was making any noise about that.

After his errant throw to the plate, however, Maury Rollins took him behind the stands and watched him pitch. "Your dad didn't teach you much in the way of mechanics, did he?"

"No, sir. He wasn't a pitcher."

"Well, you're not either, but you could be next year. There's a pitching instructional book at the library." Elgin named it. "That's the one. Get it."

The next time Rollins privately watched Elgin pitch, he said, "Difference between night and day, kid. You're gonna pitch for me some next year."

"And play short some, I hope."

"No question. For now, just see if you can make that traveling squad at the position you're in. You should have a lot of fun and get some good experience."

⚾ ⚾ ⚾

Experience was an understatement.

"What I love most about this team is the uniform," Elgin told his mother. He savored everything from stirrups to sanitary hose to colored-sleeve undershirt. He padded out in stocking feet to show her. He looked like a major leaguer, all red and gray and white from head to toe.

"I only wish I could afford to get you new shoes," she said.

"That's all right. Hardly anybody else has new ones either."

Elgin's teammates were all city kids, just able to afford the registration fees. When they traveled to the suburbs, they faced teams that had the latest equipment, bat bags, gloves, wristbands, batting gloves, glove pads, even weighted rings for swinging a heavy bat in the on-deck circle. Even more impressive, they had warm-up jackets made of brightly colored nylon that made them look professional. The Chicago kids were intimidated when the other teams ran in a line onto the field, circling the home run fence, casually displaying all their fancy stuff, doing exercises, chanting, even singing. One team chanted, echoing their leader:

"Everywhere we go...(echo) People want to know...(echo) Who we are...(echo) Where we come from...(echo) So we tell them...(echo) Who we are...(echo)!" Then, in unison, "We are Granger! Mighty, mighty Granger!"

They also practiced a chant for when they got runners on base. They would say of the hitter, "Billy is a friend of mine, he can stroke it down the line. Stroke-it-down-the-line, stroke-it-down-the-line!"

In the event of a rally, they'd practice, "Rip, a-rip-city, rip-a-rip-a-rip-city, come on now, rip!"

Elgin's eyes and ears were as big as anyone else's. He felt self-conscious. His team didn't look like more than a bunch of guys with pretty uniforms and shoddy shoes and gloves. They had no chants, no routines. A couple of them even had high-top black tennies, which drew derisive comments from their opponents.

Maury Rollins called his kids around him before infield practice. "Listen up. Some of you guys are finished already. I can see it in your eyes. Are these kids older than you?"

"No!"

"Yes!" Elgin said, breaking the tension. Everyone laughed.

"Okay," Rollins said, "but they're not older than the rest of us! And you know what? All that stuff—the chants, the equipment—none of it wins ball games, does it?"

No one responded.

"Well, does it?"

The players shook their heads.

"I don't know if you guys are scared or just jealous. You want cool stuff or you want to win?"

"We want to win!"

"Then let's show em how a real team plays ball! Take the field!"

But they were tight, and they didn't show much. They seemed to sense the suburbanites watching them, chuckling at their shoes and gloves, laughing when they made errors.

"Fortunately," Rollins said when they came back in, "we're batting first. There's no science to this. They throw their best kid; we swing the bats. The team that scores the most runs still wins, remember. There are no runs added or taken away because of how you look."

When Elgin dug in left-handed against the Granger right-hander, the opposing coach moved his outfielders back.

"This is him!" he shouted. "This is Woodell!"

The announcement that he was leading off, the eleven-year-old, nearly two years younger than anyone on the field, quieted the crowd. There was a buzz as everyone stared. Elgin, who had stepped in and stared at the pitcher as he took the sign, stepped out.

"Atta boy! Atta boy, El!" Rollins hollered. "Good thinking! A heads-up kid!"

It would be some time and several more games before Elgin understood the wisdom and maturity he had shown by stepping out, putting the pressure on the pitcher, taking some control of the events.

Elgin almost always took the first pitch of a game, and this time was no exception. He stepped and opened his hips, but made no attempt to swing. The ball was straight and hard at the waist, and it split the plate. That would be good news for his teammates. If this guy grooved it, no matter how fast, they would do some hitting.

With Elgin appearing to hit away, the first and third basemen backed up even with their bases. Elgin had a spot picked out in left center where he would hit an outside pitch, and another in right center where he wanted to hit an inside pitch. Another plate-slicing fastball he would try to send back up the middle.

The big right-hander appeared to hold the ball a fraction of a second too long, and the next fastball came right at Elgin's midsection. He spun and dropped, narrowly escaping getting hit. The whooping and laughing from the Granger bench proved it had been a purpose pitch.

Elgin stood and brushed himself off, looking carefully for the sign at third. He was on his own. He was to get on any way he could. He dug a deep hole for his left foot, trying to show the pitcher he wasn't intimidated. There was no hitting a pitcher like this if you bailed out.

This time the pitcher tried to catch the outside corner with an offspeed pitch. The speed had fooled Elgin, but the location hadn't. He'd expected a fastball and was a little early squaring around for the bunt, and here came the fielders from the corners.

The first baseman was almost on top of him when he let the ball hit the bat and directed it between the pitcher and the second baseman, who had darted toward first. It was perfectly placed. No one would get to it in time to even attempt a throw. But as Elgin raced to first, he noticed the shortstop had come over to field the ball on the first base side of second. He dejectedly swiped at it and tossed it to the pitcher, then turned his back to Elgin to trudge back to position. No one was covering second, and Elgin never slowed. He continued around first and was halfway to second before the shouting started.

"Second! Second! He's going!" The shortstop whirled and tried to get to second in time for the throw, but the pitcher tossed it wildly. It had been only a flip, so there wasn't enough on it to get it far into center field. Elgin slid in head first, and as soon as his fingers touched the bag, he pulled his feet up and headed for third. It was a long shot, probably a foolish move, but it would take a good throw to get him.

His coach wildly waved him down, so he went into another head first slide. The throw was a couple of feet high, and he was safe. Now the look came to the pitcher's eyes that had been in the Chicago team's. With no one out, Chicago had a fast man at third, leading off, faking, feinting, distracting, looking for the passed ball that would score him. It never came, but with one out, a grounder to second was deep enough, and Chicago had broken the ice.

It wasn't much of a game after that. Elgin's teammates broke it open with a five-run second that included a home run, a double, and two errors. The chanting had stopped. The fancy equipment looked fraudulent. The shabby-looking kids from the city suddenly became the team to beat in the tournament.

Three days later, Chicago finished second, losing 2–1 in the championship game to the defending state titlists. Elgin made the all-tournament team and had two homers in four games, including one that produced his team's only run in the last game. All the way home the kids pestered Coach Rollins about getting into another tournament.

"If I can get some money from the league," the coach said, "I'd love to see what you guys could do. How about that? No good equipment, no chants, and we finish second anyway, by one run to the best team in the state last year. What I wouldn't give to play that team again!"

The league told the coach that the kids would have to pitch in several dollars apiece to get into another tournament in the south suburbs, but not enough of the kids could afford it. Elgin could hardly believe the season was over already. He was still playing fastpitch every day, against the advice and wishes of his coaches. ("It'll ruin your eye and your timing for baseball.") He found it was the best thing for him. It made baseball look easy.

Elgin was sad that fastpitch was all that was left to him for another year, but his heart leapt when he noticed the return address on a letter that waited for his mother, marked "Personal and Confidential." It was from the Alabama State Penitentiary.

13

MIRIAM WAS NOT AS EAGER as Elgin to know the contents of the letter from Alabama. She set her jaw and found reasons to criticize the way Elgin had begun preparing supper.

"You should have waited to start the rice," she said. "Now it's gonna be sticky."

"Sorry, Momma."

"Please quit callin me 'Momma'! You sound like a baby!"

He squinted and turned on her. "That's what I always call you. And I'm not a baby!"

She didn't answer. She hated when they squabbled, but both had to vent sometimes. Miriam busied herself so she could ignore the letter she had put in her purse as soon as Elgin had presented it to her.

"Once I get everything rollin, I'll sit down with the mail," she said.

Elgin couldn't stand the tension. He tried to interest himself in other things, but found himself sitting at the table, drumming his fingers.

"Ain't the Cub game on or somethin?" she asked.

"Ain't! Momma, you haven't said *ain't* in months! You're excited about this letter from Daddy, too. Ain't you?"

He had tried to be funny, but he had only angered her. She stopped and stared at him, hands on her hips.

"First off, I can talk any way I want and I don't need some child prodg—some child progeny or whatever tellin me—"

"Prodigy."

"Whatever. I am not excited about the letter! It's not even from your dad. If it was it would have his lock box number in the return address. This is from some official at the prison. It's gonna be just some legal detail, and if they thought you should see it, they wouldn't have marked it personal."

"And confidential."

"Yeah."

"You think it's bad news, Momma? Like Daddy's sick again, or hurt, or dead?"

"I thought you said bad news."

"Momma!"

"Stop callin me that!" Miriam dried her hands and sat at the table with Elgin. "There's somethin you got to get straight, son," she said. "Your daddy ain't never gettin outa that prison." Elgin started to speak, but she cut him off. "I know more about it than he even remembers, and what he did is the kind of thing they throw away the key for."

"But he said—"

"I know what he says, and I also had Mr. Thatcher look into it. It was bad, El. Your dad did somethin that can never be fixed. He can be as sorry as he wants and he can come up with all his typical drunk excuses. But he was drivin without a license, drivin after a bartender told him he shouldn't, drivin after a friend had said he would drive him home. He was goin too fast, got a cop chasin him—which he probably didn't even know—and he ran full off the road, over the curb, over the parkway, past a row of trees, onto the sidewalk, and killed an old man pokin along on a three-wheel bicycle. Now I hate to have to make it so plain to you, El, but do you see why your daddy got life in prison and was lucky he didn't get death?"

Elgin was speechless. His dad had told him a much tamer story, one that made it appear the whole thing could have been the old man's fault. He talked as if appeals were in the works and that he would likely get the sentence reversed and be released soon.

"Will he get out like when he's old?"

"I believe he was given sixty-five years, Elgin. And he was in his thirties when he went in."

"Sixty-five years! He'll be almost a hundred!"

"He'll never live that long, Elgin. Prison is not a good place for livin to old age."

Elgin shook his head and the tears came. "Momma, would you just read the letter and tell me what you can?"

She nodded and took it to the living room. It was on Prison Chaplain Alton Wallace's stationery.

Dear Mrs. Woodell:

I had been under the impression that you and your husband,

Neal Lofert Woodell, were divorced. He assures me this is not the case. If he is being other than truthful with me, I would appreciate your so advising me so that I not trouble you in the future with his requests that I contact you. If there is a copy of a document that would clarify your marital situation, that would suffice. (I am sure I could ascertain the truth in his files here, but asking for such makes the administration nervous and often reflects poorly on the inmate I'm trying to assist.)

Meanwhile, Neal is hospitalized yet again, but this time not for delirium tremens. He has largely recovered from the effects of alcohol, due to time and medication and his inability to procure the same. This time, I'm sad to say, he attempted to take his own life. He used a sharpened spoon to tear a gash on the inside of his elbow and lost a considerable amount of blood. He left a note, addressed to me but concerned with you. It is enclosed, but I recommend you not read it until you've finished this letter.

I have had a chance to talk and pray with Neal and find him still despondent and, in my psychiatrically lay opinion, also still suicidal. He wants your love and attention, but this attempt on his own life was much more than just a cry for help or attention. He was serious, and he almost succeeded. Any worse and he would have to have been shipped to an intensive care unit. As it is, he is rarely lucid and only sometimes conscious.

Mrs. Woodell, I know from Neal of some of the very difficult times you endured with him. I would not be surprised to find you still bitter and perhaps, as he alleges, even hateful toward him. But as you will see from the enclosed, this is a man with a life-and-death need to hear from you, regardless whether he is still your husband.

If you would care to reply directly to me, I will honor your wishes. My prayer is that you will thoughtfully respond to Neal, but I will certainly understand if you wish to wash your hands of him. I am truly sorry to trouble you with this, and I hope you will understand that I am only trying to do what I think is right.

I remain cordially yours,

Rev. Alton Wallace, Chaplain
Alabama State Penitentiary

P.S. I have honored the request in his note.

"Well?" Elgin called from the kitchen table.

Miriam bit her lip, not wanting to read Neal's note but knowing she had to.

"Nothin to speak of yet," she said. "Just a letter from an official there."

"About Daddy?"

"Um-hm."

"Anything *from* Daddy?"

"I'll let you know, El. Now stop buggin. Those beans done yet?"

"I'll let you know," he said. "Now stop bugging."

Any other time she would have found him humorous. Now she ignored him and opened the dingy, twice-folded note from her former husband.

Revernd,

By time you find this, Ill be dead, I hope. I appricate everthing you've tried to do for me. Like I told you, I know Jesus died for my sins when I was a littel boy, but I've done so many bad things sence then, I jist don't know. Thanks for praying with me anyhow.

I cant go on. You tell me God forgives me if I'm trully sorry. I don't know how sorrier I can git. What I want is for my wife and boy to forgive me, but I cant tell my boy what I done. He knows a littel but not all and I don't want him to.

My wife knows everything I gess, and she don't want to forgive me. She hates me. I jist wish she could see that I don't want nothing from her that would make her life worse. Her forgiving me for what I done to her would just make my life a little easier. I aint going nowhere anyway. I wont be of any more truble to her.

Revernd, I got something like over a hunderd dollers in my account here. Could you use that to git my frend in Huntsvill to send my old pitching machine to my wife. She wants it real bad for some reeson.

Thanks again for everything, and I'm sorry to let you down. Tell my wife and my boy I love them and that I'm sorry. Tell my boy I wouldve wrote to him sooner if I hadn't been sick. Good by, and I hope to see you in Heaven.

Neal L. Woodell

Miriam carefully folded the letters and slid them back into the envelope. She stood and reached for the wall, shutting her eyes.

"Momma, what is it?"

"Not now, Elgin. I need to take a little walk. Do you mind?"

"No, but can I read the—"

She silenced him with a look and pulled a sweater from the closet.

"Anything from Daddy?" he tried.

She didn't look at him. "If I'm not back soon, go ahead and eat your supper. Put mine in the oven."

"But, Momma—"

The elevator was slower than the stairs in either direction, so Miriam used it only to go up at the end of the day when she was too tired for the stairs. Her senses were heightened now as she turned, turned, turned at each landing, smelled the dinners of tenants of all different nationalities, heard babies screaming, spouses bickering, kids fighting. At dinner time the smell in the old hotel was bearable, the aroma of food for once overpowering the usual stench.

"Good evening, Miz Woodell," Mr. Bravura said, standing quickly as she passed. "Everything all right?" His teeth were on the desk, and he looked as if he wished he'd known whose footsteps he'd heard on the stairs. He usually had his plates in when his favorite tenant came by.

"Good evenin, Ricardo," she said, not looking at him and not wanting to be so familiar, but tired of his insisting that she call him by his first name. "Everythin's fine."

"Anything I can get for you, ma'am?"

"No, thank you. Just out for a stroll."

"Warm evening for that, ma'am. And not the best neighborhood."

"I'll be careful," she said as she hurried out into the darkness. As soon as she was clear of the entrance, she felt the humidity, yet she shivered. The sky was not black yet, and Miriam expected no danger if she walked with assurance, as if she knew where she was going. The problem was, she didn't know. Where does one go and what does one do, what does one think or say when the problem she thought was behind her raises his head and reaches for her from inside prison bars?

She walked a couple of blocks to where Elgin played fastpitch every day, and she sat on the stoop from which she had watched him in the early spring. She peered across the street and could make out the fading chalk strike zone.

How neat and tidy, she thought, that there is a drawn box. If the pitch hits within the borders, it's a strike. If it doesn't, it's not. Why couldn't life be like that? She had not sent Neal to prison. She had not forced him to kick her and kill their unborn daughter. She had not been responsible for his killing an old man out of drunken stupidity.

She had to admit she was glad he was in prison and that he had been sentenced for life. That was tidy. Not pleasant, but final. If she could have gotten him to write to Elgin once in a while, maybe dispense some baseball knowledge or strategy, it would have been perfect.

Had she felt bad for Neal? No. He got what he deserved. He had deserved it long ago, and if he had been sentenced for what he did to her baby, he never would have been free to kill the old man.

Was she responsible to try to keep Neal from killing himself? Was that being laid at her feet too? That's what Neal had in mind, she decided. He was a manipulator to the end, even using the prison chaplain!

And what about forgiving Neal? She could not forget, but would there be any value, any harm, in telling him she wasn't holding it against him? That wasn't true, but what harm could he do from behind bars? He might get the idea that there was some hope, some chance for them as a couple. She wanted no part of that.

Miriam put her elbows on her knees and her head in her hands.

Neal, how could I have ever fallen for you in the first place?

BESIDES HAVING BEEN GREAT LOOKING and a gifted athlete, Neal Woodell had been charming in his own good-ol'-boy way. He was unfailingly polite around girls, nodding to them, pretending to tip an imaginary hat whenever one walked by, which was frequent in a large county high school. He projected enough self-conscious shyness to take the edge off his jock swagger. The girls swooned.

He was no student; everyone knew that. But teachers and coaches liked him. He was a good representative of the school. He was all aw-shucks in front of a microphone, but he knew how to draw a sympathetic laugh.

"I ain't much fer talkin here, as y'all know, but I just believe we're gon whip some, ah, Spartan tail tonight and I hope y'all'll be there to cheer us on. Thank you."

Then he would look to his buddies and give them a thumbs-up as he shuffled off the stage.

He wasn't a rich kid, so rather than the latest fashion, he set trends with how he wore his wash shirt and jeans. He was rumored to be a behind-the-barn smoker and an in-the-barn drinker and romancer. Miriam, who became his enviable steady by their senior year, grew to doubt the truth of that reputation, at least as a lover. It wasn't that he didn't want to. She set boundaries and he honored them.

As for the smoking and drinking, there was no doubt. Everyone but athletes smoked openly. Miriam hardly knew any boys who didn't drink. The problem with Neal, she decided, was not his vices, many as they were. His problem was outlook, philosophy, what some would call world view.

Miriam had little trouble making Neal behave before they were married. She gave him the silent treatment when she smelled tobacco on his breath and lectured him on his commitment as a star athlete. He never drank in front of her, but she knew when he had been drinking, and she gave him a major league cold shoulder for days.

After reveling in her amazing fortune of having landed the school's heartthrob, she discovered the real Neal Woodell. He was simple, plain, and transparent. He seemed surprised at what his body and physical abilities brought him. They became his security, his identity. But something else shaped the man.

Miriam had visited his home for the first time about six weeks after they started dating. His place was not unlike her own family's. Low marshland in the Gulf coastal plain resulted in a rich, deep green, fragrant grass covering out back, but chickens, dogs, cats, and night creatures left the front bare dirt. There was a shed, several parts of old cars, and a stone drive that led back to a chicken coop and what remained of a red and gray barn. Inside the small house, eight children—of whom Neal was the eldest—shared two tiny bedrooms. Their mother had one to herself, except on weekends when her husband returned from shrimp fishing near Biloxi, half a day's drive in a rattly pickup.

Miriam felt at home at the Woodell place almost immediately. Her family was not quite so large, just six children, of whom she was fourth. She noticed that Neal was treated with the same deference that she and her siblings afforded her oldest sister. There was a pecking order, and it started with Neal. His mother was a dour, hard woman, small with black eyes and thin lips. She never attended any of Neal's athletic events, though somehow a few of his brothers and sisters often showed up.

Despite the obvious pain and difficulty in her life, Mrs. Woodell was pleasant enough. She rarely had time to sit and chat, except at meal times, and even then she seemed to do all the running. What struck Miriam about her and her husband (when Miriam happened to catch him on a weekend), was their view of the future. To them, everything was temporary. It all pointed to a day, somewhere in the future, when their number would turn up, their ship would come in, they would get that break, that job, that phone call, that inheritance. Television and magazines had shown Miriam there was a life far beyond her own out there somewhere, and she wanted desperately to find it. But she was also a realist. What she really wanted was to marry Neal Woodell and stay in Mississippi, not necessarily in the Hattiesburg area, but maybe down on the coast or up closer to Jackson. A university town might be nice. That was the extent of her dream. Her aunt had exulted about Chicago, but to marry someone who would move to an international city like that...to even dream of such a thing would make her like Mr. and Mrs. Woodell.

There was no discretionary income in that home, not even enough to move closer to Neal's father's work. Yet they invested regularly and significantly in a local numbers racket, a sort of 16 rpm lottery, that made someone in the county illegally richer by between twenty and five hundred dollars every week and three thousand dollars richer every two months. But by the time someone had invested five hundred dollars for no return, he had been hooked on the chance at the three grand. People, including the Woodells, borrowed to play.

Four years before Miriam had even heard of Neal Woodell, his family had won a hundred and twenty-five dollars in the county game. They had been just as dirt poor then, but rather than use the illicit gain to improve their situation (one of their cars needed an overhaul, and a truck needed tires), they celebrated. The family was still talking about it after Neal and Miriam had married. What a weekend they had had in Biloxi.

The number had been played and won by Mrs. Woodell. She had chosen her number from the birthday of some dead uncle, a no-account drifter named Clovis Woodell. The story went that Uncle Clovis had looked his new niece-in-law-to-be in the eye at the church just before her wedding and told her she was about to become his prettiest relation. He shook her hand and welcomed her warmly into the family.

"I wish you all the very best," he said.

She still told the story with a sparkle in her eye. "He din't even try to kiss me like all them others done. He was just real nice, and he always treated me with respect, right up till the day he died."

"How did he die?" Miriam asked her the first of many times she heard the story.

"Somehow tripped and fell down the basement stairs over to the church. Hit his head somethin ugly awful, was in a coma for a coupla days, and never woked up. Nice funeral, real nice. He never married, so there wasn't no wife or kids or nothin to worry bout. He left us his estate, such as it was."

Miriam hadn't felt bold enough to ask, but Neal's mother told her anyway.

"Mostly just stuff from his shack. He only ever worked on the railroad, so there was some lanterns and some kitchen stuff. Nothin else worth anything. Somebody tol me once that there was some antique-buyin couple makin a swing through here what woulda give me a few dollars for the lanterns, but it wouldn'ta seemed right to me anyway, know what I mean?"

Miriam nodded, but she didn't understand. Or what she understood she certainly didn't agree with. It was beyond her how Mrs. Woodell could have been so sentimental about a dead uncle's pieces of junk and yet have the temerity to use his date of birth as a numbers racket entry.

Nonetheless, that one victory, out of the hundreds and hundreds of dollars the family had spent trying for the big one, was known—by the time Miriam had become an item with Neal—as the "Clovis Payoff." There were times Miriam wondered what would have happened if they had not won it. How many more weeks and months and years would they have gone, investing money they didn't have?

That one small bit of coincidence and luck had served to forever marry them to the game. Miriam thought some enterprising numbers racketeer may have simply decided it was time for the Woodell number to come up. Years later, having long since multiplied in expenses the paltry sum they had won, they were still playing.

That hundred and twenty-five dollars had evidenced some rockbed generosity on the part of the Woodells. They didn't hoard it, weren't selfish with it. They piled all the kids into the truck and spent two days and one night in Biloxi, not at one of the resort hotels but at a lesser one that left them enough money to play and eat.

The Clovis Payoff was anything but an end-all memory. It was a harbinger, a living, breathing piece of evidence that they were destined for good fortune. Their ship, from wherever, had set sail. Who could know when it would appear on the horizon?

It was only after she was married and working that Miriam had heard a name applied to that kind of thinking. A boss of hers on her first accounting job had referred to someone with a "blue-collar mentality."

She had resented the remark for weeks, though it had not been directed at her. Her people and her husband's people, and most of the decent people she knew, were blue collar. As far as she knew, there was no blue-collar mentality. Most were hardworking lovers of the land, and they scratched out a living the best they could.

But then she started listening more to her husband. She saw him counting on his talent alone to carry him in professional baseball. His conditioning was not what it should have been. He smoked and drank openly, and now that he had won her heart and her hand, she had no more to say about it. She had learned that quickly, violently, and completely.

He was going to get the big break, the great contract, the right agent, the right coach, meet the right executive. His four homers in a doubleheader while he was on the brink of destruction was—to her—like another Clovis Payoff. It proved to her husband in the saddest, sorriest, most insidious way that if he could just do that again, show some incredible talent, he could make it in spite of everything.

His whole life and legacy was wrapped in unrealistic hopes and dreams that had Clovis Payoffs built in. Some power, some force, some evil allowed these brief glimpses of success during his darkest hours. It reminded her of the only time she had ever tried a slot machine, at a Las Vegas Night in a local VFW hall. She had felt guilty, getting two dollars worth of quarters and starting to feed them into the mocking machine.

On her second to last quarter, she won a dollar. Rather than lose the whole two dollars and get one in return, she considered the four quarters she had won as gravy, not really hers, something with which to keep playing. And anyway, how can you do better than to play with the machine's money? She wouldn't realize until later that this was her money, that she could have reduced her losses.

Before she had finished, she had spent her own two dollars and two of the four quarters she felt she had won. Five quarters dropped into the pan, and she was hooked. One of these was going to pay off big. The bell would sound, the red light would flash, and people would gather to see her trying to contain all the quarters.

But of course that didn't happen. Those four- and five- and even another four-quarter payoffs were just Clovis tricks. Every time she seemed to be close to cashing out, she would get a reprieve to keep her in the game. Finally, she had spent her two dollars and about another three she had won in small increments. She got another five dollars worth of quarters and went through that in about twenty minutes.

When it was over, she felt sleazy, used, cheap, stupid. She had, she realized, at least for that profitless season at the VFW hall, a blue-collar mentality. She hated herself, and she saw her husband and his family in a new light.

The more Neal drank and the more he counted on dumb luck to make him a success, the more miserable he became. He had evolved into something totally other than what she had fallen in love with and married. She didn't know this man, and on the other hand, she knew him all too well.

And now, on the stoop across the street from where the new, true, real love of her life played fastpitch, Miriam knew what she would do and what she would not do. She would not tell Elgin everything; she would do that much for Neal. She would cover for him. Yet neither would she write him a letter that absolved him of his guilt for what he had done to her, to her unborn daughter, and to her living son. She would not provide him another illusionary Clovis Payoff at the most critical hour of his life.

Miriam would not be looking for any payoffs either. She would, as she had done since she left that trailer, fighting tears, make her own good fortune. She didn't want riches. She didn't want comfort. She didn't want luck.

She wanted her son to know how to work and how to think and how to set his priorities. Miriam had the feeling that everything she could see and feel and touch would blow away one day, while only the truly valuable stuff—the love, the people, the values, the honor, the honesty—would remain.

She started home.

15

THE SKY WAS NOW PITCH BLACK, but Miriam had noticed no drop in the temperature. The sweater she slung over one shoulder had been a needless precaution. She hadn't realized how tired she was until she heard her cheap sandals scuff the pavement. She wondered how old she must look, walking that way in the prime of her life.

As she rounded the corner toward the transient hotel she and Elgin made home, she passed a young couple sitting in front of their brownstone. In the light from the street lamp they sat, not moving, not even talking. They weren't looking at each other or at anything in particular. She guessed them in their late teens, maybe early twenties.

As the young man stared vacantly across the street, the woman caressed his back with long, light strokes. It was almost an unthinking, idle gesture, Miriam thought. And yet it stabbed her with pain. Did they know? Could they know what they had? She wanted to run to them, to tell them. Capture this! Keep this! This is love, casual and easy and comfortable, but not to be taken for granted! One of you will change, or his true colors will emerge, and the caresses will stop, the relationship will change. It will evaporate like the light on a summer's night, here all day, bright, in your eyes, then fading so gradually that the darkness sneaks up on you.

Miriam lowered her eyes and hurried, pain deep in her soul, the agony of loneliness and need. She wanted to sit on the steps somewhere and touch someone or be touched. She got off the elevator and sat on the wood steps within earshot of her rooms. She heard the television. Elgin was switching between a late Cub game and a show she had forbidden him to watch. He was so deprived. No movies. No good clothes or sports equipment. What was wrong with the program? She couldn't remember. Too adult, she guessed. A lot like Elgin. A generous mother, full of mercy, she made noise opening the door so he had time to switch back to channel nine.

She could see from Elgin's face that he had decided not to say anything about the letter. He just stared at her, clearly wondering if she were okay.

"How're the Cubs doin?" she asked.

"Down by two in the sixth," he said. "What else is new?"

"It's hot out," she said.

"It's hot *in,*" he said.

She smiled. "You're a sweet boy, El. A good boy." She watched as a stab of guilt passed his eyes about the TV.

"Second and third and no outs in the top of the fifth, and they don't score."

"Strikeouts?" she asked.

He shook his head. "Ground out to third. Looked the runner back. Then a liner to short, doubled off Henson at second."

"Was Henson too far off?"

"I don't think so. Clark and Sanchez both should have been trying to hit to the right side and at least get one of those guys in. Doesn't anybody ever play the percentages anymore?"

She scratched her head and shrugged. "Turn it off a minute, son."

Elgin all but ran to the TV. Normally he would have stalled and argued, but not now. He sat on the couch expectantly.

"Your dad's been hospitalized again."

"With those tremors or whatever they are?"

She shook her head and moved a kitchen chair to sit facing him. "He cut his arm and—"

"How bad?"

"Pretty bad, I guess. I don't know all the details, so don't ask."

"But—"

"Don't ask. What I wanna tell you about it is that it looks like he's gonna be all right. He sends his love to you and—"

"And to you, Momma?"

"To you, Elgin, now stop interruptin. He wants my forgiveness."

"He's always wanted that."

"Elgin!"

"Sorry."

"You may not be old enough to understand this, but I'm gonna tell you a story to explain why I'm gonna do what I'm gonna do."

She tried to tell Elgin all about the Clovis Payoff, but he wasn't buying.

"Momma, forgiveness is just forgiveness. He's not gonna go getting his hopes up about anything just because you do what you were supposed to do a long time ago."

"Oh, so I've been wrong all these years?"

"Well, it seems like it. I mean, Daddy's been saying he was sorry and begging you to forgive him ever since I can remember."

"And ever since I can remember, I've seen no change of direction, no repentance. Nothins changed cept how bad he feels. Well, maybe I shouldn'ta told you all this. You're too young to understand."

"I understand all right," Elgin muttered. "Momma, I'm not trying to say Daddy deserves it. He's probably getting what he deserves now. But it just seems like forgiveness has to be without any, um, any—"

"Strings attached?"

"Yeah, isn't that what you always say?"

"That's when you and I are squabblin about somethin and we ask each other to forgive. That's unconditional. That means there's no ifs. You know."

"So what's the difference with you and Daddy?"

Miriam stood and dragged her chair back to where she found it.

"So, we're done talking?" Elgin said.

She nodded. "I am. I wasn't askin your advice, you know. I was tellin you somethin."

He muttered something under his breath.

"What did you say, young man?"

"Nothing."

"Tell me."

"I said, 'Truth hurts.'"

"What're you sayin? Because I don't listen to you and don't do what you say, I just don't like hearin the truth?"

He turned on the TV again. "Well, it is the truth."

"Maybe when you grow up and go through a few of life's valleys, you can start tellin me how to live."

"I wouldn't even try to do that."

"Don't get smart with me, Elgin."

"I'm not trying to be smart, Momma. I just—"

"Just let me make my own decisions. There is a lot you don't know, and I just wish you'd trust me. If I can't tell you stuff without this happenin, then I just won't tell you stuff anymore."

He turned his back to her and watched the Cubs fall farther behind.

Miriam was suddenly ravenous. She set about retrieving what was left in the oven and was struck to remember that this was the same fare they had eaten the day they moved in.

She ate quickly and more than she should have. She had always been trim and never worried about her weight, but when she overate she felt uncomfortable. That's how she felt now, plus she had argued with Elgin, which she hated more than anything.

She couldn't begin to tell him what he meant to her, because she couldn't even frame the thoughts into words. How do you tell someone his age how committed you are to him and to his success, to helping make him into a man the opposite of his father? She sensed that if Elgin had any inkling of his importance to her, it would be too much for him to handle.

But how she hated to have anything between them!

She cleaned up the kitchenette and went to sit with him. He was clearly not angry. She doubted he had backed down from his position, but he wasn't the type to make her suffer, even when they disagreed. She put her arm around him and he let her cuddle him. She couldn't get interested in the game. She was thinking of that stupid pitching machine.

She had wanted it at one time, but now they had no place to set it up. Elgin obviously didn't need it. Apparently, it was on its way anyway. That would be a fun thing to see: Ricardo Bravura taking delivery of a several-hundred-pound contraption he wouldn't even recognize.

Miriam decided to write the chaplain and include a terse message. She would inform him that Neal Woodell was indeed not her husband, but that he was the father of their son. She would say that she was—what would be the right word?—upset, troubled, saddened to hear of Neal's latest troubles. She would not be mean, not say he was getting what he deserved and that she was sorry he hadn't succeeded in killing himself. She would be careful to be cool without being nasty, and yet she wanted Mr. Wallace to tell that no good—to tell Neal to write to his son

"That's all the boy lives and dies for," she would write later. "I mean, every day he looks for that letter from his daddy. And then we get this. Mr. Wallace, if you have any influence on Neal Woodell, get him to write something, anything to his son. And please look it over if you have to. I will read it before I show it to my son, and I don't want any of this mess in it.

"As for forgiving Neal, you can tell him I didn't speak to that. I'm still thinking and praying about it. Maybe someday I can get the chance to talk to you about it. It's not as simple as it seems, that's all I can say."

As Miriam sat on the couch with her son, trying to organize the letter in her mind, Elgin suddenly turned and stared at her.

"I have just one question, Momma," he said, unsmiling.

"I'm listenin," she said.

"When was the last time the Cubs had a pitcher who could be counted to get a bunt down when it mattered?"

She swatted him and went to write her letter. "I'm serious," he called from the couch. "Did you see this? All he has to do is get it down. The runners were going. He pops it to the pitcher and it was only luck they didn't turn a triple play on us!"

The game wound down as Miriam finished her letter. Elgin wandered out and sat as she folded it.

"Can I see?" he asked.

"Private," she said. "Sorry."

"If it was lovey-dovey I could understand," he said. "But you're probably just telling him how much you still hate him."

"I am not! I'm not even writing directly to him."

"I'm not either."

"What do you mean?"

"I'm not writing him again until he writes to me. I mean, I'm sorry he got hurt and all that, but why couldn't he even write and tell me?"

She shrugged and looked away.

"Momma, I want to go see him."

"Elgin! You just said you wouldn't even write him until he writes you. How can he be worth a visit?"

"It doesn't have anything to do with what he's worth, Momma. I just think he's forgotten me, and if I go see him, he'll remember me."

She embraced him. "Oh Elgin. No one could forget you."

"How much would it cost to go?"

"More than we've got in time and money."

"I'd hitchhike."

"Sure you would. And I'd just sit here in Chicago and work and eat alone and pray that you were okay and wonder about you. And then the authorities and the people in the white coats would come by and ask me if I was the mother who let her ten-year-old son hitchhike alone to prison!"

16

FIVE WEEKS LATER MIRIAM received a polite reply from the prison chaplain, informing her that he had relayed her messages to her former husband.

"I can't guarantee he will accede to your wishes in all respects," the Reverend Wallace wrote. "Your son will be pleased to know that his father is recovering and is back among the prison population. I urge you to continue praying about your own personal response to him, though I would not presume to advise you."

But advise her he had. It didn't take a brain surgeon to read between the lines. The response had taken so long, she guessed, because the Reverend Wallace was not happy with her letter. He had apparently hoped for more. From his letter it was clear he assumed she had told Elgin everything. Well, she would, as he said, keep praying about her own response, but she was at peace with her decision to not tell Elgin about his father's attempted suicide. When Elgin's letter from his father finally arrived, Miriam was convinced that the chaplain had written it and had Neal copy it. It read:

> Dear Son,
>
> I'm sorry I haven't written you in such a long time. I have been ill. I miss you and love you and wish I could see you. Maybe someday soon we can get together. Keep up the good work with your baseball.
>
> Love, Dad

"Mom! Do you think he's gonna get out after all?"

She shook her head. "I think he's hopin you'll come and see him someday, Elgin."

"Can I?"

"Maybe someday. I can't see how now, but you're growin up and he's gonna be there a long time."

⚾ ⚾ ⚾

Miriam loved the fall in Chicago, but on the occasional days when the temperature began to bite, she wondered if she could squeeze a few dollars out of her budget for a warmer coat. For each of six weeks she had put a ten dollar bill in a small manila envelope in the cabinet above the refrigerator. A couple of more weeks and she would be able to get a coat she would actually look forward to wearing. That would be nice. A reason to look forward to going to work.

In late November, the day before her four-day Thanksgiving weekend, she trudged home especially exhausted. Pre-Christmas orders for the distributing company had overtaxed everyone in the office. Tempers were short, and bosses whose passes at Miriam had been rebuffed seemed to take their frustrations out on her. She was working an hour extra each day and still getting criticized and corrected. She worried about her raise, which had been promised and then delayed, and then promised again before the end of the year.

A drunk on the bus had circulated among the female passengers, asking for money. She could not understand why these men thought women had more money or were more sympathetic than men. She had shaken her head and looked away, but the drunk had stood unsteadily, staring at her with hatred. He had scared her. The front door of the transient hotel actually looked inviting, because it was warm, because Mr. Bravura would no doubt say something complimentary (though she would ignore it and greet him cordially), and because one slow, rickety elevator ride up six floors would connect her with the reason she endured all this. Elgin.

Miriam was grateful that Mr. Bravura was occupied with another tenant as she walked past. He was saying something about the plumber being scheduled next Thursday and that he was sorry if the man couldn't make do until then.

"Oh, Mrs. Woodell," he sang out. "A word please, if it's convenient."

"I do need to get to my son soon," she said, slowing.

"Oh, ma'am, just a word. Anyway, your son only just arrived himself."

Miriam looked at her watch. It was an hour and a half after dark.

"Is he all right?"

"He's fine, ma'am, and if you could just give me a second, I'll be right with you."

Miriam thought it strange that Ricardo could be so polite in such grimy surroundings.

"So can you get by till Thursday?" he said, turning back to the man.

"Looks like I have no choice. You couldn't take a look at it for me?"

Ricardo spread his greasy hands. "Sir, I know less of such things than you do, and who would watch the desk?" The tenant hurried away without a word. "Now, Mrs. Woodell. Please, sit down."

"I really don't have a lot of time."

"If you knew what I did for you today, you would give me all the time I need."

Miriam felt the panic in her chest. Why did he have to play such games? Had he rescued Elgin from some danger? Had he caught him hanging around with gang members? What? She sat. Ricardo leaned forward far enough that she could smell him. Tobacco. Alcohol. Sweat. Breath. She fought to keep from wrinkling her nose.

"I did something for you today that I have never done for another tenant as long as I have been here, which as I have probably mentioned before has been—"

"Fourteen years," she said.

"When C.O.D.s come, I turn them away. Oh, I have paid an extra few pennies on an oversized letter or small package, but never have I done what I did for you today to save you the trouble."

He looked at her as if he expected a smile of thanks. She pressed her lips together and stared at him, waiting, determined not to beg.

"Well, it wasn't C.O.D., thank God. I would not have been able to advance you that much. But look at this."

He produced a yellow, fifth carbon sheet from a stack on his desk. It was hardly readable, but the figures he pointed out were clear.

"The total cost of shipping this, this contraption, whatever it is, is hidden under these squiggly lines, but you can see clearly the difference between that figure, which was paid in advance, and the amount that had to be paid before they would make the delivery. Well, I told them I was sure there was some mistake. That you were not here and not even your son was here and that I couldn't imagine your ordering or anyone sending you such a...a monstrosity. I mean, ma'am, it must weigh over two hundred pounds. I had to help the truckers get it to the base of the stairs, but they would not take it down for me. Not that I have any room for it, really. But you don't either. I could have, and maybe should have, refused it, but then if you *were* expecting it, then, well, what is a person to do?

"One thing is for sure, ma'am, I knew you would be good for the, let me see here, sixty-three dollars and seventy-seven cents."

There goes my coat, Miriam thought. "Elgin doesn't know about this, does he?"

Ricardo shook his head. "I advanced the money from a small petty cash fund here, ma'am, which has only seventy-five dollars to start with. So you can see how awkward and yet how urgent my need is to have you reimburse me."

"Of course, Ricardo. And thank you for doin that for me. I'll have Elgin run the money down in a few minutes."

"Oh, thank you, ma'am. I knew you were a trustworthy person, and that was why I felt confident I could do for you something I would probably not have done for anyone else."

What did he want? A hug and a kiss? She would have rather paid him double. She was just grateful he kept his clicking teeth in to talk to her. "May I see it?" she asked.

He led her down a dark hallway to a steel door that led to the cellar. She had not realized the building even had a downstairs.

"Does anyone ever go down there?" she asked.

"Only telephone and electric workers, and not very often," he said.

He stepped out of the way and flipped on a bare bulb that hung from the ceiling. He gestured toward the shipment. Miriam shook her head. She had seen the thing before, but never quite in this configuration. Every protruding piece had been twisted or pivoted or folded down and wired to keep it as compact as it was, which was not very.

"May I ask what it is?" Ricardo said.

"It's a pitchin machine."

"A pitching machine? Like a robot that throws the ball?"

"I guess you could say that. Only it doesn't look human or like a robot when it's set up. It's just a box with—oh, I don't know. It's just a machine that shoots baseballs at you."

"How much room do you need for this?"

"I don't know, Ricardo. More than we'll be able to find here, no doubt."

"I can probably find somewhere to store it for you downstairs, but again, that is something I wouldn't do for just anyone."

"I appreciate it."

"It will probably take the three of us—your son and you and I—to move it down there. But we can't leave it here, and you don't have room for it."

"We sure don't. And I don't think I'm up to movin this thing tonight.

Could we maybe do it tomorrow?"

Mr. Bravura shrugged. "Why not? I should say, however, that I would be most comfortable if I could be reimbursed even this evening."

"Oh, of course, Ricardo. I'll send Elgin right down. But do me a favor, will you?"

"Anything."

"Don't tell Elgin about this."

"As you wish."

"It's a surprise for him, and I want to tell him about it tomorrow."

"Certainly. May I ask one more thing? Does this mean that you intend to leave us, maybe to move somewhere with more space? I would hate to see you go."

Miriam shook her head. "If you can find a spot for us to store this, we'll be stayin here for quite a while, I'm sure."

Ricardo looked greatly relieved and busied himself in his cubicle while Miriam waited for the elevator.

"Why were you late?" she asked Elgin a few minutes later.

"Who said I was late?"

"Who do you think?"

"Big nose Bravura?"

"He's a nice man."

"He should mind his own business."

"I want him to look out for you, El! Now don't blame him. You were the one who was late. Where were you?"

"At a second-hand store."

"The one a couple of blocks over?"

He nodded. "Chico was looking for something. I'd never been in there before. They have everything! It's like a pawnshop. I just got to looking at everything and lost track of the time."

"You shoulda been able to tell it was getting dark out."

"I know, Momma. I'm sorry. It won't happen again."

Miriam still had her coat on as she sat in the kitchenette with her purse and the envelope of ten dollar bills. She took sixty from the envelope and the rest from her purse in exact change.

"Run this down to Mr. Bravura for me, will you, El? When you get back we'll have supper, and tomorrow I have a little Thanksgiving surprise for you."

"Turkey?"

"Better."

17

BEING ABLE TO SLEEP PAST 6:30 on a brisk Chicago morning was heaven for Miriam. She decided to stay in bed, conscious or not, until the sun was full in the sky and streaming between the curtain and the window frame. Problem was, Elgin was up and putzing around. She hoped he hadn't noticed the small turkey she had secreted to the back of the refrigerator two days before.

She chuckled at the folly of either of them trying to hide anything from the other in that minuscule two-and-a-half rooms and a bathroom. She wondered what size turkey she could have hidden in the toilet tank.

Elgin spent as much time in the kitchen, and in the refrigerator, as she did. Though she knew he had, of necessity, learned to be proficient on the stove, she still marveled to hear evidence of his ease with such things. The doors opening and closing, the match being struck, the rattle and tap of pots and pans sounded as much like a born housewife as an eleven-year-old boy.

When she smelled breakfast, she knew her reverie was over. She lay on her back with her hands behind her head, wondering what Elgin was up to. When she emerged from the bathroom in her robe, she was greeted by her son, grinning, standing by the stove and a set table. Coffee was brewing, bacon was sizzling, French toast frying, and scrambled eggs ready.

"Happy Thanksgiving, Momma," he said.

She was nearly speechless. She wanted to say something, to be eloquent. "Ain't you somethin?" was all she could think of.

"Yeah, I'm somethin," he said, for once not correcting her English. "I figure if you have a surprise for me, I can have a surprise for you."

She wondered if he had seen the turkey, though even if he had, he might have mistaken it for one of the small chickens she had used to supplement their diet two or three times a week since they'd moved to Chicago.

When she had told the grocer she wanted a turkey for two, he had laughed, but he had come up with one scrawny bird. It was frozen but less than a week fresh, he said, and should be succulent. It looked good and the price was right, but when she thought back to the turkeys her family used to share in Hattiesburg, she nearly laughed aloud. This bird was the runt of the litter for sure.

After they had eaten, Elgin started clearing. When she insisted on helping him with the dishes, he told her no, to just get dressed so they could get going on his surprise. She shot him a double take and he smiled.

"Don't trust Mr. Bravura," he said. "If you have anything you want kept quiet, he's not the guy to tell."

"Don't worry," she told Elgin as she went to get into jeans and a sweater. "He'd be the last person I'd tell anything."

She and Elgin raced down the six flights, laughing and bumping each other along the way. Just before they turned into the lobby, they heard Mr. Bravura's rumble.

"What's that racket?" he hissed, but he softened immediately when he saw who it was. "Good morning, madam!" he said. "Are we ready for our little chore?"

He said he had found a length of chain and a rubber bungee cord that might assist them in lowering the contraption down the stairs, "if one of us can guide it and the other two can hang on to keep it from getting away from us."

Elgin seemed stunned with his first look at the device. With its various metal tubes and protrusions, it made a mass of parts about six feet tall and four feet wide. It was on wheels, but not all of them rolled. Elgin put his hands on the sides and shook it to feel the weight. The thing hardly budged.

"I hope the three of us will be enough," Mr. Bravura said as he fed the chain in and around a couple of metal bars. He did the same with the bungee cord and suggested that Miriam hold it by that. "I'll hold by the chain, and Elgin, you can guide it down the stairs by the side. Whatever you do, don't get in front of it in case it's heavier than we think."

They maneuvered the machine into position, centering it in the square landing at the top of the concrete basement stairs. It took all three of them and a lot of scraping and grunting to get it facing the right direction.

"Maybe we should just let it fall down the stairs," Elgin said. "I'm gonna have to put it all back together anyway."

No one laughed.

Elgin moved down two steps while Miriam and Mr. Bravura got behind and bent to push. When the front wheels slipped over the top step, they stopped and repositioned themselves, now carefully wrapping chain and bungee cord around their hands.

"Ready?" Mr. Bravura said.

"Almost," Miriam said. "You know, we really appreciate this. It's above and beyond the call of duty."

"Well, it is true I do things for you that I would not do for most tenants."

Miriam bent and lowered her shoulder into the machine. Mr. Bravura did the same. Elgin held lightly from the side, hoping to keep the thing straight as they planned to go step by step to the cellar. But as soon as the weight of the machine shifted, the whole thing pitched forward and began to walk itself down the stairs, faster and faster.

"Whoa! Whoa!" Mr. Bravura cried, following along as if taking a gigantic robot on a walk and finding himself dragged behind.

"Don't let go!" Miriam squealed. "Elgin, get out of the way! Get up here and help us if you can!"

Elgin flattened himself against the wall as machine, landlord, and mother lurched by, picking up speed. He reached around Mr. Bravura and got both hands on the chain, but that only made Miriam's side move more quickly. The whole thing was turning to the right. Elgin let go and it straightened itself, but when he grabbed the bungee cord on his mother's side, the thing jerked that way. Now it was jumping and banging down the stairs with the three of them trying desperately to hang on.

"I'm losing my grip!" Mr. Bravura shouted.

"Hang on!" Miriam said.

Elgin was crushed between his mother and Mr. Bravura now, trying to grab the chain again. Just as Mr. Bravura's hands slipped off the chain, Elgin grabbed it. The landlord sat on the stairs, unable to hang on and help.

Elgin may have been as strong as his mother, but he didn't weigh quite as much, and now their dead weight, trailing the lumbering appliance, was all that was keeping it from tumbling end over end.

Elgin screamed that he too was losing it. Miriam felt her weight move forward, and she tried to dig with her feet to keep from rolling over the top of the machine. Now she knew what a rodeo rider felt like when he had been thrown but his hand was still locked onto the rope.

Elgin got his knee atop the machine and somehow unhooked his mother's bungee cord from the metal. She sat back and he jumped off, landing hard on the stairs as the three of them watched the thing reach the basement with a terrible crash and roar.

Elgin sat rubbing his thigh, where he had hit the edge of a stair.

"Everyone all right?" Miriam asked.

When they all nodded, she began to laugh, and soon the three of them were howling. Dust rose from the basement, along with the smell of oil and grease. They descended to survey the damage.

"I wonder if you can hurt one of these things," Miriam said.

"Two wheels are bent in," Elgin pointed out.

"I hope we can still drag or push it somewhere," Mr. Bravura said. "Somehow I think getting it out of here would be even harder."

"It's here to stay," Elgin said.

They scouted the musty, dark basement for a corner to store the thing. Every imaginable piece of junk was in that cellar, from furniture to tools, rags, gadgets, and moldy junk decades old. As Miriam's eyes adjusted to the light, she had an idea.

Just around the corner from where the pitching machine lay in a heap were two walled-off areas. Both were windowless and each had one bare light bulb that looked like it was on its last tungsten. One was a square room piled three or four feet high with junk.

"You could probably clear a corner to store it in there," Mr. Bravura said. "You know, I won't be charging you storage if the owner doesn't ever see it."

Miriam's eyes were on the other room, which ran almost half the length of the building and was about twelve feet wide.

"What would you guess was the size of this area, Ricardo?" she said idly, trying to keep him from suspecting her direction.

He straightened with self-importance and looked to all four corners. "Oh, twelve or fourteen by thirty or forty."

"I would've said twelve by forty myself," she said. "Seems there'd be even more room to store it in here."

Ricardo raised his brows and nodded, shrugging. "I don't much care. Here, there, somewhere."

"Mr. Bravura," Elgin began slowly, "is there an outlet in this room?"

Ricardo squinted at him. "Why?"

"I was just wonderin if maybe someday when I get the thing figured out and put together a little, I could plug it in and see if it works."

"Oh, I don't think so, son. This is not an inside thing, is it? And you might break something."

"What's there to break? I'd move everything into the other room."

"Maybe, Ricardo," Miriam said, "the boy has a good idea. I'll bet a thinker like you could come up with an idea of how we could make this work. Maybe I could give you a few dollars a month for your trouble and for the electricity."

She noticed the light return to Ricardo's eyes. "I will consider it, of course, ma'am. I have been an engineer in the past, you know."

"I didn't know that," she said. "But it doesn't surprise me."

Ricardo's chest expanded. "Maybe if the boy moved everything into the other room."

"That's what I—" Elgin began.

"Yes," Miriam said. "Good idea! Then you wouldn't have to even worry about what he does in here with the machine."

"Precisely," Ricardo said. "I would entrust—" He paused to consider them and chose to point at her. "You! I would entrust you with a key to the basement. You would be responsible for whatever happened down here. If you wanted to entrust him with it, that would be your risk. I would not know or care unless I needed to. Then I would come looking for you, not him."

"That's great!" Elgin said. "I'll—"

"But," Ricardo said, holding up a hand and speaking to Miriam. "I must have a rule. Just one. No one must ever be in this basement who does not live in this building. No friends. No acquaintances from the outside. I am taking a terrible risk. No boys from your team, no stickball players."

"Stickball?" Elgin asked.

"Or whatever they call it these days."

"Fastpitch," Elgin said.

"Whatever."

Mr. Bravura faced Miriam. "Are we agreed?"

"Sure. Elgin?"

"I guess. I mean, if I got the thing working, I'd want to show my friends and have them try to—"

Mr. Bravura raised both hands. "No! No! See, ma'am? He does not understand my predicament. He does not understand insurance and liability and expense and a person's job. No! Just store the machine wherever you can find room! No setting it up, fixing it, getting it to run, anything like that. And no key to the basement to either of you."

Elgin's eyes were red and filling. Miriam stepped in.

"Ricardo," she said, "you can depend on me to carry out your wishes. I understand your rule completely, and I'll make sure that's exactly what happens down here. You can trust me, and we both appreciate it."

"You'll explain it to the boy?"

"Of course I will. For sure."

18

AFTER THE THREE OF THEM MUSCLED the pitching machine from the bottom of the stairs to the wall next to the bigger room, Elgin asked his mother if he could stay and start moving stuff.

"Not now," she whispered. "Let's take this nice and slow."

Upstairs, while Ricardo fished in his desk for the extra key, Miriam was able to tell Elgin more. "He's doin this against his will, El. So when he gives me that key, let's just thank him and go upstairs."

"*Up*stairs? I wanted to—"

"You will! Just listen to me. You're too anxious about this and you're gonna spook him. Luckily that basement door is not in his sight. You can come the back way and get down there any time you want, and he won't know and be worried about you. Just don't make a big deal out of it right now, okay?"

Elgin didn't understand, but he shrugged and nodded.

Mr. Bravura made a point of giving the key to Miriam and not to Elgin. "Whenever you or whoever you designate is in the basement, I want the door locked behind you, understand?"

"Yes, sir," she said. "Elgin, understand?"

"Yes, ma'am."

"That door is always locked," Ricardo continued, "and that's the way I want it. That way there's no theft. No access to the rest of the building. No harming anyone who happens to be down there working or playing, see? That's if you keep it locked. You can always get out, but it's a big steel door, so no one can get in without making a terrible racket. I'll hear that and run them off."

"Has anyone ever done that?"

"No. But someone tried to break in the back door once. I will not allow anyone to threaten the security of my tenants."

"Elgin," Miriam said. "Would you wait upstairs for me?"

He looked puzzled and didn't respond, but he turned slowly and went to the elevator.

"Take the stairs," she called after him. "Keep you in shape."

"Oh, Momma," he grumbled. But he did what she said.

"Ricardo," Miriam said, "lemme just say again how much I appreciate this. You don't give it another thought. Next time you look in that basement, it'll be straightened up and we'll be sure your rule is followed. You made me very happy today. Can I send you and your wife down a plate of Thanksgivin dinner later?"

"Why, Mrs. Woodell," he said, beaming as if no one had ever extended such a kindness before. "I'd be more than honored."

If she didn't know him better, she might have believed she saw a tear in his eye. When she got back upstairs, Elgin was sulking.

"What's your problem, buddy?" she said, pulling him to her.

"It's just that that thing is the best thing you've ever given me, and I can't wait to start working on it. Where'd you get it anyway?"

"You don't know?"

"How would I know?"

"You can see it's not new."

He nodded.

"It's from your daddy."

"My daddy sent me that?"

She nodded.

"Momma, you gotta let me get at it."

"I don't even know if it works."

"I'll get it to work somehow."

"Listen to me, El. We've got a long weekend here, and I've got work to do for our dinner today."

"Let's skip lunch, Momma. I'll come up for a snack or something at noon and then let's have the big meal later."

"What big meal?"

"I saw the turkey, Momma."

"Not much to speak of, is it?"

He shrugged. "I love turkey. Now can I have the key?"

⚾ ⚾ ⚾

Elgin shivered when he reached the basement, but it wasn't long before he had to shed his sweatshirt. He made trip after trip from the big room to the smaller one, trying to find places to put half-used cans of paint and heavy, bulky containers of who-knew-what. There were suitcases, trunks, oil drums. It was all he could do to push them, slide them, roll them into the other room. He knew he would be tired and sore.

By noon he was getting hungry, but he kept putting off running upstairs for some fruit. He knew he couldn't last till the turkey dinner that afternoon, but he didn't want to quit working either. He could not recall having ever been so industrious. He had always thought of himself as just this side of lazy when it came to anything except baseball and school work. As he thought about it he realized that this *was* baseball work. Everything he was doing, every step he made, pushed him closer to checking out the rickety pitching machine. Trouble was, even if he could get it to fire up, he had only one bald tennis ball. Who knew if that would even work? Who knew how these things worked at all?

It was another hour and a half before Elgin had cleared the big room. He leaned against the wall and surveyed it. There were pipes overhead, a utility box in one corner, and the single bulb hanging in the middle of the room. That left the ends of the room nearly dark. He decided that the machine could be set up at either end, and since one was just ten feet from where the thing sat now, that would be the best bet.

He heard a knock at the door and jogged up the stairs to find his mother with a couple of apples. "I'm glad you're here," he told her.

"Oh, you are, huh? Need some help?"

"Wait till you see. And thanks." He grabbed the apples and chomped off a huge bite as he led her down the stairs.

"Elgin! You're ready to move the machine already!"

"Already? I've been working here forever."

"I can't believe how much you've done."

"I need your help dragging the machine over here. I'm gonna set it up at this end and have it pitch toward the other wall."

"How hard will this thing throw, Elgin, and what will it throw?"

"I have no idea how hard. I've seen em at batting cages where they throw slow and medium and fast, but I don't know how you set that. I'll have to look at it. I don't even know how to aim it."

"Aren't we gonna need Ricardo to help us?"

"I don't think so, Momma. We're on flat ground now, and the chain is still attached. We can put the bungee cord back on, and I can try to get the thing up on its wheels."

They laughed at the memory of the fiasco on the stairs.

"We can give it a try," she said as he put the uneaten apple in his pocket and tossed the core of the first one into a can in the other room.

The machine rested on its front but was not flat on the floor because one of the sides lay against the wall. Elgin hooked the bungee cord to a strategic spot, and they leaned and braced and pushed and pulled until the machine stood upright, such as it was. Two wheels were still bent, but the thing was indeed pushable now.

Every time they got it going a few inches it seemed to turn on its own and head the opposite direction. Elgin couldn't help but laugh when his mother did. As the machine started through the door, Elgin ran to the side of it and leaned into it, bumping and pushing so it wouldn't drag against the door frame. His mother had got up some speed behind it, and as it cleared the doorway it swung into the open room and spun almost in a circle.

"I've got to get back to the turkey," she said, "unless there's anything else I can do."

He shook his head. "I was just wondering if you thought Ricardo would mind if I used a few of the tools I find down here."

"I can't imagine. They look like nobody's used em for years. You be careful with the electricity now, hear?"

He nodded. "Only socket I can find is in the light fixture."

She looked up. "Funny place for it. Old building. Well, at least you know it works, cause the light's workin."

"Yeah, but I'm gonna have to rig up something so the light doesn't get hit with the ball."

"You want me to come get you at dinner time, around four?"

"Yeah."

"I promised Ricardo and his wife some turkey dinner."

"Oh, no, Momma! They gonna eat with us?"

"No, I'm just bringin them a plate. Now don't be so selfish. Havin them join us would have been a nice idea. I wish I'd thought of it."

Elgin found a hammer, some pliers, a huge monkey wrench, and a couple of screwdrivers. He started by removing the chain and the bungee cord, then loosening every bolt that looked like it was connected to something that should stick out rather than fold in. Soon he had the machine looking more like those he had seen at the batting cages. The difference here was that the ball was delivered not by a mechanical arm on a spring but by two horizontally spinning wheels.

Elgin couldn't wait to get the machine plugged in and turned on. It seemed to him those wheels must be adjustable to put different speeds and spins on the ball so you could order up fastballs, sinkers, curves, sliders, risers, whatever.

What looked like it might take days was finally finished. The machine stood there, awkward and clumsy looking. He felt around in the metal housing and found the long, coiled cord. As he pulled it out he noticed that the three-pronged plug hung by a thread.

Elgin fed the cord from the machine across the floor until he was directly under the light bulb in the center of the huge room. He felt under the machine where the cord was connected to some sort of a special box that seemed intact and solid. The connection from the box to the cord was firm.

He ran his fingers along the cord and found that the only frayed spot in more than twenty feet was right at the plug. For several minutes he sat and studied it, then used a screwdriver to separate plug from cord. He was careful to remember which color wire attached to each copper connection. There was no evidence of burning or wear, just loosening, probably from years of use or neglect.

As a man from the electric company had demonstrated at career day at school, he used the jaws of the pliers to cut away loose bits of wire and the rubber coating until he had shortened the cord by about a half inch but was left with clean, connectable wires. He wound them around their various posts and tightened the screws. Then he replaced the plastic covering with the three prongs sticking through and tightened that down.

Elgin was nearly overcome with satisfaction as he scooped up the leftover pieces and surveyed what he had done. His mother thought he was something because he could cook a simple meal at his age. Wait till she saw this!

Elgin went back to the pitching machine, located the on-off switch, and checked all other moving parts. There were few. There was a container for the balls that looked as if it could hold six or seven dozen. It appeared to be free-floating, so he moved it with his hands and found that it turned in a circle, much like the drum of a cement truck. Its proportions were uneven, and he figured that was how the balls were delivered to the short trough that led to the two spinning rubber wheels. As the container turned, the shape of the container caused the balls to stack and then emerge one at a time at the trough. The trough was balanced on a small fulcrum and dipped slightly to receive each ball and roll it slowly on its way. If Elgin was correct in his guess, each ball would drop between those spinning wheels and be thrust out toward the hitter. A series of adjustable screws and knobs determined the speed, distance, and direction of the pitches.

Elgin was filled with gratitude and forgiveness for his father. This was worth the wait, worth the days and weeks and months of hearing nothing. He couldn't imagine a better gift.

He stood at the end of the room, from where he would hit. The machine seemed to be listing to the right. He took the monkey wrench and the hammer and tried adjusting the wheels by banging on them. It wasn't the most precise or scientific approach, but every time he went back to where his batters' boxes would be, the machine looked better. It showed its age, whatever that was, but he had every reason to believe it would work.

He dragged a chair to the middle of the room and stood on it with the plug in his hand. The socket was merely part of the light bulb fixture and didn't seem that solid, but it looked newer than the building and it *was* three-pronged. He gingerly inserted the plug, half expecting to be catapulted across the room. As soon as he let go, the plug dropped out from its own weight and bounced on the floor. He stepped down, retrieved it, and climbed back up, this time pinching the copper prongs in the hope that they would grip better this time. No luck.

Electrical tape would keep it in, he decided. It was trickier than he thought to stand on a chair and use both hands to hold the plug in and wrap the whole thing with black tape. When he finished, his shoulders were sore.

Rooting around in the junk for makeshift supplies, he ran across an old, oversized bicycle basket. It was a huge rectangular thing, bent out of shape, but perfect, he thought, as protection for the light bulb. What the room needed, of course, was another couple of banks of lights, but he would never be able to afford them or talk Mr. Bravura into supplying them. He jerry-rigged the basket over the light fixture with screws and bent nails and tape.

Elgin found some sheets of drywall with crumbled corners, and he planned to use the chalky insides to outline a strike zone on the far wall and sketch in a plate and batters' boxes. He wanted them to be regulation size, so he would need his mother's tape measure.

"I was just about to come get you," she said as he burst in the door. "Get cleaned up for turkey dinner."

"Oh Momma, I just gotta finish a couple more things first. Can I have about twenty minutes?"

"I guess. You wanna run a plate of food to the Bravuras on your way back down?"

"How soon can you have it ready?" he asked, rummaging in the junk drawer. When he pulled out the tape, he dragged a bunch of other odds and ends with it and they scattered on the floor.

"Why didn't you just let me get that for you?" she asked, stooping to help him gather up the stuff.

"Momma, I'm eleven years old. I don't need you doing stuff for me all the time."

"Apparently you do."

She took a fork and a carving knife to the oven where she removed the tin foil from the little bird and sliced some turkey for Ricardo and his wife. She added stuffing, a couple of rolls, a scoop of corn, and a slice of canned cranberry mold. She applied a generous dollop of gravy and wrapped the plate in foil.

"Oh, man, is this making me hungry!" Elgin said. He stuffed the tape measure in his pocket so he could carry the plate.

Mr. Bravura was ushering a drunk out of an easy chair in the lobby. "This isn't a mission! Now get out of here! It's not that I'm unsympathetic, but go find a place that's giving out meals today. There must be a lot of them."

The old man shuffled out, swearing and trying to make an obscene gesture, which he had not quite accomplished by the time the door slammed in his face. Ricardo hurried back to his desk where a tiny black and white TV played one of his soap operas.

"Oh, young Mr. Woodell! How good to see you! And what is this? What a treat! Tell your sweet mother how grateful my wife and I are, would you?"

Elgin nodded and before he could turn away saw Ricardo remove the foil, find the silverware, and shovel a huge mouthful of dressing and gravy in as if he hadn't eaten for days. Elgin knew that wasn't true. He hurried toward the basement.

"Enjoy your feast!" Ricardo called after him.

"You too!"

Elgin carefully measured his batter's boxes and plate and drew them slowly. They turned out even better than he had hoped. He got rid of the scraps of drywall, then came back into the large room to survey his work. It looked great.

The moment had arrived. Elgin knew enough to be sure he was wearing rubber soles and that he was not touching anything metal when he flipped the switch on the machine. There was a low hum, then a rattle, then a slow acceleration until the whole thing vibrated. The motor wasn't loud, but the machine creaked and squeaked, and very gradually the ball container began to rotate. Elgin got around to the front and watched, eyes darting over the entire surface of the thing.

When the container was in a position where the first ball would have dropped out, the trough automatically dipped toward it. It stayed that way, the container turning and the trough leaning toward it, as if waiting to accept a ball. Elgin wondered what made the trough tilt the other way and the pitching wheels spin. He decided it could be only the weight of the ball. He reached for the trough and tipped it toward the wheels. As soon as it reached a certain spot of tension, the wheels kicked in and spun. When he let go of the trough, it tilted the other way and the wheels slowed and stopped.

There was so much noise that he knew the moving parts needed to be oiled. He turned off the machine, and a short search turned up some household oil in one of the cabinets in the other room. He applied it liberally to anything that looked as if it needed it.

He turned the machine on and it hummed and whirred as if it were new, until he heard a rumble and clatter that sounded like a tennis shoe tumbling in a clothes dryer. Something was loose inside the container. He moved around to the front where he could peer into the container with a sliver of light at his back.

Just as he got there the noise changed. It was no longer a bump and tumble but a rolling sound, almost as if there was a ball in the machine. He leaned over as far as he could and saw a dark, almost black, baseball-sized sphere rolling neatly around the container and edging up toward the trough. Could it be? Had an old ball been stuck in there and been dislodged by all his tinkering?

When it reached the trough he could tell it was a regulation baseball, but it was badly weathered and probably waterlogged. It moved heavily in the trough, rolling slowly until it reached the midway point, then its weight made the trough tilt forward with a clang and the pitching wheels began to spin, faster and quieter than before because of the oil.

Elgin's eyes widened as he realized he was standing directly in front of a pitching machine that was about to fire an old, heavy, rock-hard baseball right at him. He fell to the floor just as the rubber wheels hurled the ball toward the far wall. Elgin whipped his head to watch it slam off the wall near the ceiling almost forty feet away. It made a crunching sound, rebounded off the side wall, and rolled unevenly on a split side almost all the way back to him. Shaken, he picked up the ball and examined it. The seams had split on impact and much of the stuffing stuck out. The ball was useless, which angered him because he didn't know where he was going to find anything that would work in the machine.

As he rose he imagined he heard another rumbling in the container and dropped again, his heart racing. He crawled to the back of the machine and turned it off before rising. He looked and felt in the container for other orphan balls. Finding none he tossed the destroyed ball into the trash and headed up to the lobby for the elevator. He knew he should take the stairs, but his legs were still like jelly.

"Elgin, you look like you've seen a ghost!" his mother said when he came in.

He told her the story over dinner, which was wonderful. By the time he had overeaten and thought about how thankful he was for a mother who cared about him so much and a father who would send him such a magnificent gift, he had regained his courage. He knew it would be a long evening, having to keep putting the tennis ball back into the machine by hand, but it was better than nothing.

19

ELGIN AND HIS FRIENDS had agreed to play fastpitch at about 5:30, even though there wouldn't be much daylight left. Now it was the last thing he wanted to do. He got his glove and his broomstick bat and his bald tennis ball to take to the basement. In case he got tired of using the same ball over and over, he would head out and play fastpitch. He asked his mother to tell the guys he wasn't going to play today, if they came by asking for him.

He also asked if he could have five of the twenty-one dollars she was holding for him. He had been saving his meager allowance for weeks. He had no goal, though he had thought about the day when his dad's ball glove would finally give out. A new glove would take another year of saving.

"What're you lookin to buy with this?" she said.

"A baseball or two."

"Can you get two baseballs for five bucks?"

"I don't know. Maybe at the second-hand store. I didn't see any over there, but I could ask."

"Well, I'd be surprised if you could get two new ones for five," she said. "I was lookin for one for Christmas last year and I didn't see any that cheap except those rubber-coated ones."

Elgin stared at her. "*You* bought those rubber-coated baseballs?"

She hesitated. "Well, your dad told me what to—"

"He did not. You bought those, didn't you? And you told me they were from him. I knew he wouldn't buy me those."

"I'm sorry, Elgin. I was tryin to protect your image of your daddy, and I just thought—"

"It's all right, Momma. I should've known anyway. I guess I knew, but I did believe you."

"Will you forgive me, El? It was wrong, just wrong. It's never right to lie."

"Yes'm. How about the other gifts?"

"I'm sorry, El."

He plopped down on the couch and began to slowly shake his head.

"What is it, honey?"

"Now you're gonna tell me that pitching machine isn't from Daddy either."

"That pitchin machine was his, El, I swear. I wouldn't lie to you about that."

"But the shipping tag said it came from Huntsville, not Birmingham. What was it doin in Huntsville?"

"He'd been loanin it to a friend of his who coaches at a college there."

Elgin sighed. "So you're telling me it was his idea to up and send it to me."

"He had somebody at the prison tell the guy to send it."

"Who?"

"The chaplain, Reverend Wallace."

"And Daddy had him tell the coach to send it to me?"

"Right."

"To me?"

"To us. Of course it's for you. What'm I gonna do with it?"

She smiled at him. Elgin did not smile back. "The name on the tag was yours, not mine. How come it was sent to you?"

"I don't know. Maybe they thought I might have to pay for delivery, which I did, you know."

"Momma, all I want to know is, was this your idea or Daddy's?"

She looked away. "What's the difference? He had it sent and now you have it. Enjoy it."

"How'd you get him to send it?"

"What makes you think I—"

"Momma! You already lied to me about the other gifts and you said you were sorry. You know as well as I do that Daddy didn't up and decide to send me a pitching machine after not writing me or calling me for so long. How'd you get this out of him?"

"I won it as part of the divorce settlement, if you must know."

Elgin wished he hadn't asked.

He trudged down to the basement, still excited when he saw the machine, but not as thrilled as he had been when he thought his father was still interested in his baseball career. He stashed his other equipment in the corner and took the tennis ball to the machine. He dropped it into the ball container and turned on the motor. The thing whirred to life, but the tennis ball never rolled to the top toward the trough; it merely bounced around inside the cylinder. He tried to fish it out, but he couldn't predict the bounces and had to turn the machine off and let it settle to the bottom before he could reach it.

He turned the machine on and set the ball in the trough. It was too light to tip the trough and start the pitching wheels moving, so he held it in and tipped the trough himself. The wheels spun and the ball approached them, but it was too thin for the space between the wheels, and it dribbled through, being spun by just one of them and skipping harmlessly to the floor. Elgin studied the machine until he discovered what to loosen to push the wheels closer together, then he tightened it back up again. He still had to manually feed the ball into the trough and tip it toward the wheels, but this time the wheels were too close together and they caught and mashed the ball almost flat before spitting it out about ten feet to the right. It bounced off the wall and rolled into his newly chalked batter's boxes.

Elgin was frustrated. He played with the adjustment again and got it so the tennis ball fit just right, but when he sent it through with the machine on, the ball floated and looked like anything but a pitch. He finally decided the pitching wheels would work only with hardballs. He shut the machine off and went to look for his friends.

"Where you been, man?" Chico asked as he rounded the corner. "It's gettin dark and we need another guy."

Elgin took over pitching and tried to keep the ball away from the strengths of the other team of two. But he was distracted and didn't pitch well. He didn't hit well either, hitting about .300 for the hour or so he played.

"Man, you're losin it," Chico teased.

"Yeah?" Elgin said with a smile. "You want to trade me?"

"No way, man. Still you and me all the way!"

Elgin sat with his friend on the sidewalk. "Hey, Chico, you think that store you showed me yesterday would have baseballs?"

Chico shrugged. "Closed today anyway, Elgin. We can look tomorrow, eh?"

⚾ ⚾ ⚾

Miriam didn't understand Elgin's mood when he got home. The life, the excitement, the enthusiasm seemed to have gone out of him. She tried to get him to talk, but he was quieter, more sullen than he'd been in a long time. She felt terrible that she had lied to him, but she found it interesting that she felt worse now than when she had misled him in the first place. She tried apologizing again, more for her sake than for his, but he waved her off with a forgiving hand.

"I'm sure you'll be able to find somethin that will work in your machine," she said. "I'll be back in a while. Goin for a walk."

"Can I watch the football game?"

"Suit yourself."

She didn't take a wrap, and she thought that if he was thinking, he would realize she wasn't going outside. She took her key and slipped downstairs, unfortunately running into Mr. Bravura.

"Oh, Mrs. Woodell!" Ricardo exulted. "A feast fit for king and queen! Wonderful! Wonderful!"

"Did you want some more?"

"Oh, we couldn't eat another thing! You were most kind. I tried to wipe the plate clean, but I didn't do too well."

He gathered plate and silver, and though Miriam was not ready to take them back to her place, she accepted them and told him he was welcome. She didn't want to give him any wrong impressions. She hoped he wasn't any more solicitous with her than he would be with any woman he found attractive. She was certain she was nicer to him than anyone else in the building was, but she and Elgin just wanted to do the right thing because it was the right thing.

One thing she didn't understand about him and so many of her neighbors was why they didn't bathe. She felt she could hold her head high if she and her son were clean and worked and studied hard. Could the others' sense of self-worth be so base that they thought it made no difference how they looked or smelled?

When she was inside the basement door, she carefully set down the dishes and descended the stairs. She smiled at Elgin's chalk work and his ceiling basket to protect the light. She ran a hand along the edge of the pitching machine as she walked around it. If anybody could get this contraption to work, she knew it was Elgin. She wondered if the cord in the middle of the room would distract him, and if he could get the machine to pitch around it.

She found the switch and wondered if there would be any harm in starting it up. Miriam jumped when she pushed the button and the machine hummed. The container rolled and she quickly figured out how it would work. What fun, she thought. She wished she had the money to buy Elgin a dozen new baseballs. How would he see old baseballs in this dingy place anyway?

"I'm proud of you," she told him upstairs a few minutes later.

"For what?"

"For your own personal batting cage."

"It's kind of good, isn't it? I just don't know when I'm ever going to get to use it. Even when I get a couple of baseballs, it's going to take me a long time to adjust it and all that. It wasn't meant to pitch from that close up, I don't think."

"You'll figure it out, El. And I think you've got one fantastic opportunity. Once you get that thing workin, you'll be able to take battin practice anytime you want the year round."

He looked up at her and smiled. "I will, won't I?"

"It might get a little lonely, but anybody who ever did anything great had to go through a lonely time of trainin, don't you think? Fact, even if what they did wasn't that great, they needed a time to be trained. Like me with my accountin work. All that library time."

"You weren't lonely, Momma. I was with you."

"Yeah, you were, but the time in the books themselves, only I could do that. You were readin or lookin for somethin to read, and nobody could teach me that stuff but me. It's paid off so far."

She sat next to her son and put her arm around him, wondering when he would get too big and old to let her do that. For now he was warm and compliant.

"When I get to the big leagues," he said, "and make millions of dollars, you won't have to be a bookkeeper anymore. You can live anywhere you want. In fact, you can be *my* bookkeeper."

She laughed and hugged him. She didn't know whether she wanted him trying for a big league career or not.

"You know, Momma, I'll have lived again as long as I have now when that happens. I mean, I should know whether I'll make it by the time I'm twenty-two, but I might not be making millions yet."

"Oh, not right away, no," she said, teasing him. "And eleven years may be another lifetime to you, but the last eleven have flown by pretty fast for your momma. It won't be long before we know what life has for you. Just keep track of the basics and—"

"I know, Momma. Keep track of the basics and do the right things because they're the right things."

20

LUCKY'S SECOND-HAND SHOP between the transient hotel and the fastpitch diamond was a new world for Elgin. Chico took it in stride.

"I got no money, man, and less I get some money, all I can do is look or steal, you know what I mean?"

"Just like a baserunner, Chico."

"Say what?"

"A baserunner can only look or steal."

"You crazy, man."

"Yeah, but you're not gonna be stealing anything when you're with me. I don't steal, and I don't need trouble."

A red-bearded biker type was behind the counter. On his belt he wore one of the many hunting knives for sale in the store. Chico's eyes grew wide when he saw it, and Elgin knew there would be no bravado today.

"Take yer time, boys," Biker said. "Touch what you want, take what you want, pay for what you take."

"Yes, sir," Elgin said, saluting, and the boys laughed. So did Biker. Fortunately, Elgin thought.

Chico moved back into the military hardware area. Elgin was fascinated with the uniforms and fatigues until he remembered what he was there for. He looked at old ball gloves, none of them any good. He was stopped by a cardboard box full of old, brown softballs, all twelve-inchers. He tried to remember if he had been able to separate the pitching wheels on the machine far enough to accommodate such a large ball. He had seen pitching machines in batting cages that threw softballs, but he wasn't sure if they were the spring-arm type or like his own.

His own. That sounded good. He had his own pitching machine, the same one that had made his dad a big league caliber hitter. Now if he could just find something to make it work. He approached the counter. "Do you have any more baseball equipment?"

"I just got some stuff in day before yesterday that's in the back. I can't go back there while we're open and have customers in the store."

Elgin grimaced.

"You could go back there and check it out yourself. You can't get out that way anyway, so I don't hafta worry bout you stealin nothin."

"I wouldn't steal anything anyway."

"Sure. It's just through there and to the left. It's a big green canvas team bag with bats and catcher's equipment. Looks like it's from a Little League team. If you wanna know the truth, I think it's hot."

"Any baseballs in there?"

"You know, I don't think there are. You can look, but I went through the stuff real quick to give the guy a price, and that was one thing that was missin. Baseballs. Guess he had use for those. Probably took the best bats too, but take a look. You can dump out the whole bag, but put anything back you don't wanna buy. I haven't put prices on anything yet, but I know what I paid for the lot, so we can figure something out."

Chico started to follow Elgin but Biker held up a hand. "Just one back there at a time, boys."

The green bag stood in a corner of the back room, which was messier than the trash room in the basement of Elgin's hotel. He had never seen such an assortment of junk in his life. Everything from lawn furniture to old clocks and golfing equipment was stashed in that place, ready to be priced, he guessed.

Elgin wrestled the bag to the floor, opened the top and lifted the bottom. Half a dozen aluminum bats, including a long, skinny, weighted fungo bat, clattered to the floor. There was a catcher's mitt, a chest protector, and shinguards, along with several navy blue batting helmets. Elgin tried one on. Perfect.

He tried the bats. They were of various lengths and widths, and though any one of them felt okay, he was most interested in the fungo. He had seen wood fungo bats before, the kind big league coaches used to hit fly balls to their outfielders. He had never seen an aluminum fungo, though some of the suburban tournament teams he had faced probably had them. He amused himself with the thought of what a bat like that would do to a fast-pitch tennis ball. Probably rip it in two, he decided.

Biker had been right. There were no baseballs. Elgin kept the helmet on and carried the metal fungo as he looked at the other stuff in the room. In one corner were several golf bags and even a wire basket full of golf balls, each ringed with one of five colors: blue, red, yellow, pink, and orange. Nearly half had deep cuts or marks from drivers.

Elgin was in a buying mood and he had money in his pocket, but he didn't need a batting helmet for fastpitch and he couldn't use a metal fungo for fastpitch. He had his own broomstick-handle bat, which would probably not work with his pitching machine, but he didn't have baseballs for that yet anyway. He took off the helmet and put it back in the bag with the other stuff. The bat he hung onto, moving into the center of the small room where he had room to practice swing. What a great weight and feel, he thought. He wondered if teams used this as their weighted bat, or if it was just to sharpen the hitting eye. Maybe the coaches used it to hit fungoes, like in the majors.

"Findin anything back there?" Biker called from the front.

"Not much! I'll be right out!"

"No hurry!"

Elgin talked himself into the metal fungo bat. It was about an inch and a half in diameter, perfectly straight from the handle to the other end, with no fattening or tapering. When he found some baseballs for his machine, this would be the perfect bat. What a challenge! Anyway, his broomstick bat would be shattered by a baseball, he was sure.

Biker grunted when he saw the fungo bat. "Never seen one of them before. What the devil's it for?"

"Coaches use these to hit fly balls and grounders."

"But what do you want it for?"

"Just to play with."

"What's it worth to ya?"

"What do you mean?"

"What would you pay for it?"

"I don't know. I've only got—"

"Whoa, whoa, whoops, don't tell the seller what you've got to spend. You tell me how much you've got, and I'll tell you that's how much it is. You understand?"

Elgin shook his head.

"This is a second-hand store, son. I know what I paid for that bag of junk and roughly how much I wanna get for it, but there are no hard and fast prices. If I can get you to pay twice as much as I really need, good for me. If you can find out how low I'll really go, then you'll get a better deal. I'm not gonna go below a certain point, but your job is to get as close to that as you can."

"How?"

"Make me an offer and see how I react."

"You're not gonna react with that knife, are you?"

Biker found that hilarious. "You're a good kid! I like you! Now come on, let's deal on that fine bat. It's unique. I don't know where you'd find another one like it. It's in perfect condition. Lot of people come in here looking for those. I could sell that this afternoon for three, four times what I paid for it."

"You could?"

"Course not, but come on, kid. You gotta play the game. This is how I make my livin. You gotta tell me what's wrong with that thing and why it's practically worthless. You gotta try to convince me you'd be doin me a favor by takin it off my hands without chargin me to do it."

Elgin enjoyed the twinkle in the man's eyes. Chico thought they were both crazy and said so, then went out and sat on the sidewalk, his back against the metal grating that would be pulled across the front window when the shop closed.

Elgin eyed the bat and ran his hands up and down it. "Don't know what I'd do with this piece of junk."

"Yeah," Biker said. "Like that! Good!"

"Thing looks like a mistake. S'posed to be a bat, but it's just a straight metal rod. You'll never find anybody who wants this. I'll give you a dollar for it."

Biker roared. Elgin could see he loved the game, especially teaching it. "Why, I paid three times that for it, and I have to make a profit."

"Two dollars, tops," Elgin said.

"I gotta lose a dollar on the deal? I'll tell ya what, buy somethin else and I'll consider takin a loss on that...that whatever it is."

Elgin stood and thought a minute before it hit him. If he could get this bat for two dollars, he could get that basket of golf balls for three. They were hard and he was sure he could make them work in the machine. Swinging at a smaller ball with a smaller bat would be great for his hitting eye. He left the bat on the counter and headed into the back room.

When he returned with it, a man was at the counter, dickering over a fancy swiss army knife.

"That's a forty-dollar piece of merchandise I'm gonna let you have for just thirty-five," Biker said, winking at Elgin when the man looked down in disgust.

"It's not worth five," the man said, "but I can go ten."

"Ten? I can come down to thirty-two fifty."

"Fifteen is my limit."

"Well, then we got a problem. I got a limit too, and it's twice where you are now."

"Sorry, fifteen." The man turned to leave.

Biker raised his eyebrows in Elgin's direction, as if to say he was impressed.

"Ah, sir, I can meet you halfway. Twenty-two fifty and we got a deal."

"No." The man was heading out the door.

"Twenty's as low as I can go," Biker called.

The man returned. "Twenty is what I was hoping to pay."

"Pleasure doing business with you, sir."

Elgin shook his head as the man left with his knife in a paper sack.

"You like that?" Biker asked.

"It was fun."

"Yeah, for me too. You know what I paid for that knife and what I wanted to get for it?"

Elgin shook his head.

"I paid six. I was hoping to sell it for twelve. Always try to get twice what I paid for something."

"You told him it was a forty-dollar knife!"

"It is if he'll pay that."

"Does anybody ever pay the first price you tell them?"

"It happens. Not often."

"How much for this basket of useless golf balls that nobody else in Chicago would want because there's no place to use them?"

"Good! Good! Well, let me see, there must be sixty, seventy balls in that basket."

"Less than sixty," Elgin said. "I counted them."

"Oh, that was good that you didn't tell me exactly how many. Okay, if there's, say, fifty-five at a quarter apiece…" He wrote on a piece of scrap paper. "That would be thirteen dollars and seventy-five cents. Let's make it an even ten."

Elgin's face dropped. "Would you sell me just ten of them or so?"

Biker looked at him with a smile. "I want you to have the balls and the bat. We're down to two bucks on the bat if I can make a little profit on the balls. What've you got?"

"You mean honestly, not dealing any more?"

"Yeah."

"I've got five dollars and I'm not gonna have any more for a long time."

"Five will do it, buddy. Part of that goes for today's lesson. We got a deal?"

"We do," Elgin said.

The man pulled out a large paper bag for him. Elgin couldn't believe his luck. And he couldn't wait to get back to his basement.

"Where you goin in such a rush, man?" Chico called after him. "Ain't we gonna play today?"

"Later!" Elgin said. "Just like yesterday."

"You ain't hittin my fastpitch ball with that thing you just bought!"

"I know!" Elgin said, running for home.

21

THAT DAY AFTER THANKSGIVING DAWNED CRISP and windy. Elgin had eaten and hurried off to spend time with Chico until the second-hand store opened, and he had promised to be back as soon as he found, or didn't find, what he was looking for. If there was one thing for which Miriam was especially grateful, it was that she could count on Elgin. If he said he would be back at a certain time, he would be back. Of course, he might not come to the apartment first, now that he had his private hitting place. If she didn't see him by ten, she planned to mosey down there and see what he was up to. The last thing he told her was that he needed baseballs to do a final adjustment on the machine so it wouldn't pitch over his head.

As she sat at the breakfast table with her toast and coffee, she had the niggling feeling that she had never turned off the batting machine the night before.

⚾ ⚾ ⚾

Elgin let the heavy basement door shut and lock behind him and felt for the switch on the wall. Just before he turned it on he stood stock still on the steps and listened. His heart raced. The machine was on! Who would be down there in the dark with the machine running?

It could only be Mr. Bravura, he decided. No one else had a key. Elgin carefully set the paper bag in the corner. With the fungo bat in hand he crept down the stairs in total darkness. He raised the bat as he flipped the light switch in the big room. No one was there.

He trotted back up for the bag that contained the basket of golf balls. He wondered if he had left the machine on himself. He sure hoped Mr. Bravura hadn't been down there and decided he didn't like Elgin's setup. Elgin felt the machine and found the casing warm around the electric motor, but he figured it would always feel that way when it was running. He wouldn't worry about it unless it became too hot to touch.

He turned the machine off and got a wrench so he could loosen the pitching wheels and set them closer together. For the first time he became aware that the rubber on those wheels was dried and cracked, especially in the indented middles where the ball was gripped. He wondered what effect that might have on the rotation of the balls when they were hurled toward the plate.

The pitching wheels were set flat like a pair of record turntables and spun close to each other. Elgin squatted and closed one eye, peeking between the wheels as he drew them as close together as possible. Their outer edges almost touched, and there appeared to be just barely enough room for a golf ball to squeeze through. He forced a ball through by hand, and found that he could hardly make it budge. He thought about trying it with the machine on and the wheels spinning, but he didn't want to risk getting a finger caught between ball and wheels.

With the ball stuck between the two stationary wheels, Elgin turned on the machine. When it had warmed up, he tilted the ball trough, which started the wheels. They seemed to stick and grab, then they squirted the golf ball out, spinning it wildly. It landed about ten feet in front of the machine and bounced back and forth before rolling away.

Elgin wondered if he should spread the wheels a bit, finally deciding to see what would happen if the wheels were at full speed before the ball was fed through. He tilted the empty trough until the wheels began spinning at top speed. With his other hand he held a ball over the far end of the trough and let it go.

The ball rolled quickly to the wheels where there was a loud *pfft!*

Elgin had a fraction of a second to wonder if the ball had been launched. It had happened so fast he didn't see it, he only heard it. It slammed off the wall nearly forty feet away and came hurtling back past the machine and right at his face. He jerked his head left, but the ball caught him on the right side at the top of his forehead and his head snapped back as his legs buckled.

The ball hit the ceiling and dropped on his ribs as he lay on his side, dazed, not moving, groaning. He was aware of the cold cement floor on his cheek and on the back of the hand tucked under him. His other hand cradled the quickly rising bump on his forehead, which felt hot and tender.

He struggled to his knees but felt dizzy and sat on the floor Indian style.

The machine was still humming, but the trough had fallen back to its original position and he heard the wheels stop spinning. He blinked, feeling pressure on his right eye. How was he going to explain this to his mother?

The bump on his forehead felt an inch high and scared him. He knew he should get some ice on it, but how could he do that without scaring his mother and losing his privileges with the machine? He decided that though the bump was probably awful looking, he was not really hurt.

My name is Elgin Woodell and I live in Chicago, he told himself. I wouldn't know that if I was hurt bad, would I?

He stood and staggered and wondered how close he had come to losing an eye or getting himself killed. How fast must that ball have come off the wall? It had traveled more than thirty feet each way and had still knocked him off his feet. He chuckled at the thought of trying to hit or even catch a pitch like that. He hadn't seen it hit the far wall, so he didn't know about the trajectory. The way it came back at him, though, made him guess it had hit high off the wall, the way the old baseball had.

He turned off the machine and surveyed it carefully, looking for a way to adjust the trajectory. He finally found that the two front wheels at the base of the machine could be raised and lowered. When he had raised them, the front of the machine sat closer to the ground, and when he got behind the machine and lined it up with his eye, it was clearly pointing at a lower spot on the far wall.

He was tempted to try another pitch, but first he wanted to find a place to hide. He decided that if he let the machine deliver the balls automatically, the way it was designed, he could peek out from behind it.

He was still woozy when he dumped the bucket of fifty-six golf balls into the container and picked up the fifty-seventh and tossed it in too. Before turning on the machine, he walked around it, looking for the best place to stay out of the way and still be able to see where the balls hit off the wall. He was sure that once he could control where they hit and how fast they were going, he could stand in there with his new bat and take some hitting practice.

He decided to crouch directly behind the machine and peek out around the right side. If the ball came back that way, he would just duck back in and stay there until the balls ran out.

When he turned on the machine, he could hear the balls inside aligning themselves to be delivered to the trough. However, because they were so much lighter and smaller than baseballs, they rolled in a steady stream from the container to the trough, which picked them up, tilted, started the pitching wheels spinning, and drew all fifty-seven balls through the apparatus in a straight line.

The wheels never slowed and the trough never tilted back until all the balls had been fired at the far wall, sometimes as fast as two a second. It was as if the pitching machine had been transformed into a submachine gun.

It was deafening, and Elgin was sure he saw one ball hit off the wall and then collide with the next one just a few inches behind. Two of the first five balls skipped off the cord hanging down in the center of the room and made it swing and sway, creating a weird shadow in the semidarkness. Two balls banged on the wire cage around the light, and it came loose and began rocking.

But then the machine settled into a cadence and began firing the balls every half second or so, right to the same spot, low on the far wall. The balls smashed off the wall and rose quickly over the machine on the rebound. Elgin kept watching until he heard a ball strike the wall behind him and felt the thud between his shoulder blades. He couldn't believe it. And here came another, and another.

Six balls hit him hard in the seat and back, and he covered his head and curled up behind the machine. He rolled to his left, getting hit a couple of more times. Finally, he gave up caution and scrambled to the door, peeking at the far wall as he went. He had made the mistake of pushing off against the machine as he made his break, and he had redirected it to shoot into the far corner. Three balls struck Elgin as he reached the doorway and three more bounced low off the far wall and came back high, two hitting what was left of the cage and the third knocking it loose and banging it into the light fixture.

Just as the last few balls were being fed into the wheels, two hit the fixture and the cord, bringing the whole assemblage crashing to the floor, cutting out the light, and shutting down power to the machine.

Elgin lay there, dazed and hurting all over as he heard the machine slowly wind down to a hum and a whine and then stop.

That was unbelievable! When I get this thing figured out, it's going to be great!

22

Miriam knocked on the basement door but didn't hear anything at first. Then she heard footsteps, and the door opened.

"Elgin!" she shrieked. "What happened to you?"

He shushed her, and she was certain someone had attacked him. "Tell me!" she insisted.

"Upstairs," he said, leading her to the elevator.

As the doors shut, she examined his head under the light. "What in the world?"

"It's just not working yet, Momma. It's my own fault. I'll get it right. Just don't worry about me. My basket didn't work either, and I broke the light. I'm sure it just needs a new bulb. I hope."

"I hope so too, Elgin, because we've got no more extra money for this thing."

"This thing was your idea, Momma."

"Don't get smart with me or you won't see it again."

"I wasn't being smart! I just don't want you acting like this is some crazy idea of mine that you have to pay for."

"Did the ball hit you?" she said. "Were you trying to bat before you knew where the thing would throw the ball?"

"Not exactly."

"Not exactly what? Did the ball hit you or what?"

"A ball hit me."

A minute after they were in their apartment and before Elgin could explain, Miriam heard a knock at the door. It was a tiny black girl with pigtails.

"Scuse me, ma'am, but Missuh Brava say he wanna see you right now. Say you know where to meet im."

"Thank you, honey," she said. She shut the door and turned to Elgin.

"What would he have found in the basement?"

"You don't want to know."

"Yes, I do. I want no surprises."

"I haven't got time to explain."

"You comin with me?"

"I better not, Momma. You'll do better without me there."

"True enough," she said, and she ran down all six flights to the basement door. She had forgotten to get the key from Elgin, so she had to knock. It seemed to her as if she were asking to be bawled out.

Mr. Bravura was huffing and puffing when he reached the door. "I gave you a key. Why do you knock?"

"I forgot it. I'm sorry. It sounded like an emergency."

"An emergency is right! This will not do! Look at this mess!"

"I know about the light," Miriam said, following him down the stairs. "Elgin told me about the light."

He shined a flashlight into the big room. "And what did he tell you about the golf balls?"

"The golf balls?"

"I am telling you something, Mrs. Woodell. You know I think the world of you and the boy, I really do. I have tried to treat you with more than courtesy."

"I know."

"In fact, I think you are most charming and beautiful, and you have been wonderful to me."

"I know. Forgive us."

"Forgiveness is not what this is about, ma'am."

"Mr. Bravura—"

"Call me Ricardo, but for now, don't call me anything and let me finish. I want this place repaired, the light replaced, and the cord plugged in somewhere else. There is a socket in the smaller room, but you will need a heavy-duty extension cord, which I don't have. I want the glass swept up, and I don't ever want balls left on the floor when the boy leaves the basement."

"That's certainly fair, but he injured himself or I'm sure he would've cleaned up the—"

"If that is too much to ask, then I must ask for the key back."

"It's not too much to ask."

"Good, because we're talking about my job here. You know my wife is ill and in bed upstairs all day. I get my room free plus my small salary which puts food on our table and gives us medicine for her. I cannot be without this job. We would be homeless and she would die."

"I understand."

"I don't think you do. You have a good job and can pay your rent and buy fancy sports equipment for your boy. I wonder if you know what it means to be desperate, to have a life-and-death need to keep a job. I know for certain that if the owner of this building came through here and saw this, I would be out. Out! No severance pay. No warning. No notice. Out, gone, finished, over and done with."

Miriam had gotten a glimpse of what the room looked like with a broken light and several dozen golf balls all over the place. She thought it looked ten times better than before Elgin had cleaned it up.

"Ricardo," she said, "please accept our apologies. We'll get this cleaned up right away and you'll never have to worry about it again. I'll talk to the boy about what you've said, and I know he'll be careful to follow your orders, because he thinks so highly of you."

"Well, I like him too," he said. "But this, this will just not do."

⚾ ⚾ ⚾

Elgin had figured out a few things. First, ice hurt before it helped. His forehead throbbed. He had taken off his pants and shirt and looked at his back and legs in the mirror. Several red spots would become bruises, he knew. He looked like the victim of a stoning. He was standing before the mirror with a washcloth full of ice on his forehead when his mother returned.

"Guess I shoulda told you about the golf balls, huh?" he said.

"That would've been nice. You can imagine what he said."

"Is he throwing us out?"

"No, he's not, no thanks to you."

Elgin's mother recapped the whole encounter with Mr. Bravura.

"I'm sorry, Momma," he said, and he told her how it had all happened.

"How is your head?" she asked finally.

"It's all right...and why are you smiling?"

"I'm not," she said, but then burst into laughter. "I'm sorry, El, but that musta been a sight! I wish I could've seen that!"

"Sure glad you care about me so much," he muttered, but he couldn't help laughing too.

Over the weekend, Elgin worked on the light fixture, which needed only a new bulb, and the machine. He added a few pieces to help balance the trough to make up for the weight of the golf balls, but he wasn't ready to try the machine just yet. He was able to pick up a used extension cord for fifty cents (after hard bargaining at the second-hand store). He decided to make a smaller protective cover for the light bulb that would be harder to hit, and he knew he could adjust the machine so it wouldn't pitch the ball at the light or even have it bounce off the wall and hit the light. The only way to hit the light after that would be if he hit it with a batted ball. He couldn't imagine getting the bat around fast enough to do anything more than just bunt a ball.

Most important, he was doing odd jobs for his mother and for Mr. Bravura, saving a little each day so he could afford some large sheets of canvas. These he would hang from the ceiling on the back wall behind the pitching machine. If a pitch got past him—as he assumed most would—and banged off the far wall, that was fine. But he wanted the canvas at the other end so a ball would hit and drop near the machine.

His only problem was that the canvas sheets at the second-hand store, cheap as they were, were white. He probably could have had his mother dye them, but by now he had resigned himself to making this the most difficult batting practice area he could.

He was not going to slow down the machine. He had no idea how fast it could throw the golf balls, but he knew it was faster than anything he had ever seen before. No pitcher and no pitching machine threw the ball so fast that it looked like a white streak.

If he could get it to throw strikes, with a white canvas background, while he swung a skinny but heavy aluminum bat, well, that would be some kind of training. He hoped it would make live pitching with a bigger ball, and hitting with a bigger bat, look slower and easier. He didn't know if anything like that had ever been tried before, but it seemed logical.

He washed the golf balls until they were gleaming. He was grateful for their colored stripes or he would never have been able to see them against that background.

His last purchase was the batting helmet that had fit so perfectly in the second-hand store. His new friend, the man behind the counter, showed him how to cut down the foam rubber around the ears as he got older and bigger. "That should fit you for three or four more years, if you do it right. If you have any questions or problems with it, just bring it in here when it needs cuttin, and I'll do it with my bowie." He patted the blade at his hip, and Elgin decided that was something he would like to see: a man who knew what he was doing, adjusting sports equipment with a hunting knife.

By the time Elgin had rearranged the room, hung the canvas, and made all the repairs, he was back in the swing of things at school and had only a few hours after homework every night to make final adjustments. He kept making excuses to his friends who played fastpitch, but the fact was, he was not getting good enough competition there. He didn't want to tell them that, but it was true. The game was still fun and challenging, but he was hitting about .700. And after a lot of dry swinging with the heavy fungo, the broom handle seemed like a toy. He could smash that fastpitch ball.

Every afternoon Elgin played an hour of fastpitch, went home for supper, did his homework, and tinkered with the machine in the basement. He finally got it to fire the golf balls, one every few seconds, right into his strike zone. By adjusting the wheels, he could make the balls curve in or out or up or down, but of course he had to have it throw all the balls one way before adjusting it to throw them another way.

He had not yet stepped into the box against the steel monster. He was waiting for final adjustments and lots of time. That would come at Christmas break when he would have almost three weeks to take his cuts or, he hoped not, his lumps.

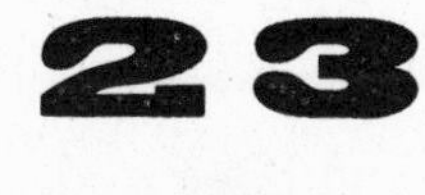

THE CHICAGO SNOW CAME as a lake-effect dump during the first week of December. Despite expert predictions of only minor flurries followed by Indian summer days that would clear the white stuff, the city was frozen nearly to a halt till March.

One day the sun would melt the drifts to slush, making citizens on the side streets hope for plows to clear them with the same enthusiasm that streets in the Loop and the expressways were cleared. But as evening fell, so would more snow, and everything reverted to the way it was. Soon even those sunny days became rare. Little flags on long metal rods were attached to fire hydrants so they could be found in the snow. People took to attaching the same to their car antennae so other motorists could see them at corners over the five- and six-foot piles and drifts.

Miriam found it depressing. Walking was a treacherous chore. The wait for the buses seemed interminable. The shipping charge for Elgin's pitching machine had eaten most of her coat money, so she opted for a pair of cheap boots and a shawl she wore between her sweater and her old coat.

⚾ ⚾ ⚾

Elgin liked the snow. He enjoyed running and jumping in it, climbing the piles, making snowmen with his friends. There was no fastpitch in this weather. Their "field," such as it was, had to be flat from the pitcher and outfielders on one side of the street to the hitter on the other. Drifts and parked cars obstructed the playing area.

Elgin had located one of his rubber-coated baseballs and adjusted the pitching machine to see what it would do with the ball. Mostly, he was curious to know if the machine only appeared super fast because it had been throwing golf balls, or if it was malfunctioning. He wasn't sure he would know, except to try to compare it to his memory of what he had seen at batting cages.

One night after school and homework and dinner, he fired up the machine and fed the ball into the pitching wheels. To his amazement, even though the ball hit the floor about three feet in front of the wall, the machine put the same English on it as it had the golf balls. The baseball flashed toward the wall, spinning and sweeping to the right. When it hit the floor and then the wall, it bounced high toward the light and blasted into the canvas at the far end, dropping to the floor.

Elgin shook his head. There had to be something wrong with this machine. It was throwing the ball faster than he had ever seen. As he reset the wheels to accept the golf balls, he inventoried the reasons he did not expect to be able to hit them:

They would come in faster than it was humanly possible to react.

The machine itself was a third closer to the hitter than it was designed for, even if it had been throwing at normal speed.

There was no clue to the rhythm of the deliveries, as there was when you could watch a pitcher wind up. Arm-style pitching machines provided that same advantage. He would have to learn to anticipate each pitch from the spinning wheels by watching the tilting of the trough.

The room was dark at both ends. He would see the pitch better when it passed under the light than he would when it left the machine or reached the plate.

The balls were small. They were white, except for their rings of color.

The backdrop he had installed to keep the balls from attacking him from every angle, was white.

The bat was skinny, like a fastpitch bat, but heavy, almost like a weighted on-deck bat.

Why, Elgin wondered, do I think I even have a chance of getting the bat on the ball?

The question was better and more valid than he realized, until he finally ran out of reasons to not try it.

Elgin dumped the entire basket of golf balls into the container. He had already determined that with all of them in there, he could turn on the machine and run to the batter's box in time to set himself and take a practice swing before the first pitch came.

Before turning it on, however, he adjusted everything he wore. He untied his shoe laces and pulled up his socks, then tied his shoes again, firm and tight. He loosened his belt and tucked his shirt in. He put on his batting helmet and shoved it all the way down, banging the top of it until it was snug.

He swung his bat above his head and stretched it across his shoulders. He felt as nervous as if he was facing the toughest pitcher ever. His dad had always told him to think only about looking for his pitch, having a plan, and attacking the ball. He was to work for bat speed and confidence, not just trying to get the bat on the ball. That seemed impossible now.

As he put his fingers on the switch, his mind tried to talk his body out of this. Was he sure the machine had not shifted? Would it start throwing several balls every few seconds, despite his adjustments? Would he be hit, drop to the floor, and be unable to evade the continuing fusillade? He pressed his lips together and told himself this was no time for more excuses or stalling. He had forced himself to become a better-than-average player for his age by doing the tough things, working on the fundamentals, running longer, working harder. Anybody could get along on his talent, but he was Elgin Woodell, son of a man who had almost made the Pittsburgh Pirates.

He flipped the switch and ran to the other end of the room. He heard the machine whirring as he went, and he stepped in right-handed. A tingling sensation ran from his seat to the back of his head and made him shudder.

"You'll learn to hit the off-speed stuff," he remembered his father telling him. "The curves, the changes, the sliders—they say that's what separates the big leaguer from the amateur, but don't you believe it. The day comes when you hope a guy throws you junk because it's the only thing you can catch up with. What really separates the men from the boys is that drop dead, freight train fastball that's in on you and hoppin before you can move. That's the pitch you dream about. That's the career-ender, right there. Show me a man who can stand in there against a big league fastball and I'll show you a man who can hit a curve in his sleep."

The balls were tumbling, then rolling smoothly but loudly in the container. Elgin had reached the box more quickly than he expected. He took a couple of desperate practice swings while trying to position himself where he could reach the ball with the bat but wouldn't jeopardize his future.

He was as close to the back wall as he could be without hitting it with his bat, and he was as far from the plate as he could be without being out of the box. If he couldn't reach the first few pitches, he decided, he would just creep in until he could. He had fifty-seven pitches worth of adjusting available.

The trough tilted back, picked up a few balls, and tilted forward. Elgin saw and heard the pitching wheels whine into action. He heard the *pfft!* and the *whoosh!* but hardly saw the pitch before it slammed the wall behind him, flashed to the other end of the room, and smacked into the canvas.

Elgin had not even flinched. There was no swing, no half swing, no step, no thought except, Don't let that thing hit you. He could tell from the sound that the ball had come through the strike zone, but he probably would not have been able to reach it if he had swung. He was tensed and ready for the next pitch.

He squinted and told himself to at least pick up the flight of the ball this time. He heard the first two sounds almost simultaneously, cocked his head and bat, and almost stepped. He saw the blur, heard the bang off the wall, and watched the ball fly to the other end. He had just enough time to appreciate his own handiwork with the canvas and wonder if he would hit any of the balls before the sounds came again and another blur hit the wall.

He had hardly stepped, still hadn't swung, and was almost as amused as he was scared. For the briefest instant, every few seconds, the brute seemed connected to the wall by a flash of white. The ring of color on each ball disappeared in flight, and Elgin wondered if his mind and his eye would ever adjust. If they did not or could not, he would be forced to modify the machine and find some baseballs.

As the flashes kept banging, Elgin realized he might be hundreds or even thousands of pitches away from actually making solid contact. Yet somewhere deep inside him was the feeling that if he could somehow catch onto this, practice it, master it, it could make him as a ballplayer.

What the eleven-year-old did not know and could not have realized was that he was facing pitches at speeds of more than 113 miles an hour. All he knew was that the machine was an inanimate, brainless, muscleless, tireless thing that threw a ball tinier and harder than a baseball from less than two-thirds the major league distance.

After about the tenth pitch, Elgin made up his mind to start swinging. He stepped and swung at waist level, regardless of where the pitch was, and tried to pick up the cadence so he would at least be stepping and swinging in rhythm with the machine, even if he wasn't making contact.

He stepped and swung, stepped and swung, stepped and swung. Not hard, not overpowering, not much bat speed. He quickly came to where all he wanted was to get lucky, to hit a foul tip, to dribble one away.

Step and swing.

Step and swing.
Step and swing.
Step and swing.
Miss.
Miss.
Miss.
Miss.
Step and swing.
Miss.

Thirty, maybe forty pitches into the ordeal, Elgin felt anger and frustration rise in him. He swung harder and faster, telling himself that he could and he would catch up with a pitch. He seemed to be swinging through a couple of the pitches, convinced it was only a matter of time now. But then his timing would leave him and he felt as if he was swinging after the ball had already hit the wall.

The room was filling with missed golf balls, some rolling lazily almost back to the batter's box. He would have to do something about that, maybe drape a blanket or extend a rope across the floor to stop those so he wouldn't have to worry about stepping on them.

He was determined to keep his head down, his swing level, his step the right distance.

"Perfect practice makes perfect," his dad's advice rang in his ears. "No matter what the drill—running, hitting, fielding, throwing—you do it right every time. Even if you swing and miss, make sure your mechanics are right, that you're puttin in your mind's computer a perfect picture of how it oughta be done."

Elgin imagined he was hitting line drives with every swing, but he couldn't beat back the frustration of reality. He was missing, missing, missing, not even coming close. He guessed there were about ten balls left when he squared around.

I am going to make the ball hit this bat at least once, he told himself. At least once.

Squaring around allowed him to pick up the flight of the ball better. Man, that thing was moving! He carefully stuck his bat out and kept it level. The pitch was rising. He followed it, still keeping the skinny aluminum bat steady.

No dice.

He tried it again and again. Just a few pitches left now. He just had to touch one, foul one off, get something on it, anything.

But he didn't. Elgin was just afraid enough of the slamming golf balls to keep him a few inches from touching them with his outstretched bat, even to bunt.

His anger and frustration exploded. He was madder than he had ever been. All the work, all the adjusting, all the waiting and anticipation, and he hadn't even been able to bunt or foul off or even tip one of the fifty-seven pitches.

He drew the bat back into his normal swinging position and whipped it through the strike zone, letting go with both hands. The metal bat clanged off the side wall and whirled toward the machine. Elgin hoped it would bang it, but it didn't. He couldn't hit anything he wanted to that day. He wanted to kick something, but everything he looked at was cement or metal.

As he cooled down, he got the wire basket and gathered up the balls. This time, he decided, he would hit lefty. The balls were moving from left to right across the plate, so he told himself he needn't be afraid, even if the pitches seemed to be coming at him.

As if I can see them at all, he thought.

But from the left side, he could. On the first several he bailed out without swinging. It was one thing, he decided, to tell yourself you didn't have to be afraid, but it was another to stand in there. He was grateful to find that the machine was consistent within inches, firing every ball to almost the same spot on the wall. A couple of times he looked back as it hit. Eventually he became aware that the machine jarred itself slightly out of position with each pitch and that he would have to readjust it with every two or three buckets of balls.

After more than twenty pitches, with no better luck than he'd had from the other side, Elgin began wondering why he had made it so difficult for himself. He wondered if he could adjust it to throw the old, torn-up baseball, his bald tennis ball, that box of softballs he'd seen at the second-hand store. Mostly he wondered how his mind could mull over all those things while streaks of light, as if from a laser, blasted off the wall behind him. Concentrate, he told himself. Concentrate.

Elgin was mad, frustrated, and sweating a half hour later, after he had stood in from both sides twice and never touched a pitch with the bat. He wondered if the pitches were catchable, let alone hittable. He got his glove, stood in the left-hand batter's box, and kept reaching farther and farther, getting closer and closer to each pitch.

Finally, one touched the web of his glove and he felt the thing almost fly off his hand. Five more pitches flew past before he touched another with the thumb and got the sensation that his glove could come flying off at any moment. How his father would ridicule him if he saw him like this!

"Only sissies step out of the way and catch the ball to the side," Neal had always said. "They're afraid it's going to hit them or bounce off their gloves and catch them in the nose. You watch me and you watch your pros; we catch the ball right out in front of us. Does it ever skip off and get us in the ribs or the face? Sure. But have you ever seen a guy go to the hospital because he missed a ball in a game of catch? Nah! Maybe hit by a pitch or a big throw by accident, but not from playin catch. Only guy I ever saw get hurt from a ground ball was Tony Kubek when he took one in the throat for the Yankees in the World Series years ago. A Cub got hurt with a thrown ball playin catch in front of the dugout, but that was only because he was talkin to somebody and the guy throwin to him didn't know he had looked away. He turned back just in time to take it in the mouth. Cost him a few teeth, but then he played eight more years. Catch it in front of you, El."

But here he was, standing gingerly in the batter's box, reaching out on tiptoes. By the end of that basket of balls, he had caught two, but the first had made him overconfident. He reached a little farther for the second, and it smacked into the palm of his glove just below his index finger. He yanked his hand out of the glove and shook it, waved it, stuck it between his legs, jumped, and hollered. "Nice pitch, you..."

Meanwhile, the machine just kept firing. Elgin decided to try one last basket of balls to see if he could just hold the bat out with one hand, moving it and adjusting it ever so slightly with each pitch, trying to guess where it would be coming. He flexed his left hand all the while he was picking up balls. He knew, as his father said, that he wouldn't be going to the hospital, but this was a painful injury, maybe a bone bruise, and it would be a long time healing.

Elgin took a different approach with the machine this time. He dumped the balls in and turned it on, staying behind the machine for the first few pitches to study the trajectory. By now he knew exactly where the ball would fly off the wall and where to walk to stay away from it.

When he was ready, he walked to the other end. He wondered if he was being foolish. He knew guys who had been hit in batting cages because the machine inexplicably threw a wild pitch right at them. He prayed this one would never do that. He guessed that the spring-arm machines were more inclined to that than this type.

He stepped into the box and took his normal swing for the second dozen or so pitches. As he expected, he didn't come close. Now he crouched low and held the bat in his left hand from the lefty side of the plate, stretching it out horizontally in the direction of the pitches, which swept away from him over the outside corner. He could tell he was within a half inch of touching a few.

Finally he reached far enough and held the bat level enough so that a pitch ticked the end of it on the top side and skipped back to the left off the wall. It cracked into his helmet, hit the wall and helmet again before Elgin went down, and he found himself in the righty batter's box.

He was not hurt, just stunned, but he knew he had to get out of there. When he tried to step, he slipped, so he lay flat on the ground and felt a pitch miss him by a foot. He tried to get up and move to the other side again, but he was too panicky and didn't get traction and had to spread-eagle himself again. Eventually he was able to roll out of the way.

A dozen or so balls were still left in the machine, so he got back into position. If he could tip one, maybe he could get more of the bat on another. He missed several, but the second-to-last pitch hit the top side of the bat about six inches off the end, hit the wall, and slammed into Elgin's side, just under the shoulder and above the rib cage in a fleshy area that seared with pain. Elgin hit the deck again, this time in the lefty box.

How many times am I gonna do this before I learn that fouling off a pitch makes it bounce off the wall and try to kill me?

The last pitch sailed past him, hit the wall, and flew to the other end. Like all the others, it was a screamer. It wasn't as if he could see it in slow motion, he decided, but because he had watched hundreds of pitches already, he was able to break this one down as it came. He was aware of it snaking its way from the container to the trough, the tilt of the trough toward the wheels, the wheels grabbing and shaping themselves around it, seeming to mash it between them before slinging it out. It spun wildly and darted more than a foot and a half from left to right as it traveled less than forty feet to the wall. It swept past where a left-hand hitter would stand, breaking over the outside corner and seeming to rise from just below the knee at its lowest point to about thigh level.

Elgin had seen it all the way. He longed for the day when he could not only swing at that pitch at the right instant but also be able to hit it. He wasn't thinking about just getting his bat on it. He wanted to attack the pitch, hit it with authority, drive it somewhere.

He had seen film clips of George Brett turning with that ferocious left-hand power stroke on the then fastest pitcher in baseball, Goose Gossage, and actually pulling a fastball in the high nineties into the upper deck in right field. That was the way he wanted to hit. Not just spraying the ball, but turning on it, driving it, sending it to the gaps or to the seats, no matter what it had on it when it left the mound. Elgin slowly gathered up the balls, occasionally reaching to rub the sore spot on his side. That would be another bruise. He was sure glad he had invested in the batting helmet. He wondered if he needed a piece of canvas on the batting wall too.

He decided against it. He imagined foul balls and missed balls hitting a tarp and dropping at his feet. He couldn't imagine rigging up some sophisticated device to keep the balls from rolling forward and tripping him. That would be all he needed: to be sent to the floor while swinging at a demon pitch. He'd be killed for sure.

Something nagged at Elgin as he retrieved the balls. Had this been a perfect practice? He had swung hundreds of times, and always tried to do it right. He had stood in against unbelievable pitching, and though he was frustrated at not hitting, it was understandable that he hadn't.

But had it been profitable? He decided not. When the balls were in the basket, he dumped them in the container in the machine and left the machine off. He dug out his rubber-coated baseball and stood by the machine. For the next half hour he threw against the far wall, aiming at tiny spots in the strike zone and fielding the ball as it came back to him.

When he threw the ball high, it came back in two or three bounces. When he threw it waist high off the wall, it came back as a skipping grounder. When he threw it low, it skittered along the floor, hardly bouncing. When he wanted a liner, soft or hard depending on how he threw it, he made the ball bounce on the floor just before it hit the wall. The harder he threw, the harder it came back.

There was little challenge in catching balls you threw yourself, but Elgin was a perfectionist. He wanted to cleanly field a hundred in a row, every time with his left leg forward, head down, glove down, butt down. The glove was like a vacuum cleaner, his dad had said. There was only one right way to do it.

"Lots of guys can bend at the waist and spear a ball one-handed," his dad had said. "They might even have a big gun of an arm and be able to throw the guy out at first. But that was the wrong way to do it. Do it right, same way every time. Head down, glove down, butt down, left foot forward. Move to the ball, keep the hands and arms relaxed and out front. Play the ball, don't let it play you. Gather it in, pulling both hands across your body to the right as you take one step and make a crisp hard throw, all in one motion."

Elgin repeated the motions over and over and over. He huffed and puffed and sweated profusely. Off the wall, to the glove, you can always come up on a hopper; you can hardly ever get the glove down if you started in the wrong position. Do it right, every time. Be in a position to whirl and start the double play. Don't be lazy. Perfect practice makes perfect.

Perfect practice. Perfect practice.

MIRIAM HAD SWEET-TALKED Ricardo Bravura into a second key to the basement. That way, she assured him, she could check up on Elgin and make sure everything was tidy. It also, of course, allowed her to go and find the boy when he had been in the basement too long. Like now. It was bedtime.

When she opened the door and peered down the stairs, she saw him turn from where he was sitting, on the bottom step with his back to her, and smile. He looked beat.

"What're you doin with that helmet still on?" she asked.

"Just forgot," he said, pulling it off.

"Have a good workout?"

"In a way."

"Do any hitting?"

He laughed. "I tried."

"No luck?"

"That's for sure. Look at this." A purple spot had already risen on his palm.

"Did you try to block a pitch with your hand? You know what your daddy always said about that: only block it with your hand if it's comin at your head or face. Protect those hands."

"I know, Momma. I was trying to catch a pitch."

"Barehanded? A golf ball?"

"Not barehanded, but yes, a golf ball."

He explained his entire evening.

"So, you got in some good fieldin practice anyway, huh?" she said.

He nodded wearily.

"You need a shower, buddy."

He nodded again. "It's fun to work out alone, Momma. But I don't know how long I'm gonna be able to stand not hitting the ball."

"What kind've an attitude is that, El? This thing got you beat?"

"Momma, you should see it. I feel like I'm a year away from really hitting the ball."

Miriam sat next to her son and put her arm around him. He was wet all the way through his sweatshirt. "Boy, you're hot."

"Um-hm. Be careful."

"Of what now?"

"My side. Look at this." He lifted his shirt.

"Elgin! I can see the imprint of the dimples from the ball!"

"I was hitting lefty and reached out and tipped one. It bounced off the wall and got me."

"If anybody at school sees your bruises, they're gonna send the authorities after me for child abuse."

He laughed. "I'd love to see that!"

"I'll bet you would. Now get upstairs."

"I gotta turn that light out."

"I'll get it. I promised Ricardo I'd check up on you, anyway."

He turned and started up the steps, and Miriam moved into the batting room. Tidy, she thought. She saw the empty wire basket in the corner, but didn't think anything of it. She idly flipped the switch on the machine and heard the container begin to turn and the balls begin to roll.

"Momma!" she heard from the stairs. "Get out of there now! The machine is loaded!"

She froze, not knowing what to do or where to go. Elgin appeared just as the first ball was being fed to the spinning wheels. He raced to her yelling, "Get down!" and she ducked behind the machine. For the first time, she heard the sounds of the grab, the pitch, the flight, the wall, the second flight, and the canvas behind her.

"Whew!" was all she could say.

"Whew is right," Elgin said. "Lucky for you, they're all flying that way." He reached around and turned off the machine.

"They do go fast, don't they?" she said, her voice weak.

He laughed. She didn't know if she could laugh until she saw him. He sat there, smiling, sweating, bruised, tired. She knew he was frustrated at not having been able to hit the pitches, yet he still seemed excited at having tried. Had anyone ever loved baseball as much as this boy? She couldn't imagine.

He was like a newborn calf that wanted to run, a new bud reaching for the sun, a tender shoot eager to sprout and blossom. For the briefest moment, in the middle of a miserable Chicago winter that had arrived before the calendar called for it, she was still glad she had moved there.

⚾ ⚾ ⚾

Elgin's bruises turned ugly and were hot to the touch. They stung whenever he brushed against anything. His limbs ached from the harder and longer than usual workouts, but after a few weeks, he was in shape and could handle them. In fact, he looked forward to them.

He forced himself to stand in the batter's box for three buckets of golf balls from each side of the plate before he did his fielding and throwing work. Though he tipped only one pitch, batting lefty, in several days, he kept swinging and felt he was getting his timing down. There were times, of course, that he wondered if swinging over or under or ahead or behind thousands of pitches was doing anything for him. But his chest and back and arms grew stronger.

When he had gone several weeks with just a few tips of the ball from each side, he added something to his regimen. He began taking one hundred swings from each side as hard and fast as he could with no pitches coming. He wore himself out, tore down his muscles, and built them up again doing that, hoping to increase his bat speed. That had to be it, he decided. The only reason he was missing those pitches was because they were so fast and the ball and bat were so small. He had to learn, to force himself to catch up with the pitches.

Chico came by one day to lament the snow and the sad state of the fast-pitch area. "Man, I could use a good game of catch, you know?"

"I hear you, Chico. It gets lonely working out alone."

"You're workin out?"

"A little."

"Where?"

"The hotel. Our sidewalk is cleared. Let's play a little catch."

"With what?"

"I've got a rubber-coated baseball."

"It's cold outside, man."

"We'll take it easy. I need to throw just like you do."

Chico ran home for his glove. He returned with a big grin. "My mother and my brother think we're crazy."

"We are!" Elgin said, following him out.

They began about twenty feet apart, throwing easily. Elgin knew it wouldn't show yet, but he felt good and strong. He had wanted to get into some kind of game or at least throw with someone just to see if his workouts were paying off. The first thing he noticed was that the ball looked huge to him, much the way it did when he threw it off the wall after watching more than three hundred golf balls whiz past him.

But outside, playing catch with someone he had been used to throwing a bald tennis ball to, he really got the perspective. Chico seemed tight, almost awkward. Elgin threw like he meant business.

"Hey, man," Chico whined, "back up if you're gonna throw like that."

Elgin smiled. "You loose, Chico?"

"No, but I'll put an arch on it or somethin. Just don't make me stand here and catch fastballs."

Elgin had not been aware he'd been throwing that hard. He felt he had some snap on his delivery, but Chico had always been able to catch him. Of course, they had always played with a rubber ball. This one, despite its coating, was hard, especially in this weather.

As they backed up from each other, Elgin still felt strong. He whipped throws right to Chico's glove, hardly making him move. Chico shook his head with every throw.

"Man, you're hot!"

Hot was exactly what Elgin felt. He loved this, but he was also sweating. He shed his coat and put it next to the building. The only time the boys broke their throwing rhythm was when someone walked by. The frigid air felt good on his face and neck, and as it breezed through the thin material of his long-sleeved shirt, he felt invigorated.

Elgin threw long and straight, popping Chico's glove. Chico smiled, shook his head, and lofted the ball back. Every time Elgin caught it he imagined a different game situation. A runner was tagging or leading off too far or in a rundown or represented the second half of a double play. Catch and fire, catch and fire. How he loved the game, the sheer joy of it, the great fun of throwing a baseball!

But he lived to regret his foolishness. He had not known he was being careless, of course. He felt a dull ache in his arm, near the shoulder, at bedtime. He had just been telling his mother how great it had been, how strong he had felt. He said nothing about the pain.

In the middle of the night he awoke with a burning shoulder and biceps. His elbow hurt too. He ran the bathroom sink full of cold water and submerged his arm to the shoulder. By morning, he could hardly bend it. Dressing and eating was a chore. He felt like an old man with, what was it his mother called it? Bursitis?

Throwing in cold weather was not something he'd ever had to worry about in Mississippi. And the winter before had been mild enough that the guys got used to the weather because they played in it the whole time. It had been nearly two months since he had played fastpitch, and they all had worn warm jackets.

What had he been thinking of? He thought he should have known better, even if he hadn't ever had to worry about it before.

His teacher grew tired of his excuses for having to write with his left hand. He may have been able to switch hit, but ambidexterity with a pencil was not one of his strengths. He felt like an idiot and knew he had brought all this on himself. He hated the idea of not being able to practice his fielding religiously, but there would be no stopping his hitting practice, though he had to swing with one hand.

Who knew? Maybe he would start hitting these crazy pitches when he could come at them with just one hand.

The first night he tried working out with his bad arm dangling, it was futile. He couldn't even stand the pain that came with swinging with his left arm. Eventually his mother found an Ace bandage and rigged him a sling. He felt more comfortable with the arm bent and close to his body, but he felt more like an invalid too.

It took longer to set himself to swing with one hand, and he was able to swing at only every other pitch. When he began fouling off one of every ten or so, he knew he was making progress.

He missed terribly his throwing and fielding workouts, and he vowed to never again risk injury because of enthusiasm. Nothing was more frustrating to a perfectionistic athlete than not being able to train properly.

He guessed his arm was a month away from being back to normal, and then he would have to build the muscle again. That seemed an eternity away.

25

MIRIAM NEVER HAD REASON TO DOUBT ELGIN BEFORE, but neither had she ever experienced a cold-weather arm injury. Elgin had gone through the typical childhood stage of duplicity, but it had been two full years since she had caught him in an outright lie. Still, she had to ask.

"El, are you sure all you were doin to hurt that arm was throwin without your coat on? I mean, you weren't wrestlin or roughhousin or somethin, were you?"

He insisted he was not. He told her how he had felt so good and how his throws were crisp and right on the money. "I got warmed up, the cold air felt great, and I guess I just got carried away."

She had insurance at work, but the deductible alone would have threatened her various weekly savings programs. She was willing, of course, to take Elgin to a doctor, but he told her he was sure the arm was just strained.

"I don't think anything's broke or pulled," he said. "I just got to wait it out."

Waiting it out was as tough a thing as the boy had ever done. It was two weeks before he could use his right arm to pick up the golf balls at the end of each hitting session, and two more before he could start throwing easily. The muscles had atrophied, and he couldn't fully straighten the arm for a few more days. It wasn't long, however, before he could bat with both hands again.

That was what he had been waiting for. The Christmas vacation had been lost to what he considered profitable workouts, though even standing in against the pitching machine with one hand and fouling off a few did more for his eye and his timing than he imagined.

For a few days after resuming his normal right and left batting stances, he had as much trouble catching up with the pitches as he always had. But after weeks of being rigid and tense in the box, he had learned the rhythm and cadence of the machine and knew what the pitches would and would not do. It didn't bother him—as it once had—to just wait on a few pitches, not swinging or even looking at them, but simply getting himself set.

Finally the day came when Elgin took a few practice swings from the right-hand side, ignored a few pitches without moving, then set himself and drew the bat back. He stayed in his crouch with knees bent, eyes on the ball, stepping slowly, about six inches, when he heard the sound from the spinning wheels. He opened his hips and turned on the ball, driving his bat through the strike zone and keeping his chin down, eyes level. He smacked the ball on a direct line past the machine and into the hanging canvas. Elgin dropped to one knee just to savor it. It had not been luck. He had gotten to where he thought it might be possible. Pitch after pitch came banging off the wall as he knelt there, smiling. Man, that felt good! It had been a solid line drive, maybe a homer.

He couldn't wait to do it again, and he didn't mind that the machine emptied itself of golf balls while he reveled in his success. It had been almost worth the wait. Almost, but not quite. If he could get a shot like that during each set of fifty-seven pitches, then he might consider the lengthy ordeal worth it.

Batting lefty a few minutes later, Elgin found he could reach the outside corner by forcing himself to step into the pitch. He would rarely try to hit a pitch like this into left field because he simply couldn't get enough on it, but until he was ready to adjust the machine to either start spinning the ball the opposite way, redirecting it so the ball cut across the inside or the heart of the plate, he would try this.

Elgin hit four foul tips and what would have been a weak pop-up, probably to the third baseman. In a way he felt better about that performance than even the solid shot from the right side. He felt he had come a long way, getting his bat on five pitches. It was less than ten percent, but it was so much more than he had ever done before. His goal was to be able to drive the ball from both sides the way he had—one time—from the left.

He refilled the machine and used his rubber-coated baseball for a little infield practice. His arm was still delicate and he felt feeble, not being able to snap the ball on the throw. Still, he knew it was good for the arm to just loosely arch the ball to the wall and then play the easy hops. He would take it slow, not try to hurry his comeback. He wanted to be ready by spring to become the best player on his team and maybe in the league.

Miriam was glad Elgin had found some success in the basement. She loved to hear him tell of his progress. Occasionally she stood in the doorway and watched him, ready to duck behind the wall when necessary. The difference between the first time she had done that—just after Christmas when he was able to foul off maybe ten pitches out of a whole set and hit grounders on one or two more—and the second week in March was amazing. By then he was at least tipping every other pitch, and he hit a half-dozen solid every time. Only once in every two rounds of pitches would he hit a hard liner, but Miriam was still astonished by his progress.

As the weather cleared and Elgin's fastpitch buddies began making noises about starting up the games again, Miriam cautioned him about throwing too hard too soon outside.

"Oh, don't worry," he told her. "I don't ever want to go through that again. If I play, I won't pitch, at least till next month."

The only problem Miriam had with Elgin's obsession was that it made her lonelier. He was doing homework or reading when she got home, for which she was thankful. They talked during dinner, and he helped her with the dishes. Then he finished his homework and headed for the basement, usually not returning until bedtime. They talked a little more when she was getting him settled in, but still she felt she had less and less time with him and for him. He didn't seem any the worse for it, but she felt deprived.

He was becoming a charming, quick-witted kid. He was sensitive, though a loner. She worried that all that time alone would affect how he got along with people, but his teachers said he was an outspoken leader in class and that everyone liked him. He had a reputation as a local baseball star, but he assured Miriam he had said nothing to anyone about his private training room and regimen.

Miriam used the time in the evenings to read and sew, and she watched more television than she felt she should. She worried when she began to pretend there was a man there, one she could talk to about anything at all. More than once she caught herself thinking aloud, imagining that someone who loved her cared about what she had to say. She spoke of Elgin, waited for a reasoned response, then talked some more. She knew it was silly, wondered if she was crazy, and eventually went to sleep trying to picture the man who would come into her life.

Her bed was lonely and cold until she curled into a ball and embraced the extra pillow, often waking in the morning in the same position, feeling as if she had hung on all night for her very life. But when she saw her son, her precious son, the one who was worth any sacrifice, she decided every morning to postpone her own needs for his. He didn't know this, she recognized. He seemed to take life as it came, believed that baseball was all there was and, she hoped, realized that she loved him. That was all she wanted for now, for him to know that he was loved—to know something she had never really known or felt.

There had been too many children in her family, too many sons, too many daughters. She felt as if she had slipped through the cracks, as if she was just one of the kids and not a special person to her parents. Being one of the younger, she was convinced her parents had run out of time and energy for her. She was not a rebel, not a troublemaker, but she was a troubled soul. She had desperately needed and wanted attention, and not being a socialite or a rich kid, she settled for dating the campus heartthrob. That was almost enough, but it had evolved into a nightmare.

Miriam had read and seen and experienced enough to know what it meant to be a caring parent. She didn't want to overdo it, but she compared herself to TV moms, movie moms, even moms of her friends. Few had experiences any different from hers, but she had one friend whose mother was fun and funny, who listened and seemed to care. This was a woman who didn't embarrass her kids by trying to be like them or by trying to impress their friends. She just was who she was and seemed comfortable with it. She was a mother who didn't spoil her kids or let them run her, but who cared deeply for them—and it showed.

That was the kind of mother Miriam wanted to be. She had friends and acquaintances in the work world, as she grew older and got married and divorced, who liked to blame their troubles, and hers, on the way they were raised. They commiserated about neglectful parents, too harsh parents, too permissive parents, too busy parents. Miriam grew sick of it. She believed in her soul that your adult life and what happens to you does not have to be a result of the way you were raised, but rather can be a result of how you responded to the way you were raised. For a while, especially when she doubted herself and believed she had brought many of these marital troubles on herself, she believed that her upbringing had a lot to do with it. Had she become an enabler? Was she making it convenient for Neal to be alcoholic, abusive, self-destructive?

Eventually she separated herself from that kind of thinking. She convinced herself that she would be a good mother and could have been a good wife. She told herself that, yes, perhaps her family was dysfunctional and never learned to interact properly, but she had known all along it was wrong. She had a brain, she had eyes and ears, she had experience and years, and it was time to grow up, to take responsibility for her own actions.

She still didn't know whether her divorce was right in the eyes of God. She assumed it probably wasn't, and she hadn't felt good about giving up on marriage, or giving up on Neal. But he had bled from her every vestige of energy and dignity. She decided that a God who allowed people to divorce because of adultery would not expect one of His children to live in fear for her life or those of her children, born or unborn. She wasn't sure she was right, but she knew she had to take control.

In just eight or nine years she would see her son off to college and maybe he could help her financially after that. Maybe she could be open to another relationship then. For now, though, she was content to devote herself quietly and almost secretly—for eleven-year-olds rarely sensed such things—to giving her son a life she would have died for as a child. She didn't want to be blind and spoil him; she didn't want to center her life on him to the point that she would have nothing to live for when he was gone. But in her small ways, with her humble financial means, she intended to deny herself—and him in many ways—so that in the long run he would have opportunities she never had.

Then, regardless what he did with those opportunities, he would know what she had tried to do. He could have obscenely expensive athletic shoes and other equipment now, and then have to work and not go to college one day. But she would not do that to him. She knew the day would come—in fact, she was amazed it hadn't already—when his values might not be her values and he might start badgering her to give him what everyone else seemed to have. Then she would just try to explain things to him. She would tell him of her budget and why they lived beneath their means on a salary that would be poverty level for most. Unless she missed her guess, Elgin was one kid who would understand. He may not like it or agree with it at first, but he would be grateful for her and for her philosophy one day, the day that it counted. He would not be looking for any ship to come in. He would know the value of love and family and work and diligence, and he would know that you make your own way in this world. He would become a man of responsibility and discipline. That she prayed for above all.

⚾ ⚾ ⚾

Chico came by looking for Elgin late one afternoon. Elgin was in the basement, but Miriam didn't want to tell Chico that and make him feel bad that he couldn't join him. "I'll tell him you came by."

"Tell him we gonna play fastpitch till dark today. First game of the season."

After Chico left, Miriam hurried to the basement to give Elgin the news.

"I think I'm ready for a little fastpitch," he said. "I'm not ready to pitch though. Chico always wants to pitch. I'll get on his team."

An hour later, just after dark, Miriam heard Elgin on the stairs from a couple of floors below. He was the only person in the building who could run up that many flights. He rarely did it at the end of the day, though. Usually, especially after playing hard and long, he took the elevator. He must, she decided, have news.

Did he ever.

26

MIRIAM WAS SURE IT WAS ELGIN banging on the door, but the rapping was so insistent that she peeked through the peephole just to be safe. "C'mon, Momma! Open up!"

She removed the chain and twisted both dead bolts. Elgin had already turned the knob and the door swept in at her. She stepped back just in time to miss being slammed in the nose. "Elgin! What's wrong?"

Nothing was wrong. She could see that from his face, but she wanted to send him a message. Nothing but an emergency should require that kind of enthusiasm at this time of day.

"Momma, you've got to come with me right now. Chico is waiting."

"Why? Waiting for what?"

"Please, Momma, get your coat."

"Dinner's on the stove, El."

"Turn it down, turn it off, put it in the oven. Just come on."

"No, you gotta tell me first."

"You just have to see this, Momma, what I can do in fastpitch. You will not believe it. Chico promised to throw his hardest and to do whatever he can to get me out, but you gotta watch."

"It's after dark! You can hardly see the ball now!"

"It didn't make any difference when the sun went down. I could still see. I mean, I see it leave his hand and—"

"I thought Chico was on your team."

"He was, but we won so big that the other guys finally left. Chico said he thought the other pitcher must have been throwing me candy pitches, because he sure couldn't hit the guy. Momma, I must've made only three outs in an hour, and there were only two guys on our team, just Chico and me."

"Just three outs?"

She could see there would be no bargaining. She put the pans in the oven and turned it to low, then grabbed her coat. They hurried a couple of blocks, and sure enough, there sat Chico.

"I try to get him out, ma'am, I really do. I pitch after dark, my best, my fastest. I can't even see the ball after the pitch, but he hit it and then I see it, very high."

"I'm watching," she said. It was unlike anything she had ever seen. If she hadn't been there herself, she would not have believed it. It wasn't that Elgin was one to stretch the truth, but this would have been hard to swallow. He stood up to the chalked-in plate.

"Tell her what happened first, man," Chico said, grinning.

"Oh, yeah, that," Elgin said, laughing. "Well, when we first got here, nobody else was here, so we pitched to each other."

"You weren't going to throw in this weather," Miriam scolded.

"Oh, I was just lobbing it."

"Yeah, he was, ma'am. I was hitting him pretty good!"

"But then when I tried to get some practice hitting against Chico, I couldn't hit a thing. The bat seemed so light I couldn't control it, and I was way out ahead of everything. He started throwing harder and harder, and just before the other guys showed up, I got used to it."

"Yeah," Chico said, "and then—well, watch this!"

Chico wound and fired, a high fastball, outside and right about at Elgin's chin. Elgin turned and smashed the ball high off the eighth or ninth floor of the twenty-story building across the street. Chico chased the ball by listening for the bounce, then both boys looked to Miriam.

"What's a home run again?" she asked.

"Anything over the fifth story, ma'am," Chico said, grinning and pointing.

She raised her eyebrows and nodded.

"That's nothing," Elgin said. "I can't miss!"

Chico fired again, hard and low. Elgin golfed the shot from his ankles, another fastpitch homer. Chico changed speeds. Elgin was way ahead of it.

"Strike one, man!" the pitcher yelled.

The next pitch nearly hit Elgin in the knee before he hit it for a homer.

"Watch this!" Chico said.

He bounced the ball to Elgin as hard as he could. Elgin hit it for a homer. Chico threw sidearm, then submarine, then an overhand pitch that dropped through the strike zone. Elgin hit them all out.

"If he don't quit this, ain't nobody gonna want him to play fastpitch anymore!"

"Okay, Chico," Elgin said, "let's show her the biggie."

"You sure?"

"Yeah. Come here."

Chico cut the pitching distance almost in half. He was now throwing from about twenty feet away. His first couple of pitches were over Elgin's head. Miriam could not imagine how the boy could see them. They bounced off the wall behind him and almost all the way back to Chico. Miriam heard the slap against the wall and then several echoes. From the sound of it, Elgin's friend was throwing as hard as he could.

"Be careful of your arm," she cautioned.

"No problem."

He finally found the range at the new distance. Of the next ten pitches, nine were hittable. Three were lined right past Chico for doubles low on the wall. One was slightly higher for a triple. The rest were homers.

"Momma, usually I at least have a strike or two before I get a hit. This is unbelievable!"

"It sure is," she said. "It most surely is."

Elgin was still wound up on the brisk walk home. Miriam tried to slow him, trudging along with her hands deep in her pockets.

"How do you account for this, El?" she asked.

"I don't know! I just think it's fantastic!"

"Now, hold on. You can't tell me, baseball mind that you are, that you haven't tried to figure this out."

"I don't want to think about it. I just want to do it."

"Think about it, El. Tell me. What's happening?"

She stopped under a street lamp. Elgin leaned back against a building. "Well," he began, "I've been doing a lot more swinging with a heavier bat since the last time I played fastpitch. So I'm getting the broomstick bat around a lot faster."

"But you're hittin fastballs pitched close up in the dark."

"I know. I guess that's from hitting in the basement with the low light and the golf balls coming so much faster than the tennis ball. You know, the pitching machine must be throwing two or three times faster than Chico and the other guys."

"But you could see it almost in the dark! How?"

"I wasn't really seeing it all the way, Momma. It was strange. You know

I've always had good eyes. That school doctor told you that."

"Yeah, better than twenty-twenty he said, which I didn't even know was possible. But how were you picking up that tennis ball in the light of a street lamp a half block away?"

"I saw just enough of it as it came out of his hand that I could judge the speed and where it was going to be. I don't know how I do it, I just do. I guess trying so hard to watch the golf balls makes this easy."

"It looked easy," Miriam said. "You made it look like you were tossin those balls up and hittin them yourself."

He nodded. "I felt like I could hit anything I could reach, and I could smack it anywhere I wanted. The ball looked huge and slow to me."

Miriam signaled with a nod that it was time to keep moving. "Do you think this is gonna affect how the golf balls look to you tomorrow?"

"I hope not. I'm gonna do both every day and see if I can get used to that."

"What if nobody can get you out in fastpitch? You won't like that, will you?"

"I'll probably get tired of it. But I love it. When I first tried to play this game I couldn't even hit a foul ball. Now it seems like in one day I'm hitting better than even the best kids. I've never seen *anybody* hit like this. After about ten homers in a row, the guys were laughing because I seemed so lucky. They'd change pitchers and move closer, which isn't even fair—but nobody cared, not even me—and I just kept hitting them. It got scary after a while. The other guys finally went home shaking their heads. Even if I never do this again, they'll be talking about it for years."

It was all Miriam could do to get Elgin settled down enough for bed that night. All he wanted to do was talk about his feats. She could hardly blame him. She lectured him on humility and steered the conversation to something else. As usual, it came back to baseball.

"They say Willie Mays learned to hit playing stickball. They used a ball made out of rolled up tape, so it was small and moved a lot, but he got to where he could hit it hard no matter where it was pitched or how hard or what it was doing."

⚾ ⚾ ⚾

Three days later Elgin came home early from fastpitch, looking glum.

"Have you lost it?" Miriam asked.

He shook his head. "Maybe I should. Couple of the guys told me it really wasn't fair anymore, that my home runs could count but they would also be outs. Otherwise, whatever team I'm on stays up too long."

"What did Chico say?"

"Same thing. When a guy on your own team thinks you make the game too long, you start seeing what they're saying."

"What are you gonna do?"

"Quit, I guess."

"Do they really want that?"

"I think they do."

"You still have friends at school, right?"

He nodded. "I think the fastpitch has been hurting my basement practice," he said.

"Really? You're having a tough time adjustin?"

"Yeah. But you know what, Momma? I have a new goal, and it's real important to me. I want to start hitting the golf balls off the pitching machine the same way I can hit fastpitch."

"Lofty goal," she said.

"I mean it," he said. "I'm gonna work like crazy till I can do that. Think what that's going to make baseball pitching seem like to me."

27

AS A RETURNING PLAYER, Elgin was not required to try out for his baseball team that spring. He attended and watched and was struck by how big and slow the ball looked. He still had not had the opportunity to test his theory of whether a baseball would be easier to hit because of his secret golf ball training, but his facility with a fastpitch broomstick-handle bat had ended his brief career in that sport.

Occasionally Chico or one of the others would pull him over to the fast-pitch street and show him off, but nobody wanted him unless he could be on their team. Occasionally someone would pair him with a player who couldn't even hit the ball, thinking that would make the teams even, but that just made Elgin mad. He would coach his teammate until he walked or scratched a hit, then Elgin would homer.

He eventually grew as tired of those kinds of games as his friends did, and even when he agreed to bat same-handed as the pitcher, he couldn't be stopped. He quit showing up for the games and they quit asking him. It had been a game he was at first intimidated by, then had fun learning, then got good at, and finally mastered beyond comprehension.

From then until the first day of practice with the Tigers, Elgin spent every spare moment in the basement, working on his fielding or standing in against the monster. He had begun to experiment, to change the speed of the wheels and get the thing to throw pitches that broke in and out, up and down. He even rigged it to throw all the pitches in the dirt to see which were hittable and which he should take.

He still was not comfortable. The best he had ever done in a 114-pitch stretch, fifty-seven from each side of the plate, was to hit three pitches solidly from each side and foul off more than a dozen. The greatest part of that was about midway through the left-hand batting segment when on three straight pitches he smashed two solid line drives and what would have been a clear pop-up.

He had stepped and driven the ball, quickly moved back into position and done it again, and recoiled in time to get a good part of the fungo bat on the tiny ball. The rush that gave him was almost like what he had felt when he realized how he could hit fastpitch. It gave him a foretaste of the possibilities. He wanted to drive and drive and drive the ball off the machine someday. His only fear was that he would tire of the discipline years before he developed that kind of ability. Till now, however, his enthusiasm had not flagged.

He had instituted a new training regimen. He stood in the middle of the room and threw as hard as he could in all four directions, having to lunge and jump to catch the balls, depending on how they came off the walls. He did this sometimes for more than an hour at a time, running, jumping, lunging, crouching, coming up throwing. He sweat till his clothes were soaked through. After a few weeks, he was used to the effort and didn't ache the next day. He looked forward to the workout and felt jumpy until he had completed it. He never missed a day. Hour after hour after hour on weekends and for at least two hours every night after school, chores, dinner, and homework.

His twelfth birthday passed with no word from his father, and true to her word, Miriam did not try to cover for Neal. She gave Elgin a few dollars and took him out for a fast-food meal. He loved it.

"Sometimes I wonder, El," she said, "if you're not in better shape than most of these kids just because you don't eat this junk all the time."

"Oh, Momma," he said, "it's only because I work out. Who do you know who plays ball as much as I do?"

She shook her head. "Who'd have ever thought you'd have your own place to play in this city?"

⚾ ⚾ ⚾

The Tigers' first practice was called for a Saturday late in April. It was still blustery and wet, but Elgin couldn't wait. He had badgered his mother into taking him to the local library, several blocks away by bus, just before closing the night before. He had gotten everything done, including his workout, just in time to shower, change, and get there. He checked out a how-to book on hitting like a big leaguer, one he'd heard about and privately wished his mother might buy him for his birthday. She probably would have, he decided, if he had dropped a few hints. But it was expensive, and he didn't know if she had planned to spend that much.

"I know I need my sleep before practice, but I'm too excited anyway. Can I read till I fall asleep?"

"You may never fall asleep. Lights out at eleven, no matter what."

It was more than he had hoped for. He read the book quickly, then went back to the crucial chapters and studied the series of photographs until eleven. He was pleased to see he had been doing almost everything right. If anything, he decided, he might have been over-striding lately. He would concentrate on keeping his step to between six and ten inches. He was intrigued that though much is made of a level swing, the best hitters swing level only on pitches at the waist. Otherwise, their bats are angled as necessary. Ted Williams, probably the best hitter of all time, thought a hitter had to have a slight uppercut to make up for the height of the mound.

Nervousness was not the issue the next morning. Eagerness was. Elgin was starved for competition, starved for the real thing. He wanted to play baseball.

Barry Krass seemed to have grown a foot since Elgin had seen him. He hit several home runs his first time up in batting practice. Everyone knew he would be returning to his powerful form now that he'd had a year in the older league. Elgin just hung around in the infield, filling the position of whoever was hitting. He wondered why Mr. Rollins's assistants were throwing so slowly.

"Is that all the faster you'll be pitching?" he asked.

Fred, an assistant coach, turned. "This is the first day back for us too, Elgin. We don't want to wake up with no arms tomorrow. I'll see if I can crank it up a little just for you, but you're gonna find your eye and timing are off too. We want to build confidence today. We're just loosening up, seeing where everyone is."

When it was Elgin's turn to hit, Fred was still on the mound. He had found his control, but he was still throwing easy. The first pitch was directly down the center of the plate. Elgin, batting left-handed, turned on it and swung viciously. He hit it off the tip of the bat and sent a foul ball dribbling down the third base line.

"See?" Fred said. "Your timing is off. Just swing easy and make contact."

The next pitch was over the outside corner. Elgin hammered it so hard foul down the first-base line that players waiting to hit had to scatter.

"See? You're way out front. You been playing fastpitch?"

"Not for a long time, Coach."

He pulled another outside pitch, this time even farther foul, banging it off the bench and sending it skipping back to the mound. Fred fielded it and put his hands on his hips. "You're so far out front that you're pulling outside pitches foul! You know to go with the pitch! C'mon!"

Elgin wanted to tell him the pitching was too slow, that the baseball looked like a basketball. Apparently, just to cross him up, Fred came inside the next time, and if Elgin hadn't swung, the pitch would have hit him. He swiped at the ball with a bat two and a half times bigger and several ounces lighter than he had been using for months, and drove the ball high and deep, but on a line perpendicular to where he stood.

Players and coaches watched until the ball landed on a soccer field where spring players stopped their game and glared toward the baseball diamond.

"That's the dangedest thing I've ever seen," Fred said. "All right, Elgin, I'm ready to throw some heat. I don't know if I can throw it hard enough to keep you from fouling it off, but then I don't know if you're ready to catch up to my best stuff yet or not. Let's see."

He wound and fired. The pitch was high and outside and Elgin laid off it. Strangely, that seemed to relax him. One of his goals was to become a selective hitter, not because he wanted a lot of walks, but because he knew that to be a great hitter he had to hit his pitch. Even some strikes would not be the best pitches to hit, unless he had two strikes. He wanted to discipline himself to wait for that one hitting-pitch per time at bat that he'd read Boog Powell had looked for in his prime.

The next pitch was low and inside, about an inch off the plate. "That's a batting practice strike," Fred complained. "You're not in there to walk."

"Sorry," Elgin said, and dug in, ready to go after anything close.

Fred threw him his best fastball, hard and just below the knees, maybe two inches off the outside corner. Elgin stepped short, kept his chin down and eyes steady. He knew the swing was perfect even before he made contact. The aluminum bat rang as the ball leaped from the bat and was still rising as it cleared the fence in dead center field. The ball easily traveled three hundred feet.

Even Elgin couldn't help but admire it. He stood in the box, bat in one hand, and watched till it stopped bouncing and rolling. No one said anything. This was beyond exclamation or praise. No one there had seen a kid that age hit a ball that far and with such a beautiful, perfect swing.

Though Coach Fred had several baseballs on the ground near him, he turned his back to the plate and waited until the home run ball was retrieved and delivered to him. He examined the ball, held it up for Elgin to see, and threw it again. Elgin hit an opposite field home run, and Fred went through the same routine.

"I have to keep looking at that ball," he hollered to Elgin. "I want to make sure it's regulation. It's flying off your bat like a golf ball. I know I'm not that bad a pitcher. Hit this out again and I'll switch balls on you."

Elgin did, and Fred did. But the choice of ball had little to do with what Elgin was able to do with the pitches. He rocketed line drives to all fields, making infielders back onto the grass, just as he had done in his first year. He cracked a couple off the fence and hit two more homers.

"Not a bad first batting practice," Fred said. "Not a bad first BP at all."

After that Elgin played third and short and was all over the infield, fielding grounders and liners and pop-ups and firing hard to first, so hard that the first baseman complained. He took a lot of ribbing from guys who reminded him how much older he was than Elgin.

"Just keep throwing," the big kid said.

Elgin knew he shouldn't have, but on the next one-hopper, he carefully placed his fingers across the seams and threw sidearm. The ball swept across the diamond, appearing to be headed up the line. But to catch it, the first baseman had to cross his legs and fall into foul territory. Elgin could tell he wanted to cuss him out, but apparently he didn't want to take any more heat for not being able to catch a throw from a twelve-year-old, nearly two years younger than he should have been to be on this team.

When the team ran the bases and took a lap around the football field, Elgin was again dominant. Mr. Rollins approached as practice ended. "It doesn't surprise me to see you keep improving," he said. "It is a little scary to think about how good you could become. We'll try you pitching next week and see if we can get any mound work out of you this year."

That excited Elgin until he thought of the arm trouble he'd had in the winter. He would have to practice his pitching in the basement. Though it would be from closer in, he could at least get his mechanics down. He was looking forward to this season like no other. And he could hardly wait to tell his mother about the first practice.

28

EXCEPT IN BATTING PRACTICE, Elgin never got a chance to pitch in that league. It was just as well. No one could hit him anyway. His teammates complained when he threw BP, and so he backed off from his fastball and let them hit. The reason he never pitched in a live game was that he never appeared in one. That first practice had been the last time he'd had trouble adjusting his timing from his own BP in the basement to hitting the coaches and other players. And the way he hit astounded anyone who had ever had anything to do with the game.

Elgin himself was shocked. He had seen what trying to hit super fast golf balls had done to his fastpitch hitting, and he hoped the same would happen in baseball. But since he was still not hitting more than three or four golf balls per session against the machine, he didn't expect to see so much improvement in baseball.

During the fourth practice of the preseason, Elgin lined a pitch directly back at the face of Coach Fred, who took the ball just below his left cheekbone and went down in a heap. The concussion was heard all over the field, and in an instant, the team surrounded him. Fred had reached for his face with his gloved hand as he went down, but by the time he hit the ground, he was out. His unseeing eyes were open and an ugly raspberry quickly formed.

"Think if that had hit him a little higher," Barry said. "Would have broke his cheekbone for sure."

"Bet it's broke anyway," someone offered.

"Out of the way!" Maury Rollins said, shouldering in. He knelt by Fred and gently rolled him to his back. The stricken coach had not blinked since he had fallen. Rollins pushed Fred's eyes closed and someone gasped.

"Gee, he ain't dead, is he?"

"Shut up!" Rollins said. "Somebody call an ambulance."

Elgin wanted to make the call, but he couldn't drag himself away. Barry was right. A little higher and that ball would have broken a bone, and any higher than that could have put his eye out.

"Fred, c'mon, buddy, talk to me," Rollins said, holding his friend's head. "Water," he commanded, and someone passed him a plastic cup. Rollins poured ice water on his hand and applied it to Fred's face, causing him to flinch and stir. He coughed and tried to sit up. Blues and purples were already replacing the red hues near his eye.

He swore. "What happened?" he said. "I'm all right."

"No, you're not," Rollins said. "Just sit there."

"I'm okay, really."

Rollins had someone run after the boy who had gone to call for the ambulance. "I'm taking you to the emergency room myself," he said.

"For what? I'm all right."

He tried to stand and fell back to his seat. Rollins told him what had happened.

"Never saw it," Fred said. "Nice goin, Woodell."

Elgin could tell Fred was sincere, but he didn't find that encouraging. He felt terrible. Maybe this golf ball business was making a hitting freak of him. He didn't want to hurt anyone.

When Fred was finally standing, he wanted details.

"Listen to me, Fred," Rollins said, "that ball came off the bat like I don't know what. I mean, I can't even tell you. I was hitting fly balls to the outfield between pitches, so I was watching to see when the ball either went past Elgin or he hit it. Man, did he hit it."

Fred moved his lips and jaw. "Wow, was I out or something?"

"You didn't know you were out?"

"Well, I figured I missed something because I threw a pitch and then saw a bunch of faces. Some idiot was touching me where it hurt the worst."

"Sorry," Rollins said. "I was hoping you were still alive. Let me get you to the hospital. That looks nasty."

"Can I come?" Elgin said, unable to hide the whimper in his voice.

"No need," Rollins said. "We're done for the day anyway."

"Then let me come."

"Then I'd have to give you a ride home," Rollins said.

Fred whispered to Rollins and the coach turned back.

"Okay, but I can only bring you back to the L, all right?"

Elgin nodded, glad he had change in his pocket so he could call his mother from the hospital. Somehow, getting to ride along didn't make him feel any better. Even his apology was brushed off.

"Hey, champ, it happens, you know?" Fred said. "If I thought you did it on purpose I'd ask you to teach the other guys. What've we been trying to teach you guys for two years? To hit right back up the middle."

Elgin nodded, but he wanted to sob. He had seen that ball crash into Coach Fred's face as if in slow motion. He wondered when he would ever be able to erase that image from his mind.

After Fred was treated with painkillers and an ice pack, the threesome rode in silence most of the way to the L.

"I have to ask you something," Coach Rollins said finally, turning to the boy. "How is it you seem to have so much strength? I mean, you're big for your age, but you're not big for this team. I consider myself a baseball man and I can see you've got the tools and the coordination, and I don't guess I've seen as good a leg coordination and upper body movement in a kid, but is that giving you this power?"

"I don't know," Elgin said. "I guess."

"Where'd you learn to hit like that?"

"My dad."

"He must have been some coach. You have a compact step and swing, you keep your head down, your eyes level, you don't swing at bad pitches. You hit like you know what you're doing, and it's working."

Elgin didn't know what to say or even if he was supposed to say anything. "I sure hate hitting people," he said softly.

"That's part of the game, part of the risk," Fred said. He laughed. "You know, this is the worst I've been hurt in a baseball game in my life. Wouldn't you know it would come off the bat of a fourteen-year old kid."

"Twelve," Elgin corrected, then wished he hadn't.

⚾ ⚾ ⚾

Elgin didn't hit in the basement that night. He moped around the flat and appreciated his mother not trying to make less of the incident than he did.

At practice two nights later, everyone stopped and watched as usual when it was Elgin's turn to hit. He had selected the only wood bat in the bag, a wagon tongue of a relic that looked like a heavily grained softball bat. It was hefty and felt soft in his hands, compared to the sleek aluminum ones.

Mr. Rollins pitched while Fred joked about hiding behind the backstop. Elgin smiled, but he was not amused. He was scared to death of hitting someone else, especially Rollins.

"Why are you batting righty?" Rollins asked him.

Elgin shrugged. "Just want to. Might hit righty against righties sometime."

Rollins threw easily and Elgin worked on his timing. As each pitch came, the boy thought about keeping his body rigid, his bat still, his stance open enough to allow both eyes to see the pitch. He stepped and swung, not hitching, keeping his hands relaxed, the bat whipping through the strike zone, the sweet spot meeting the ball. Elgin was swinging at about half his usual speed and power. He knew it was bat speed that provided the thrust to his hitting. He was not a weight lifter, and while he worked out ten times more than anyone else his age, he knew his bones and muscles were still developing and that he should keep from straining them with overwork.

So the answer to the coach's question two nights before about where he got his power should have been "bat speed." But for some reason, Elgin felt that would have sounded too know-it-all. And now he was pushing bat speed aside to loft easy flares into the outfield, going with the pitches. Outside pitches went to right. Inside pitches went to left. Down-the-middle pitches went up the middle, but in lazy arcs over the mound and past second.

After a dozen such hits, Rollins slapped his glove at a throw in from the outfield and whirled to face Elgin. "I can pitch just as slow as you can swing, kid, and then what'll you have? One wasted batting practice! C'mon, hit the ball!"

Elgin's face burned. The next pitch was outside, yet Elgin pulled it to left.

"You're the best I've ever seen for going with the pitch!" Rollins said. "What're you doing?"

Elgin shrugged, fighting tears, and stood in. The next pitch was right down the middle. He pulled it foul down the third base line. Rollins pursed his lips and made a great show of doctoring the mound with his foot. By now, everyone was quiet, watching.

"I'm going to throw you a fastball, Elgin. I'm going to throw it as close to seventy miles an hour as an old man can, and I'm gonna split the plate with it. Normally, you'd drive a pitch like that all the way to tomorrow, and it'd be right up the middle. Now, are you gonna hit, or are you gonna be a pansy because you gave somebody an owie? C'mon, Woodell! Quit bein a baby! This game isn't for wimps!"

Elgin swallowed and dug in. The pitch was just as Rollins had predicted. Hard and fast and splitting the plate. Elgin couldn't make himself swing. Rollins shook his head in disgust.

"Another!" he said, and threw an identical pitch. Elgin checked his swing.

"Unbelievable," Rollins muttered. "One more and then you can go play on the swings."

Elgin was more humiliated than mad, but he decided he'd better swing. If he could just relax, not think about anything, make it all automatic...

Elgin felt as if he were floating. He was aware the pitch was coming and that his front foot was off the ground. The bat was back, his hands feathery on the handle. His weight was back, now moving forward. His front foot touched the ground, his hips opened, his back foot pivoted. The bat flashed through as if it were a weight on a rope rather than a stick of ash.

The sound of the bat on the ball brought Elgin back to reality. The sound of the ball on Coach Rollins's left knee made Elgin burst into tears. He slammed the bat on the ground as the coach screamed and everyone came running. When the bat didn't break, he beat it against the backstop post. He ran across a parking lot to escape the scene of his coach writhing on the ground. Had he heard bone breaking? Had he destroyed the man's kneecap? He didn't want to know. He hurried to the corner of the brick school building and swung the bat as hard as he could, driving the trademark into the bricks. The bat began to split and the handle snapped back into Elgin's chest.

It hurt but he was glad. If he'd had the courage and known what he was doing, he would have hurt himself. As he beat the bat to pieces on the corner of the building, he imagined that he was the target. Why had the coach made him do it? He could hit .500 in this league without hitting hard line drives. How could he ever hit again on this team? If he hit a kid in the face or in the head, he could kill someone. What would happen when parents found out what had happened?

Elgin felt like a coward when he could not force himself back to the field. Tonight was different. No one was trying to move the fallen coach, who still moaned. Elgin hung back, waiting in the parking lot. Then he ran home, all the way, nearly three miles. He bounded up the steps, carrying only his glove.

His mother waited in the open doorway, her face grave.

29

MIRIAM HAD BEEN SEWING Elgin's tournament shoulder patch onto his new uniform when the message came from Mr. Bravura that she had a phone call. It was from one of the boys on Elgin's team.

"Coach asked me to call you," the boy said.

Miriam panicked. "Why?"

"He just wanted you to let him know when Elgin got home. Wants to make sure he got home, I mean."

"Why wouldn't he?"

"He left before practice was over, and Coach wants to talk to him."

"About what?"

"I don't know."

"What happened?"

"I don't really know. All I know is Coach Rollins got hurt and he wants to come over and talk to Elgin."

"How'd he get hurt?"

"Line drive."

That was the extent of the message, but Miriam knew. In the economy of young teens, the boy had told her all she needed to hear. It had happened again, and Elgin would be tormented. When she saw him reach the top of the stairs, she saw a man-child who was exhausted.

"You run all the way home?" she said, taking him in her arms.

He nodded, saying nothing. He was boiling, his soaked sweatshirt steamy to her touch.

"Mr. Rollins is on his way over here."

"Here? He's coming here? Please, Momma, anything but that."

"You ashamed of where you live?"

"Momma, I need to quit baseball. I wasn't even thinking. Just like with Coach Fred, I just swung hard and nailed him."

"Why'd you run, El?"

"I can't stand it! It hit him right on the knee and probably broke something."

"I told you he's comin over, so at least he can walk."

"I'm still quitting."

"Elgin, you can't quit," she began, as they heard a knock at the door.

It was Mr. Rollins, Coach Fred, and Ernie, an outfielder from a couple of miles further south. Rollins limped in, a heavy bandage bulging from beneath his jeans. Miriam offered ice, which he refused. Fred was strangely quiet, and Ernie busied himself nosing around the flat, looking at everything Miriam had on the walls.

"Elgin," Rollins began, "I wanted you to know I was okay and that it wasn't your fault."

"Wasn't my fault? Who hit the ball?"

"Who dished up the candy fastball?" Rollins countered.

"That was no candy; that was heat."

"Well, sure it was, but a straight fastball is no challenge for a hitter like you. It's candy, am I right? Huh?"

Elgin wanted to nod but caught himself. "I don't want to hurt anybody else ever."

"You won't. We're going to get one of those little fences like they have for big league batting practice. You've seen them at Wrigley."

Elgin hadn't ever seen the Cubs play live and wanted to say so, but he didn't.

"You can adjust them for righties and lefties, and the pitcher is completely protected during his follow-through."

"You're getting that just for me? I'm going to feel like a freak."

"Let me tell you something, Elgin: You are a freak. I don't mean that in any unkind way, but you hit like an adult, son. Better than most. But we'll leave that barrier up for everybody; it won't be just for you."

"But everybody will know why it's really there."

"I can't argue with that. But boy, you've got something nobody should be ashamed of. You've got talent and ability that should make you proud."

Elgin shrugged. He had nothing to say. He was proud of his ability. But he had no interest in injuring anyone.

"You've got that quitting look on your face," Coach Fred said. Ernie yawned from across the room. "You're not thinking about quitting this team, are you?"

"I'm thinking about it."

"We don't want you to quit," Rollins said. "We're the two guys you've hit with line drives, and we're saying, stay, you're good, we need you, we want you. Okay? Got it?"

Elgin nodded but he didn't return their smiles. He still wasn't sure he wouldn't quit. He wanted to ask about the danger of hitting other people, other kids, but he knew what they'd say. They would keep the kids back, warn other teams, all that. He wanted to be a ballplayer, a good one, even a powerful hitter, but he didn't want to be a monster.

His coaches were still talking on their way out. "So, don't give it another thought, El. We'll have our BP screen before next practice, so you won't have to worry about hitting anybody else."

"Not even during games?" Elgin said quietly.

"Well, that's a different story," Rollins said. "I don't know what to say about that."

Elgin reached to tap fists with Ernie as he followed the men out the door. "You sure live in a hole," Ernie said so only Elgin could hear. It bothered him almost as much as having hit both coaches. He couldn't imagine Ernie lived much better, but he had dreaded the day when coaches or teammates saw the sparse rooms he and his mother called home.

He wasn't about to tell his mother about the comment. He wanted to talk to her about his future in baseball.

"I guess it wouldn't have bothered me as much if it had been kids who didn't know how to play. I mean, I'd hate to hit a kid, but you know what I mean. If I could say it was just someone who hadn't caught up to my speed yet or something like that, that would be one thing. But these guys are men! They would have caught those shots if they were catchable."

"Elgin," his mother said, "listen to yourself. You're hittin uncatchable liners up the middle. Even I know enough about the game to know that's what hitters want to do."

"If it means hurting people, it's not what I want to do."

His mother sat next to him on the couch. "You hardly ever hear of big leaguers being hurt by line drives, do you?"

He shook his head. "And those guys have to be hitting a lot harder than I am. I guess it's just the difference in the distance between the mound and the plate."

"Is it possible you're already too good for this league?"

He shrugged. "Could be. But who's gonna let me play in an older league?"

"Whoever tries you out and sees what you can do."

"Well, I'm not gonna keep this up, I know that. You know what I feel like doing?"

She shook her head.

"Hitting where no one can get hurt but me."

"Downstairs?"

"Uh-huh."

"Go ahead. You didn't hit last night, did you?"

"Nope."

"Do it, El. Your chance will come to play where people can compete with you. And you want to be ready."

Elgin didn't know if it was because he had taken one night off or because his mother had encouraged him much more than his coaches had, but something was different in the basement. He seemed more relaxed, more comfortable. The machine was beginning to look like, if not a friend, a companion in training. It was no longer the dangerous ogre that could take his head off. He even turned it on and strolled to the other end of the room while it began firing golf balls. He knew where to stand to avoid being hit, and he didn't have to watch it every second for fear of his life.

While in the batter's box he was able to let pitches come within an inch of him, though he could hardly see them for their size and speed. He remembered the early days when he kept his distance from the menacing thing. Now he didn't try to hit every pitch. He waited for the ones that broke just so, spun just right, came into not just *the* strike zone but his strike zone.

That night he hit six solid shots in one session and five in the next. He found himself smiling broadly in the damp solitude of the cellar. He would not have guessed that he could hit that many line drives off the machine in two sessions. If just standing in against the thing had made him such a dangerous hitter, what would happen if he became proficient at it, even mastered it? Was it possible? Six hits out of fifty-seven chances was just a shade over ten percent. He was a long way from mastering it. But he went upstairs to bed in a much better mood.

⚾ ⚾ ⚾

More than just the batting-practice pitcher's screen was new at the next practice. Several fathers and even some mothers showed up. They wore grim faces, and Elgin was aware of his teammates pointing and parents staring.

From his position at shortstop he studied the protective screen, a piece of wire mesh with a cutout. The pitcher threw over the short half and his follow-through carried him completely behind the rest of the gadget.

The first eight hitters seemed to be trying to hit the thing, despite Coach Rollins's urgings—from a folding chair behind the backstop where his swollen-kneed leg was elevated—that they ignore it and hit as usual. Coach Fred was on the mound. It took him a while to get used to the screen. His first dozen pitches were high.

Elgin was embarrassed that he was the reason the man on the mound had a purple blotch that now extended from just above his mouth all the way to his eyebrow. What used to be the white of his eye was blood filled—but, he insisted, not painful—and his eye socket, especially next to his nose, was a deep blue that looked black from five feet away.

The adults associated with the team were walking wounded, and the bigger-than-average twelve-year-old, two years younger than the next youngest, was the reason. No wonder there was a crowd.

Elgin made a couple of good plays and all the routine ones, but he knew as well as everyone else that people were there to see him hit. By the time he was called on—and a hush fell over the park—he had made a decision. He was not going to hold back. He was going to muster his courage on the strength of that protective screen and that his teammates in the infield knew enough to play deep for him.

He wished he hadn't ruined the wood bat and thought it interesting that the coach had made no mention of his having to replace it. He wanted to, of course, but that would take time. Now he found his favorite aluminum bat and felt all eyes on him. He felt himself rushing, stretching, swinging his bat with the lead ring on it, then hurrying to the plate.

"Give me a second," Fred called. "You know I throw a little harder to you, and I want to make sure I've got a few left."

Elgin thought about stepping in right-handed, but his mind was made up. People came to see a show; they would see a show. Part of it was for the rush the attention would provide, but he also wanted to push things off dead center. Wasn't it obvious to everyone that he was too much for this league? He appreciated their placing him in it, because he should have been with a younger team. But if he had already passed up everyone here, what could he do about it?

He knew the coaches would want to keep him, and that was flattering, but they would be thinking of themselves rather than what was best for him.

He knew he was thinking of himself ahead of the team, but in a way he was also thinking of his teammates. Someone was going to get hurt bad, and he wasn't about to risk that just so his coaches could keep their best hitter.

Fred carefully prepared to pitch with Elgin waiting about six feet from the box. A fastball whistled to the plate, the hardest he had seen from Fred all year. It was better than the stuff Fred had been throwing the night he'd been hit, and if Elgin was correct, the warm-up toss was also a few miles an hour faster.

Interesting, he thought. *Fred's thinking about the audience too.*

Elgin stepped in carefully and set himself just so, as always. He wanted to explode on the first pitch. Start with a homer. Set the pace.

30

THE CATCHER SAID SOMETHING APPROVINGLY to Coach Fred, but Elgin's mind was somewhere else. He was thinking how he had hit instinctively at the last practice, just before cutting Mr. Rollins's leg out from under him. That was the way he had hit in the basement the night before too. It was a secret, an answer, something that would enhance his already astounding ability. If his mechanics could become natural, something he didn't even have to think about, he would be even better.

All he had to do, he told himself, was program his mind to get around on that fastball, then put himself in neutral and get into the box. He felt ready and—he had to admit—he loved the idea that there was a crowd, small as it was. He was going to show them something, something they feared, something they hoped couldn't be true. He was going to show them their sons were in danger when he was at bat. His hope, his plan, was to drive a home run to center that rose no more than fifteen feet off the ground. He tingled with excitement, with confidence, with concentration.

Fred wound and fired, or did he? Elgin unleashed himself just as he realized that the coach had pulled the string, let the ball roll out of his palm and off his fingers. It floated tantalizingly before Elgin's eyes as his swing carried him in a circle and spun him to his seat. He had been two feet in front of the ball, burned big time by a first-class change-up, and as he sat in the dirt he heard the laughter. First from Fred, then the catcher, then Rollins, then a few parents, a few players, a lot of parents, and then everybody.

He could only smile and shake his head. So that was how it was going to be? He would be fooled, tricked, put off balance, even in batting practice? Well, he figured he had it coming. Either he was a good hitter or he wasn't. Anyone could hit in batting practice. Barry Krass had hit four out, two in a row, and received applause from the parents. They had seen nothing yet,

Elgin told himself. In truth, he liked it better when even BP was a game situation. No candy pitches, not all fastballs, not all in the same location. Hitting against a thinking pitcher was even tougher than facing the basement machine, no matter how hard it threw the tiny balls. At least those were consistent and predictable.

Elgin was wondering now, thinking, plotting, guessing. Maybe putting his mind in neutral was not the way to go after all. He wanted his basics, his mechanics, to be automatic, but he had to stay alert to outguess a good pitcher, especially with people watching. Watching and expecting something.

As he dug in again, Elgin thought he noticed something. Had Fred's smile faded? Was that a look of apology? Was he trying to communicate something? To say, all right, I'm sorry, that was cheap; here's a hitting pitch?

Elgin studied him carefully as Fred toed the rubber. As he rocked back, he waved his glove at the catcher the way pitchers signal they are throwing breaking balls during warm-ups. So this was it? A peace offering, a pitch of apology, a pitch that would make them friends again? No hard feelings for putting you on your can; here's a real batting practice curve. If Elgin was wrong, well, he'd be wrong. He'd be on the ground again, and people would laugh again. But this, just like any other time he stepped into the box, was an at-bat. He would catch up to this guy and his stuff and show who was better.

He guessed curve, set himself for curve, and got curve. So many things raced through his mind as that spinning, high and outside pitch came in. He knew he couldn't take it to right. Even if he succeeded, he would likely hit it too high. A long, loud fly out was not what he was after. As he uncoiled his swing he was not trying to pull the ball but to drive it to center. Fred was safely tucked behind the new pitcher's screen. The shortstop and second baseman were sufficiently deep and straight-away. The outfielders were deep and pulled a little toward right.

He realized as he hit the ball that it had not dropped as far as he hoped. It would have been an easy pitch to foul off or pop-up, had he not been on autopilot. He had reached up far enough to hack at it, swinging down on the ball. And he got all of it. He drove it two hundred feet to left center, and before the fielders could react, it hit the ground and bounced high and far, all the way over the fence.

Who had ever seen a ground rule double that hit that far from the fence before bounding over? Certainly not Elgin. And from the sounds of the crowd and his teammates, they never had either. Fred smiled as if he had engineered the whole thing.

Elgin had no time to admire his handiwork. Fred was into his wind-up again, signaling another curve. This one broke on the inner half of the plate at the belt. Elgin ripped it over the right center-field fence. A slider resulted in what would have been a triple down the right field line. A fastball screamed back up the middle, just over the pitcher's protective barrier.

"Trying for the other eye?" Fred teased. Everyone laughed.

He threw the change-up again. Elgin was fooled, off stride, but recovered to hammer a ground ball to the second baseman, playing in shallow right center.

Fred came back with a fastball inside and Elgin's baseball career changed forever. He turned on the ball and smashed a one-hopper to the first baseman in shallow right. Raleigh Lincoln, Jr., a skinny, slick-fielding black kid, stabbed at it and caught it, but was turned completely around by the force. He lobbed the ball in to Fred, then held his hand over his heart to a chorus of nervous laughter.

A gigantic black man emerged from behind the backstop. "Can I pitch to this kid?" he said.

"Be my guest, Raleigh!" Fred said, tossing him his glove and pointing to the bucket of balls at the mound.

"Know who that is?" the catcher asked.

"Must be Raleigh's dad," Elgin said, staring.

"Raleigh Lincoln, Sr., threw the only no-hitter in an Olympic game. Almost made the big leagues with the Red Sox."

The catcher was taking off his gear.

"Where you going?"

"Deep," the catcher said. "I can't catch him, and I'm not gonna try to stop your shots."

"Hey, whoa, stay there," Mr. Lincoln called. "At least warm me up. It'll take me a while to get loose. If nobody can catch me, we'll move the hitter back and I'll pitch to the backstop."

Mr. Lincoln looked to Elgin to be at least six-three and well over two hundred pounds. He was a pleasant-looking man with big eyes and high cheekbones, but he looked menacing on the mound. He yanked down the pitching screen and set it aside ("One thing I don't need is this!"). He put Fred's glove awkwardly on his right hand and began throwing easily lefty. From the first pitch, Elgin knew he was watching in person a type of pitcher he had seen only on television. Everything about the man's mechanics were fluid and rhythmic. He wore deck shoes, casual slacks, an expensive pullover shirt, yet looked at home on the mound.

"You know who that is?" Mr. Rollins said to Elgin, motioning him over.

"Geoff just told me," Elgin said.

"This guy still pitches, you know."

"Looks like it. Where?"

"City league. They say he can still throw in the eighties."

"Uh-oh."

"Well, hey, Elgin, I never saw anybody you couldn't hit. Give it a try."

As if he wouldn't have. Elgin couldn't wait. He didn't care if the man made him look like a fool. He wanted competition, wanted to know where his level of ability really was. Even if he couldn't get the bat on the ball, he would know that he fell somewhere between the league he was in and a man who had been an almost-major leaguer in his prime. And Raleigh Lincoln, Sr., looked to be still in his prime.

As he got loose his fastball began to pop, pop, pop into Geoff's glove. Everyone seemed mesmerized. The man began to sweat, dark circles appearing under his arms and in a line down his back. Elgin decided that Mr. Lincoln was going to enjoy this as much as he did.

Finally Geoff had had enough and no one else was willing to catch the fastballer, so Lincoln moved several feet in front of the mound and began throwing at the middle post of the backstop. He came close with every pitch, banging at least six out of ten off the post.

"I'm ready!" he bellowed. "Get in there and take your cuts."

"His ERA is under one," Mr. Rollins said finally as Elgin moved away. "You know what that means?"

Elgin nodded. Of course he knew what an earned run average was. What it meant was that he was about to face a real pitcher. He only wished he could have come to this moment having just faced the pitching machine in the basement rather than Coach Fred. Fred's fastball was better than any of the kids', but Raleigh Lincoln threw harder warming up. And Elgin knew he wasn't going to be seeing any of those warm-up pitches once he stepped in. If there was anything readable in the man's joyous, bemused face, it was that he was not about to signal any pitches or make things easy on the hitter.

It was written all over him, Elgin decided. He just wanted to show that there was one man in the crowd who didn't have to be intimidated by some kid. Raleigh, Sr., waved him in and began to throw. There was little ceremony about it, no pretending to take a sign, no waiting between pitches. He held four balls in his glove hand and just kept throwing. It was, Elgin decided, a little like facing the machine. But this machine had a brain and a heart and pride and experience and savvy and intelligence.

This machine was one mean pitcher.

31

MIRIAM ENJOYED AN OCCASIONAL WALK alone on early summer evenings. It was light enough out that she didn't feel afraid, and she stayed close to home anyway. Tonight she was looking for Chico. Elgin had lost touch with the boy when fastpitch became too easy for him. Chico lived several blocks east of where the kids played fastpitch, and Miriam didn't want to walk that far. She hoped to catch him nearby.

A fastpitch game was in progress, but Chico was not there. Miriam sat on the stoop across the street and watched the tiny United Nations of the game. At least four nationalities were represented among the six players. That was something she had not been used to in Hattiesburg. She wondered if it had not been for Elgin and his ease at talking with anyone, whether she would have been out looking to chat with a Puerto Rican.

Chico was a nice enough kid. She had been surprised that though he had an accent, he was fluent in English and understood everything she said, something she couldn't say for all her Yankee coworkers.

Miriam was also surprised that her exposure to baseball had taught her enough about the game to recognize different levels of ability. These kids, for instance, had probably been playing fastpitch for years. Yet they hacked at the ball, moved around in the batter's box, didn't plant their back feet, hit with hitches, didn't follow through on their throws. She hadn't seen it so much before, but when she imagined Elgin in this game, she knew it would be like watching a pro with amateurs. Not only had he mastered the fast, unpredictable pitches, but he also looked like he knew what he was doing. He didn't goof around. His stance and swing were the same every time. It was like watching those good golfers on television and then remembering when she first clubbed at a bucket of balls on a driving range at a church outing.

A crazily spinning foul ball dropped to her right and skipped into her lap. She surprised herself and the boys by catching it. When she tossed it back, however, she was chagrined to have thought these kids were less accomplished. They were, of course, compared to Elgin, but her throw was awkward. Why was it that women couldn't throw like men, she wondered. Some could, she knew. She had seen them play. But she always felt conspicuous when she tried.

The ball had drawn attention to her, and now she was aware that the boys were talking about her. They tried not to make it obvious, but they would whisper and one would look, then others would whisper and another would look. A big black kid looked defiantly at her, but she just stared right back at him. Surely none of these kids meant her any harm. She recognized a couple as old acquaintances of Elgin's. They had to be the ones who told the others who she was. Maybe they were just sharing wild stories about Elgin's exploits. He was already a legend on the fastpitch diamond.

Then she noticed it. The aluminum bat the tall black kid would not allow anyone else to use was leaning against the wall near where the kids hit. Occasionally one would plead with the boy.

"Ricky, c'mon, man, let me use the bat, huh?"

"No way!"

"Yeah!" someone else would chortle. "You stole that a long time ago. That boy's gonna come bust you for that."

"Uh-huh," big Ricky said. "He send his mama already."

Miriam felt a chill. So this was the boy who had stolen Elgin's bat. Anger rose within her. She wanted that bat back. It was only right.

Ricky looked to be about sixteen, hard and wiry as a grown man. When it was his turn to hit, he grabbed the bat, stared menacingly at Miriam, and stepped in. He took the first pitch, then skied the next one for a home run near the top of the building across the street. As the ball caromed about the street, Ricky let the bat clang to the pavement and went into his home run trot. Coming around first brought him as close to Miriam as he would get. He stared at her as he passed, then stopped dead in his tracks when she whispered something.

"What'd you say?"

"I said you ought to bring me that bat. It belongs to my son."

He squinted. "My bat belongs to your son?"

"Yes, sir, that's right. His name is scratched in the end of it."

"What's his name?"

"Elgin."

"I'll tell you what, lady. You want that bat, you can come and get it."

That sounded like a challenge, but there was also a note of sincerity in it, as if maybe he admired her spunk.

"I can?" she said.

He laughed and continued his home run trot. "You can try."

Miriam stood, but Ricky had his back to her as he headed toward third base. When he reached the base, he saw her coming, slowly, carefully. She stared at him and walked toward the bat. He stopped trotting and walked briskly to meet her. She wondered what she had gotten herself into. She heard a slamming door a block and a half away and the rattle of a shopkeeper dragging the steel grate across his storefront. She hoped he would walk her way.

Ricky beat her to the bat and held it by the barrel in both hands.

"That's my son's bat," she said evenly.

"Yeah?"

"His name is scratched into the end there."

Ricky turned the bat on its end and read aloud, "E-L-G-I-N. Hm."

"Hm, what? May I have it please?"

"What's it worth to you?"

Miriam heard the jangle of the shopkeeper's keys. "It's worth what I paid for it," she said.

"Which was what?"

"I don't recall."

"I'll take half," he said.

"You'll take half of what I don't recall? I recall paying a penny for it then, how's that?"

Ricky's eyes grew dark as the other boys giggled. "Ten bucks'll buy it, honey."

"I don't have ten dollars and I wouldn't pay for a bat twice anyway."

The keys stopped. "What's the trouble here?" a bearded man asked.

"Nothin that's none of your business," Ricky said.

"Just give her the bat," one of the boys said. "You know it's hers."

"Maybe I'll give her a beatin with the bat."

"You'd better be kidding," the man said. "Because to hurt her, you're going to have to hurt me."

Ricky turned on the man and glared at him. "What *is* your problem, man?"

"People stealing stuff in my neighborhood is my problem. And people threatening people is my problem. Let me just tell you something, son, and I'm not trying to make you mad. You don't want to tangle with me, and I'm serious as a heart attack. Give the woman the bat if it belongs to her, and we'll be on our way."

"You're together?"

"We are now."

Ricky swore and handed Miriam the bat. "C'mon, guys. The air stinks around here." He started off, but no one followed. "Well, come on!" Still no one. He waved at them derisively and swore again, disappearing around the corner.

Embarrassed, the boys resumed their game. Miriam turned to the stranger. "I can't thank you enough."

"No need," he said. "Glad I came by when I did. Can I walk you home?"

"I'd appreciate it. I live just—"

"I know where you live."

"You do?"

"Course. You live in the hotel over here, right?"

She nodded.

"I know your son. I sold him some baseball equipment."

"Oh! You're the one he calls—" She stopped, fearful the moniker might offend the man.

"What? What does he call me?"

"Biker," she admitted softly.

He threw his head back and laughed. "You know what he told me once? That I had the same hair color as his mother. I saw you come over to watch him play once, and I thought, Hey, the kid's right! Almost the same length, too."

Miriam stopped at her corner. "I'm grateful," she said, taking a good look at him in the fading sun. His face was ruddy and freckled. He appeared in good shape, mid-to-late thirties, a generous smile. She extended her hand. "Miriam Woodell."

"Lucas Harkness," he said. "Friends call me Lucky or Luke. You can call me Mr. Harkness." He was laughing.

"I will," she said.

"Do me a favor. Tell Elgin that Lucky has some more stuff he might want to see."

"Sure. What've you got?"

"Well, a wood bat for one thing."

"Really?"

"Yeah. They're hard to come by. I couldn't give him much of a deal on it, but wood bats are used only in the pros, so it's the real thing. A light thirty-three incher. Probably too big for Elgin, but he said he was looking for one."

"He sure is. That sounds like a great surprise. Maybe I could come over and see it and he wouldn't have to know about it."

"You know where my shop is?" She nodded. "I'll look forward to seeing you. You should be safe now, especially with that bat."

He smiled and walked away. She watched to see if he would sneak a glance back, but he didn't. At home she looked in her cash stash to see if she could afford a no-occasion gift for her son. She had less than twenty dollars.

She was watching television when Elgin came in. "I've got something for you," she said.

"Good. Listen, Mom, I've got to tell you about practice."

"Let me show you what I got you first."

"What is it?"

"Something you thought you'd never see again."

"Daddy?"

She scowled. "You'll see him again someday."

"When?"

"I don't know, but knowing you, you'll think of something."

"So hurry up, Momma. I've got a lot to tell you."

She reached behind the couch and produced his aluminum bat.

"I don't believe it," he said. "Where in the world—? Did Chico bring it? He said he knew who stole it."

She shook her head. "I got it myself."

Elgin turned it on its end to be sure it was really his. "This I've got to hear," he said.

32

"CALL ME STUPID, MAMA," Elgin said when she finished her story, "but I never put together the name of the shop with Biker. Lucky, huh?"

"Lucky," she said. "And is that all you have to say about how I got your bat back?"

Elgin sat shaking his head. "I can hardly believe it. I mean, I know you're tough and brave, and you always stood up to Daddy, and to me."

"Standing up to you is nothin like standing up to your father."

"Yeah, but what if that guy Ricky had started beating you with the bat?"

She shrugged. "I could see in his eyes he was scared. He didn't want to do anything. He just wanted to play big and he hoped I'd let him off with some dignity. I almost didn't. It's lucky for me Lucky came along when he did."

Elgin snorted and held the bat with one hand, balancing it. "Who knows what would've happened?" he said.

"I don't wanna think about it," she said. "It's one thing to do it and another to worry and wonder about it. I just hope you appreciate it."

"I do."

"So what happened today?"

"Nothing as scary as your story. Well, maybe it was."

Elgin told her how he had hit off Coach Fred and how Raleigh Lincoln, Sr., had taken over after Elgin had nearly knocked his son down with a line drive.

"He didn't even use the pitching screen," Elgin told her. "He didn't need it. I proved it."

"Oh, no. How?"

"I'll get to it. Anyway, he waves me into the batter's box and tells me, 'I'm gonna say only two things, kid. You don't have to worry about me knockin you down or even brushin you back. I wouldn't do that to anybody, especially a kid. I'm not lyin, so you can just stand in there. I've got better control than anybody you ever saw.' And then he says, 'Also, don't feel bad if you can't hit me. Nobody can really.'"

"So did you?"

"Well, at first I couldn't because I didn't know whether to believe him or not. I mean, what if the guy was bustin my chops and I hang in there and get beaned? I'd never met him before. His kid is a good guy, but you never know. So he throws the first three right past me, and all three of em bang right off that center post of the backstop about waist high."

His mother smiled. "Bet you wished you'd been swingin."

"He says to me, 'Trust me, boy. Swing the bat. Anybody can look. Show me what you can do.' So I ground the next one right back to him. The thing is, I know he took something off the fastball, because the pitch was way outside and still I was out in front of it enough to hit it back up the middle."

"Hard?"

"Not really. In fact, he caught it behind his back."

"You're kiddin."

"Really. Both Fred and Mr. Rollins start hollering at him, telling him not to try that when I get my timing. Rollins points to his knee and Fred points to his eye and everybody laughs. 'He ain't gonna get no timing!' Mr. Lincoln says, and he blows another one past me. I mean he was throwing smoke. It didn't hit the center post, but it was a strike. I say, 'Give me another of those.' He says, 'Just like that one, same speed, same location?' and I say, 'You wouldn't dare.'"

"Tell me you didn't say that," his mother said.

"I did! I had to, Momma. If I had just said yes, he might have tried to fool me, and I wouldn't have had any idea what was coming. Well, he thinks that's the funniest thing he's ever heard. He's laughing and jumping, and he keeps repeating it. 'You wouldn't dare?' he says. 'You wouldn't *dare!*'

"I say, 'Yes sir, I dare you.' He laughs and says, with this big grin on his face, 'Okay, white bread, here it comes, and I mean you're gonna get all of it.' Well, that makes *me* laugh and I'm stumbling out of the box when he throws the pitch, and Momma, I swear it was in exactly the same spot. Right there, same speed, and I know I could have killed it. It was as hard as the first one, which was the hardest anybody live had ever thrown to me, but I could have hit it."

"But now you couldn't."

"No! I was falling out of the box, laughing at him calling me that. I say, 'Come on, throw the same pitch without making me laugh.' He starts laughing again, but I know he's gonna throw that pitch again. I drove it right back at him."

"Oh, please."

"It was a hard shot, too. I just about died. For the split second before he snagged it I was sure I'd hurt my third pitcher in a row. I would have quit; I swear I would."

"What did he do?"

"He did like this," Elgin said, mimicking Lincoln's double take. "He was surprised. He really was. That ball almost took his glove off, and you knew he had to have caught it on instinct because there wasn't time to think. Then he did something that made me feel great. He could have said it was a fluke, right? That anybody could get lucky seeing the same fastball three times in a row?"

His mother nodded.

"Well, he went and got the pitching screen while all the parents laughed. While he was adjusting it and kicking it into place, he said, so everybody could hear, 'You're gonna see nothing but heat now. No curves, no changes, just power. I'm gonna change locations and that's all.'

"I nodded and dug in, and he put on a show. Almost every pitch was in the strike zone, and they were all the same speed. I loved it, Momma. I just loved it. Zing, zing, zing, they came barreling in there. Some were tight, some were outside, some were up, some were down. He set me up, made me reach, jammed me, everything the big leaguers do."

"How'd you do?"

Elgin sat back on the couch, grinning. "I hit him, Momma. I hit him pretty good. I swung and missed maybe six times, fouled off a bunch, took a few. I only popped up a couple. I hit at least five off that pitching screen, one that would have killed him. I hit two over the fence, both to right center. Lots of grounders and weak liners too."

"What'd he say?"

"Not much for a while. He just got silent and seemed more determined. Then he said, 'Folks, I'm not kiddin you. I'm throwing my best hard stuff. This is as fine a hitter as I've faced in a long time, and I mean of any age.'

"Somebody hollered, 'Mix in some offspeed stuff and breakin balls, Raleigh, and then see where he hides!' Mr. Lincoln wiped his face off and said, 'If he can hit this, he can hit that.' Then he turned to me. 'One more pitch, boy,' he said. 'You hit this and we'll make room for you on the city team.' Well, I knew he was kidding. You have to be out of college to play in that league. But I sure wanted to hit that pitch."

"And...?"

Elgin shook his head. "I don't know what he put on it, but it was his best pitch of the night. He busted it in on my hands and I just couldn't get my arms out away from my body to get the bat on it. He made me look bad on that pitch. I beat the bat on the ground and a few people clapped and cheered him. He came off the mound pointing at me. 'Be clappin for him,' he said. 'We all will be one day.'"

"What did he mean by that?"

"I don't know. I guess he thinks I'll make it to the majors some day."

"You know the odds, don't you, El?"

"Yes, Momma, I know."

"And you'll keep your—"

"Grades up so I can get into something else if I can't make it in baseball. Yes, Momma."

She smiled at him apologetically. "I just don't want you to be disappointed."

"I know. You wanna know what Mr. Lincoln said to me after practice?"

She nodded.

"He said he was going to tell Mr. Rollins to not let me play this year."

"What?"

"He told me the whole thing was a setup. A bunch of the kids told their parents about how I'd hit both the coaches, and they got together to come and see if I was really that dangerous. The deal was that if I was the kind of hitter they'd heard I was, they wanted Mr. Lincoln to pitch to me. He told me he didn't bring his glove on purpose because he wanted it to look like he'd just thought of it."

"So what are you supposed to do if they don't let you play?"

"Mr. Lincoln said there's a high school summer team for kids who are gonna be juniors and seniors next fall."

"Oh, Elgin, I don't know!"

"Momma, I need this! I don't want to bat .750 in a league that's too easy."

"Don't get too big for your britches."

"I'm not, but I don't want to hurt anybody, and I want to see where I should be playing."

"But high schoolers," she said. "Some of them will drive. Some will be working. Smoking, drinking, running with girls."

"I won't. I just want to play ball."

"Isn't there another step up in the league you're in?"

"There was, but they didn't have enough guys. The best players play on the high school traveling team, so I guess the other one just fell apart."

"These teams travel?"

"Yeah, that's the best part!"

"I'm not so sure."

"Mr. Lincoln said he would be happy to work with me on my pitching and stuff. I asked him if he would pitch to me. He said he'd like to see what I'd do against all his pitches. I don't want to just work out, though. I want to play for somebody."

"What did Mr. Rollins say?"

"Well, he said nice things about the way I had hit and then he asked me if I knew why so many parents were there. I told him I had an idea and that I didn't think it was just to admire me. He thought that was pretty funny.

"He said, 'Elgin, I'll be real surprised if the league lets me keep you. You're a secret we can't keep. I can't ask a boy to stand on the mound or even ninety or so feet away from you when you're at the plate when I would be unwilling to do it myself without a screen.'

"I told him what Mr. Lincoln had said, and he said, 'Son, you'd better not get your hopes up about that high school team. It's carrying fourteen all-stars right now, and even if you were the best of them, there's not one who would be willing to give up his spot, nor should he. The team is set, it's winning, and they wouldn't let a big leaguer into that lineup or even on the bench right now.'

"I said, 'Really?' He said, 'Well, that's a slight exaggeration to make a point.' I said, 'Well, what am I supposed to do if I can't play for you and I can't play for the high school summer team and there's nowhere to go in this league?' He said he didn't know. He said lots of people would be happy to coach a kid like me. But he also said he couldn't promise I'd be playing ball at all this summer."

"Oh, Elgin."

33

WHEN THE OFFICIAL WORD finally came that he could not play for Maury Rollins's team anymore, Elgin went to a last practice, threw a little, ran a little, hit not at all, said his good-byes, and heard his good-lucks. He would miss these guys.

Coach Rollins told him the way had been paved for him to try out for the summer high school traveling team. "Raleigh Lincoln Sr. put in a good word for you, and Hector Villagrande is looking forward to giving you a look. No promises now, hear? He told me just what I expected. That team is set and winning and full."

"I'll make it," Elgin said.

What he didn't say was that he had been running, throwing, doing sit-ups and push-ups, practicing his fielding, and of course, hitting. He had adjusted the machine so it would throw him a variety of pitches. By finagling with the axles and collars for the spinning wheels, he could adjust the machine to throw high, low, inside, outside, and breaking balls from two directions. With each new setting he had gone through hours of not being able to even foul off a pitch, but slowly and eventually, he caught on. He was at a point now where he could hit nine or ten decent shots off the thing at its original setting and two or three from each of the new ones for every basket of golf balls he poured into it.

Mr. Rollins gave him a slip of paper with the name and phone number of Hector Villagrande. "They're practicing at the old Lane Tech field Saturday morning at ten. Hector will give you a look at noon."

"I'll go early."

"Good idea."

"Find out what the competition is like."

"You just worry about yourself. It doesn't make any difference what anyone else does. You show well and you've got a chance. It's a long shot no matter what. Understand?"

Elgin just smiled. He was twelve years old and too good for a team of thirteen- to fifteen-year-olds. He had injured two coaches and had sent the rest of the team backing into the outfield when he came to the plate. Parents had come to see for themselves. He had hit well against a great adult pitcher who was past his prime but still better than most kids—even in their teens—ever face.

During the few days before his tryout with Hector Villagrande, Elgin did more than his usual working out. He read more than ever. He saturated himself, even more than usual if that was possible, with baseball. He read and reread how-to's, biographies, statistical compendiums, everything he could find.

Miriam had never seen him like this. As it was, living with him had been like living with baseball history personified, but now his constant chatter and expressions of confidence were getting even to her. She attributed it to nervousness and excitement, and she could hardly blame him. This was the break of a lifetime. Elgin predicted that making this team would get his name in the papers, maybe even in *Sports Illustrated.*

"I'd have to be the only kid on a high school team who's not even in junior high yet, wouldn't I, Momma?"

"I guess."

"You guess? You know I would."

"I s'pose you would."

She wondered how he could sleep. But she didn't hear him tossing or turning or getting up in the night. It must have been those grueling workouts. She rarely watched him hit in the basement because there was nowhere to stand or sit where she felt safe. But she had watched his hour-long run-through of calisthenics, throwing, fielding, and pitching off the walls. Sweat dripped off him, even in that cold, damp cellar, and she imagined she could see his musculature maturing, growing, tightening. He carefully avoided weights because a teacher had told him his frame and muscles and ligaments were not yet mature enough to respond the way he wanted.

"Give weights a couple of years," he was told. "When you're fourteen you can start slowly. Don't start too early."

He was so far ahead in everything else that Miriam worried he might want to jump the gun on weight training too, but clearly some instinct had told him his teacher was right. He was as strong and as bulked up as a lean, somewhat over-tall-for-his-age kid could be. She just knew he would shine for Mr. Villagrande on Saturday.

"I want to go with you, she said. "Can I watch?"

Elgin shrugged. "Why?"

"I won't say anything. I won't even let on who I am."

"Momma, you'll probably be the only woman there. They'll figure it out."

"So you don't want me to come?"

"It's all right. The more people, the better I do."

"Elgin, what size is your bat?"

"Fungo or regular?"

"Regular."

"Thirty-two inches, twenty-seven ounces. Why?"

"Just wonderin. Will you be using that one Saturday?"

"I might. It's been a long time since I used it. The one I used on the team was a thirty-three. I don't know the ounces, but it was probably in the high twenties. Pretty light for a bat that long. I used it against Raleigh's dad."

"You should've asked Mr. Rollins to let you borrow that bat for Saturday."

"Oh Momma, this high school team will have more bats to choose from than I've ever had. I'll tell you what I need. I need metal spikes."

"You've never had metal spikes."

"I've never been in a league that allowed them."

"How much are they?"

"I don't know, but I know I have to have some. Is there any way I could get some by Saturday?"

She shook her head and closed her eyes. "I'll tell you what, El. You make this team and we'll figure out a way to get you some metal spikes."

"If I make this team? Momma, how could I not make this team? I'm hoping to bat second or third and lead the team in hitting!"

"Well, I hope you do, but let's not get ahead of ourselves."

⚾ ⚾ ⚾

Friday was payday, and Miriam was home a little early. Elgin was watching the end of the Cubs game.

"They're down four-two. Momma, the Cubs need a third baseman. On two sacrifice bunts he was right in the hitter's face and could've got the lead runner but went to first anyway."

"Whatever that means."

"Momma, you know what that means! The players at the corners should always be thinking, Get the lead man, and come up throwing. They can always stop and go to first if they have to."

"Whatever."

"Momma..."

"Did you work out today?"

"Yeah. Everything but hitting."

"How long were you down there?"

"About four hours total."

"Don't wear yourself out before tomorrow."

"Wear myself out? Momma, I'm in the best shape of my life."

"Still planning on doing some hitting?"

"When the Cubs are over. Maybe I'll hit for an hour before dinner."

When the Cubs came back to win on a clutch triple in the eighth by none other than their third baseman, Miriam was amused that Elgin took it as a sign.

"Everything's gonna go right this weekend," he said, grabbing his aluminum bat, the one that had been gone so long.

"You working out with your regular bat?"

"A little," he said. "Wanna get used to it."

As soon as he was gone she hurried out. Lucky's Second-hand Shop was a little farther away than she had remembered, but it was still open. As she had hoped, Lucky himself was there.

"Mrs. Woodell!"

"Mr. Harkness!"

He laughed, apparently at her memory. She had carefully not given him permission to call her Miriam, and she did not now either.

"I came to look at that bat."

"I've never weighed a bat," he said a few minutes later. "But it measures thirty-three inches, like I said. And," he added, balancing it carefully on a small postage scale, "it appears to weigh twenty-nine, maybe thirty ounces."

"Hm," she said. "Sounds too heavy."

"It may be a bigger bat than he's ever used, but it is very, very light for its length, I know that. You can see it's signed by Frank White, a former Kansas City Royal who used light bats. Even used a thirty-two-incher for many years, one of the smallest in the big leagues. The way I understand it, these bats are usually the same number of ounces as they are inches, so a wood bat this light should be fragile. You can see that it's not. Elgin chokes up on this baby and he'll be able to get it around. I've seen him play fastpitch, and he tells me about his exploits with the ball team."

"Oh, I'm sure he does. You wouldn't believe he used to be humble."

"He's got nothing to be humble about, ma'am. Kid that age makes a team for older kids, well..."

She told him about the next day's tryout. He whistled through his teeth. "Makes me wish I could give this bat to you at my cost."

"Which was?"

"I could have paid thirty dollars for it. It's not used, but because of its weight, I have to believe it's the real thing, that it actually belonged to White."

"But it's stamped, not personally signed. Does that mean it's hot?"

"I have no reason to believe it's hot."

"I heard on TV that bats like this, even for big leaguers, go for a little more than fifteen dollars, half what you're sayin."

"You're offering me twenty?"

Miriam smiled. "No, sir, but I just found out you were lyin about the thirty, didn't I?"

Lucas Harkness looked stricken. "I never said I paid thirty! I said I could have. In fact, if I had paid what the guy wanted, I would have been out fifty, but for a genuine big leaguer's bat..."

"I have twelve dollars," Miriam said. "And if I was a bettor, I'd say that would double your investment."

"Well, it'd be more like breaking even."

"Oh, come on," Miriam said, still smiling. "You telling me I couldn't go to K-mart and find this same bat, same model, same name imprinted on the end?"

"Not the same length and weight, no, ma'am, and I'm telling you that honestly. The bats they make for the public are mostly same length as ounces, like I said."

"And you're telling me that honestly."

He put his hand on his heart. "Absolutely."

"But everything else you've said is dishonest?"

"No! Now why do you want to say that?"

"Well, you're the one who said you were telling me something honestly as if the rest was just—"

"I know, okay. You drive a hard bargain. Let me show you my original receipt. I'll prove I paid more than six dollars for the bat." He rummaged in a cardboard box behind the counter.

"You have to prove to me that twelve dollars would make you only break even."

"I didn't say I would break even. I said twelve dollars would be more like breaking even. It would be closer to breaking even than doubling my investment. Here, see? I paid eight dollars for this bat. Proves it."

The twinkle was still in his eye, and Miriam enjoyed the repartee. "I'v finally caught you in a lie," she said.

"No, please. You didn't. I don't lie. I bend and twist and imply to get th best price I can, but don't accuse me of that."

"Well, maybe you didn't intend to."

"Yeah, that's it, I didn't intend to. What'd I say, when I wasn't intending to?"

"You said that twelve dollars would be more like breakin even than doublin your investment, which was what I predicted it would do."

"And you see? You were wrong, ma'am. Twelve dollars does not double my investment."

"Right. Sixteen dollars would double your investment, which is four dollars more than I said would double it."

"Yeah?"

"And my offer of twelve is also four dollars more than what it would take for you to break even, right?"

"Right," he said carefully, clearly trying not to be sucked in.

"So I made you an offer that is just as close to your breakin even as it is to doublin your investment."

He thought about it for a moment. "You figured all that out just standing here?"

She smiled at him.

"I want to give you the bat."

"No way, Mr. Harkness. Twelve is a fair offer. Take it or leave it."

34

ELGIN STOOD IN AGAINST THE PITCHING MACHINE with his fungo bat, hoping to break his personal record of ten solid shots in one session of fifty-seven balls. In truth, he was too eager to get to his old aluminum bat, the one that had been too heavy for him when he lived in Hattiesburg. He hit only five good drives and grabbed the lighter, fatter bat.

Elgin started by fouling off a half-dozen pitches, then hit four line drives in a row. By the end of the first basket of balls with the aluminum bat, he had hit fourteen solid shots. It had taken him a few pitches to get used to the new weight and the lesser power required to get it around, but then that and the larger sweet spot had contributed to better performance.

Elgin felt guilty somehow, as if he had cheated. He would never give up primarily using the skinny, heavy fungo bat, but this was a fun, new experience. He hit from both sides of the plate, then ran through a short throwing workout so he could save endurance and sharpness for his big afternoon the next day.

When he trudged back upstairs to the apartment, his mother seemed different, as if she had something on her mind. She asked him the usual questions about his workout, and he gave the usual responses, except to report about the use of the bat she had retrieved for him.

"You can control the ball better with the bigger bat?"

"Sure."

"Wonder how you would do with a wooden bat."

"Yeah. That would be something. It would sound different, feel different. That would be like being in the big leagues. Course I don't know if those pitches would dent a wood bat. Wood bats are softer, you know. I don't think a golf ball could break a wood bat, but the pitches sure come in quick."

"They still look fast to you after all this time?"

"Oh, yeah. It's not so scary, but they're just flat out fast. I wonder what would happen if I took that old piece of plastic railroad track, from the train that kid traded me, and stuck it between the wheels when the machine was turned on."

"Don't you use it anymore?"

"I haven't played with that train for a year."

"What would that track do?"

"It seems like it would fit real tight between those wheels, underneath. It would jam them when the little ties came through, then it would release before the next tie. That would make the wheels start and speed up and then slow down and speed up again. Some of the balls would just drop through, but other ones would have all different speeds and directions."

"You think of that yourself?"

He nodded.

"I have something else for you," his mother said, smiling.

"What, another bat?" he teased.

Miriam's smile disappeared. "How'd you know?"

"Oh, right! I'm sure you got me another bat."

"I did!"

"C'mon, Mom!"

"I did!"

"Let's see it."

She pulled it from behind the couch. For once, Elgin was speechless. He could only shake his head as he hefted the new wood bat.

"Where?" he managed finally.

"Lucky's," she said.

"He rip you off?"

"Nope. He paid eight dollars for it. I paid him twelve."

"No way. He lied to you. If he paid eight, he would have sold it for sixteen."

"Hey, I'm a good bargainer."

"Not as good as he is. Did he *show* you what he paid for it?"

She nodded.

"He's got a lot of phony receipts he can pull out from under the counter," Elgin said.

"That scoundrel!"

"Ah, he wouldn't lie to you, Momma. He asks about you all the time."

"How do you like the bat?"

"I can't believe the bat," he said. "Can I go down and swing it a few times? There's no room in here."

Elgin rummaged under his bed for the piece of plastic railroad track, then headed for the basement. He ran through a couple of dozen practice swings, finding that he had to choke up about an inch to make the bat feel as light as his aluminum one. But what a wonderful feel! His dad had always told him he should switch to wood bats as soon as he could afford it, even if everyone else in his league was using aluminum.

"It'll cost you in your batting average," his dad had told him, "because you can get hits off the handle of a metal bat that would break a wood bat. And you can figure a metal bat is gonna push the ball about twenty percent harder. But the sooner you get used to wood bats, the better it'll be for your career."

Elgin smiled at the memory. He had been so young when his dad said that, he didn't even know what a career was. Now, he thought, the advice sounded good. He would use the wood bat in his tryout the next day.

It was getting late, but he wanted to see if his experiment would work. He poured a basket of balls into the machine and started it up. After the first ball had slammed off the far wall and flown to the hanging fabric at the other end, Elgin fed one end of the plastic track through the underside of the spinning wheels.

The machine whined and groaned and nearly stopped. Then it seemed to heat up as the plastic was drawn through in a slow, herky-jerky motion. The contraption smelled of electricity. Elgin counted sixteen pitches affected by the track. What those pitches did amazed him.

Some hit the ceiling, some hit the floor, some shot out either side. But about five whipped through the mechanism and broke three or four feet before banging into the wall for what would have been strikes. Elgin knew it would be weeks before he could figure a way to make the machine throw predictable pitches. He didn't want to go through another series of beanings and bruisings.

The machine was still spitting out pitches, so Elgin pulled the plastic strip from the floor and inserted it again. The machine slowed and strained, and then began to smoke. Elgin tried to pull the strip out, but it was already halfway through and would go in only one direction. One of its bent-out-of-shape ties caught between wheel and axle and slowed the machine nearly to a stop. Yet the motor kept grinding, emitting a gray plume of smoke.

Elgin yanked at the plastic from both ends. Now it wouldn't go either way. By the time he thought to turn off the machine, the acrid smell had sickened him and something had been damaged inside the switch. Nothing was happening. The machine was still running. The cord! He yanked it.

Elgin found his tools and loosened a wheel so he could dig out the mangled strip of plastic. Though he had other pieces upstairs—he had hoped to attach them to each other so he could drag plastic through the mechanism during a whole bucketful of pitches—he could see they would be useless to him now.

He quickly reassembled the machine, only to find that it would not rumble to life when he plugged it in and flipped the switch. There was only a low hum, heat he could feel from a couple of feet away, and that tiny column of smoke. He was heartsick. What did he know about fixing an electric motor?

The last thing he wanted to do was worry about his pitching machine when he was supposed to be getting a good night's sleep before the next day's tryout. With a huge screwdriver he removed the whole self-contained motor, amazed at how heavy and still hot it was. He had to make two trips back to the apartment, first to carry his glove and rubber-coated baseball and two bats, then the heavy, cooling motor.

"What're you going to do with that?" his mother asked.

He told her the story. "I'm hoping Biker can maybe fix it for me."

"You'd better start callin him Mr. Harkness, don't you think?"

"Well, maybe Lucky."

"You know better than that. You don't call your seniors by their first names unless they insist on it."

"Yes, ma'am."

"Anyway, what makes you think he knows anything about motors?"

Elgin shrugged. "He knows everything about everything."

⚾ ⚾ ⚾

"How bad do you need this?" Luke Harkness asked him the next day. He had plugged in the motor and flipped the switch.

"What did I do, ruin it?" Elgin asked.

"Likely. Smells like somethin's melted in there. It's froze up good. I got a friend who works on these things, but I could probably get you a good rebuilt one for the same price, maybe better."

"How long would that take?"

"A week or so."

"How much?"

"For you? Thirty, forty bucks."

Elgin scowled.

"I could carry you for a while."

"You mean let me put a little on it each week?"

"Yeah, or you could even work it off. Do odd jobs for me, that kind of thing."

"I'd love that! Only thing is, I'm trying out for the high school summer league traveling team this afternoon, and I don't know when they practice and play and all that."

"Just let me know. We'll work around it. Just see if you can give me a couple of hours a day."

"All right!"

"Listen, just because you're a good kid and you have a nice mom and I'm not payin you real money doesn't mean I won't expect you to be here on time every time and work hard."

"You just wait and see."

"One more thing, buddy. You didn't say anything about that bat."

"I love the bat! Thanks!"

"I gave your mother a good deal on that bat. Didn't do more than four bucks over breakin even."

Elgin laughed. "Which worked out to a fifty percent profit."

Harkness smiled sheepishly. "You *would* be the kid of a numbers woman."

35

ELGIN'S MOTHER WAS UNDER THE WEATHER Saturday morning, which was okay with Elgin. He had decided he'd rather go alone anyway and didn't know how to tell her.

"You need me here?" he asked. "I can call Mr. Villagrande."

"I'll be all right, honey," she said. "You just go and do good."

"You know I'll do good."

"And don't forget Mr. Lincoln's warning about getting your hopes up."

"I'm not gonna make this team by hoping anyway, Momma. They're gonna be wondering how they ever got along without me."

His mother did not appear amused, and he wasn't really kidding. He had learned how important confidence was in baseball. He was super confident, but not overconfident. He had a reason to be.

⚾ ⚾ ⚾

Elgin felt conspicuous at the dusty practice field across the street from Lane Tech. A dozen of the fourteen all-stars had shown up for practice that morning, and they were impressive. All had metal cleats, of course.

Elgin was struck by the distances. The mound was the major league distance from the plate, sixty feet, six inches. The bases were ninety feet apart. A strangely shaped outfield fence was precisely three hundred feet from home plate all the way around. That made center field look deceptively short. It was still a long poke, about as far as Elgin had ever hit a ball.

He introduced himself to the coach, who asked him to sit in the stands and watch until noon, when he would get his tryout.

"Could I sit in the dugout?" he asked the stocky Mexican who wore a straw fedora with a black band, expensive loafers and jewelry, and a pullover shirt and shorts. He sported a precisely trimmed mustache. To Elgin, Hector Villagrande looked like a successful businessman.

The coach studied him. "In the stands, *por favor.*" His accent was thick.

"Will I be facing you or one of your best pitchers?" Elgin asked.

Villagrande hesitated before responding. "I will decide when I decide. In the stands, please."

"I brought a wood bat. I hope that's okay."

Villagrande looked at him and then back to the field. He did not respond.

"I mean, I can hit with either, but I'd like to get used to wood, a better feel and all that. My dad told me that. He was a ballplayer. Almost made the majors with the Pirates." The coach had turned his back on Elgin. "Um, do you think someone could warm me up a little before noon, so I don't have to start cold?"

The coach called out an instruction to the batting practice pitcher, an extremely tall man in his late twenties who threw hard and straight with little effort. Then Mr. Villagrande turned back to Elgin and looked at him with dark eyes.

"This is not the stands, is it, Señor Woodell?"

Elgin's face burned. "No, sir."

"Let us see how well we can follow instructions and respect a man's time and responsibilities; then we will see what kind of a ballplayer we are. Okay?" Elgin felt terrible. "At about ten to noon, I would take a slow jog around the field. Don't wear yourself out in this heat."

"Where should I leave my stuff?"

Elgin knew as soon as it was out of his mouth that his just-one-more-question had angered the man. Villagrande's eyes narrowed. He tilted his head and sighed.

"I never have to tell high school ballplayers where to leave their equipment," he said carefully. "Anyone who qualifies to play for this team takes care of certain things himself."

Elgin wanted to apologize, but he didn't want to open his mouth again. He trudged to a high perch in the stands, where he sat sweating in the sun until almost noon. From that vantage point, the players still looked huge. Even the youngest were well developed and long armed. Throws were crisp. No one was criticized for an error, but woe to them if they were out of position or threw to the wrong base. Hector Villagrande's rage was hottest for anyone who didn't hustle. They were to run out everything, run on and off the field, hustle, hustle, hustle.

"We have ballplayers," Villagrande said, emphasizing the second syllable, "taking numbers for your jobs!"

Elgin just sat, waiting for his chance. When the time came, he clambered down the rickety wood benches and dropped bat and glove next to the first base dugout. As he jogged slowly around the field, outside the fence, he watched the last few hitters.

Apparently, this team took batting practice in order of age. The strapping seniors, whose goal it was to get college scholarships or even play minor league ball the following summer, were hitting.

They crashed hard liners and long fly balls all over the field. Two were switch-hitters, hitting both ways against the big right-hander, who was throwing harder now. Elgin hoped to face him. There was not a pitcher alive he feared, and he daydreamed about standing in against a major leaguer. He knew it was folly and that he would probably bail out at the first sight of a big-time dust back pitch, but so far he had not been stopped by anyone.

Shortstop and second base were played by twins who looked as smooth and strong as any double play combination Elgin had ever seen, even on television. He wondered where he might play. Maybe in the outfield, as he did in his first year for Mr. Rollins.

Hector called in his boys and addressed them on the bench in the third base dugout. Elgin retrieved his equipment and walked across the diamond to hear the coach. When Villagrande noticed him he stopped and spoke quietly.

"Señor Woodell, if you would excuse us a moment, please."

When will I learn? Elgin wondered, humiliated. He stepped out of earshot. As he waited, he realized there was little fooling around and no talking back to the coach. The kids seemed to be having a good time, but they were not typical of kids their age. They quietly did what they were told and did their jobs right. Elgin decided he would enjoy this team if he could just quit irritating Mr. Villagrande.

The boys filed out of the dugout and took a hard lap around the field. As they drifted toward their cars, a couple approached Elgin, which drew a small crowd.

"You're the rookie we're supposed to worry about?" one said.

"I guess," he said, smiling.

"What position?"

"I can play any position."

"Oh, really?"

"Yup."

"What's your batting average?"

Elgin shrugged. "Haven't found anybody who can get me out yet."

"You're batting a thousand?"

"No, but nobody can get me out regularly. Not even adults."

"Whoa. Excuse us! Well, we'd stay and watch you take our jobs, but—"

"Yeah, all our jobs! He can play every position!"

"—we were told we couldn't. Guess you'd make us feel bad, or we'd make you nervous or something."

"You wouldn't make me nervous. I do better with more people watching."

"Oh, he does better with more people watching! Let's stay!"

"Coach said no. We gotta go. How old are you, kid?"

"Twelve."

"Sure you are."

"I am!"

"Yeah, okay. Well, good luck."

Elgin took the wish seriously and said thank you, but the players laughed as they left.

"Mr. Woodell," Hector said, "what time is it?"

"I don't have a watch, sir."

"It remains your responsibility to be on time. You are four minutes late."

"Sorry."

"Coach Michaels will time you around the bases. One chance and one chance only."

Elgin moved to the right-hand batter's box and took off with the command from the assistant coach. He slid around each base in the dust, but he felt fast. Coach Michaels raised his eyebrows and showed the watch to Hector, who pursed his lips.

"Do you own metal cleats?"

"If I had metal spikes, I would've brought them."

Hector Villagrande glared at the boy. "Was that supposed to be an answer, or are you a smart aleck?"

"No, sir. I was just saying that if—"

"Do you own metal cleats, yes or no?"

"No, sir."

"Thank you. I am curious to know how fast you would be with real baseball shoes."

"Where do I rank on your team in speed?"

Hector looked as if he didn't want to say. "Fourth or fifth," he admitted.

"And I'm not even thirteen yet," Elgin said, beaming.

"Run two more times, but this time—"

"You said just one chance."

The coach squinted. "Listen to me. Here is something I want to say to you. If I say something that sounds not like something I already said to you, you do the last thing I say, okay? You don't argue, you don't ask, you don't explain, okay? You just do."

"Okay," Elgin muttered, looking at the ground.

"And with a good attitude," Hector added. "Now I want you to run around the bases two more times, as hard as you can, without stopping, and not for time. I will watch you for speed, endurance, and technique. Go!"

The command caught Elgin off guard but he knew better than to question or hesitate. He sped twice around the bases as fast as he could, hitting each sack with his left foot. It did not surprise him to see that Coach Michaels indeed had a watch running, and that when Elgin was done, the coaches conferred over the watch.

"Very impressive," Hector announced. "Are you not winded?"

Elgin shrugged. "A little. But I could run it again if you wanted."

"I will let you know."

Coach Michaels swore, just above a whisper. "Man, any one of our kids, except maybe O'Mel, would be on the ground suckin air right now! He got faster as he went and he could go again!"

Elgin smiled.

"Want to do some hitting?" Hector asked.

Elgin ran for his bat.

"You are a switch-hitter, right?"

Elgin nodded.

"Bat righty against the righty, anyway."

The tall hurler hurried to the mound with a huge plastic bucket of balls.

"Uh, sir, do you have a screen to protect the pitcher?"

Hector stepped close to Elgin. "You worry about getting your new wood bat around on Neil's fastball, and I'll worry about his safety, okay?"

"Okay, but I've hit two adult pitchers, and I—"

"Were they throwing from this distance?"

"No, sir."

Elgin shrugged and stood in. Coach Michaels had pulled on the catching gear. It would be a game situation, signal calling and all. Hector moved to the third base coaching box, but rather than giving signs, he merely hollered out what he wanted Elgin to do.

Neil, accurate as he was, was not nearly as strong or powerful or fast or intimidating to Elgin as Raleigh Lincoln, Sr., had been. And he certainly was no match for the pitching machine. The pitches looked fat and inviting, and the feel of the wood bat made Elgin as comfortable at the plate as he'd ever been.

36

MIRIAM WAS NOT ONE FOR PREMONITION OR SUSPICION, though her family and her husband's family had been. Yet she knew her logy feeling that morning had as much to do with impending dread as with anything physical. She had awakened depressed, not eager to start the day, definitely not interested in going with Elgin to Lane Tech.

She padded around the flat in her robe and slippers most of the morning, not eating and feeling faint by noon. She finally talked herself into a shower and grubby clothes, making a sandwich and a pot of coffee, then sat reading an old issue of a magazine Mr. Bravura had saved for her from the lobby.

Her lonely vigil of love for Elgin had been colored somewhat by how little she had seen him lately. She admired his devotion, his brain, his physical abilities, but they were also taking him away from her. During the school year he had studied hard, though maybe not for as long as she would have liked; he was always on his way to or from the cellar. When his homework and his workout were done, he read baseball books or sat in the library reading sports magazines. She wanted to order him a subscription for Christmas until she saw the prices.

She was excited for Elgin at his progress, and she was intrigued by his confidence. It didn't seem to make him lazy as it had his daddy, but she didn't like the new cocksuredness in his tone. Self-confidence was one thing, but his superior attitude had crept up on her. It didn't wear any better on him than it does on anyone, she decided. What should she say? How should she say it? Confidence, she knew from personal experience, was fragile. Self-image could be wrapped in tissue. Even constructive criticism could tear self-worth to shreds and expose an illusion of confidence.

And yet Elgin's certainty was based on incredible physical and mental talent he had honed. How could she fault him when he was so devout, so obsessed, so unwilling to compromise or take shortcuts? It wasn't his methods she was questioning; it wasn't even his self-confidence. That was well placed and valid. It was his expression of it.

But was such braggadocio merely typical of his age? Kids like him loved to talk about themselves, to boast, to see where they fit in. Certainly he could not brag much on his daddy, except to say what he used to be, could have been, might have been, almost was. He couldn't brag on his momma, except to say she gave him his stick-to-itiveness. She barely got along, provided him a home more humble even than all of his friends'.

Others said she was pretty, and she had seen him beam over that, but a kid his age didn't brag about that kind of a thing. It wasn't something that would come from his mouth.

So maybe he had a right to be a little proud of what he had done with his interest, his inclination, his skill. He had, she knew, done this himself. Reading, studying, watching, analyzing, trying, doing, developing, he had turned himself into a hitter and fielder and thrower far beyond his years.

Miriam couldn't shake her foreboding. She flipped on the TV and found herself staring, unhearing, at a vapid local talk show. She went down to get her mail. Sometimes Mr. Bravura brought it up to her if she let it sit for more than an hour on a Saturday. With Elgin not there, she'd rather get it herself.

"Ah, lovely Mrs. Woodell," the manager said as she approached the glassed-in cubicle. "You have something we never get here." He pulled a few pieces of mail from her pigeonhole, including a receipt he had signed for a Federal Express envelope. "And from an unpleasant place," he added, muttering.

Miriam was pricked with fear and irritated at Mr. Bravura's noticing, let alone commenting upon, where she got an important piece of mail. She had never received a personal Fed Ex delivery, though she knew from her office work that they usually arrived in the morning.

"What time did you sign for this?" she asked coldly, noticing the return address: the Alabama State Department of Corrections.

"This morning," he said. "I do not let delivery men up to the apartments, as you know. I would have run it up to you myself, had I not been swamped."

"I would have appreciated that," she said, turning. A thank-you was the last thing on her mind.

"No need for a tip," Ricardo Bravura said softly.

She spun to face him.

"Just kidding," he sang out. "Next time I will personally deliver it."

The first two pitches were high and outside, and the third was tight at the letters. Elgin stepped but didn't move his bat on any of them.

"Reachable?" Hector Villagrande asked Coach Michaels from the third base coaching area.

The catcher shrugged and nodded, as if to say, not great pitches, but yes, reachable. Hector held up a hand to keep Neil from throwing and moved up the line toward Elgin. "Here's what I want you to do. You have a good eye, but this is batting practice. I—"

"I thought it was a tryout," Elgin said, with sincerity. "If you want me to hit like I have two strikes, I will."

Hector nodded slightly, not smiling. "That is what I want you to do."

Elgin took a low, inside pitch right down the line at Hector, who skipped out of the way. He was not amused.

Elgin grinned. "Sorry."

"Did you do that on purpose?"

"Not really. I was trying to hit it fair."

"You can come that close to where you want to hit it?"

"Even on an outside pitch."

Hector thrust out his chin, as if thinking. "Neil," he said, "move the ball around. Elgin, I will tell you where to try to hit each pitch. No matter where it is pitched, hit this to center field!"

The ball split the plate. Elgin barely swung, lofting a soft liner over second base.

The next pitch was hard and low, off the outside corner.

"Same spot!" Hector shouted.

Elgin stepped farther than usual, bent his left knee, and got around quickly. He pulled the ball directly over Neil's head into center. Elgin looked at each of them. He could read nothing on Hector's face. Neil was clearly impressed, and perhaps a little embarrassed. He threw the same pitch, maybe a little harder.

"Left field," Hector said as it left Neil's hand.

It had been a chore to hit a low outside pitch to center, but to pull one to left, one with more on it…

Elgin did it. He was pumped. He loved this idea. Throw me anything, tell me to hit it anywhere! he thought, and only the winding motion from the mound kept him from saying it aloud.

"Right field!"

The pitch was outside, just what he was waiting for: the chance to hit a pitch where it was thrown. He drove it on one hop to the fence.

"Left field line!"

Elgin took a waist-high strike down the line, his hardest shot so far.

"Now," Hector said to Neil, then shouted to Elgin, "hit this one out o here, wherever you can."

Was Hector calling for a pitch? Elgin guessed breaking ball or a change of speed. He could barely keep from grinning as Neil's arm swept toward him and he saw the turn of the sweeping curve.

Elgin was so pleased with himself for guessing correctly that he got out in front of the ball and got under it a little too much. He sent a 275-foot towering fly ball to left, then stole a glance at Hector.

The coach's face had softened. He pointed at Neil who nodded. The next pitch was a fastball right at Elgin's rear end. He felt himself bailing backward, then stopped himself and skipped across the plate, avoiding the ball. The next pitch was at the back of his head. Elgin ducked and glared, first at Neil, then at Hector. Neither was smiling. The next pitch was at his feet. He danced to avoid it. He had hit pitches like that from the machine. He hoped Neil would throw that same pitch again. He laughed aloud, as if to say that anyone could get out of the way of a pitch like that.

Neil wound fast and quick-pitched him, a fast ball in the same location and, if anything, a little lower. Elgin stepped and swung as if golfing. He ripped a shot at Hector who had to dive to the ground to evade it. He came up dusting off his shirt and shorts. Elgin wanted to smile, but he didn't.

Neil came in under his chin with the next pitch, and Elgin blasted it back up the middle on one hop. Neil somehow got a glove on it, and without winding up, fired it right back at Elgin. He fought it off, fouling it back. And here came another pitch, right at him. He stepped back and lined it back to Neil's glove.

Now he was scared. What if these guys didn't let up? Were they really trying to hurt him? All rules were out the window. He jumped around to the left-hand hitting side of the box and drilled the next pitch into the outfield. He fouled off a few more, swung and missed a few, and felt tears rising in his eyes. He willed himself not to cry.

Hector began calling out fields again. Elgin tried, not as successfully as before, to hit the balls where Hector said. But Neil's control, intentional or not, had left him. Elgin swung at everything—pitches in the dirt, over his head, behind him. He was huffing and puffing and sweating, and he was mad. He wanted to fling his bat at the hulk on the mound. Oh, for a few good pitches!

And with the thought came the pitches. He hit four towering fly balls into the outfield.

"Routine fly outs," Hector said.

Elgin tried hitting harder. He wanted to hit one out. That was a mistake. He was not a power hitter except against kids his age. He knew his long hits would come naturally with the right mechanics on his normal swing. He hit a few shots, a few liners, and a lot of hard grounders. He fouled off a half-dozen pitches and missed three more.

"One more pitch," Hector said. "Give him a home run pitch, Neil."

For some reason, Elgin didn't suspect any treachery. They owed him a home run pitch. And here it came.

⚾ ⚾ ⚾

Miriam set the colorful cardboard envelope on the kitchen table and avoided it like some malevolent intruder. Of course it had to be from the chaplain, and of course it had to be bad news. She picked through her bills, a form from the personnel office, and a silly, no-occasion card from Lucas Harkness. What a nice friend he had become to Elgin.

37

ELGIN KNEW HIS POWER did not extend to three hundred feet. Otherwise, he might have hit the fat pitch over the center-field fence. His choice now was to take off someone's head. But whose? Neil seemed like a nice enough guy. He had done only what Hector had told him. Hector was the choice, the target. And Hector had been warned. He said he was in charge of safety, and Elgin assumed that meant his own as well.

He did not want to hurt the man and would have felt terrible, though justified, if he had. Yet he wanted to produce a purpose line drive, just like the purpose pitches he had seen. He lashed Neil's letter-high, inside fastball down the third-base line, and Hector's eyes grew wide as he ducked.

Elgin didn't smile. He didn't even look at the man. He could tell Hector was glaring at him.

"Are there any more balls in the bucket?" Elgin said.

Neil looked to Hector who shrugged. "A half-dozen or so," Neil said.

"Bring em on!" Elgin said, wondering if for once Hector would allow him to do something Hector had not thought of.

Hector nodded to Neil again, and the big right-hander reached into the bucket. All seven pitches were fastballs on the inner half of the plate. Elgin swung rhythmically and easily, driving each on a line into right field, almost into the same area. When the bucket was empty, Elgin ran for his glove and waited for instructions.

Coach Villagrande motioned to all the balls in the outfield. "Fetch them and loosen up your arm by tossing them easily to Neil, please."

When Elgin had finished, he was hot and dripping, but he felt good. Surely, this strange coach had to be impressed. Could any of his regulars have done what Elgin did?

Neil stood at first base. Hector hit grounders to Elgin at short. The first few were easy and right at him. He charged slow rollers, angled back on ones away from him. His throws to first were fast and true, though each took tremendous effort. He had never played on a field this size.

Soon Hector was smashing liners and grounders at him harder than anyone had ever hit them to him in practice or a game. Elgin enjoyed diving for them. A couple skipped off his glove. One bounced off his chest, causing him to grunt. He recovered the ball and threw to first. On about fifty ground balls, he had three bad throws, two over Neil's head and one that pulled him up the line off the bag. Otherwise, Elgin was flawless. He was getting tired, but he would have done it all day.

Hector waved him in, and as Neil and Coach Michaels loaded the equipment into Hector's car, Elgin sat with the coach on the first row of the bleachers.

"You are very young," Hector began quietly.

"Yes, sir, I know, but—"

"Señor Woodell, I would like you to not speak until I am finished. Do you understand?"

"Yes, but—"

"Yes or no is all I need. Do you understand?"

"Yes."

"I want to talk about what I saw today and a little about my team. First of all, I saw a young boy, big for his age, but not big for a high school team. You are a better-than-average fielder with a better-than-average arm, but I do think your arm is at its limit from shortstop on a regulation field. Were you to play for me, I would probably not risk putting you anywhere in the infield other than at second base."

Better than average? Elgin thought. What was I supposed to do, catch everything?

"Your range and mechanics are good. You show tremendous potential as a fielder. I like the way you use your feet and your glove. You have been well trained and coached. You are a fine hitter, very strong for your size and age. Power will come with growth. You have a little boy's immaturity, and I would wonder about team spirit and attitude."

Elgin took a breath to speak, to assure Mr. Villagrande that he had always been and would always be a team player, even on those teams where he was the star. But the coach kept talking.

"You are full of yourself, that is clear. I say this not because you nearly hit me with batted balls. It is seen in your face, your walk, everything. You know how good you are, and I fear you will be satisfied to remain at the level you are now. That would be a tragedy, for you have unlimited potential. But I do not have a place for you on my team."

Elgin felt paralyzed. His head buzzed; his breath came in short gasps.

"I know this is a disappointment to you, and I know also that it puts you in a position where you may not be able to play ball at all this summer. That is not good but not all bad either."

Elgin was barely listening. How could this be? How could this fool have watched him hit and field and throw and run and not realize what he could do for this team? Surely he was better than half the players he had seen that day.

"You should continue working out. Look for a league that will accept you. I know Mr. Lincoln was impressed enough with you that he would be willing to pitch to you occasionally. I would, if I were you, work on humility. You are not the best ballplayer who ever lived."

Not yet, maybe, Elgin thought.

"You did not see anyone congratulate himself on this field today, no matter what he did. My players encourage each other, but there is no self-promotion. Do you know what that means?"

I'm an honor student, Elgin wanted to say, but he was in shock. He merely nodded.

"Many a player has come to me the best on his high school team. There are only two players on this team from the same school, so you see what I mean. They have their sights set on college and the pros. One player every five years gets a contract. The odds are tremendous. But each comes to me thinking he is the best. Those who learn quickly what it means to be a humble team player are the ones I keep. The others go elsewhere and I have never seen one succeed in the game. You have a great advantage because of your youth, but let me warn you what happens. I have not seen someone so young so gifted, but almost. What happens is you may plateau while everyone else catches up to you. That will take some pressure off you. If you keep improving, you will be something special.

"If you are convinced you are already something special, you will probably be a better-than-average high school player someday. Then, because you are not better, you will be more interested in cars and girls and money, and you will drift from the game."

"Never," Elgin said, noting the man's surprise that he finally interrupted. "No way, ever. I may have a lot to learn, but I will never drift from the game."

"Well, good for you," Villagrande said, slapping Elgin's knee and rising. "I wish you the best and I invite you to try out for me again next year."

"But what if I—?"

"That's all I can offer, *muchacho*. I am sorry."

Sobs were dammed in Elgin's throat. He was angry, humiliated. He wanted to scream, to threaten, to accuse. Who was this man who thought he knew so much? Elgin moved stiff-legged to the field where he picked up his glove and looked for his bat. He found it outside of the third base dugout. He was suddenly weak and tired. He put his back to the end of the dugout and slid to the ground, letting the tears come silently.

Elgin could hear the two coaches chatting near their cars. "The mask?" Neil said. "Where would Michaels have left it?"

"I thought I saw it in the dugout."

"Let's check."

They found the mask and stood talking, apparently unaware that Elgin was on the other side of the dugout wall.

Hector sighed. "Was that kid something today, or what?"

"Good, huh?"

"Good? Neil, that was the most unbelievable hitting exhibition I've ever seen, especially for a kid that age."

"Who you tellin? You made me stand sixty feet away from him. Almost cost me my head."

⚾ ⚾ ⚾

The only time sunlight streaked between the close buildings and bathed Miriam Woodell's kitchenette counter was in the early afternoons, so of course the only time she saw that was on weekends. In a few minutes the sun would be hidden again, and she sat there idly in the thin beam, feeling the warmth move across her face and neck. How she wished that warmth had come from a hand—one other than her own.

She took her time opening the Fed Ex package, first studying the air bill. Neither Chaplain Wallace's name nor initials appeared anywhere, but when she pulled the tab and removed the business envelope, her expectation was confirmed. It bore his return address.

Re: Neal Lofert Woodell (092349)

Dear Mrs. Woodell:

I thought for the sake of your son that you would want to be informed of your former husband's condition. He has suffered acutely from a new attack of delirium tremens, apparently brought about by yet another difficult withdrawal from alcohol. I know this comes as a shock to you, because he was not assumed by anyone, myself included, to have access to alcohol here.

As you can imagine, such substances can be smuggled in, unfortunately only by prison employees. He was supplied with vodka, which could not be detected on his breath, though it was detected in blood and urine samples. He denied knowing how his system could evidence signs of the same.

Apparently he ran out of whatever mode of payment he had been making, and his supply was cut off. An investigation continues here to determine who was bringing in the liquor. Meanwhile, your former husband's condition is not good. For several days he suffered the typical hallucinations, which he now tells me were more vivid and terrifying even than last time, which was the worst I had seen anyone endure. He may wish to inform you of the details, but I will spare you that for now.

More important, according to the physician here, Neal suffered dehydration, a dangerously elevated heart rate during convulsions, and a blood pressure reading in the critical danger zone. He has suffered two heart attacks, one severe and the other not so severe except for a man in his condition, and also kidney failure.

He is on heavy medication to sedate the central nervous system, is on IVs for constant hydration, along with whatever fluids they can get him to take orally, electrolytes for salt, multi-vitamins, and a strict diet. Of course, his strict avoidance of alcohol is key, but I fear he has no self-control in that area and would eagerly take a drink if he could get one.

The doctor is most concerned with the kidney and heart failures and, I must tell you, is pessimistic about Neal's survival regardless. Were you to elect that your son see his father again, the doctor urges that you consider a trip within the next thirty days.

Very truly yours,
Rev. Alton Wallace, Chaplain
Alabama State Penitentiary

P.S. Neal is not aware that I have written you. While he has not specifically asked to see his son, he has mentioned that he wishes he could see his family again.

38

A WEEK FROM THE FOLLOWING MONDAY, Elgin and his mother sat on a train from Chicago that would snake them all the way to Birmingham, Alabama.

"Bet you don't like wasting your first week of vacation on a trip like this," Elgin said.

His mother shrugged. "It's for you. It's okay."

"Can't we see anybody else when we're down there?"

"We'll not be close enough to Hattiesburg. Maybe some of your dad's people will come by. I don't know."

"Am I still going to be able to go to college?"

His mother smiled. "I didn't take *all* your college money, El, and I shouldn't have told you that anyway. Let's say I just borrowed it from that fund and that I will be payin it back, okay?"

"I'll help put money in that fund someday," he said. "Soon as I get my electric motor paid off, maybe Mr. Harkness will start paying me."

Elgin had walked all the way home from Lane Tech after his tryout more than a week ago, hiding his tears from passersby but letting them flow when he was alone. With every step he determined to work harder than ever to show Hector Villagrande and anyone else who doubted him that he was ready, that he could play with anybody.

"I hate to say it," his mother had told him, "but I've seen the same things in you lately. You used to be the sweetest, most selfless child. You're still a good kid. But you've become impressed with yourself."

"I'm impressive," Elgin said.

"I know you are. But you're only impressive until people know you're aware of it. Then it's obnoxious, and it's only going to get you what you got today. Let people discover you, El."

He had thought about it constantly, even talked with Luke Harkness about it. Luke had little to say, except to confirm Elgin's own conclusions.

Elgin began trying to become again the kind of kid he had been before everyone started raving about him. He still enjoyed attention and was heartbroken to have no venue from which to display his gifts. It would not be easy, but from now on, he was determined to let his play do his talking. The shot between the eyes from Hector Villagrande had awakened him, and painful as it was to be turned toward the light of self-awareness, he would try to face himself. His mother's confirmation of Hector's conclusions was just as painful, but down deep Elgin missed the original Elgin Woodell just as much as she did. Maybe he *would* like to play for Hector someday.

One day at the second-hand shop, a few days before Elgin and his mother were to leave for Alabama, Lucky's electrician friend showed up.

"I gotta talk to the boy about this motor," he said. They sat in the back room, just Elgin and the tall, skinny man with a bobbing Adam's apple. "This here is a good motor," he said. "It's not new. Fact, they hardly make em this good anymore for less than several hundred dollars. My question is, what's it from and how did you burn it up?"

"I can't tell you what it's from," Elgin said.

"Because you don't know, or because it's somethin illegal?"

"Neither. I just don't wanna tell."

"Well, okay, let me try it this way: Were you jammin the thing somehow?"

"Yeah."

"With what?"

"Plastic."

"Why?"

"I can't say."

"Well, give me a general idea what you were trying to get it to do."

"Start and stop at different speeds without turning it off."

"Oh, well, see, that's all I needed to know. Problem is, you probably put your resistance out here, am I right?" The man pointed to the end of the spinning shaft.

"Actually, I put it out at the axle that's driven by a belt."

"Oh, that's even worse. Puts too much torque on the—well, you don't need to know all that. So what you want is a pretty heavy-duty motor, this size, that you can turn on, get warmed up and running, and then have it change speeds, what, sort of at random?"

Elgin nodded. He thought he understood.

"What you want is a bit of a different animal," the man said. "It's got a clutch in it, and a cooling system, and I can build right into it your random, spring-loaded metal resistor. It shouldn't ever jam or overheat or break down, as long as you let it warm up before you start askin it to change speeds."

"That sounds fantastic."

"Well, it is fantastic. Industry has some uses for motors like that, mostly for mixing food and such, but I can't for the life of me figure out what a kid would need one for. I'd sure like to see your contraption."

"Maybe someday," Elgin said. "How long before I can have the motor?"

"How long? I'd say two weeks and a hundred dollars. It'll be a rebuilt one, but old enough that it'll be almost indestructible."

Now, on the train, Elgin said, "Wouldn't it be something if that motor was fixed when we got back home?"

"Don't get your hopes up," his mother said idly, looking out the window.

⚾ ⚾ ⚾

Miriam phoned Chaplain Wallace from the train depot near the taxi stand.

"Get yourself a room nearby," he said, "and I'll be happy to come and get you. You may see Neal at four this afternoon. You'll be happy to know that he is ambulatory and will be able to walk into the visitors' picnic area to greet you."

Miriam was grateful that Elgin didn't have to see his daddy in a hospital bed with needles and tubes running in and out of him. She wasn't sure she was up to seeing Neal herself, after an overnight train trip and not sleeping well. But there would be no putting it off. The chaplain had said Neal was on his own feet. He didn't say the prognosis was any better. Which it was not. The chaplain explained that in adult language on the way to the prison that afternoon. Miriam and Elgin had showered. He was dressed up. She was dressed down. There would be no encouraging Neal on this trip, though it felt strange, she had to admit, to think she might be seeing the last of him.

"The incarcerated individual," Rev. Wallace began, looking at her over the tops of his glasses to see whether she was following, "remains in a negative prognosive state. This current ambulatory ability is not uncommon, according to the attending physicians. He must be very careful, however, to avoid anything that would exacerbate his hypertension or threaten his cardiovascular system."

"Uh-huh."

Rev. Wallace was a kind-looking man, perhaps softer and plumper than she expected in a prison chaplain. He had fleshy hands and thick glasses, and he spoke with an articulation his letters had evidenced.

"It's so good of you to come, ma'am," he said. "Have you thought any more about the matter about which we corresponded some time ago?"

"Yes," she said. "I'm not prepared to reconcile, if that's what you mean. I don't plan to be nasty, but I'm here for the boy. I don't mind seeing Neal again, but I will not be encouraging him."

"Ma'am, I think he knows what's happening here, and I doubt he's looking for any romantic encouragement."

"I know what he's looking for, sir," she said, not unkindly but directly. "He's not gonna get absolution from me."

"I was not under the impression you folks were Catholic," the chaplain said, pulling onto the prison grounds.

"We're not, but isn't absolution what Neal is after?"

The chaplain showed his card to the guard and began the long process of getting himself and his guests inside the maximum security facility.

"Yes, I suppose he is," Wallace said when he had the chance. "And a little mercy or grace to a terminal patient is an inexpensive but precious commodity."

Miriam fell silent. Wallace turned his attention on Elgin. "So, I'll bet you'll be glad to see your dad after all this time."

Elgin nodded. "Momma said he was sick."

"Yes, he might not look like what you remembered, but you'll recognize him." He led Miriam and Elgin to a picnic table beneath a huge tree.

"I am happy to stay but will be just as happy to make myself scarce," he said.

"Thank you," Miriam said. "I think we would prefer to see him alone, if you don't mind. That won't upset Neal, will it?"

"I don't think so."

"Would you mind staying within sight in case I want to let Elgin and Neal spend some time together? I don't think I'd know what to do with myself here."

The chaplain agreed. "I'm going to go get him, and after I have pointed you out to him, I will be over there." He gestured to where several tables had been pushed together.

Miriam found herself strangely nervous. She had once taken some solace in the belief that she would never have to see Neal or deal with him again. What would this man look like, now near death, his body ravaged by attacks on his major organs?

Elgin said something she didn't hear. She had watched the chaplain's back until he disappeared from sight. Now she watched other families, wives and children, embracing men and laughing and crying. She planned to do neither, and she certainly would not touch the man.

"What?" she asked Elgin.

"There's Rev. Wallace," he repeated. "Where's Daddy?"

Miriam saw the chaplain sitting where he said he would wait. He waved at her with a small flick of his meaty hand and proffered a polite smile. Several prisoners milled about, looking for people, striding purposefully. A few hesitated, some perhaps with no one to see but checking out the scene anyway. Miriam did not see Neal.

She raised her palms at the chaplain in a question. He pointed past her to the corner of the building. She told Elgin to wait as she hurried to the chaplain.

"Where is he?" she asked.

Rev. Wallace smiled tolerantly and pointed back toward Elgin. "Right over there," he said. She looked. "Right there."

He was pointing past a group of families and about twenty feet from Elgin. Slowly, carefully making his way toward his son, was Neal Lofert Woodell, number 092349. Over his prison blue dungarees he had a drab green woolen blanket around his shoulders.

Miriam stared and burst into tears. Her knees buckled and the chaplain caught her as she sank awkwardly to the bench beside him.

39

SINCE SHE HAD SEEN NEAL LAST, there had not been one clue that she could ever lose her resolve to continue holding against him the loss of her unborn daughter. The man had cost her a child, her dignity, her security, a normal family life, her childhood dreams. He had lied as a matter of course, even when lying benefited him nothing. He was, she had finally decided, evil and worthless.

But now as she saw the broken husk of the boy she had fallen in love with in high school, she was overcome with pity. Perhaps he deserved this. Perhaps she should be glad he finally got his due. But what a sad and sorry price! She had not even recognized him, had looked right through him looking for the powerful frame of the former athlete.

Former was right. This man, barely into his thirties, clutched the blanket around his shoulders as the wisp of a ninety-year-old would. His gait was deliberate, his step unsure. Miriam felt the warm, soft hand of the chaplain on her shoulder and fought to control herself. She hoped Elgin wouldn't bolt from his father.

She dabbed at her eyes and forced herself to watch the encounter. Elgin had stiffened and now stared as his father approached, prison-issue hat mocking the baseball caps that had looked so smart on him in his youth.

Elgin stood as his father approached, and Miriam felt herself rising too. She pulled away from Chaplain Wallace, insisting she was all right, and hurried to within a few feet of her son. Neal glanced at her but then turned to Elgin.

"Dad?" Elgin said, his voice thick.

"El," Neal said, and the boy rushed to him, embracing him. Neal put one arm around his son and held the blanket up with his other hand. "How ya doin, boy?"

His voice was weak, his face dark and shadowy. He looked as if he had lost more than thirty pounds. His eyes were sunken and dark, his teeth bad, and thin strands of hair poked out under the cap. Miriam was impressed when Elgin helped his father get one leg under the table so he could straddle the bench. The boy hurried around to the other side to talk to his dad.

"Did we surprise you, Dad?"

Neal hesitated, thinking. "No, I believe the chaplain told me you might come." A flicker of amusement came to his eyes. "I never was much for bench sittin."

"Me either," Elgin said, and went into a long explanation of why he was not playing on a team this summer.

"That's a crime," Neal managed. "I oughta write somebody a letter and tell em I'm gonna sue em if they don't let you play."

"It's all right, Daddy," Elgin said. "If I don't get to play till next summer, I'm gonna be something because of that pitching machine," and he proceeded rapid-fire to bring him up to date on that. Neal, whose attention seemed to flag frequently, merely smiled and nodded occasionally.

Miriam knew that what she felt for the man was compassion and sympathy, not love. Still she felt as if she wanted to embrace him. What would be the harm now? There would be no false encouragement in it. The man was clearly dying. Anything and everything he had ever done had caught up with him, and now he was in an irreversible spiral toward the end, years before his time.

"El," he whispered, "there's some things I got to tell you, and then I want to talk to your momma. Listen to me. I want you to remember me for the good things, you hear? For what I could do on the ball field when I was healthy, for teachin you all that stuff. You know what I mean?"

"I inherited my baseball from you, Daddy."

"Well, it sounds like you're already better than I was at your age. But let me tell you somethin, boy. I been a liar all my life. I two-timed your momma from the day we started dating. You know what that means?"

"You had another girlfriend?"

He nodded miserably. "She wasn't someone you'd marry, just have fun with. Bad news. Bad thing to do. I even had other girlfriends after we was married."

Miriam wished Neal had spared Elgin this. It was little surprise to her, though she had tried to believe otherwise all her adult life. Now she would not begrudge Neal's one last attempt to have some positive influence on Elgin.

"I been an alcoholic since high school. Not just drinkin, but needin it, doin anything to get it, lettin it run my life. There were times when I controlled it a little, sometimes in the minors, just after your mom and I got married. But I never got a handle on it. My job was drinkin and everything else was just to finance it, right up till the time I killed that old man."

"You said that was an accident."

"Elgin, I'm tellin' you I was a liar. Believe what I told you about baseball. I never had to lie about my career or how to play the game. But everything else I ever told you, you can take to the dump. You know your mom believes I killed our baby."

"Yeah, but I know you—"

"Well, I did. I never doubted that from the minute it happened. I didn't kick her to hurt the baby. I was just drunk and not thinkin and ragin mad. As soon as I did it I knew, and just because they never busted me for it don't mean I didn't do it. I know I did and I live with it every day. That baby girl comes to me in the middle of the night sometimes and—"

Miriam stepped from behind Elgin to put her hand over Neal's. His lean, cold fingers twitched under hers.

"Neal, he's just a boy. Be careful, please."

Neal's lips had begun to quiver. "I just wanna tell you, El, don't ever even try booze. It'll kill you just like it's gonna kill me. I'm sorry for everything I've ever done that's made life hard for you. I wanted to give you everything and see you be whatever you wanted to be."

"I want to be a ballplayer like you, Daddy."

Neal shook his head and held up his free hand. The blanket slid from his shoulders. Miriam pulled it up around him again. He smelled of the infirmary.

"Be a ballplayer, El. But don't be like me."

He turned to force his other leg under the table, rested on his elbows, and held his face in his hands. Miriam went around and sat beside him, her knees facing away from the table. She pulled the blanket up around his shoulders again as his body jerked with his sobs.

"Daddy, I forgive you," Elgin said. "I forgive you for everything."

"You always have," Neal whined. "Even when I was still makin excuses and lyin about bein sorry."

Elgin looked at his mother and she felt the accusation in his glare.

"Give us a minute, honey," she told Elgin, but he hesitated. She looked to the chaplain, who hurried over. She signaled him with a nod toward Elgin.

"Son, let's give your mom and dad a couple of minutes, hm?"

"I'll be right back, Daddy."

Neal remained hidden behind his knuckly hands, weeping. "I'm through lyin, Mir," he said. "I never convinced you of anything anyway, but I'm through."

She could not look at him, and she knew he would not look at her. Something in her needed to hear this, yet she took no joy in his pain as she once had.

"Oh Miriam," he whimpered, "can't you forgive me? Everything you ever accused me of was true. I'm sorry for the other women, I'm sorry about the baby, I'm sorry about the old man, I'm sorry for what I've done to Elgin and to you."

She took his head in her hands and pulled him to her, cradling him like the baby he was, the pitiable, helpless, hopeless infant she had longed to rock in her arms since she lost her own at his hands.

"I need to hear you say it," he said, but she could not speak. How could she tell him what he wanted to hear? Why should he die in peace when she had to live in turmoil? He would not die in peace regardless of what she said. She would not lie. Why was the onus on her? He could apologize for a year and cry twenty-four hours a day and it would not bring back to her the treasures he had ripped away.

She did not doubt his sincerity. There was no more profit in his lying. Otherwise, he would lie. Unless he'd had some real transformation, he had simply come to the last dead end on the road of deceit. His alcoholism was beyond a character weakness by now. He could not be sorry for the hold it still had on him; he could be sorry only for the choices he had made that had brought him here. She held him and rocked him and heard his pathetic, woeful weeping.

He pulled back from her and looked into her eyes. His were the eyes of a dead man. "Call me a liar every time before. Say I was bein phony every time I turned over a new leaf, and you'd be right. Sometimes I thought I meant it, but I could never make it stick. This time, Mir, I got nothin to gain except your forgiveness. All you'll be sayin is that you won't hate me forever. That's all I want. Tell me you'll think about me sometime without hatin me and everything I was. At least remember that by the end I realized what I'd done and was truly, truly sorry."

Miriam held him again, pitying him. Forgive him? She would not be phony. That would be worse than anything he had ever done to her. "O God," she said silently, "only You can forgive this man. It's not in me."

How long, she wondered, has it been since I prayed?

Miriam felt Neal stiffen. He was trying to stop crying, maybe trying to regain some dignity. It was as if he realized his begging had been in vain, and now he wanted to stop groveling. In his now rigid shoulders she read the attitude, "If she doesn't want to forgive me, I don't want her pitying embrace either."

She let him straighten and pull away. He wiped his eyes with his fingers. He did not appear angry. Just frustrated, as if he didn't know what else to say or do and he knew she couldn't stand a weak, blubbering man.

Miriam remained leaning close to him, her left arm on the table in front of him. "You were one good-lookin high schooler," she whispered, feeling a smile play at her lips.

Neal backed up and looked at her in surprise. "I was, wasn't I?" he said, a painful grin forming.

"I was the envy of every girl in that high school when I landed you."

His face contorted again and the tears came. "Yeah, and look what I did to you. I was so proud to have you as my girl, and I spent the rest of my life ruining yours." He struggled for composure. "When I see what kind of a strong mother you've become, I only wish I'd somehow been able to stay with you. But I've got nobody but myself to blame."

He tried to bury his face in his hands again, but she took them in her own and set her face before his. "Neal Woodell, you were one scoundrel of a husband."

"I know I was."

She shushed him. "But it's all behind us now, isn't it?"

He nodded.

"Isn't it?" she repeated.

"Well, I'm sure sorry for it, I know that," he said.

"I know you are. But you snuffed out every last flicker of love I could have had for you."

"I'm not even hopin for that. I just want you to believe I'm sorry and to forgive me."

"You have been sorry so many times—"

"No, I wasn't. I was lyin then. I'm not lyin now."

She held him, and his neck and shoulders felt bony in her hands. God, help me. Who was she to be an agent of mercy and grace?

Neal's breath came as if he were exhausted. "Forgive me, Mir. Believe I'm sorry and forgive me."

She took a fluttery breath and pressed him closer. "I believe you, Neal. I believe you...and I forgive you."

40

NEAL DIDN'T STIR, DIDN'T SAY ANYTHING. His breathing was even and deep, almost as if he had fallen asleep.

Miriam felt an airy lightness, as if she herself had been forgiven. Some dignity had been restored. She had for years been in control in this relationship. She had held the key to the lockbox of a debt of guilt. Now she had allowed the guilty to pay her. She felt as if she could fly.

She gently nudged Neal away from her until he was sitting straight, staring. He seemed spent, as if he had nothing more to say or ask or do. He didn't smile, didn't thank her, didn't do anything but sit. Perhaps, she thought, she had made him wait so long for what he wanted to hear that he had convinced himself it was not forthcoming. Now it had come and he was stunned to silence, unable to take it in.

"We need to go soon, Neal," she said gently, wanting to run and jump and shout. She did not understand her own feelings. Was she finally, truly free of her albatross of all these years? And had it not really been him all along, but her own reaction to him?

"Would you like to talk to Elgin one more time?"

Neal stirred and squinted at her. "Awful tired. Yeah, I'd like to see El one more time."

She began to go get the boy, but Neal touched her arm and she stopped to face him. "One more time is probably it, you know," he said. "I'm probably never gonna see y'all again."

She pressed her lips together and nodded. She was past playing games with Neal. What was the point of polite dishonesty at this stage of a man's life?

"I'm never gonna see y'all again," he repeated.

⚾ ⚾ ⚾

His mother stayed with Chaplain Wallace as Elgin approached his father again. "Are you gonna be all right, Daddy?"

"Oh, I'll be all right, El. I'll be just fine now. Your mom and I got some things straight between us."

"Did she forgive you?"

"Yes, sir, she sure did."

"I didn't know if she ever would, Daddy."

"She probably shouldn't have."

"Why not? You were sorry. I knew that."

"Sometimes sorry isn't enough. And I was never as sorry as I am now, I know that."

They sat in silence for a while. Elgin wanted to talk baseball or anything but this. Somehow asking his dad about hitting the cutoff man didn't fit now.

"El, I'll probably never see you again. I—"

"Don't say that!"

"Well, it's true."

"I'll come see you again, Daddy. I promise. And I won't wait till you're sick again."

"Listen to me, boy. You ain't never goin to see me alive again. The next time you come see me, I'll be in the ground."

Elgin began to cry.

"I know that's no way to tell a boy somethin, but I've been a bad enough father as it is by not tellin you the truth. Well, that's the truth. I'll fight this thing, but they can't fool me. It's already whipped me and I can feel it."

"Daddy, please! We can't afford to come back down here soon! If you die, I won't even be able to come back for your funeral."

His father laughed a miserable laugh. "You want me to die today so you'll be in town for the fixins?"

"That's not funny."

"I just wanted to tell you, that's all, El. Now you can go on and blubber about it, and I guess I can't blame you. Except I was such a bad dad you shouldn't miss me too much. But it would make me feel a lot better, almost as good as your mom forgivin me, if I knew you were gonna be a better man than I ever was."

Elgin didn't know what to say. He decided on silence.

"Just tell me you'll take care of your ma, and—"

"Oh, Daddy!"

"—and that you'll be honest and not get mixed up with drinkin."

Elgin nodded and tried to stop crying. "I love you, Daddy." He hugged Neal's neck.

"I love you too, El, even though I was never good at—"

"I've already forgiven you, Daddy, so quit talking about it, okay?"

Neal laughed and sighed. "Okay, El. Okay."

Elgin pulled away from his dad and took a deep breath. "Daddy, I'm going to be the best ballplayer I can be, and I'm going to make the major leagues. I'm going to make you so proud you won't be able to stand it. When I play in my first big league game, they'll let you out to come see me, won't they?"

"I don't know. I guess they might."

"You keep thinking about that, and I'll keep thinking about that. We'll make it happen, Daddy. I'll remember everything you taught me and told me."

"Especially today?"

He nodded. "Especially today."

Neal rose uncertainly and put a hand on the table to steady himself. "Do me a favor, will you, El? If I can't make it, will you tell em you owe a lot of your baseball success to your dad?"

"I'll tell them I owe all my success to my dad!"

"No, no, now, that wouldn't be honest. You know I didn't give you that skill and that mind. And you know your mom deserves a lot of the credit for all she done for you without a man in the house."

"I know."

"So you tell the whole story. I'll be listenin. I'll wanna hear how your old man, Neal Lofert Woodell, helped make you what you are that day."

⚾ ⚾ ⚾

The next day, though their train was not scheduled to pull out of Birmingham until early evening, Miriam made the difficult decision to not return and see Neal before they left. Being closer to Hattiesburg, she made a few calls to relatives.

Her mother told her, "Word we get here is that Neal is dying of AIDS. Don't you dare touch him."

"That's a lie," Miriam said. "He's not well, but it's alcohol related."

"Alcohol. Well, how in the world does he get booze in prison? I mean, I—"

"Momma, I gotta get off the phone, if you don't mind. My love to everyone."

Such irresponsible talk was one of the reasons Miriam had moved to Chicago, and now she couldn't wait to get home.

Home. She had thought of Chicago as home. That, she knew, was significant. She had made the final break. She didn't let her mother's comment interfere with her joy. She was no less heartbroken or full of pity for Neal, but she sensed that some transaction had taken place, some closure. When she allowed herself to think about it, she shuddered at what her future might have held, had she not resolved this with him one-on-one.

"I don't see why we can't see him again," Elgin said in their tiny hotel room. "We have time."

"Someday you'll understand," she said.

"You always say that."

"And I'm always right. Honey, he'd look even worse today. We wore him out. We've said all we could say, and he has done the same. Let's let it be for a while."

"But he doesn't think he's going to live much longer."

"He looks pretty sick," she admitted.

"You don't think I'll ever see him again and you won't let me see him today?"

"Elgin, sit down." He sat on the bed. "I don't think any of the three of us needs the distress of another meetin just now. There's nothing more to say or do. Let's let him try to get stronger and see if he can turn this health thing around. Then when we get some more money we can come back and see him again."

Elgin lay on his side. "You don't believe that. You know he's going to die."

"I don't know for sure."

"But you think it."

"Yes, El, I do."

"Then why can't I see him?"

"Remembering the way he was yesterday is going to be difficult enough, Elgin. Why would you want to risk seeing him even sicker? Anyway, he wants you to remember his last advice."

"I'll never forget it."

"Then let's leave it at that."

"Can I write to him?"

"Of course. We can give it to the chaplain when he drives us to the train."

Elgin wrote a note, rehearsing what his father had said and renewing his promise to make the majors, to make his dad proud, and to be sure to give his dad credit for his success.

"I still want you at my first game," he reminded him. "Try to be there."

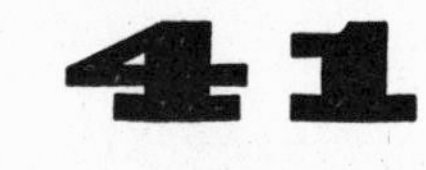

THREE DAYS LATER, WHEN THEIR TRAIN finally pulled into the Illinois Central station in Chicago—and while Miriam was running over in her mind the reverse trip to their place by bus and L—she heard her name.

"Mrs. Miriam Woodell, paging arriving passenger Mrs. Miriam Woodell!"

The message was from Rev. Wallace: "Please phone me collect immediately at your next stop." Miriam strode to a wood bench to collect herself, Elgin right behind her.

"What is it, Momma? Did Daddy call?"

"I'm to call the chaplain," she said.

"Why?"

"I'm afraid to think why, El," she said.

"If he died, I have to go to the funeral."

"I'm sorry, Elgin. You simply cannot."

"Can't we borrow the money? How can I miss my own dad's funeral?"

"Elgin, please don't make this more difficult. Goin would be the only right thing for me too. But we cannot and we will not be goin, and that is the end of it. Don't pretend I have a choice. If I could manage it, I would get you down there. But you saw him, you talked to him, you got things said—and so did he—that needed to be said. You can't feel bad about missing the funeral."

"Momma, I'll feel bad about it the rest of my life. We should've stayed down there."

"We couldn't have known how long he would linger. I can't say this surprises me, but I wouldn't have been surprised if he'd lasted out the year either."

"Momma, you've got to call that chaplain. I have to know for sure."

"Wait here," she said, "and watch our stuff."

Miriam moved to a pay phone where she could still see Elgin. He sat crying. The prison switchboard took a long time reaching Rev. Wallace.

"Mrs. Woodell," he said finally, "I'm so sorry I was unable to reach you earlier. They could have called the train directly. Well, I suppose you know why I'm calling."

"Yes, I'm afraid I do."

"He had an uneventful night and seemed to rally the morning after you were here. I did not tell him you were still in town. Late the evening your train left, they tell me about midnight, he had a seizure that led to a coughing spell. I'm sorry, ma'am, but I don't want to burden you with these details unless you want me to."

"I do, please."

"Well, it seems this seizure and the coughing caused a blood pressure crisis and eventually another heart attack. That did not kill him, but his kidneys failed by dawn. He was put on dialysis, but there is only so much a system can take. He was gone by noon."

"We were not that far away by then," Miriam said. "I might have thought about coming back."

"That was my hope and my intention," he said. "I'm sorry."

"Sir, my son gave you a note for him when you took us over to the train—"

"I gave it to him and he read it."

"Oh, thank God."

"Yes, ma'am. He said he wanted to answer it in the morning. He had it with him, in his hands, when I left him that night."

"Would you do me a favor and tell my son that?"

"Certainly."

"I mean, I know this is a collect call, but—"

"Put him on. Please."

A few minutes later, when Elgin handed the phone back to his mother, he did not return to the bench but stood and buried his head in her chest as she finished up with the chaplain.

"I want you to know, ma'am, that I believe Neal did make his peace with God sometime back. He was never terribly knowledgeable or articulate about his faith, but apparently he had been a churchgoer in his youth. I feel his devotion at the end was genuine."

"Well...yes, sir. Thank you for telling me that."

"And how about you, ma'am? Can I be of any assistance to you in that regard?"

"In regard to...?"

"Your own faith?"

"Well, I...we, we've only just recently found a church in Chicago."

She felt like a little girl, confessing to her pastor that she had been bad. Her church attendance had begun to decline when she first had problems with Neal. She gradually drifted even from making Elgin go to Sunday school. When they moved to Chicago she had made no attempt to find a church until Elgin had mentioned it once.

"Let me just say this, ma'am. I don't know how you're responding to your former husband's death, but I can tell it's difficult for the boy. I would encourage you to get some spiritual counsel up there. God cares personally about you. I'll not say any more. If you're unable to get to the funeral, I'll send you whatever documents are appropriate. I'm sorry Neal's life ended this way, ma'am. You should know that he was very thankful he got to see you both again. And I very much appreciated your comments to him."

"I meant them, sir. I wasn't just talking."

"I sensed that when he shared them with me. Good-bye, Mrs. Woodell."

It was a lonely, silent trip home from the train station. Miriam saw Elgin clenching and unclenching his fists, his eyes dark and narrow, his lips pressed tight. She didn't want him to grow bitter or angry. "You understand why we can't go to the funeral," she said as they approached the hotel.

"Uh-huh. I know."

"You gonna be okay, baby?" she said.

"I don't know. I'm not sure. This sure feels weird."

"Let me ask you something before we have to answer Ricardo's questions about our vacation. Do you like that church we visited, and do you want to keep going?"

He looked at her and tilted his head. "I guess."

"Does that mean yes?"

"It'd be okay. I wouldn't want you to go alone. I wouldn't go without you, if that's what you're thinking."

"No, it would be you and me, El. Like we used to a long time ago."

"Not tonight, though, right?"

She laughed. "No. Not tonight."

⚾ ⚾ ⚾

"Ah! You're back! And how was the trip? Let me help you with those!"

"Thank you, Ricardo. I'm afraid we have suffered a death in the family, so we're not much in a talking mood."

"Oh, how horrible! May I ask whom?"

"Elgin's father."

"Not an old man. Sudden?"

"Heart attack and complications." She put her finger to her lips and glanced at Elgin, who was studying the floor.

"Well," Mr. Bravura said, "I am so sorry."

He helped with the bags without another word, not even of farewell. He didn't pester to know if the return address on her Fed Ex package had anything to do with her former husband. He didn't gush about deaths in his family or about how time heals wounds. He just carried the suitcases from the elevator to their apartment, set them in the middle of the floor, bowed to her without a word, and slipped out, closing the door behind him. Just as Miriam was wondering if he'd had a transfusion of sensitivity, he knocked lightly and poked his head back in.

"Forgive me, I almost forgot. A small but heavy package came for your son from Lucky's Second-hand Shop. May I run it up?"

"Oh, don't bother. Elgin can get it in the morning."

"No bother, ma'am. No bother at all. I'll leave it outside the door and knock. Okay?"

"Thank you, Ricardo."

⚾ ⚾ ⚾

Elgin had undressed and was sitting on the couch when the knock came. His mother fetched the package. It was a shoe box wrapped in brown paper, and it was indeed heavy. A note inside read:

> Master Woodell, Mr. Harkness has already paid me $120 for this rebuilt motor with the clutch and gears you desired. You'll notice that it can be run with or without engaging the gears. If it works as you hope, you may settle up with him. Any problems, call me at the number below. It's been a pleasure.

Elgin set the box aside and thought about turning on the television. That didn't appeal either. He didn't even want to talk to his mother, who seemed to be watching him carefully.

All he wanted was to sit and think about his dad. As if he had a choice. No matter what he thought about, his thoughts came back to Daddy.

Well, he thought, he won't make it to my first big league game. But he'll be the reason I'm there.

For Elgin Woodell had determined on the ride home, when his mother had noticed his clenched fists, that he would turn up the heat. He would do anything and everything it took to become the best baseball player possible. And he would start as soon as he felt like working out again.

42

MIRIAM'S SYMPATHY CARD TO NEAL'S PARENTS crossed a scathing note from her own mother about her not getting Elgin to his father's burial—"I can understand your not wanting to go, though you should have anyway, but to keep that boy away is shameful."

Miriam didn't feel like defending herself. Her own grieving for Neal was a strange, unpredictable progression of emotions. Sometimes at work, sometimes at home, sometimes alone, sometimes in a crowd, sometimes with Elgin there, sometimes with him in the basement, she was overcome with melancholy. The distant memories didn't seem so distant now. The man she had prayed to be rid of was now more a part of her life than when he was alive and in prison. He dominated her thoughts, reminded her of how things had been. When she found herself weeping, sometimes sobbing, she knew it wasn't over missing him or merely longing for a man in her life. She wept for Neal, for the sad, frustrated, miserable lonely man he had become.

She found it difficult to draw out Elgin now. His face was more sober, his eyes darker. He was, she knew, nearing puberty. She looked forward to how manly that would make him, and she dreaded the mysterious new interests and passions it would engender in him. She'd seen, heard, and read enough to know that she was ill equipped to deal with an insolent teenager. She prayed he would keep his sweet innocence, though she knew she was dreaming.

⚾ ⚾ ⚾

Elgin suffered but somehow knew to channel his grief and a strange anger into his goal. He wanted to be the best baseball player he could be. Not the best of all time, unless that was what was in him. As his dad had drilled into him: "Find your level, find your limit, push it until you know. Don't worry about who's better or different. Your job is to be the best you can be, because you can't do more than that."

Elgin knew he was the best ballplayer of his age he had ever seen. He wondered if there were any others like him anywhere, but he didn't invest much time pondering it. Even if there were, he knew what they were thinking. They didn't want to compete with kids their own age any more than he did. Sure, it would be fun matching skills with someone like himself, but how many could there be? And once the two or three of them who might exist decided which was the best, they would want to get on a team—of teens, collegians, adults?—where they could forget who was best or who was ahead for his age and merely play some ball. Competitive baseball. That's what he wanted, and that's what he missed. He was frustrated beyond comprehension to be unable to play on a team.

He worked every day at Lucky's, and he worked out every night in his private arena. The new motor for the pitching machine was so good it was frightening. Not only did Elgin use it with the gear sometimes engaged and sometimes not, but he had also figured out that he could tighten a screw halfway and cause the machine to throw hundreds of random pitches with zero predictability.

It was like facing the monster for the first time again. Elgin had no idea which pitch was coming, how fast or from which direction. The gears could fire a straight pitch at his head so fast he could barely evade it, then come back with a dancing, sweeping curve that looked as if it might hit him in the rear but would then break across the outside of the plate. There was no more hitting a half-dozen or more solid shots for every bucket of fifty-seven balls. He tried to read the spin and location of each pitch in time to dive for cover or get a bat on it. He was light on his feet in the box, knowing he had to keep the back foot buried for a perfect swing, yet always ready to leave the floor for a fastball at the shins.

Elgin used only his heavy, skinny fungo bat, but he fought through the frustration of hitless buckets knowing that, just as with his introduction to the contraption months and months before, he would catch on. Better than that, this would make hitting a baseball like breathing. Elgin hung around the fastpitch street but was not allowed to play except to show off. He could hit virtually any reachable pitch for a home run. It was fun only as long as the other players oohed and aahed. He got some of the guys to occasionally play catch with him with his rubber-coated baseball, but Chico had moved on to other pursuits, and most of the others didn't see the point of just throwing a ball around.

Lucky sometimes hit balls to Elgin, but he couldn't hit hard enough to challenge him. Elgin had to compare everything with what he could do in the cellar. Somehow he knew that nothing could compete with that until he found a whole team he could match in ability. He sensed that Hector Villagrande had such a team, and his goal was to make that team the next year when he was thirteen. What both drove him and made him crazy was that he knew he was ready now.

He stood at the plate in the basement with his glove on, trying to catch as many pitches in a row as possible. Once he caught fourteen straight before seeing a wicked curve skip off his glove, bang off the wall, and hit him in the triceps. He jumped and howled and rubbed it vigorously, then flung his bat at the machine. As had happened before, the impact moved the thing an inch or so and caused it to throw its unpredictable pitches into the corner, and he had to dive out of the way.

Eventually he learned to catch fifty pitches per bucket, sometimes standing near the machine and catching the grounders and liners after they came off the wall. He dove and lurched and reached and stretched until he sweat through his clothes, and he was getting into incredible shape, matching the growth of his frame with hard muscle and coordination.

He had hoped to take Raleigh Lincoln Sr. up on his offer to pitch batting practice, but that worked out only twice. He didn't feel bold enough to push it, and the man was busy with his own playing and coaching. The two times they got together, however, were heavenly. The cellar was driving Elgin crazy, and the need for some competition, and especially some feedback, some strokes, was crucial.

Though by the middle of the summer he was hitting only a dozen or so balls solid from each bucket of offerings, he hit Mr. Lincoln like he owned him. He took any pitch he sensed was a quarter-inch off the plate, and he drove hard nearly everything else. The man shook his head.

"It's like facing a big leaguer," he said. "I don't want to puff you up and mess you up, but you hit me like nobody ever has, and I mean nobody. I know I haven't got the stuff I once had, but no local adult hits me good. I can't believe your eye. Where in the world did you develop that?"

"I guess I just have a sense of where the plate is," Elgin said softly. "My dad said good hitters will walk a lot, not get too eager. And my stance gets both my eyes on the pitch."

"I feel like I need to have a talk with Hector," Raleigh said. "He doesn't know what he's passing up."

"His team's doing okay."

"I should say they are! They've only lost two and they're going to win the state. But I never knew a team that couldn't be improved. You could start on that team, boy."

"Maybe next year."

"Maybe? You don't make that team next year, and I'm gonna get Hector fired and take it myself. You don't make it next year, and I'll get you on the city league!"

Elgin laughed. "You have to be eighteen for that."

"Even so, you'd be one of the best hitters in that league, son, and I'm not putting you on."

That was the kind of encouragement Elgin needed, though it was not news to him. He could see how he was hitting, even if Raleigh Lincoln had said nothing. How he wanted to play in a live game! Several times he thought about pleading with Hector Villagrande to let him work out with his team. He dreamed of being so dominating, so impressive that the man would have to make room for him, not just on the bench but in the lineup.

But he had already shown Hector his stuff. The man himself had said he'd never seen a hitting performance like that. So Elgin would wait, continuing to work out for as many hours as his mother would let him every day. He continued to read and think and dream baseball.

One day in the dead of winter, everything seemed to miraculously fall together for him. A bad cold had kept him away from the cellar for two days. That break was somehow what he had needed. It made him sharp, allowed him to focus on the precise skills necessary to watch, gauge, and hit. Though it had taken him hundreds of thousands of pitches, he seemed to have succeeded overnight. He began to hit consistently off the monstrous machine he had tamed.

Elgin began to focus on March when tryouts would be held for local teams.

Miriam didn't know what to think anymore about Elgin's obsession. It was as if his disappointment at not making the team and the devastating loss of his father had driven him deep into himself. There was a determination, a dedication in him that frightened her. Had anyone anywhere ever been so unbendingly committed to anything?

One night at dinner, as the snow outside turned to slush and the spring tryouts and his thirteenth birthday approached, he said, "Momma, I think I'm ready for you to come to the basement with me and see something."

"I thought you'd never ask," she said. "What in the world have you been doing down there?"

"What do you think?"

"Oh, I think I know. But I decided a long time ago not to come down there until you were ready to ask me."

"Well, I'm ready. But you're not going to believe it."

⚾ ⚾ ⚾

The basement workout cell was as dark and foreboding as ever. That skinny little bat looked heavy and impossible to hit with. The machine was ugly and noisy. She had not seen it work with the new motor, but she had heard him talk about it enough.

But what was this? The machine looked closer to the batter's boxes.

"Elgin?" she said simply as she approached it.

He was nodding. "Yup. Closer. By more than ten feet."

"You used to have it as close to the back wall as possible. You said—"

"I said it was only two-thirds of major league distance. Now it's half."

"Well, is it that much slower with the new motor?"

He said it was faster, then told her where to stand: with her body outside the door frame, her face peeking in.

"Nothing should hit you there, but be ready to duck," he said.

She stood obediently outside the door frame, her head poked around the corner. He cleared the room of everything but himself, his helmet, his bat, and the machine. Everything else he tossed past her near the stairs.

How long could it have taken him to get used to the new motor, the new speed, the new distance? How much tinkering would he have had to do to get the thing to throw balls that were reachable? It had to have been hours, yet she knew he would have never given up, no matter how long it took.

The machine whirred to life, but Elgin did not hurry to the batter's box. He watched the first pitch slam so hard off the wall that it carried all the way to the other end and whapped against the canvas drop. Miriam jumped, ready to get out of the way, but Elgin seemed to casually study the ball. He stood just outside the left-hand batter's box, his bat dangling from his right hand, as the next pitch swept at him and in over the plate.

With that he crisply stepped into the box and set himself. The next dozen or so pitches were a variety of demon darts that flew all over the place. One started high and dropped into the strike zone. One appeared to be ankle high until the last instant when it flashed up to his knees. The only pitch he didn't swing at came in right under his chin. He moved only a fraction to elude it.

On all the other pitches, Elgin turned with a controlled but mighty swing. The sound of metal on plastic resounded from the walls and each pitch was driven hard to the canvas. As far as Miriam could tell there was not even a pop-up or fly ball. All sped to the other end of the room on a line, most of them directly over the machine.

Elgin slipped around to the other batter's box. Now batting righty he continued his barrage, stepping, swinging, driving, recoiling, and doing it again and again. His eyes looked alive, narrow, piercing in the dim light. He seemed to watch and see nothing but the ball. At that distance each pitch came in what seemed like milliseconds. How could he react? How could he hit with such authority? She knew it could be only the hours and hours of practice. This had cost him bruises and frustration, but now they had paid off—if being able to hit the hideous machine was payment enough.

Elgin was high after the performance. He had hit fifty line drives as if he and the pitches were part of the same script.

"Help me pick em up!" he exulted. "I want to show you something."

He had already shown her something. Miriam gathered up a few balls as if in a trance and dropped them into the bucket as Elgin hurried past. She wanted to compliment him, to express her wonder, to ask what the future might hold. Words would not come. Elgin just looked at her and grinned and didn't demand any response.

He knew, she decided. He knew how she would react. There was nothing to say, nothing to be said ever. He had made himself into a miracle. She wondered if an adult athlete could have done the same. Surely a big leaguer could do this. But would he have the patience to teach himself?

As she picked up three balls in a corner, she envisioned her son on television, on programs about people who do amazing things. Could he make a living at it? Would other people copy him and get better at it than he?

"Watch this!" Elgin shouted. "Take cover!"

He poured the balls into the machine, which was still running. She skipped out of the way. He leaned past her and traded his fungo bat for his glove. He stood on the plate, his eyes wild, as the first pitch came.

He was not quite ready and it swept above his head, hitting the wall within inches of him. He whooped and hollered, and she wondered if he had lost his mind. She wanted to tell him to stop, to quit showing off, to not try to do something he couldn't do. It was enough that he could hit this crazy pitching; he didn't have to catch it too.

Who was this child? Had he come from her womb? Yesterday he was a baby, a kid who, like most kids, loved baseball. Now he was a contrivance, a marvelously gifted and trained and honed and polished machine with a brain.

The pitches bounced in, swept in, sped in, dropped, rose, danced, curved, slid, broke. He caught one after the other, his face set, eyes afire. As each slammed into his glove, he casually shook it loose and let it bounce away like a too small fish, then set himself again.

"How do you know?" she shouted.

"Know what?"

"Where the ball will go! They all look different!"

"They *are* different! You never know. You have to be ready for anything and watch where it goes and what kind of a spin it has!"

Catch and drop, catch and drop, catch and drop. He looked like a big leaguer. What team could possibly be good enough for him?

Half an hour later, as he sat at the table in the kitchenette eating popcorn, she could tell he was thrilled that he had impressed her. He never asked, "So, what do you think?" He just sat and watched her, his smile huge, his eyes wide. He knew. She could tell he knew.

"What are we going to do, El?" she managed finally. "You have got to do something with this."

"Do something with this? This is nothing. This is just for baseball. This is what I'll do every day for the rest of my life to keep me sharp for hitting live pitching. That's all."

"You don't think people would pay to see you do something that no one else anywhere could dare even try?"

"Momma! I'm not a freak."

She wasn't so sure. "But you could challenge people, make them guess whether or not you could do it. Show it to them, demonstrate it. Then get them to bet that you wouldn't dare even stand in against it, let alone be able to hit it with a skinny, heavy bat."

"Momma, even if I could do that or wanted to—which I don't—what do you think it would pay?"

"A lot."

"Like millions a year?"

"Well, no, of course not, but—"

"That's what I can make as a big leaguer."

"That's a lot of years away."

"I know. But by then I'll be able to make even more. You know what? I'm on a schedule."

"To become a big leaguer?"

"To move the machine even closer to the batter's boxes."

"Oh Elgin, no."

"What? You think I can't do it?"

Would she ever again think he couldn't do something, anything?

⚾ ⚾ ⚾

She didn't want to watch. She didn't want to see that machine taking aim at her son from twenty or even twenty-five feet away. She just listened to him tell of it every day for the next several weeks.

"Just for fun," he told her, "I moved the thing to about fifteen feet away. I think I finally found out what I can't hit."

They both laughed.

"What about from twenty and twenty-five feet?" she asked him.

"I can hit almost every pitch. They don't have time to move out of the strike zone. If it's in there, I get around on it. I'm swinging faster than ever. Bat speed is more important than power, you know."

"I know," she said. He had told her enough times. Before he could say it, she quickly interjected, "In fact, bat speed *is* power."

"You're learning, Momma. You coming to my tryout a week from Saturday?"

"If you'll let me."

"I want as many people watching as I can. Lucky's bringing his family."

Miriam's heart seemed to stop. "His family?" She knew her voice was weak.

"Yeah. He's got two younger brothers and a bunch of nieces and nephews in the suburbs."

"Is he married?" She tried to sound casual.

"I thought I told you, Momma. His wife died when he was in Desert Storm. Cancer or something like that."

"Right."

43

LUKE HARKNESS, HIS TWO BROTHERS, their wives and six children, and Miriam were not the only spectators at the high school all-star summer traveling team tryouts. Hector Villagrande had eight spots to fill, and he required his six returning players to try out again too. There were no guarantees, he had always said, and he proved that nearly every year by cutting at least one returnee.

It appeared that the parents and a few other relatives or friends of every hopeful showed up to sit in the rickety stands at the old Lane Tech practice field. Several of Elgin's former teammates were there, including Raleigh Lincoln Jr. He wasn't trying out. ("My dad says I'm not ready, and if anybody should know, he should.") Of course, Raleigh Sr. was there too.

Elgin guessed there were a hundred in the stands. About twenty ballplayers, plus the six returnees, had been invited to the tryout. Elgin finished second in the wind sprints to one of the returnees, the six-foot, two-hundred-pound shortstop. He finished fourth in throwing for distance, behind the shortstop, his twin brother second baseman, and a stocky Mexican pitcher. When they ran around the entire field, Elgin leaped to an early lead and held off a small, skinny outfielder he guessed would not make the team.

Elgin tried pitching and estimated he was in the top half-dozen contenders. His control was excellent, his speed above average, but his pitches did not move like those of the bigger, stronger players. He knew his pitch selection would probably be among the best, but pitching was not his priority.

He had a little trouble running down everything hit to him in the outfield workout, but that was the one area in which he had the least experience. The few times Lucky had hit him flies, he had done all right, but

Hector and his assistants sent them back to the fence on almost every shot.

It was in infield practice where Elgin shone. His throws from short were straighter and truer than they had been the year before, but he knew he could not compete against the huge twin. He felt much more comfortable at second, where the throw was shorter and he quickly picked up the double play pivot. But the other twin seemed to have a lock on that spot as well. His only hope was to hit so well that Hector would be forced to find a place for him.

Coach Villagrande had saved the hitting tryout till last. He called all the players around him and assigned them to various spots in the field. Fourteen of them would trade off at the infield and outfield positions with every hitter. His returning catcher would handle all of batting practice. The nine remaining players would get ten pitches each.

The pitching would be handled by a quartet of huge hurlers from a local college team. Elgin knew who they were from having read about them. Each was a big league prospect. The youngest was twenty, the oldest twenty-two. Three were right-handers. The other was a bald lefty. He didn't even have a rim of hair, nothing showing beneath the cap line.

Elgin couldn't wait to face any one of them. But first he had to play the field. He was sent to second where he traded off with the veteran with each new pitcher. One of the right-handers was on the mound, and apparently he and his cohorts had all been told the same thing.

No mercy.

⚾ ⚾ ⚾

Miriam had not brought a warm enough wrap to the tryout. Wrap. She smiled as she thought of the word. In Hattiesburg the elementary school teachers had warned the children that during the winter months, even though they had never seen snow, they still needed to remember their wraps for chilly mornings.

Though the sun was high and bright in Chicago, Miriam sat shivering in a light jacket, one she was embarrassed to be wearing in front of Lucky anyway. But he was not a wealthy man and had never put on airs. She knew he knew her situation, where she lived, where she worked, what she had, what she didn't have.

"Should have brought my winter coat," she said idly, but she was certain he hadn't heard. He was a mother hen with his nieces and nephews and always had an eye on them, even when conversing with her.

"Uh-huh," was all he said. But as she stared at Elgin, who was apparently failing in an attempt at small talk with the other second baseman, Luke Harkness draped his wool-lined leather jacket around her shoulders. His hands did not linger. She smiled a thank you at him and he looked away.

"I don't want *you* to be cold now," she said.

"I've got a higher thermostat than you," he said. "I'll probably have to get rid of this sweater, too, before long."

⚾ ⚾ ⚾

"Nobody seems to be able to hit these guys," Elgin said.

"Yeah, well, my brother and me'll hit em," the second baseman said. "Just watch."

"I expect to hit them too," Elgin said, but the boy didn't respond. "What's your name, anyway?"

"Dirk," the boy grunted. "My turn."

"My name's Elgin," he said as Dirk glided into position to field a weak grounder. It was the only fair ball hit off the four pitchers. Five hitters had gone down weakly, and the pitchers kept rotating, sometimes two or three would throw to the same hitter.

"We all know your name, buddy," Dirk said, not unkindly. "You've got a lot to prove today."

Elgin wanted to say he had nothing to prove, that he had proved all he needed to prove last time he had tried out for this team. But he said nothing. It couldn't be better, he decided, that they knew who he was and were watching to see what he could do.

"You're not going to get any baserunners this morning," Hector Villagrande hollered, "so play every grounder as if you've got a guy on first and less than two outs!"

"Lefty pitching, Dirk," Elgin whispered. "This guy gets a bat on Baldy, it's coming to you."

Dirk turned to glare at Elgin. "Baldy happens to be my cousin!"

Elgin wanted to apologize, to say he hadn't meant anything by it. But the fair, thin kid who had been so impressive in the distance run—who had swung and missed weakly at Baldy's first three offerings—had somehow got his bat on this one, and it rocketed between second and first.

Dirk heard the impact just before Elgin shouted his name, but he whirled back too late and couldn't get his glove down or his foot out of the way in time to avoid taking the liner off the top of his shoe. He spun and danced and howled as the ball skittered into right field.

"You all right?" Coach Villagrande screamed, marching from the third base dugout to the foul line.

"Yeah! Woodell was distractin me!"

"Well, get out of there!"

Elgin thought Hector was talking to him. He was not.

"If you can't keep your head and your glove in the game, let somebody in there who can! Get in there, Woodell!"

"Sorry, Dirk," Elgin said sincerely as he traded places with the red-faced, swearing boy. The look he got was of pure hatred.

Two batters and a couple of dozen pitches later, a left-handed hitter, fooled and out front of a change-up, grounded sharply to the left of first. The first baseman raced to his right, but Elgin hollered him off. Elgin speared the ball to his left, spun all the way around, and fired to the right of second. Dick, Dirk's twin, arrived just in time to drag his trailing foot across the bag as he gathered in the throw and rifled the ball to first, as hard as any pitch thrown all day.

Elgin crouched to avoid it, then had to go face-first into the dirt to keep from being hit. The first baseman had not gotten back in time to be in on the bang-bang play, but the pitcher had come over to take the throw.

The crispness, speed, and power of the play left fans and prospects speechless. The pitcher jogged over to slap gloves with Elgin, who beamed, and Dick, who did not. He was scowling at Elgin.

⚾ ⚾ ⚾

In the stands, Lucas leaned close to Miriam and bumped her with his knee. "That boy is gonna be your security someday, you know that?"

She smiled, not entirely sure what he meant.

"He's got big league written all over him. I don't expect he'll hit these pitchers any better'n the rest, but he won't do any worse. And he's so much younger."

Miriam just smiled. She liked the idea of Elgin as her wrap in the cooler, fall years of her life, almost as much as she would have enjoyed Lucky's arm around her shoulder. She had a delicious secret, too. She had a feeling Elgin could hit these guys, all of them, any one of them, even the left-hander.

Elgin was called in to hit. Miriam saw him pick up both his wood bat and his aluminum bat. She hoped he would chose the metal one, but she was not surprised when he tossed it away and stepped in with the wood. He was a purist, a single-minded, obsessed player with his sights on the future. There was no sense getting anywhere with an advantage he could not carry with him to the majors someday.

He looked like a big leaguer to her already, the way he dug in on the left side, pressed his helmet down with a free hand, and studied the pitcher. He took the first pitch, which was at the waist but outside by about two inches.

"Close enough to hit!" Hector called.

The next pitch would have split the plate if Elgin had not driven it to the left center-field wall on one hop. The pitcher smiled and began to work harder. Elgin took every pitch that was off the plate, and none were off by more than a couple of inches. Hector barked his disapproval with every taken pitch, but the line drives to all fields kept him mostly quiet.

Elgin hit six liners, a foul homer, and two foul tips, swinging and missing once against the first right-hander. He started to leave the box when the pitcher tossed the ball to the bald lefty, but Hector told him to stay in.

"I want you to take four pitches from each of the other three pitchers," he said. "And I want you to swing at every pitch, even if it's two feet off the plate."

Elgin nodded.

"Do you understand, Woodell? Because I am serious."

Elgin nodded again, keeping his eye on the pitcher.

"Let me hear you!" Hector hollered.

Miriam wondered why he had to be so mean. It was clear Elgin heard him and would obey. What had the boy done during the tryout the summer before that had made the coach so nasty to him? She prayed Elgin would do as well against these other pitchers as he had done against the first.

⚾ ⚾ ⚾

Elgin was so excited he could hardly stand it. He knew he was facing the best pitching of his life, even better than Raleigh Lincoln Sr. These guys were big and young and strong and fast and smart. Their pitches moved. They had pride. They didn't want anyone hitting them, and they didn't expect many high schoolers would. Of course, they hadn't yet faced Dick, who had hit over .400 the season before. But they surely didn't guess the almost-thirteen-year-old would make them look like batting practice pitchers.

Their assignment had been—as Hector had told everyone—to show these kids what real pitching was all about. He had told the players to not expect to get a bat on the ball off any of these guys.

"Then you won't be disappointed. And when they're done with you, we'll throw you some real BP and you can show us what you've got."

The plan had gone as expected until Elgin had stepped in and made the first right-hander look hittable.

"The other guys wore him out for you," Hector said as the pitchers traded places. But that comment brought laughter from the crowd. They had to wonder if anybody could get this kid out.

"You want any warm-up pitches?" Elgin asked the left-hander.

"Just get in there," Baldy growled. "All I want is you."

Elgin skipped around to the other side of the plate and dug in. He looked up just in time to see the first pitch sailing at his head. He ducked just a couple of inches and the ball skipped lightly off the top of his helmet and banged off one of the backstop posts, rolling all the way back to the mound. With more fortitude than even he thought he had, Elgin pretended not to have seen or felt the pitch. A collective gasp had been sucked in by the crowd, and Elgin would learn later that both his mother and Luke had been fooled.

From the corner of his eye Elgin saw Baldy pick up the ball and go into his wind-up again. Elgin was ready and correctly guessed the pitch would jam him. He stepped toward third and dragged his bat through the strike zone, drilling the ball straight back at the pitcher, right to his glove. The pitcher stared at him. Elgin stared back. The next pitch came flashing toward the outside corner with as much movement as Elgin had seen on a live pitch. It was nothing like the machine could do. It looked big and slow compared to that. But Elgin had wasted too many hundredths of a second convincing himself it would be a ball. He had intended to take it, then remembered he was supposed to swing at everything. He swung late and missed.

The pitcher looked pumped, but the strike had served only to get Elgin into his rhythm. He knew the left-hander could not get another hittable pitch past him. He was in sync, ready to hit, eager for the lefty's best stuff.

Just before Baldy went into his wind-up, Hector Villagrande shouted, "Last pitch!"

Elgin backed out of the box and stared at the coach.

"I mean with this pitcher," Hector said. "You still face the other two guys."

Elgin stepped back in, but now Baldy was glaring at the coach.

"Okay!" Hector said. "What do you want?"

"I want to strike him out!" Baldy said.

"Try," Hector said, and Elgin heard bemusement in his voice.

Elgin cracked a high, outside pitch into right center. He sent a low pitch, which would have nipped the corner, screaming past Dirk at second base. When he did the same with an inside curve, Hector chirped at him, "Hey, hey, hey, you're not trying to show anybody up except the pitcher. You take the inside pitch to left. You can spray the outside pitches to the right side."

Elgin had been caught. He liked seeing Dirk bend and stretch and grunt after a ball just out of his reach.

These pitches, moving and impressive in one sense, looked big and slow and fat compared to those from his pitching machine, whipping tiny golf balls at him from twenty-five feet away. Here he had time to think, to calculate, to see the rotation, to make his judgment. He knew experts would think he was crazy if he ever said aloud that he hit different pitches at differing points on the ball.

But it was true. Though most people believed it was impossible for hitters to really see 85 m.p.h. and faster pitches hit their bats, Elgin knew he could. This guy was easily throwing that hard, and Elgin hit on top of the ball to create a top spin that curled it over the infield and to the ground before the outfielders could get to it. He felt as if he could do that all day. When he wanted height and distance, say for a deep sacrifice fly, he hit under the ball. And with every swing, he believed he was seeing the ball and the bat meet.

Baldy was sweating on this chilly morning. He made Elgin swing and miss once and foul off three pitches. At one point he had him down one-and-two, before Elgin flied deep to left. Hector waved the lefty out of there and let the other two righties have a shot. From the other side of the plate, Elgin missed a few good change-ups and popped weakly twice, but mostly he continued to flare solid hits to all fields. He hit several grounders just out of the reach of the infielders, and when he hit one each right to Dick and Dirk, they were so eager that one overthrew first and the other muffed the play.

Other prospects tried to hit the four aces that day, but the Elgin Woodell legend had accelerated. No one would talk about anything else that happened there. Hector brought in a true batting practice pitcher and let everyone have his raps. Everyone except Elgin. Hector asked him to go across the street with Raleigh Lincoln and take infield practice. Raleigh's son played first. Elgin played short and second. Luke Harkness caught for Mr. Lincoln.

⚾ ⚾ ⚾

Miriam stayed in the stands at the practice diamond. She could see the private workout from where she sat, and she sensed something significant was going on. At some point soon she would want to be in on it, to know what was to happen with and to her son. But for now she sat in the bright, late morning chill, wrapped in Luke's leather jacket, breathing the fresh maleness of it and wondering. Lucas Harkness was not a natural. He could catch the ball and toss it to Mr. Lincoln but he wasn't born to the diamond, didn't glide around it and adjust automatically to short hops or high throws. He wasn't a klutz either, and he did know the game, but neither was he a player. Still, she could see in his demeanor that he was excited. He wasn't the type to chatter. He wouldn't be over there asking the big black man if he wasn't impressed with this kid. No, it would be more like Luke to just enjoy being in on it.

Mr. Lincoln drove hard grounders and liners at Elgin. The boy ran, crouched, dove, speared, pivoted, threw. He wasn't perfect, but he was something, Miriam decided. What other kid that age could catch such missiles off the bat of an adult who was pushing to see how good he was?

The tryout broke up. Coach Villagrande addressed the adults, telling them when the next session would be, telling them that some would be getting calls during the week informing them that their sons need not show up again. He told them not to feel bad, that everyone had done well, it was a difficult decision, choosing between better and best, all that.

While the other parents and guardians had moved down closer to the coach as he spoke, Miriam had stayed where she was. She listened, but somehow she knew she was no more a part of this group of parents than Elgin was part of this team. There was no way he could be cut this time. He was the best hitter already. From what she could see on the other diamond, he was one of the best fielders and throwers too. He didn't have the range or the arms of the twins, but then they were eighteen.

As adults and players drifted from the stands and the field, Miriam remained, cozy and excited. Luke's relatives waved their good-byes to her and to him and left with everyone else. The workout across the street continued.

Hector spoke briefly with his coaches before they gathered up the equipment and headed for their cars. He cast a brief glance her way before kneeling in front of the dugout to talk to the four American Legion pitchers. When they left, only Hector and Miriam remained in the rickety old park.

He moved to the fence and peered across the street.

"Had enough?" Raleigh bellowed.

"I can play all day," Elgin said in the clear, high-pitched voice of youth.

Hector looked up at Miriam and held up an index finger, as if asking her to wait where she was. She felt honored. He could have beckoned her to talk to him, but he was going to come to her. Raleigh Lincoln Jr. was sent to wait in his father's car while his dad, Luke, and Elgin returned to the practice field. Hector asked Elgin and Luke to wait for him, and they trudged up to Miriam. Luke looked as excited as Elgin, who also looked exhausted. Miriam offered Luke his jacket.

"Are you kidding?" he said, squinting and smiling. He took off his sweater and sat huffing and puffing.

"What's happening?" she said.

"Coach wants us to wait here," Elgin said. "He'll be up."

Miriam was disappointed to see Raleigh Lincoln leave. She had wanted to meet him. She stood as Hector approached, climbing gingerly up the wood steps.

"Please," he said, in what she thought was a charming accent. "Sit down. I need to talk to you privately."

Luke moved away with Elgin.

"Mrs. Woodell, I have sent Mr. Lincoln to see if he can get hold of Jim Koenig, coach of the local summer collegiate team. I would like him to be in on our discussion."

"Why?"

"I know it will sound strange to you, ma'am, but I believe Elgin is ready for that level."

"Not totally strange," she said. "I could see what was happening today. He can compete at this level."

"Yes, but we would be holding him back."

"You know he's had very little actual game experience. Just parts of a couple of seasons and one full one."

Hector smiled shyly. "And part of that is my fault, is it not?"

Miriam shrugged.

"Of course it is," he said. "But if my not finding him a spot last year—on my team or any other—had anything to do with the determination that made him work as hard as he has, I deserve some credit."

Miriam smiled and said nothing.

"Elgin!" Hector called out, "come join us for a moment. I need to know if you felt you could hit the ball anywhere you wanted off those four pitchers."

Elgin nodded as he rejoined them.

"You *were* hitting, in other words, at my shortstop and second baseman on purpose?"

Elgin hesitated.

"You can tell me. I know they can be difficult. Both are excellent players and you made them look bad."

"I'm sorry."

"But you did it on purpose."

"I shouldn't have. I'm sorry. They could have looked just as good if they had fielded those balls."

"You were hitting them just out of their reach."

Elgin nodded apologetically again.

"You showed hints of being able to do that last year when I thought you were not ready. But you were not hitting off the caliber of pitchers you hit off today. Do you have any idea of the limits of your potential?"

"No, sir, and that's just it. I want to play games. I need game situations. I mean, I know the game and I think I know what to do and when to do it, but it's killing me not to be able to do it in competition."

"I wish I could help you."

"You're telling me I'm not going to make this team again?"

Hector held up a hand. "Last year you had the ability and not the attitude. This year you have the attitude but you're way ahead of us. I could use you. I could win the state again with you. But I would not be being fair with you."

"But I want to play for this team! Put me anywhere! I need game experience."

"I know you do. But what good will it do you to hit .800 or .900 in a league you're too good for?"

"I wouldn't mind that."

Hector laughed. "I wouldn't either, but it wouldn't be fair. Not to our opponents. Not to your teammates. Not to you. But anyway, son, listen. You're going to be playing somewhere this summer."

That was a relief to Elgin, though it scared him to think he might have to jump two or three levels just to find a place to play. What if he wasn't ready? A few minutes later, when Jim Koenig showed up, Elgin was in for another pleasant surprise. ("It's pronounced *Kay*-nig," he said. "Don't ask me why.") Koenig was a tall, thin man with short black hair. He whispered privately with Hector and Raleigh before approaching Elgin.

"So you're the one who humiliated my pitchers today, huh? I was tempted to come and watch, but I decided it would be a waste of time. Apparently it wouldn't have been. Hector and Raleigh here tell me you've got skills in the field too, though you're not as far ahead of your age there as you are at the plate. Switch-hitter."

He said it rather than asked it, so Elgin didn't respond.

"I could use a switch-hitter. Frankly, we had our eyes on Dirk for second base, but we hate to break up the twins. Dick is actually a better ballplayer, but we won't need a shortstop for two years. Hector tells me Dirk is better than you in the field and has a stronger arm, but if you can hit my pitchers, you'll hit a couple of hundred points higher than he would at this level."

Elgin was so excited he could hardly sit still. He wanted to talk, to discuss baseball with this man. But he couldn't speak.

"I'll make sure my guys treat you right, and past that I won't make any promises. If this was luck, if you're a fluke, a flash in the pan, you're headed back for Hector's team in a New York minute. Got it?"

Elgin didn't know what a New York minute was, but he got it. He nodded.

"We have ten preseason games. They mean nothing to standings, averages, anything. I play everybody. I try a lot of pitchers. I'll try you at second. Probably hit you seventh or eighth. Your first tryout was here today. My pitchers tell me you're for real. They're all superstars. How you do in those preseason games will tell us where you fit. I'll tell you this, though. Based on what Raleigh and Hector and my pitchers say, I'm willing to start you and play you every inning of every preseason game, even if you bat zero. Get comfortable, find your rhythm, and show me what you've got. I'm as amazed as anybody at what I hear about you. We start workouts Monday night and we practice or play every day for the next three weeks."

He turned to Miriam. "Can he be there, Mom?"

She smiled. "He'll be there."

"And how do you feel about all this, ma'am?"

Miriam thought a second. "I may never be able to say. Proud, for sure. But I can't tell you how marvelous this is."

"Well," Jim Koenig said, "I just hope I'm not doing something that will be bad for the boy. He deserves a chance, but I'd sure hate to ruin him for the future."

44

THREE WEEKS, FIVE PRACTICES, and ten games later, Elgin had made a believer out of Jim Koenig and fourteen skeptical teammates. As the only player on the team to play every inning, he had racked up a personal stat sheet as follows:

AB	Runs	Hits	Doubles	Triples	HRs	RBI	Sacrifices	Average
33	11	26	12	3	0	14	3	.788

He had gone hitless in his first game but had driven in two runs on two sacrifices—one a fly and one a bunt. In the next nine games he had no fewer than two hits per game, twice went four-for-four, and finished with ten hits in his last eleven at-bats.

That performance prompted another meeting with Coach Koenig, this time at the hotel with only Miriam and Elgin present.

"I don't know quite how to tell you this, ma'am," the coach began, "but your son is a phenomenon, almost a freak of nature. I've been in the game a long time, and outside of all-star big leaguers, this boy is the best hitter I've ever seen. He doesn't get fooled. He doesn't strike out. Well, you struck out once, right?"

Elgin nodded.

"But in that at-bat he had hit foul his farthest ball of the year. He's not a home run hitter yet. His power takes him only about three hundred feet. But, heck, he's a child. They shifted on him, pulled in on him, threw at him, walked him intentionally. But they couldn't stop him. The only game he went hitless in was the first, but he had two runs batted in on two sacrifices and lined out twice."

"Once into a double play," Elgin muttered.

"You can line out into all the double plays you want for me, buddy," Koenig said.

"I've enjoyed watching him," Miriam said. "It's been as exciting to me as to anyone. I'm thrilled and I'm proud. I'm a little scared though. What am I supposed to do with a child like this?"

"Just let him keep doing whatever he's doing. He's a natural who also works hard. What can I say? If he doesn't get sick and tired of the game, he's going to be a superstar someday."

"He's a superstar now, isn't he?" Miriam asked.

"Well, yes, ma'am, at this level. But I'm talking about the big time. The majors. This boy has unlimited potential."

Miriam guessed she knew that. Clearly Mr. Koenig had come to tell her more than this. She decided to wait and let him say it.

"Ma'am, I need to tell you a little about summer collegiate ball. It's top-drawer amateur baseball. Some of the best teams in the country come from Illinois. The Arlington Heights team is a contender in the state and national tournaments every year, and we've been beating them the last few seasons. Stars from this program play college baseball in Arizona and California and Florida. Many of them make the pros and a few have become big leaguers. What I'm trying to tell you is that big league scouts watch our games."

Miriam nodded. Was he going to tell her they would laugh at a thirteen-year-old on the field? That Coach Koenig will look silly counting on a kid to carry his team?

"Ma'am, we won all ten of our preseason games. I've never seen crowds like that before, and I've never seen scouts at games that don't count. They were there with their radar guns and their stopwatches. Sure, I know they were looking at our pitchers, who, I might add, didn't allow as many hits all of the preseason as Elgin got off them in Hector's batting practice. Do you understand what I'm trying to tell you, ma'am?"

"No, sir."

"You need a lawyer, is what I'm trying to say."

"We need a lawyer?"

"An adviser. An agent. Someone to represent you. These guys are like vultures, and you've got a lot of legal things to think about."

"Like what?"

"Like the fact that I had to jump through all kinds of hoops just to get permission for Elgin to play collegiate ball. Can you imagine what it would take to allow him to play professionally?"

"Oh, Mr. Koenig, when that time comes, I'm sure Billy Ray Thatcher from Hattiesburg would be happy to—"

"Ma'am, that time has come! I know of three scouts who want to talk to you now. I don't think you should talk to them alone. Don't sign anything, don't agree to anything. I don't know if anyone anywhere could ever clear the way for someone who hasn't graduated high school to play professionally, but if they can they will, and Elgin will be so much fresh meat. They'll grind him up, use him, and discard him."

"You're scarin me, Coach."

"I'm trying to. Can you imagine how noisy it would be if a child—and I'm sorry, but that's what Elgin is—starts on a big league path at his age? It'll be the biggest thing that's ever happened to the game. No one will believe it until they see it, and if Elgin can keep doing what he's been doing, he'll be the rage."

"What about school? What about travelin? I can't afford to go with him on big trips."

"Yes, you can. You see, that's what you negotiate. If someone wants Elgin, you're part of the package."

"But I have a job."

"You won't need a job."

"But what if he loses it? My husband did. What if he's injured? What if he gets tired of it?"

"Momma!"

"Well, you could. There are no guarantees. I know the odds against a player makin a living at baseball. What are the odds for a child who just turned thirteen?"

Jim Koenig leaned back on the couch and sighed. "Now you're asking the right questions. Now you know why I think you need counsel."

"Would you help us?"

He held up both hands. "No way. I'm not taking any credit for what Raleigh and Hector discovered, and none of us can take credit for honing or polishing what God gave the boy. I don't want to be accused of making money off a talent, and you need to have someone you're paying to look out for your best interests. It has to be someone you know, someone you trust. This man from Hattiesburg you mentioned—"

"Billy Ray Thatcher."

"Does he have any experience with this type of a thing?"

"Matter of fact he does. He's Bernie Pincham's agent."

"No kidding? And you know him?"

"He's a dear family friend."

"Well, there you go. If I were you, I'd talk to him right away. The best I can do for you is to keep these scouts away from Elgin and you. I won't give them your name or address or phone number."

"We have no phone."

"All the better. Once you have Mr. Thatcher as your representative, I'll send everybody to him. Uh, could I speak with you privately for a moment, ma'am?"

Miriam cocked her head and thought for a moment. "No, sir, I think anything you want to say to me, Elgin can hear."

"Suit yourself," Koenig said. "I just want to tell you that you're looking at some huge money here."

"I gathered that."

"I'm talking potentially millions." He sneaked a peek at Elgin.

"Sir?" Miriam said.

"Millions."

"I understand. I'd say that's a long shot, but let's say you're right. We'll just make sure Elgin gets good counsel."

"But, Mrs. Woodell. You'll likely never have to work again."

"Oh, I expect I'll be plenty busy."

⚾ ⚾ ⚾

Elgin went to bed that night unable to sleep. His mind raced with his pulse. His dream had always been to be a big league baseball player. How soon could it happen? How old did you have to be? He knew of big leaguers who had begun in their late teens. Joe Nuxhall had pitched for the Reds when he was fifteen, but that was when a lot of the regulars were fighting in World War II. Things were different now.

What appealed to Elgin most about all this was that even if he didn't make it for several more years, at some point along the way he was going to find his level. More than anything, he wanted competition. He didn't enjoy dominating a league. It was nice to be noticed and recognized as a great player, a prodigy they were now calling him. And if the day came when he tore up the big leagues, he guessed that would be all right. But something inside told him that he was simply ahead. He wasn't the best ballplayer anywhere; not yet, not already.

Mr. Koenig's offer to keep the scouts away from him was welcome and necessary. Elgin started the regular season batting second and playing second base. He had a little trouble in the field, sometimes getting taken out of the double play by bigger players sliding into him. He made a few more errors than someone older might have made. But as usual, he was hitting from the start.

Three games into the season he was five-for-eight with a double. He went two-for-three the next game to send his average well over .600, then saw how quickly the numbers can change when he went one-for-four the next game and was eight-for-fifteen on the season, or .533. That put him third on the team and eighth in the league after five games, but no one dreamed of what was coming.

Elgin had already been made famous by local newspapers and television stations, who sent crews and interviewed him. It was interesting and newsworthy that a boy of thirteen had been cleared to play in a league where the next youngest player was eighteen. His mother had had to sign all kinds of forms and waivers to absolve the league of any responsibility for his health. But as one of the TV reporters said, the league should have signed a waiver of its rights to sue Elgin Woodell for damage inflicted by his hits.

No one had been seriously injured, though a first baseman had to leave the game with a bruised ankle off one of Elgin's liners. And a pitcher had a one-hopper back to the mound skip off his glove and into his forehead, though he stayed in the game. But it was the stretch of the next five games that really put Elgin on the map. He became known even nationally as he led the Chicago collegiate team—which had begun the season with a record of four-and-one—to five straight victories. He came to the plate twenty times, walked three times (twice intentionally), and was otherwise seventeen-for-seventeen.

He went three-for-three three times and four-for-four twice, with three doubles and a triple. He had eight RBIs and scored five times. The five games were played in an eight-day span, causing Jim Koenig to say, "The kid had a nice season last week."

In the eleventh and twelfth games of the year he was oh-for-two and one-for-three, dropping his average to a mere .702. The second best hitter in college ball in the state was hitting .505. Media swamped the games, and scouts from nearly every major league team began to trail the team. Stories in the daily papers covered behind-the-scenes maneuvering to somehow get around all the prohibitions against a minor playing professional baseball. Everyone agreed: the kid deserved a chance to start moving up. The city league was considered a step down from collegiate ball, and he could not play for a college team during the school year unless he attended that college. He was a smart kid, but no academic prodigy. The only logical next step was the pros, and that didn't seem logical.

Elgin talked with his mother of nothing except the future. And he still spent just a little over an hour every night in the cellar with the machine he had come to love. He would never stop that daily regimen, he told himself. He knew it was the secret. And it was a secret he planned to take to his grave. In Elgin's next eight games he went twenty-for-thirty with thirteen RBIs, three triples, eight doubles, and fourteen runs. Best of all, he had a three-hit game that included a triple and a home run. He had thought he would never hit one out of a big park. He had a couple that bounced off the wall, but it was a thrill to see one drop straight down over the right field fence, just inside the line 305 feet from the plate. He would not swing for the fences. He knew better. Until he grew up, he would not be a power hitter, but with the solid contact he always made, he knew the occasional home run had to come.

Batting .687 and becoming a flawless fielder, Elgin was the heart of a fifteen-and-five team on its way to the state championship. He began to wonder if there was a pitcher anywhere who could get him out consistently. The best hitters in the majors were out almost seven times out of ten. He wondered what that would feel like.

45

BILLY RAY THATCHER SAT in the Woodells' transient hotel flat with his briefcase on his lap, knees together, the toes of his wingtips pointing at each other.

"What I need to know, Miriam," he said, in his deliberate way, "is exactly what you want. I'm retiring, as I said, but I will gladly represent you for as long as Elgin plays the game. That could be a long time, but it could just as easily be a short time. I would advise you to move cautiously with his best interests in mind. If there is money to be made in short order, I would hope and expect that you would be much wiser than your late husband was with his little windfall."

"I'm assumin that's not a question, Mr. Thatcher," Miriam said. "I'm assumin you know me well enough."

"I know you all too well," he said with a smile. "I know you probably wouldn't want a penny of Elgin's money." She nodded. "The fact is, neither do I, but we're both going to be very involved in it until he's of age. I will not take a percentage but will charge you only my hourly rate for whatever I do on his behalf. That will not come due until he has realized some income, but I will prepare a document stipulating that. You need to know that litigation can be expensive, even at just an hourly rate."

"Litigation?" she said. "Goin to court?"

"Very likely," he said. "I'll get to that."

"Excuse me, Mr. Thatcher," Elgin said. "But I've been reading a lot about this. Are you sure you don't want a percentage? I mean, it could be millions."

"Oh, it likely will be millions," Mr. Thatcher said. "But I don't need it and I don't want it. There will be enough people coming to you with their hands out, and I'll want the freedom to advise you to ignore them as well. Very few people from here on out will have your best interests at heart. I never want to be accused of being one of them."

Miriam had sent Billy Ray Elgin's stats twenty games into the regular season:

AB	Runs	Hits	Doubles	Triples	HRs	RBI	Sacrifices	Average
67	24	46	14	4	1	23	6	.687

He had called her at her office.

"You say this is in a league where the minimum age requirement is eighteen?"

"Yes, sir."

"And Elgin is thirteen now?"

"Just turned."

He had whistled through his teeth. "Yes, ma'am, I think I had better visit you."

Now, as he sat awkwardly with that briefcase in his lap, he told her his plans. "Baseball rules, as they stand now, say a team can't draft a young man until his high school class graduates. Then if he doesn't sign and goes to college, he can't be drafted until after his junior year."

"Is there any way around it?" Elgin asked.

"It's never been tested in baseball. Back when I was representing Bernie Pincham things had already changed in basketball."

"What changed them?"

"Spencer Heywood. He was signed by Seattle out of the American Basketball Association without having ever gone through the National Basketball Association draft. The NBA said Seattle couldn't keep him. His agent sued the NBA, won, and Heywood was allowed to stay with the Supersonics. That led to the hardship rule where a kid could inform the league if he was an underclassman and wanted to be entered in the draft. For years they called it the poverty or hardship draft. Now it's just standard procedure. The NBA can't keep a kid out of a draft just because he's young."

"Well, that's the issue here, isn't it?"

"In the extreme, yes. I wonder if there's even a junior high rule. Everyone knows you can't draft a high schooler till he graduates, but what about a junior higher? It's never come up."

"So, what do you plan to do?"

"I'm going to take the gentlemanly, and inexpensive, route first. I will inform the commissioner's office that we would like to enter Elgin in the June draft. If that is laughed off or refused for any reason, I will establish the hardship situation."

Miriam stiffened and Thatcher noticed. "Now, Miriam, I know you're a hard-working, independent, strong, and proud woman. I know you're solvent and even saving money. But the fact is, your income qualifies you for food stamps if you'd ever apply."

"You know better than that."

"Of course I do, but don't be so proud that you stand in the way of your son living out his dream. Your humble financial means as a single parent may help make Elgin the youngest player in the history of professional sports."

Miriam sat thinking. "Are we sure that's what we want?"

"I'm sure," Elgin said.

"I'm sure you are," Miriam said. "The question is whether I'm ready for it."

"Only you can answer that," Billy Ray said, "and hardship is one way to approach it."

"But you won't go that way unless we have to, right?" she said.

"Right. Meanwhile, I'll set up temporary headquarters at the Hyatt Regency downtown. I want you to steer every request, every offer, every approach to me. It wouldn't surprise me if more than one team has already been in the baseball commissioner's office trying to convince the man it would be in the best interests of baseball to allow a child into the June draft. Baseball doesn't need this, but the public may force baseball's hand."

Miriam scowled. "I just feel it's a shame that Elgin can't play ball at a level where everybody else can compete with him," she said.

"Then you want me to push the commissioner on making an exception and getting him into the draft?"

"Well, I want Elgin to keep his priorities. He can't travel till school's out. And he's goin nowhere without me."

Mr. Thatcher was taking notes. "I need to know all this, and I think you're right. This is good. Elgin, how is your team going to feel if it loses you halfway through the season?"

"I don't know," he said, "but I don't think I'd like it."

Thatcher raised his eyebrows. "If you do get into the draft and some team signs you, you're theirs."

"But I don't have to sign, right?"

"No. But ethically you should tell a team in advance so they won't waste a pick on you. Because of who you are, a team might sign you just for the publicity. But if they come up with an offer you shouldn't turn down, you have to be prepared to leave this team and go to whatever rookie league they want to send you to. Nobody could fault you for that."

"Maybe nobody could fault me, but it still wouldn't be right."

"Somebody told me," Miriam said, "that the rookie leagues aren't much better than summer collegiate ball. In fact, some of them are not as good."

"That's probably true," Billy Ray said. "Are you saying you don't want us to sign with a team that starts you lower than, say, A ball?"

"How about double-A?" Elgin said.

"How about going for the whole enchilada?" Thatcher said.

"What do you mean?"

He set his briefcase on the couch. "Try this on. Let's say we get you into the draft. I don't want to make that sound easy. It will be the hardest work I'll have ever done, and I can't guarantee anything. It'll be noisy. You may be on *The Tonight Show* and on the cover of *Sports Illustrated* before the summer is over."

"That'd be okay," Elgin said.

Thatcher smiled. "Then you go on record that you can't sign with anybody until the summer collegiate season is over. That'll get lots of attention, make you look wonderful."

"Hey! I *am* wonderful, because that's how I feel. I mean, I'd go to the majors right now if I thought they would let me, but nobody's going to do that. I owe it to my team to stick with them to the end."

"That's going to be good for the summer league too, because the crowds will start showing up for your games. Anyway, what I'll lobby for on the side is letting a team get a commitment from you that you will sign with them after the summer season, provided they start you no lower than double-A, and that you are invited to spring training with the big club next spring."

Elgin sucked in a huge breath. This was getting crazy. He'd been enjoying being phenomenal, a prodigy, better than anyone his age or up to ten years older. But spring training in the majors? Maybe Mr. Thatcher was getting ahead of himself. Elgin's skepticism must have showed.

"Let me explain it this way, Elgin. Everyone will think it's a lark, a publicity stunt. I will look like a bad guy. But if you're, say, a first round pick, you deserve a huge signing bonus, and we'll get it for you. I'll argue that all this attention and premature speculation risks all kinds of damage for you that needs to be compensated for in advance. A double-A first-round pick who goes to spring training, publicity stunt or not, gets a certain amount.

"Do I think you're going to earn a starting spot on a big league club before you're fourteen years old next spring? Of course not. For one thing, your mother won't let you play until school's out. But you can go to spring training during spring break, and if you perform even marginally well, your stock will rise."

Miriam brought iced tea from the refrigerator. "Mr. Thatcher, I need your help and your counsel. I don't want to have to rein you in, you understand?"

Billy Ray laughed. "I hear what you're saying. But you recall that I have talked with his coaches. I can't wait to see him play tonight. Frankly, I am just as skeptical and even more realistic about his chances than most baseball experts will be. But Miriam, you have a chance here to cash in, no matter what happens to his abilities in the future, and I'd be a fool if I didn't advise you to take advantage of it."

"I know you mean well," she said. "But if I know Elgin, he's not interested in cashin in."

"I don't mind cashin in, Momma. But you're right. I'd be doing this to play ball, and I would be fighting to make the big leagues."

Miriam shook her head. "I hope, sir, that you haven't caused more of a problem than you're here to solve."

"I do too," Thatcher said seriously. "Forgive me if I've been premature."

"Well, it's just that we're all of a sudden sittin here talkin about Elgin Woodell, my son, tryin to hook on with a big league baseball team. He's thirteen years old!"

Billy Ray leaned forward and held his sweating glass in both hands. "I want what you want, Miriam. If you'd rather I simply tell everyone to leave the boy alone until he's sixteen or even eighteen, I will do that. There are no guarantees about his health or even his ability as he grows taller. He has a wonderful opportunity, getting to play at the level he's playing at. He has a chance to break all kinds of records in summer collegiate ball, just because of the sheer number of years he can invest. Maybe that's the best."

Elgin shook his head. "I hate to say this, but I think this league is going to get too easy for me before it's over. I'm really looking forward to the state and regional and national tournaments, because then maybe I'll get tested."

Miriam stood and paced. "I'd like to think about alternatives. We need to know whether there is some other league he can play in without becomin a professional. This is too much too soon. I don't want him becomin an adult overnight."

"He's already apparently an adult ballplayer," Thatcher said.

"Don't I know it. Elgin, you'd better start gettin changed. Mr. Thatcher offered to drive us to the field in his rental car. Won't that be fun?"

"Oh, Momma!"

⚾ ⚾ ⚾

It was a good thing Billy Ray Thatcher was at the game that night. He saw things he otherwise would not have believed.

More than a thousand crowded an intimate if wobbly stadium with a full-sized diamond and shorter-than-minor-league fences. At least a dozen scouts were there, some with video cameras. On the way to infield practice, two suited men in their forties asked to see Elgin.

"Mr. Woodell, a word please."

Elgin turned, having forgotten Coach Koenig's warnings.

"Son, I just need a second," one of the two said, and several others crowded around.

"I'll want a minute too, Elgin."

"Me too, son."

"Ho! Hey! Wait a minute over there!" It was Koenig, face flushed and on the dead run. "Woodell, get to your position if you want to play tonight! Now!"

"We just need a second with him, Coach," one of the men said.

"Yeah, sure you do. I told you, he's not talking to anybody during the season. And when he's available, he will have counsel."

"Coach?" Elgin said.

"I told you to get on the field!"

"I will, but I just wanted you to know that I have counsel. He's here."

"You have an agent?" one of the scouts demanded.

"He didn't say that!" Koenig shouted.

"He did too! Now where is he?"

"He's not an agent," Elgin said, as Koenig dragged him away. "He's an attorney, and he's right up there with my mother."

"Oh, Elgin," Koenig said as the scouts scampered into the stands, "you never should have told em who your mother was."

46

MIRIAM HAD JUST BEGUN TO TELL Billy Ray Thatcher about Lucas, and that she hadn't said a word to Elgin about him yet. She was irritated that Billy Ray looked past her and seemed to ignore her. She stopped and waited for his attention, but when he spoke, he was still looking elsewhere.

"Forgive me, Miriam, but if I'm seeing what I think I'm seeing, we're about to have company. I believe I am about to start earning my money."

Miriam followed his eyes to a group of well-dressed men, some old, some young, some in the shapes of former athletes, some clearly not. They all seemed to hurry up the stadium steps while pretending not to. Mr. Thatcher leaned toward Miriam.

"Don't say one word, understand? Don't even acknowledge who you are."

She watched wide-eyed as the men approached, notebooks and business cards in hand. Some had radar guns bulging from sportcoat pockets. Others carried them. Most had stopwatches around their necks.

"Are you Mrs. Woodell?" two asked in unison.

It was all Miriam could do to keep from nodding. Whatever could be wrong with admitting who she was?

"That depends," Mr. Thatcher answered the men, rising. "Who may I say is calling?"

The men looked at him, then at her, then back at him. He pulled a wallet from his pocket and began distributing his own cards. "Thatcher's the name. I represent the Woodells. You may reach me by phone, fax, or mail at the numbers and address on the card, or you may reach me for the next few days at the Hyatt Regency downtown. For now—"

"Well, I'd like to speak with you right now, if possi—"

"For now," Mr. Thatcher repeated, "I am engaged in a private conversation and do not wish to be disturbed."

"Can you tell us when you might be available?"

"During the game when Chicago is in the field. But not in the first inning."

The scouts looked at each other and began to take seats near Billy Ray and Miriam.

"Gentlemen, please," Billy Ray said, sitting again next to Miriam. "Give us some space. I will talk with each of you, I promise." The scouts moved down a few rows. "I'm sorry, Miriam. You were saying..."

"I was sayin that Lucas will be here a little later. He would like me to start preparin Elgin for the news about us."

"And that news is that you are to be married?"

"Oh my, no! But the other day, we uh, held hands for the first time and—"

Billy Ray grinned. "Perhaps you need me to break that news to your son?"

Miriam pretended to be hurt. "Don't mock me. Now Lucas and I have talked for hours about how seriously we take each other, and we had said long ago that we would just be friends, sort of like buddies."

"I don't need to tell you that doesn't work for long, Miriam."

"Well, we thought it might. He told me I would know if he ever changed his mind, and I asked him how. He said he would want to touch me. I asked him didn't he already want to even touch me and he said no. He said he didn't look at me the way he looked at most women and that he wouldn't ever even so much as hold my hand unless he was in love with me."

Mr. Thatcher looked away again. Miriam had told this man some of her deepest, darkest secrets in the past. She'd had to. He represented her during her most difficult seasons of life and walked her through her most dire circumstances and decisions. She thought she could talk to him about this. He was the closest thing she had to a father.

But he was clearly embarrassed. Or preoccupied. She didn't want to bother him. She quit talking.

Presently he turned to her. "Don't misunderstand my discomfort, Miriam. I miss my wife."

"Don't tell me somethin's happened to Miz Thatcher!"

"No, no. And I was with her just this morning. But Miriam, when you have a long, happy marriage like ours, you miss one another whenever you're apart, especially when you know it's going to be a few days."

"That's beautiful."

"Well, maybe it's beautiful and maybe it's a little clingy. But what got to me was your story there. You see, Shirley and I felt the same way when we courted. There was no doubt we were dating and looking and available. We were the right age, in college, and all that, but we were very serious. We weren't pretending to be just friends. We were checking each other out, sizing each other up. She was a law student too, you know, so we're talking about an analytical mind. Anyway, she felt the same way Mr. Harkness feels. I'll be pleased to meet him."

"I feel the same way," Miriam said. "But I'm a little embarrassed about how it's all come about. See, I wanted to hold his hand long before he wanted to hold mine."

Billy Ray looked at her and she looked away. "Don't be too sure," he said. "After saying what he said about how serious holding your hand would be, he probably waited a long time after first wanting to, making sure you were ready."

Miriam looked down and shook her head. "It all seems so juvenile."

"No, it doesn't. Juveniles would have been in bed together already, pardon my directness."

So, it was okay, Miriam decided. She and Lucas had taken a walk while Elgin had been in the cellar. They had laughed a lot, talked a lot, been quiet even more. They stood closer to each other, brushed shoulders as they sat and laughed. She had held his gaze a little longer than normal, just enough to increase her pulse and wonder if her face had reddened.

On the way back to her flat, he had held her elbow as they crossed the street. How she wished he would not let go when they were safely across. He let his hand slide down to hers and they walked on like school chums, not looking at each other and not talking.

"I wouldn't even hold your hand unless I was in love with you," he had said, and that echoed in her mind. Now he had silently declared himself, unless he had a bad memory. She hadn't told him that her allowing him to hold her hand signified the same. She hoped he knew that she had heard him, that she knew how important this was to him. She hoped he knew that if she found his gesture of love premature or inappropriate, she would not have allowed it. Had he been tentative, waiting to see if she would shrug off his hand? She didn't give him the chance.

Miriam had so longed for his touch that her hand in his was every bit as meaningful and warm and loving and sensual as an embrace. She gripped his wide palm firmly, trying to silently convey all she wanted to say. It clearly embarrassed them both, and when he let go as they rounded the corner and came within sight of her building—she assumed because he didn't want to risk Elgin's discovering them holding hands—she was relieved. She did, however, look forward to the next time.

Neither she nor Lucky said anything about the incident, and they didn't touch each other again when he was saying good-bye, though they held each other's gaze. The next time they were alone together they did not hold hands again. She searched his eyes in vain for that same flicker of response.

She worried, but not for long. Perhaps he was waiting for her to make a move. Was she willing? She was.

Miriam had agreed to take Elgin's spikes to Lucky's for a little repair. When she walked in Luke looked up and smiled. She set the shoes on the counter then thrust out her hand as if to shake his. He looked puzzled, but shook her hand. When he did, she covered his also with her other hand.

"I'm Miriam Woodell," she said. "You must be Lucky."

"I am today," he said, also covering her hands with his. And there they stood, four hands entwined, looking into each other's eyes. When another customer entered they went back to business, but Miriam was encouraged. Apparently he had wanted to know he wasn't pushing too far too fast. She smiled to herself. They were like school children, not like grownups who had been married, divorced, widowed.

She wanted to confirm he was coming to Elgin's next game, so she waited. He had tagged Elgin's shoes and was waiting on the next customer. Miriam busied herself looking over new merchandise.

"Yes, sir, every price you see here is right at double what I paid for it. That's how I cover my overhead and make my profit. If you have to talk me down, I can usually find about ten percent in the price. If it's something I know will go for full price soon, I'll fight you on it, but if it's something that's been sitting a while or that I should cut the price on anyway, you might have a little more luck."

"How do I know you're telling the truth about what you paid for it?"

"You don't. But if you can't trust me, you probably shouldn't shop here."

"Well, that's true enough," the man said. "And I don't expect you to feel obligated to tell me the status of every piece of merchandise."

"I'm glad, because I wouldn't," Lucas said. "I got to make my margin somewhere, you understand."

The man nodded. He was looking for a real but defused hand grenade for his son. Lucas produced one from under the counter.

"I get these in lots of a dozen for twenty-five dollars. I sell em for four bucks apiece."

"Would you take three?"

"No, but thanks for asking. I wouldn't feel I was doing my job or that you were doing yours unless you tried. I run a brisk business on these babies. I fix em myself so they can't be recharged. I would feel bad if someone tried to make these work again and succeeded."

The man forked over the money and thanked Luke.

"Now, if you want a deal, you can have that glass bowl over there for two dollars."

The man looked at it. "You'll never sell that monstrosity.

Luke laughed heartily. "Yeah, I'll probably have to pay someone to take it off my hands. Would you believe I paid nine dollars for that and had it priced at twenty for a while?"

"No!"

Luke held up a hand. "Honest. Proved I was human, didn't I?"

"Proved you were an idiot, more likely," the man said. He was smiling.

"We've all got those ugly glass bowls in our lives, don't we? Sure you don't want it? I'm willing to take a seven dollar loss on it."

They both laughed as the man left.

Miriam approached again. Luke was still smiling. "Do you believe that?" he said. "Maybe it looked pretty in the dim light of the estate sale."

She looked at the piece and shook her head. "It's so ugly it's cute."

"You like it," he said.

"I kinda do."

"You're not serious."

"No, but sort of. I mean, I wouldn't use it for anything but a conversation starter."

"Oh, it would serve that purpose well," he said. "I'd be willing to sell it to a beautiful woman like you for what I paid for it. Nine bucks."

"You are a rascal," she said.

"Hey, if you were a friend or something I could cut you a deal, but if I remember correctly, we just met."

"Indeed," she said.

"Buy that piece before someone else snaps it up at full price, and we can shake hands again."

"A rascal," she repeated, winking at him as she left.

47

FOR THE FIRST TIME, Elgin was fully aware of the uproar he was causing. "I don't want to bother you before the game, Champ," Jim Koenig said, "but not all of those guys were scouts."

"What were they, agents?"

"No, no agents yet. They'll come later. Good thing you've got your friend representing you, because agents will descend upon you like vultures. I'm not saying there aren't some very, very good ones, but how would you know?"

"So who were the guys that weren't scouts?"

"Well, only one that I know of. He's from *Sports Illustrated.* I mean, he's local, but he works for them. He was supposed to do a 'Faces in the Crowd' thing on you. You know what that is?"

"Sure, of course."

"But now he says they're asking him to do some full-blown deal on you. I don't know what to think about it, but you'd better have your friend, uh—"

"Mr. Thatcher."

"Yeah, you'd better have Thatcher talk to him, huh?"

"I guess."

"If he comes back around here, I'll tell him. If he's a good enough reporter, he'll find out from the scouts that Thatcher is here. You just concentrate on getting some hits tonight."

"Right," Elgin said. "For a change."

He jogged out to second for the start of the game before Koenig could respond. For a change? Elgin was only five for his last seven.

In the top of the first Elgin covered first on a bunt up the line and was run over by the Arlington Heights leadoff man. Not only was he unhurt, but he was the first off the ground and helped the runner up.

"That was bush," Elgin said, smiling and patting the runner on the rear.

"Maybe next time you'd like a mouthful of cleats."

The runner turned and stared at Elgin. "You lookin for trouble, Pee-wee?"

"No, I'm just looking to stay on my side of the baseline on a play like that. Old veteran like you ought to know how to do that by now."

The kid made a move toward Elgin and the benches cleared. There was no way Elgin really needed to be held back. He had plotted his escape if the big guy had taken a swing at him. But with teammates holding their arms, Elgin was brave enough to go nose to nose with him.

"You'd better stay outa my face, little man," the Arlington Heights boy said.

"It's tough when Pee-wee helps nail you by two steps on a Little League bunt, isn't it?" Elgin said.

The Chicago players roared, and the Arlington leadoff man struggled to break free. The umpires broke it up and conferred, then the plate ump approached the visitors' bench.

"There was an infraction. The runner was inside the line and would have been out regardless. So that's the end of it. Any more and somebody's walkin!"

But there was more. With one out and no score in the bottom of the first, Elgin had to duck out of the way of a purpose pitch behind his ear. The ump came charging out from behind the plate.

"Oh, don't call that!" Elgin said. "That easy of a pitch had to be an accident!"

The umpire pointed a finger at the pitcher but said nothing.

"Slipped," the pitcher said, shrugging.

"Don't let it slip again," the ump said.

The next pitch was in the dirt, a foot in front of Elgin's feet. He danced to elude it and here came the ump again.

"That's a warning, Arlington! You're a better pitcher than that!" He repeated the warning to the coach, who waved disgustedly.

The outfield was shallow, as usual. Elgin decided to try to rifle the next pitch over the pitcher's head, but he didn't want it to hang up long enough for the center fielder to get it on the fly. The pitch was perfect for what he had in mind. Low, down the middle, and hard.

Elgin laced the ball about two feet above the pitcher's head. He had time only to duck and whirl to see if it was catchable. The center fielder took a step in, a critical mistake. The ball was still rising when it flew over his head, and he stumbled trying to reverse himself, backpedal, and turn around at the same time.

Elgin was off like a shot. He saw the ball hit near the bottom of the center-field fence as he rounded first. It skipped to the right and the right and center fielders converged on it. Elgin never slowed. He'd never had an inside-the-park homer, but he could smell this one. And with all the right people in the stands. Concentrate, he told himself. No mistakes. Shortest distance. All speed. He hit second with his left foot and shifted his eyes from the ball to his coach.

Then the lights went out. His breath escaped in a huge grunt and he could not inhale. He was not on solid ground, could see nothing, felt the cool summer night air on his head as his helmet flew away.

What was happening? Was he dreaming? There was no pain, just that whoosh of air and breath. He hit on his heels first and rolled backward, winding up on his back with pain in his sternum and still no breath.

He opened his eyes and grimaced, panicking. He needed to breathe! What had happened? He felt his face turning blue. Was he going to die right here in front of his mother and Mr. Thatcher and all the scouts?

Jim Koenig bent over him, screaming at everyone to back off and threatening the Arlington shortstop's life. So that was it, Elgin realized. Their leadoff man was the shortstop. Elgin had thought the shortstop might try something if Elgin tried to steal second or break up a double play, but he was not thinking of him at all with an inside-the-parker on the line.

Koenig loosened Elgin's belt, but the boy began to thrash, desperate for air.

"You'll breathe, buddy. Give me a second. This happens all the time."

The coach reached under Elgin and put a huge palm beneath his lower back, lifting his rear off the ground. Elgin felt a stretching along his chest, a building of pressure. It seemed an eternity since he'd had air in his lungs.

"Relax!" Koenig commanded, grabbing Elgin's ankles and pressing them forward to his seat, forcing his knees up to his chest.

When Koenig straightened Elgin's legs again, his lungs expanded and he sucked in cool, sweet air. His head cleared, his pain intensified, and he was mad. It all came to him. That shortstop had driven an elbow into his ribs when he rounded second on the dead run, knocking the wind from him and blowing him into left field. Elgin's eyes darted among the Arlington players while he was still on his back in the grass.

"Don't even think about it," Koenig said. "He's already been ejected."

"Do I get third?"

"Of course you get third. I'm arguing for home. You'd have made it. They hadn't even touched the ball yet."

Elgin stood and buckled his belt, then quickly scanned the stands for his mother. She stood next to Mr. Thatcher, her hand covering her mouth. Elgin waved at her to set her mind at ease. He was as scared as she must have been. Worse than the pain, worse than the shortness of breath, worse than the disappointment of not legging out the homer, was not being able to breathe. He wanted to cry. But he had held his own against this kid in the top of the inning. And he had stood up to the pitcher who had tried to hit him. He would have taken on the shortstop again if he were still on the field. But being unable to breathe, that was terrifying.

Elgin rubbed his sore chest, took several deep breaths, and bent over, hands on his knees. The umpire awarded him the plate, which threw the Arlington coach into a tizzy.

"No way you can give him two bases! You've already kicked out my guy!"

"I'm sayin in my judgment he would have scored. So he scores."

"This game's under protest!"

"Protest all you want. If he's healthy enough to touch third and home on his own, he stays in the game."

Coach Koenig looked at Elgin. "Don't feel obligated. You can sit the rest of this one out."

"No way. I'm all right."

He didn't want to just walk around third. He broke into a trot, which produced a long ovation, even from some of the opponents. It was then he noticed that both teams were on the field again, glaring, posturing.

"Let's go, guys!" he shouted as he rounded third, his breastbone smarting with every step. "Let's get back to winning this thing!"

He was glad he had a chance to sit while Arlington brought in a new second baseman and moved their original one to short. The pitcher lost his control and walked two of the next three hitters, then had words with his coach on the mound. A new pitcher had to warm up, so Elgin had time to regain his strength. Nothing was broken. He wouldn't miss any action. But he would not soon forget that feeling, that fear of being on the brink of death.

At the end of the dugout stood a solitary figure with a large paper sack under his arm. He wore a leather jacket and sported a bushy red beard.

"Anything had happened to you, El, I would've been out there swinging," Lucas said.

"Hey, Lucky. I'm all right. Thanks for coming."

"Are you kidding? I wouldn't miss a game if I didn't have to."

"Get out of here. You just came to be with Mom."

"You noticed?"

"No, I'm blind."

Luke smiled and looked away. Elgin was startled. He had been simply talking. He hadn't expected Lucky to confirm his suspicions. He liked his boss all right. He even liked how his mother was when Lucky was around. But now what were they trying to tell him? He looked at Lucky to see how serious he was. Maybe he had just been putting Elgin on.

"Woodell! You in or out? You watchin or gabbin?"

It was Koenig. Elgin stood. Was it time to take the field again? No. What was he hollering about?

"Stay in the game, buddy!" the coach said. "No extra points for owies, you know."

Elgin smiled and sneaked a peek back at Lucky. He had already headed into the stands.

48

MIRIAM FOUND LUCAS—as glib as he was in his own shop—a shy, soft-spoken man in private. He was awkward and quiet as she introduced him to Billy Ray Thatcher.

"I've heard a lot about you, Mr. Harkness," Thatcher said.

"Yes, sir, same here. Thank you."

It was the top of the second, and as expected, the scouts began burrowing their way back up to Billy Ray.

"Is this Mr. Woodell?" one asked.

Lucas laughed. "No, sir!" he said, now bolder with an audience. "Lucky Harkness. I run Lucky's Second-hand. Come on over and I'll make ya a good deal."

He had lost their attention. They were clearly not interested in anyone not related to or representing Elgin Woodell.

"Excuse me, kids," Mr. Thatcher said to Miriam and Lucas, and he led the scouts to the end of the bleachers like a pied piper.

"Brought something for you," Luke said shyly when he and Miriam were alone.

He thrust out the brown paper sack, and she knew when she felt its shape and weight what she would see when she opened it. She giggled and set it in her lap, pretending to be as excited as she had ever been. In fact, she was.

She unrolled the folded-down top and was about to pull apart the opening when Luke said, "Grounder to Elgin."

Her eyes darted to her son, who was racing to his right. He backhanded a three-hopper near second and had to fire to first to nip the runner by a half step. The crowd reacted noisily, but Miriam knew it had been routine. She couldn't count the times Elgin had told her, "Teams who win make the routine plays. The tough ones usually won't make you or break you if you make the rest."

Miriam pressed her knees together and felt the cool night air on the back of her neck as she pulled the hideous glass bowl from the bag. "I'll cherish it forever," she said, laughing.

"I knew you'd love it," Luke said. "It's not so ugly in the dark, is it?"

"Oh, I don't know," she said, holding it up and turning it toward the ballpark lights. "Even if you couldn't see it at all, it feels ugly."

"Like me," he said, still smiling.

"Like you, what?"

"Ugly even in the dark."

"You don't believe that," she said, suddenly serious.

He shrugged.

"Lucas, tell me you don't believe that."

"You don't need to patronize me," he said. "I've never been much to look at."

"Lucas," she said carefully. "I admit I've never seen you without your beard, but now with your hair shorter and your beard trimmed, you look younger and very attractive."

"Younger than what?" he said, eyes dancing.

"Younger than, um, you looked when I first met you. I had you pictured older. And you're in great shape."

"I'm no jock, but I like to stay healthy. I didn't mean to get into this, Miriam."

She loved the way he said her name. He said it more quietly than any other word in a sentence, almost as if he revered it. She hoped he did.

"I just hope you're not embarrassed to be seen hangin around with a broken-down old veteran your kid thinks looks like a biker."

"He doesn't still think that. I have to admit, when I first saw you, I could see what he meant. You had a flannel shirt on, untucked, and your hair was as long as your beard."

"You still let me walk you home."

"You had just saved my life, as far as I was concerned. I felt safe with you."

"You are safe with me," he said.

"I know."

She slipped her hand into the crook of his elbow and turned her face to the field. He pressed his arm close to his side, and she loved him.

"No more talk about looks," she said, still watching the game. "I'm proud to be seen with you."

"But you're so pretty. Heads turn everywhere you—"

"No more," she said firmly. "That's always bothered me. One of the things I liked about you was that you didn't leer at me."

Luke looked away and laughed.

"What?" she said, turning to face him.

"Nothing."

"No, you laughed. Now what? You didn't leer at me, did you?"

He laughed again. "Apparently not when you were looking."

She shook her head and used the excuse of putting the bowl back in the bag to remove her hand from his arm. He watched her as she rewrapped it and set it on the bench beside her. She returned her hand to his arm and slid closer.

"Thanks for the bowl," she said in mock seriousness. "It'll be hard to top that."

"Hey!" he said. "The tag might have said two bucks, but I know what I paid for that lovely piece."

She conked his shoulder with her head to shut him up and wondered what was happening with Mr. Thatcher.

⚾ ⚾ ⚾

Elgin sat on the bench next to the only other player on the Chicago team who seemed to care as much as he did about statistics. He was a reserve outfielder who hardly ever saw action, but who knew everyone's averages.

"So, what am I hitting now, Doyle?" Elgin said.

"Still under .700, but two more hits and you'll be back up there. You're forty-seven for sixty-eight. You have to have forty-nine hits by your seventieth at-bat to hit .700 right on the head."

"Not a bad goal," Elgin said.

Doyle snorted. "There's nobody else in the state over .500 anymore. That guy from Peoria, the power hitter that plays for USC, is at, like, .495."

Elgin pressed his lips together and nodded. "I can't start worrying about the numbers now. All I think about is one pitch at a time."

"You think about the count?"

"Course I do. The count, the score, the number of outs, who's on base and where; they all go into what kind of pitch I can expect and where I want to put it."

"I wish it was that easy for the rest of us."

"What makes you think it's easy for me?"

"Well, if it isn't, you're sure a good actor. I can see those wheels turning from the time you're on deck to the time you're in the box. It's like you decide you need to take a pitch down the line or to the other side of the diamond for a hit-and-run, and you just wait for your pitch and do it."

"It's kind of like that, yeah," Elgin said.

"You want to know what it's like for humans?"

"What?"

"For humans, the rest of us. People who can't just do whatever they decide to do."

"Sure," Elgin said smiling. "What's it like for you humans?"

"It's like just hoping not to get killed, hoping to get a bat on the ball, hoping to do anything but strike out so you can fling your bat away in disgust on a grounder as if you can't believe you didn't hit one out."

"Is that why you do that, Doyle?"

"Sure! We all like to act like we can't believe we're not hitting a thousand. And then you come along and make us all look sick."

"Sorry."

"Don't be. We don't mind winning. I wouldn't mind playing more, though."

"You will. You're a good ballplayer. I see you starting in the outfield when Andy and Toby are gone next year."

Doyle fell silent and Elgin wondered if he had said something wrong. The boy went and rearranged the bat rack.

"You're in the hole, Woodell," Doyle said when he returned. There was no eye contact.

"What'sa matter, Doyle?"

The boy sat heavily next to Elgin. "Let me tell you something because I like you, Woodell. That last thing you said was a little obnoxious, okay?"

"What? I said I thought you'd be a starter next year."

"Well, thanks a lot, okay? I'm nineteen years old, was a superstar high school player, started on a junior college team, and hit in the high three-nineties. I'm impressed with you. We all are. I'll probably never play with anyone as phenomenal as you, and to top it off you've got to be thirteen years old. I know you know the game, and I know I should be encouraged when an expert like you tells me what a great future I have with this club, but you'll forgive me if that didn't make my day."

"You want to start this year, of course," Elgin tried, knowing he had messed up but not sure exactly how.

He eyes followed the crack of the bat. An easy double play was muffed when the third baseman dropped the liner.

"You're on deck," Doyle said.

"I'm sorry," Elgin said. "I don't know how to talk that good to people."

"Don't worry about it. It's all right. I'm just in a mood."

"Can I make it up to you somehow?" Elgin was moving for his bat.

"Yeah," Doyle said. "Yeah, you can. Sacrifice fly to right. Drive in Burke from third."

"Wish that was a righty on the mound," Elgin said. "Then I could just try to pull one deep. With a lefty, I have to get an outside pitch to push the other way."

"The guy'll be trying to keep stuff away from you, anyway," Doyle said. "Should be easy."

"That's true," Elgin said.

The hitter ahead of him grounded sharply to third. The third baseman looked the runner back at third, saw he had no play at second, then threw across to first for one out. Elgin hurried back to the dugout from the on-deck circle.

"Doyle, with two guys in scoring position I'd rather try to drive em both in with a hit. Okay?"

"Geez, Woodell, I was only kidding! Do what you have to do! Be sure to get one of them in anyway."

"Right!"

Elgin knew if he hit anything to the right side of the infield, at least one run would score. A single to center or right would likely get both men in. He fouled a pitch straight back, then took two close pitches for balls. He looked for a hitter's pitch, got it, but pulled it foul down the left field line. He kicked the dirt.

Stupid! he told himself. Stop trying to pull!

He guessed the pitcher would try to keep the ball away from him after that loud foul. With two strikes he had to protect the plate, even on a pitch low and away as the next one was. He golfed it into right, sending the fielder down the line into foul territory. Both runners tagged up and broke with the catch. The throw skipped past the cutoff man and both runs scored.

When Elgin returned to the bench to the backslaps of the runners and his other teammates, Doyle sat shaking his head.

"You are incredible," Doyle said. "You hit your sac fly to right and still drove both runs in!"

"Guy should have let that ball drop foul," Elgin said. "Really a stupid play."

"He made a nice catch. With you hitting, he's got to try to get the out."

"No, he lets that ball drop and I've still got a two-two count. There's still a chance to get me out with no damage. He had to know at least one would score if he catches that ball with his back to the infield."

Doyle stared at him. "You still need a couple of hits to reach .700, Coach."

49

ELGIN GOT THE TWO HITS HE NEEDED that night. In fact, he got three more, but he was also out once on a fly to deep center. His average climbed to .704, but that was the least momentous happening in his life that night.

When the game was over, and Chicago had drubbed Arlington Heights 13–2, Elgin was surrounded by photographers and reporters. With Coach Koenig at his ear, reminding him to answer only questions about the season and that night's game, Elgin was learning to ignore questions about his future, his agent, his history.

"Is it true your dad was Neal Woodell?" someone asked.

That stopped him cold. He looked at his coach, who shrugged.

Elgin nodded, a lump in his throat. "That's my dad."

"Is he here?"

"No, sir. He's dead. He died in…in Alabama. I don't want to talk about it." After a few more questions about the game, scouts pretending to be reporters asked him where he went to school, where he lived, and about his family. He dodged them all, and Koenig ended the impromptu news conference. Mr. Thatcher, Elgin's mother, and Luke waited at the edge of the crowd for him. When reporters saw him with them, they surged to try to talk to Billy Ray.

"I'll not be answering any questions tonight, ladies and gentlemen," he said. He pulled cards from his wallet and again distributed several.

When Elgin, Miriam, and Lucky were all in Thatcher's rented car, Billy Ray asked if they would enjoy room service dessert at the Hyatt Regency.

"You can just drop me off at the L," Luke said from the back seat, next to Miriam. "I got an early morning tomorrow."

"Oh Lucas, no," Miriam said softly. "You're welcome. He's welcome, isn't he, Mr. Thatcher?"

"Absolutely. And I'm not just being polite, sir. Miriam confides in you, and I have a lot of news for her this evening. I won't infringe upon your schedule, however, if you really have to get home. In fact, I'll drop you at your place."

Luke was silent for a second. "If I really won't be intruding—"

"Of course not," Miriam said.

Elgin was still high on the game. He twisted in his seat next to Mr. Thatcher to talk to Luke. "Did you see my hit in the first?"

"I was just getting there," Luke said. "I saw the outfielders chasing it and someone circling the bases. I wasn't sure it was you. I was just hopin. You would've scored. No doubt. Those guys ran past the ball, one of em from each side."

"You see that guy knock me over?"

"Sure did. I was runnin to get there, but by the time I got to the fence at the third base side they were already kickin him out and your coach was screamin at him."

"I showed that guy," Elgin said, sighing. "And we've pretty much pushed them out of the race too."

Miriam leaned forward and put her hands on Billy Ray Thatcher's shoulders, whispering in his ear as her son and Lucas talked baseball.

"I can't wait to hear what's going on," she said.

Billy Ray turned his head to the left so he could speak without the other two hearing. "Let me just say that your lives will never be the same. I should have known this, or at least figured it, but Rafer Williams is already more than aware of Elgin."

"You're not serious."

"I am."

"I'll wait for the rest," Miriam said, and she sat back.

Lucas was rhapsodizing about a play Elgin had made in the fourth inning.

"Yeah, but that doesn't make up for my error in the sixth."

"Hey, you got to prove you're human!"

Elgin laughed. "Doyle was talking about me not being human tonight."

Miriam was lost in her thoughts. Rafer Williams! The first former player, and the first black man to become commissioner of baseball. He had proven himself in all kinds of crises, and, if anything, he had a reputation as a hard-nosed traditionalist. How in the world could he have heard about Elgin?

Miriam loved the beauty of the city at night when she couldn't see the grime and the crime. She also loved the smell of a new car. The last thing she wanted was to feel conspicuous in the lobby of the big hotel, but she knew she would. She wouldn't know whether to open her own door when the valet came to park the car. She wouldn't know where to stand, who to be next to, what to do when they entered.

Her jeans and sweater and jacket fit her nicely and drew compliments, but they were out of place at a fancy, formal hotel. Maybe that's why Billy Ray had suggested room service. Surely he wasn't ashamed of his company, but maybe he knew she and her son and her friend would be more comfortable in private. She left her glass bowl in the bag on the seat of the car.

When she saw the place Billy Ray had rented, she knew why he wanted to eat there. It was the type of a room you had to show off. And it wasn't just a room. It was a suite with a parlor and a kitchenette. It was, she quickly realized, not only a hundred times more opulent than her flat, but twice as large as well. She couldn't help but mention it, realizing she sounded like a gee-whiz hick.

"It probably costs half as much a night as your place costs for a month too," Billy Ray said. "I worked a lot of years to travel like this, and as a matter of fact, flying first class and staying in a suite is company policy for senior partners, even retiring ones."

"Must be nice," she said, still gawking.

"Get used to it," he said. "It could become an everyday thing for you."

"I'm not sure I'd ever be comfortable."

"You might surprise yourself."

Billy Ray took dessert orders and phoned them in. He also asked the front desk to hold all his calls for a couple of hours. He then waited to break his news till room service delivered and everyone finished looking around and trying the bathrooms. Miriam wanted to remember everything about this night. Later she might tell Elgin that her feelings for Lucas had become more serious. She wouldn't do that in front of Lucas, not without his permission.

Mr. Thatcher amused Miriam by eating his huge strawberry shortcake with a tiny, long-stemmed spoon clearly intended for something else. It made the big man look dainty, and she thought of how he missed his wife, how they had courted, and what a sentimental and romantic man he was.

"You called me none too soon," he said finally, between bites and careful dabs at his lips with a napkin. "It's darn good I was at that game tonight. You were sitting on a bubbling caldron and didn't even know it."

"I had an idea," Miriam corrected. "Or at least Mr. Koenig did."

"Well, wait till you hear this," he said. "These scouts have been on Elgin's trail since the preseason. Koenig has done a magnificent job of keeping them away from Elgin and from you. They're all aware of the problem of Elgin's age, and every one of them came to watch him with a good deal of skepticism. They all thought it was a fluke the first several times they saw him, but once they got over the shock and the sheer mountain of numbers he was racking up, they started studying him seriously. Was he strong enough to drive a big league fastball? How were his mechanics? Did he work hard? Was he a smart player, a good baserunner, have all the tools?

"They've all decided, of course, that he's pro material, but they know they've got a selling job ahead of them. What's a real stitch is that they're all telling each other that he's a myth, not worth pursuing, an interesting aberration, all that. In private they're begging their bosses and the front offices to come out and see him. What's happening with almost every club is that the brass has made inquiries to the commissioner's office. What they're asking is, if we found a kid who was underage, what could we do about signing him? I doubt if any of them have had the guts to admit up front that they were referring to a thirteen-year-old."

"So what does the commissioner think?" Miriam asked.

"The word I get is that he pieced together about a half-dozen of these requests and then called in the parties and demanded to know just who they were talking about. When it came out that it was a Chicago-based kid who was playing summer collegiate ball at Elgin's age, he hit the roof. He told them to get serious, that he was not going to be party to any publicity stunts, child labor controversies, or gimmicks. That scared everybody off for a while until more and more teams heard about Elgin and began checking the Chicago papers for statistics. Now the commissioner has a problem."

"What's that?"

"He has to realize there's something to this. He may not believe Elgin's age, but then I suspect few ever have. He wants to check Elgin out for himself, but he doesn't want to draw any attention to the situation. What's the guy supposed to do? He can't sneak into Chicago for a private tryout. Right now he's trying to make a decision. Apparently the statistics for the first half of the season have convinced him Elgin is for real. He knows if the press and the public find out about it, he'll be expected to make a decision about Elgin's eligibility for the June draft."

"So eligibility has nothing to do with just whether he's good enough?" Miriam said.

"Miriam, let me give you an example from our own neck of the woods. A few years ago one of the guys on our staff took a case from Huntsville, Alabama. This guy specializes in sports stuff—still handles some of Bernie Pincham's deals and such. Seems six batboys for the Stars, the double A team in Huntsville, had to quit working every night before nine o'clock because of a state statute that says kids under sixteen, and these boys were all fourteen and fifteen, can't work that late."

"But surely batboys have been doin that for years," Luke said.

"Right, until the parent of a boy who wasn't selected as a batboy complained to the Department of Industrial Relations. Then they had to enforce the statute."

"What do they do about paperboys or kids who work in family businesses?"

"Well, there are laws like this in almost every state, and almost every state has certain exceptions. Obviously the law is there to protect kids from unscrupulous employers. If a kid wants to work and has parental permission, the authorities usually look the other way. These were kids living a dream, making a few dollars a game. With Elgin, we're talking about a kid, even younger than those batboys, who stands to make millions and travel and work in several states."

"I already told you, Mr. Thatcher," Miriam said, "Elgin will not be playin ball during the school year, either in the spring or in the fall. And he will not be travelin anywhere without me."

"And I won't be playing for an American League organization either," Elgin piped up.

"We're getting picky now, are we?" Luke said.

"Those guys know I'm way ahead at the plate but that I don't have the speed or strength or range or arms of older players. I can see them making me a designated hitter."

"Not a bad idea," Thatcher said.

"Oh, yes it is," Elgin said. "I hate it. I've always hated it. And unless there was no choice, I'd never want to be a DH."

"Well, honey," Miriam said, "that's certainly something we can talk about when the time comes."

"No, Momma. I think we should talk about it now. I think it's something that Mr. Williams should know about and that all these scouts should know too. There's no sense them going to all this trouble trying to sign me if I won't play for them."

Miriam was embarrassed, but Thatcher was apparently not thrown by Elgin's opinion. "How serious are you about this?" he probed.

Elgin shook his head as if he couldn't find the words. "I wouldn't want to be a designated hitter for all the money in the world."

Thatcher chuckled. "That may be how much you'll be offered. But if you're dead set that way, I will definitely communicate that."

"Let me ask you this," Miriam said. "If I decide that my son can sign and travel and be up late enough to play in night games durin the summer, why should anybody be able to keep me from doin that? I mean, is this age discrimination or somethin?"

"Now, I've never heard it argued over a young person before, but you may have a point. If the only criterion is age, Elgin is being discriminated against. You're stipulating that he will not miss school and that he would travel and play (or work, as the law would call it) only with your supervision, so to deny him that privilege would be wrong."

"Of course it would," she said.

"And you know what?" the old lawyer said. "We've got something else wonderful going for us. Baseball is a law unto itself. That's not all good, but in our case, it's not all bad. We'll have to wrangle with a lot of opponents, no doubt, but if Rafer Williams can be convinced, we're halfway home."

"Are you going to talk to him?"

"I'm thinking about it. Right now I'm of a mind to let him call me. Lots of reporters and scouts have my name and number, so it won't be long before I begin hearing from people. I expect his office will contact me."

"Your phone light's been blinkin for quite a while," Luke said.

"Well, I won't be returning any calls this late. And anyway, one of the things you'll learn about negotiating is that the silent one is the one in control. And the one with the commodity everyone else wants need not appear eager in the least."

"So now," Miriam said, "Elgin is a commodity."

Billy Ray looked thoughtfully at her. "He is exactly in the position he wants to be in. If you don't want him to be a commodity, you can take him off the trading block any time you want."

50

AS THE FOURSOME EMERGED FROM THE ELEVATOR on the second floor, Billy Ray Thatcher excused himself and stopped at the front desk.

"Take the escalator and wait for me at the front door," he told the others. "Mr. Harkness, if you wouldn't mind giving this to the bellman."

Luke took the ticket for the car and snorted. "Ha! I'm sure they're gonna bring somebody who looks like me a car that looks like it belongs to someone like you!"

But before they reached the escalator, Luke, Miriam, and Elgin met several men Elgin recognized as scouts. "You must be looking for Mr. Thatcher," Elgin said.

"Exactly."

Elgin pointed to the desk, where Thatcher stood with a stack of phone messages in his hand. As soon as he saw what was happening, he hurried over. "I'm sorry, gentlemen. Not tonight."

The men demanded to know when he would be back.

"Please, call me in the morning, after ten."

Once in the car, Mr. Thatcher kept staring disgustedly in his rearview mirror. At a stoplight he leaped from the car and stomped back to talk to the driver behind him. He returned before the light changed. "Really!" he said. "It's like these guys are living in an old movie."

"A scout was followin us?" Miriam said. "What for?"

"They want to know where you live. They'll try to get to Elgin through you or around you if they don't get satisfaction from me. If anyone approaches you when I'm not around, keep insisting that everything come through me. That is, if that's the way you want it."

"Don't give that a second thought," Miriam said. "I'd have either bopped someone or signed my son's life away by now."

"Well, the first thing they'll want to know is whether I have any idea how much Elgin might be worth. When they find out I represented Pincham, they'll know I'm not intimidated by big numbers. This is a whole new frontier though. Who could ever calculate the worth to a ball club of signing the youngest professional athlete in history?"

Mr. Thatcher dropped off Luke at his third floor room near the second-hand shop, then wheeled around the corner, rode the elevator with Miriam and Elgin, and walked them to their flat. "I don't want to come in or keep you up any later," the lawyer said. "I just wanted to make sure there weren't any scout gremlins roaming the halls."

"The man at the desk downstairs would not allow that," Miriam said.

"The one who slept through our arrival, you mean?" Thatcher said, chuckling. "He gives me a great deal of confidence."

"Do you have a plan?" Miriam asked.

"Just to wait and let things build. We're in the best position we can be in just now. All I need to know from you is exactly what you want. I'll have the office draw up an agreement between us, but before I get serious with the baseball people, I need to know we're all on the same page."

Miriam looked at Elgin, whose eyes were heavy. "You know what I want, Momma. I want to go as far as I can as fast as I can, and no DH."

She turned to Thatcher with her brows raised. "You heard him. What he wants is what I want. You know my rules."

"And do you want me to do my absolute best for him financially?"

"Mr. Thatcher, I don't even know what that means."

"It means that if he's as good as he appears, he should be worth millions and millions."

"You'd better come in a minute. I want this boy to go to bed, and I need to talk to you." Miriam spent the next half-hour telling Billy Ray Thatcher about the Clovis Payoff. "The last thing I want is for Elgin to be my ship that's come in. If he gets his mind messed with all this money, it'll affect his game. But more than that, I don't want to look like a mother who's used her kid to get rich. That's not my motive and not my wish. I wish I could do like you and take an hourly fee, just so people would know. But I realize all this is going to have to be in my name until he's of age. Mr. Thatcher, I can't even get my mind around that kind of money. I work with dollar figures all day, and they mean nothing. The biggest check that ever had anything to do with me was one for around ten thousand that was part of Neal's signing bonus. That was on your desk one minute and spent the next. If Elgin comes into a lot of money—which it sounds like he will, even if he never gets past the first level of minor league ball—I am not going to let it get squandered."

Billy Ray removed his suit coat and draped it over a chair. He loosened his tie. "That's really all I need to hear, Miriam. I'd like to do for you what Neal would never let me do for him. We have people in our office who will manage your money for you, saving it, investing it, accounting for it. I'll keep you informed all the way. You're going to have every fast-buck artist in the country on your doorstep if anything comes of this, and you need to send all of them my way too."

"I'm grateful," she said.

"I'm tired," he said.

⚾ ⚾ ⚾

Miriam was awakened before dawn by persistent thumping on the door. She sat up groggy and panicked, reaching for her robe. "Elgin?" she whispered as loud as she dared.

He hit the floor and hurried to her. "Who's that?" he mouthed.

She held him. "If it's an agent I'm gonna beat him with a pan. Ricardo's supposed to protect us."

The pounding continued.

"It's me, Mrs. Woodell! It's just me, Ricardo! You have to see this!"

She ran a hand through her hair and began unlatching all the locks. "This had better be good," she muttered.

Elgin hid behind her in his underwear as she cracked the door and squinted at the light from the hall. Why had she ever thought it too dim?

"Look, look!" Ricardo said, shouldering his way in and then realizing that with the couch unfolded, this was his tenant's bedroom. "Excuse me. Forgive me. But I knew you'd want to see this. A light, please."

Elgin threw on a shirt and pants and returned to the now bright room where his mother stood in robe and slippers and Mr. Bravura leaned over a table in his sleeveless undershirt. He spread the *Chicago Tribune* so they could both see it. Elgin's picture appeared on the left side of page one, announcing a story in the sports section: "Teen Phenom Sets Sights on Majors."

In a huge story inside—with photos from the previous night's game—Elgin's saga was played out. Somehow, the reporter knew everything. Everything except about the pitching machine and the name of the "family friend" who attended the game with his mother. Most amazing to Elgin were quotes attributed to the Arlington Heights players, including the leadoff man and shortstop.

> "He's a player," Brian Ewart, 20, said. "I ran him over on a bunt in the first inning and he came up scrappy. After his inside-the-park homer, I got booted and he stayed in and killed us. He's got it all."

The article made much of Elgin's batting average and raised the question of whether he was too good for summer collegiate-level baseball.

> "Of course he is," Coach Jim Koenig says. "You only want to hit over .500 in a softball league. These few kids who run up astronomical numbers are showing they're ready for the next step."
>
> But the next step would be college, and Elgin Woodell just turned thirteen. He won't be eligible for the professional baseball draft until he graduates from high school, five years from now.
>
> There is the possibility of some genetic advantage from the boy's father, a short-term minor league standout in the Pittsburgh Pirate organization. Neal L. Woodell died last year of an alcohol-related illness at the Alabama State Penitentiary in Birmingham where he was serving a lengthy term for reckless homicide while driving without a license.

Elgin was thrilled, but his mother was in tears.

"All our business, right out there for everybody."

"You should be happy," Ricardo said. "Somebody famous right under your own roof. They even have the address here, but not the name of the place."

"That's a relief," she said. "Otherwise your phone would be ringin off the hook, and we'd have to move. We may have to anyway."

"Oh, no, we don't want that!" Ricardo said. "You stay here and I'll protect you!"

"May I keep this?" Miriam said.

"Of course! I'll order more. I'd like to post this in the lobby, let people know who they're living with! Royalty, Elgin. You're like royalty."

Elgin didn't feel so special. He had dreamed of this kind of a story, but the last thing he wanted was for it to hurt his mother.

"I have to get goin," she said. "I can just imagine what kind of a day I'm gonna have at work."

"I'm sorry, Momma," Elgin said as Ricardo excused himself.

"Oh, I guess I knew this was coming," she said. "I just didn't expect it to wake me up and slap me in the face this mornin."

"I know we left Mississippi because you didn't want everybody knowing our business."

"Well, it's not so terrible now that your dad is gone. It's all in the past. I know if you keep on doin what you're doin, my privacy will be a thing of the past too. You'd better get some breakfast and get ready for work yourself, young man."

"Momma, you think I still have to work when we're so close to going professional?"

Elgin could tell by the look on her face that she was not amused. "You are an employee, Elgin. You don't quit without notice, and you don't quit without knowin where your next check is comin from. You could be years away from makin money in baseball. I know everybody believes different, and I s'pose I do too. But don't start—"

"I know, Momma. Don't start counting your chickens and all that."

"Anyway, you want to just leave Lucas high and dry? He's grown very fond of you, El, and he won't be happy if you up and quit on him."

"Lucky has grown fond of *me*? C'mon, Mom, you think I'm blind? I think I'll be seeing a lot of Lucky whether I work for him or not. Right?"

She didn't respond.

"Right?"

He could see she was fighting a smile. "Right, Momma?"

"You're obnoxious sometimes, Elgin, you know that?"

"Course I do. Doyle told me that last night. I'm obnoxious and rich."

"Get some breakfast."

51

I'VE GOT A COUPLE OF ERRANDS TO RUN this morning," Luke Harkness told Elgin. "Could you watch the place while I'm gone?"

"Could I?"

Elgin loved the idea of selling, of dealing, of negotiating. He only wished it was his responsibility in his own career. Luke told him how to call for help if needed, what to do and what not to do.

"Your mom will probably kill me when she hears I left you here alone, but I'll only be gone about two hours. I'll call you in an hour or so, okay?"

"Don't worry about me, Lucky."

Elgin strapped on the apron Luke often wore. He had to take it halfway around his body again before he could tie it. Luke wasn't a big man, but he was sure bigger than Elgin. The boy waited expectantly behind the cash register, rehearsing his lines.

"I can let that go for fifteen. The boss paid about ten for it, so it'd be a real deal."

But no one showed up. Not one customer. Two or three peered in the window and kept moving. One did some window shopping, but scowled and walked away. After an hour, Lucky called.

"One more stop and I'm on my way back," he said. "I should be a little earlier than I thought. Any customers?"

"Nope."

"None?"

"Nope."

"What do you think of that?"

"I think they see a kid here and they don't want to come in," Elgin said.

"Nah. Hey, if nobody comes by, I'll try to buy somethin off ya when I get there."

Elgin smiled. "Good-bye, Lucky."

About ten minutes before he expected Lucky, a middle-aged woman stopped at the window, looked at the door, looked through the window again, then knocked tentatively, her eyes on Elgin.

"It's open!" Elgin called.

She pushed the door slowly, ringing the bell. "You're open for business?"

"Yes, ma'am. May I help you?"

"You're open then?"

He fought the urge to shout. Was she deaf? "Yes, ma'am."

"Well, you might want to turn your sign around then. It says Closed."

"Oh, man!"

Elgin hurried over and turned the sign around. He smacked himself in the head.

"Was that your responsibility, son?"

"No, but I should've noticed when I got here."

The woman asked about used clothes.

"Not for women, ma'am. I'm sorry. We just have sports clothes and military surplus."

She thanked him and passed Lucky on the way out.

"I see you noticed the sign," Luke said sheepishly.

"Not till that woman showed me. You do that?"

"Yeah. Sorry. I figured if you noticed, hey, okay. If you didn't, well it was just a slow day and I didn't do something stupid by leaving you here alone."

"Lucky, what'd you do to yourself?"

"You can't tell?"

"Your beard is gone! Geez!"

Lucky had had some gray in his red beard, but now with it gone, including his sideburns, he looked younger. He was red-haired and freckle-faced, just like Elgin's mom, and he was a good-looking guy. He had left only a bushy mustache.

"I like it!"

"Really?" Luke looked self-conscious as he took the apron from Elgin and slid a crisp, new manila envelope under the counter.

"What's that?" Elgin asked.

"Personal. Listen, don't feel bad. You know we don't get much business in the morning anyway."

"Yeah, but I feel like you don't trust me."

"Elgin, listen to me. You've been great. I know you won't be here much longer, but I'll tell you one thing: If you ever need a job, you've always got one here."

"You mean like if I get into a slump?" They both laughed. "You were gonna try to buy something off me."

"Right! Where's that glass bowl, that ugly one I couldn't get rid of?"

"You know where it is as well as I do," Elgin said. "You think Mom wouldn't show me that?"

"You never know."

"You guys in love?"

Luke didn't say anything. He looked at the floor. "I can't speak for he he said finally.

"Then speak for you."

"I like her an awful lot. She's a wonderful woman."

"I know that."

"I know you do. Your ma and I have a lot in common."

Elgin chuckled. "Well, you look a lot alike. You're awful pretty together she's pretty and—"

"I know, and I'm awful. Very funny. Great junior high humor there, Elgin."

"You gonna get married?"

"Slow down, cowboy," Luke said. "She doesn't even know how I feel about her yet."

"The heck she doesn't. Guy gives a girl a present like that, well—"

"Shut up."

Elgin giggled. "Ugly thing."

"I know, but she loved it. She wanted it."

"So you gonna get married or not?"

"You're way ahead of me, pal."

"Going to our church was smart, Lucky."

"Hey! I went to that church long before you did. Don't accuse me of that. That's something I'd never do, fake something like that."

"I know. Mom knows too. You mean a lot to her."

Luke couldn't hide his pleasure. "I do?"

Elgin nodded. "So what's the deal? Mom won't tell me anything. You guys serious, or what?"

"I'm tellin ya, I don't know! We haven't even talked about it yet."

"Honest?"

"Honest."

"What'd you cut the beard off for?"

"What's that got to do with anything?"

"That's what I'm askin you."

"C'mon, Elgin. I cut my beard because I've had it more than twenty years."

"That's no reason. That's a reason to keep it. You cut it for Momma, didn't you?"

"Doesn't she like it?" Luke asked.

"She's never said, but you must think she doesn't like it."

"I don't think that."

"Then why'd you cut it?"

"I don't know."

"C'mon."

Lucky moved around to the front of the counter and leaned back on it. "Don't you have some sweepin or somethin to do?"

"Are you kidding? With all that free time you gave me this morning?"

"Sorry. I owe you."

"Tell me why you cut the beard and we'll be even."

"Man, Elgin, if Billy Ray Thatcher could play ball like you can pester, you two could trade jobs."

"I'm waiting."

"Your mom said something about never having seen me without the beard, so I thought maybe she deserved a peek."

"So! I was right! I knew it!"

"So am I gonna regret it? Is she gonna take one look and wish she'd never met me?"

⚾ ⚾ ⚾

When Miriam arrived home late that afternoon, she was disappointed to find that Elgin had nothing on the stove for dinner.

"I had it all ready in the refrigerator. All you had to do was—"

"I had some of it, Momma. And you don't need any."

"Elgin, I'm famished! All day interrupted by everybody stickin that newspaper under my nose, askin me how much longer I was gonna be workin there. I am so glad to be home—but what am I supposed to do for dinner?"

"You've got a date."

"I know. But Mr. Thatcher's not comin by till nine-thirty. I can't wait that long to—"

"Not that one. You've got another date."

"I do?"

"Yeah, Lucky told me to tell you."

"Tell me what?"

"That he's coming by for you at about six."

"You're supposed to tell me or ask me?"

"C'mon, Momma. You know you want to go out with him."

"Well, maybe I do and maybe I don't. But that's no way to ask for a date."

"So stand him up."

"What do you know about standing anyone up? Why didn't he call me at the office?"

"He said he didn't want to embarrass you. He knows how you hate having people know your business."

"He said that?"

Elgin nodded.

"How sweet."

"So, you'll be ready at six?"

"I might. What am I supposed to wear?"

"Dress up."

"He said that?"

Elgin nodded. "Maybe he's gonna pop the question tonight, huh?"

"Elgin! Lucas and I hardly know each other! We're a long way from being that serious, so don't be worryin about that."

"I'm not worried."

"You're not?"

"No. Should I be?"

"I don't know, El. Do you like him?"

"Sure I do, Momma. Do you?"

"You know I do."

"Do you love him?"

"Well, that's none of your business."

"It is if you're gonna marry him."

"I'm *not* going to marry him! Now will you quit sayin that?"

"Well, don't marry him if you don't love him."

"Elgin!"

"At least tell me if you love the guy."

"Well, I certainly wouldn't tell you before I tell him!"

"So you do."

"I'm not saying another word about it."

"Don't you think I deserve to know?"

"Certainly not before he does."

"Have you kissed him yet?"

"Elgin!"

"Well, have you?"

"No! And I wouldn't tell you if I did!"

"Mom, this is my business."

"It most certainly is not."

"You're my business, aren't you?"

She shook her head and pressed her lips tight. In truth she was impressed and amused by this kid. She had worried what he would think, and she still wanted to know. She had imagined very seriously discussing with him how he might react if she and Lucas grew more serious about each other. Now here he was, bugging her, interested in their relationship.

He had to be wondering what it would be like to have a new man in the family. He had to wonder whether he was going to be adopted by a new father. He didn't seem apprehensive. She relaxed in the hope that he seemed excited about the possibilities.

And she was anxious about her date.

52

ELGIN HEADED FOR THE BASEMENT at about a quarter to six, not wanting his mother to feel embarrassed about answering the door to the new Luke Harkness. He had said nothing to her about his newly smooth-faced boss. Who knew? She might want to hug Luke or something, and she would feel conspicuous with Elgin there. She had argued that Elgin should be there because it wouldn't look right, a man coming to their place when she was alone.

"Well, Momma, he wouldn't any more want to come in than you would want to invite him. He's more particular about that than you are."

Luke was the type to be on time. That's how Elgin guessed that the machine had painfully injured his wrist even before his mother had left on her date. He had set the machine up closer to the plate than ever, hoping that his excitement over what was happening to him would give him that extra surge of adrenaline that heightened his senses. It did, but it had also made him forget to double-check the aim of the thing before getting into the batter's box. The irony was, he thought about it at the last minute, as he stood in, helmet on, fungo bat in hand, hitting lefty. As the first golf ball rolled down the trough toward the spinning wheels, he thought, I sure hope this thing is throwing straight.

There was no time to move, even to flinch. He took the first pitch on his right wrist, an inch above his hand. Elgin dropped to the floor and scooted to his right, settling back against the wall where he knew he was safe. He was still within four feet of where the next fifty-six pitches slammed off the wall, and his ears hurt from the noise.

He couldn't tell if the wrist was broken, but the spot where the ball drilled him was hot to the touch. He held it hard with his left hand, and every time he let go to look at it, he nearly screamed with pain.

He knew he needed to treat it somehow, but he didn't want his mother to see it before she and Luke left. He figured they would be long gone by five after six. He would wait till ten after to be sure, and those proved to be long minutes. He rotated his wrist to check for a break. It didn't feel broken, but he'd had no experience with such injuries. He'd been hit enough times, but all he cared about now was how long he might be out. Of all the times for such an injury, and he had no one to blame but himself.

⚾ ⚾ ⚾

"Lucas! You shaved your beautiful beard! Did you save the hair?"

"You're kidding, right? I knew you wanted me to cut it, but I didn't think you'd want me to save it. I thought you hated it."

Miriam squinted at him. It seemed only right to invite him in, but she knew he would feel funny if he knew Elgin wasn't there.

"I never said I hated your beard," she said as she pulled the door shut behind her and they started down the hall. "I just said I had never seen you without it."

"Well, here I am," he said, smiling self-consciously.

"I like your face," she said, knowing that sounded crass.

"You should. Your son says I look like you."

She let out a laugh. "Then you'd better stop talkin bad about your looks." She noticed he was carrying a manila envelope. "Now what's this all about?"

"I just thought we ought to have a formal date," he said. "We never really have, you know. You didn't have to accept."

"I wanted to accept, though your invitation wasn't exactly traditional. How would I have refused? Sent our courier back to you?"

Luke shrugged. "Sorry. I didn't want to call you at work."

"I know. So, Elgin already saw this shave, huh?"

"Yes, ma'am. He didn't say anything, did he?"

"No."

They boarded the L a few blocks away. Miriam had dressed as if for church. It was the only thing she had to wear other than what she wore to work. Luke wore a tie and a corduroy jacket. Neither looked new, but they were new to her. He looked great, but Miriam thought she had complimented him enough for one evening, maybe too much.

He took her to a family restaurant a few miles west. She tried to be calm, but she felt like a teenager. It wasn't the date, though this was more awkward than just hanging out with Lucas and her son, as they usually did. Even their private walks were casual. This was different. And that envelope intrigued her. She had been amused at Elgin's mention of Lucas's popping the question. Some men might be presumptuous enough to jump that far ahead, but not Lucas.

They talked less than they ever had, and Miriam decided she didn't like this date so far. If it wasn't for the promise of the envelope, she might have admitted that to him. But he had said he needed to talk to her, so she hung on to that.

The food was plain and moderately priced. She worried about Lucas spending money on her. She knew he was self-sufficient, and it seemed he was comfortable for a man who didn't own a home or a vehicle. Because he was frugal and careful, he seemed to have discretionary income. He was not extravagant in the least, but this meal alone would have been a burden for Miriam's budget.

"Everything I need is in the neighborhood," he'd said more than once. She hoped he still thought so.

⚾ ⚾ ⚾

Elgin left the fifty-seven golf balls strewn about the floor and ignored too his glove, bat, and helmet. His workout was over for the evening. Cradling his right wrist in his left hand, he went upstairs to the elevator and let himself into the flat. His wrist had begun to swell, scaring him. He held it under the cold water tap.

He thought he should have it x-rayed, just to be safe, but he assumed he shouldn't do that without his mother knowing. The Cubs were on TV, so he turned them on and took to the couch a large bowl and a supply of ice cubes wrapped in a washcloth. He sat there, his wrist throbbing and his head aching, the cubes turning to water as the Cubs lost big. The swelling may have been slowed, but it did not reverse.

When the ballgame became a laugher and Elgin's fear reached a crescendo, he rummaged for some change and headed downstairs to call Mr. Thatcher at the Hyatt.

⚾ ⚾ ⚾

Miriam was impressed when Lucas paid the waitress and asked if she minded if they sat and talked awhile. The girl noticed the generous tip and smiled as she left.

"Well," Luke said, focusing on Miriam, "I can't put this off any longer."

"You make it sound like bad news."

"Oh, it's not. At least I hope it's not. This morning, just after I got my beard shaved, I visited Mr. Thatcher."

Miriam's mind raced for a possible reason.

"I just wanted to make a few things clear to him and ask him to help me make them clear to you. I gotta tell ya, one of the things I like about you and him is how unselfish you're bein with Elgin. I mean, we can all see what's happening here, and I think it's great that you're worried about the money and what people will think of you because of it. And Billy Ray's, uh, Mr. Thatcher's workin for just his hourly fee, well, that's just incredible."

"Yes, Mr. Thatcher is a wonderful man. Of course, his hourly fee is about half a week's salary for me."

"But you know he's not going to charge you unless there's some income for Elgin."

"I know that," she said evenly.

"And he's not charging you expenses, like his car and hotel and travel and all that."

"I'm aware of that too." Miriam stared at Lucas. Something bothered her about his having thought all this through.

Luke reached for her hand. "I'm sorry, Miriam. I don't mean to be telling you anything you already know. It's just that I become more and more impressed with Mr. Thatcher. He's been really kind to me, and I'm just a friend here. When you said something about his fee, I just wanted to defend him, but of course I know I don't have to defend him to you."

Miriam nodded. Luke still covered her hand across the table, but she was not responsive. He noticed and pulled back, producing a folder from the manila envelope.

"Miriam, I asked Mr. Thatcher to help me draw this up today, and I told him I wouldn't do it unless he let me pay him. It was hard to talk him into it, but I finally did get to pay for having the typing and copying and notary public stuff done by a service in the hotel."

Lucas handed her the folder with a smile and a look of excited anticipation. Twenty minutes before, she would have returned his smile and eagerly read the document. Now she dreaded knowing what it was about.

The two pages were filled with legal mumbo jumbo, but she recognized her name and Elgin's name and "To all parties concerned as of this date and following re: present and future earnings of one Elgin Neal Woodell."

She saw several "whereases" and "wherefores" and "therefores," and a "Be it known to all that..." and her heart sank. Her eyes darted back and forth over the pages until the words swam together. Anger and disappointment rose in her and she wondered if she could speak. If he had spoken just then, she would not have heard him for the pounding in her ears. Her first impulse was to jump and run, to get away, to leave the document, to find Billy Ray. How could Lucas reduce their relationship to words on paper and then try to benefit from it?

⚾ ⚾ ⚾

The hotel operator told Elgin Mr. Thatcher's line was busy.

"Is there any way I could leave a message?" Elgin didn't have much change.

"Certainly, son. We can turn on his message light and ask him to return your call."

"Well, I'm at a pay phone and I know he sometimes doesn't even ask for his messages until later."

"Is this an emergency?"

"Um, yeah. It sort of is."

"Sort of?"

"Yeah, it is."

"Emergency or just important?"

"I don't know the difference, ma'am."

"Well, if it's an emergency I can interrupt the call he's on. If it's just sort of important, I can try to keep an eye on when he hangs up and ring him right away."

"Yeah, that would be good."

"Let me have that number."

Elgin hung up and turned to lean against the wall. Then he slid to sit right under the pay phone. He stayed there even when smelly old Mrs. Majda ordered her nightly smelly old pizza. He was still sitting there when Mr. Bravura's holler came from the ground floor that she had a delivery. She gave Elgin the same dirty look on her way by in her robe that she had given him when she was on the phone and he was still sitting there.

On her way back by with the pungent pie, she ignored him. He only hoped Mr. Thatcher had not tried to reach him while she had been on the phone.

53

MIRIAM GRADUALLY REGAINED HER COMPOSURE, though she was no happier. She placed the documents back in the folder and handed them across the table. Luke was still smiling.

"Lucas, why don't you just tell me, in your own words, exactly what this thing says? I don't understand the language, and I want to hear it from you."

"Okay," he said, "just so you know I went about it the right way, got it done up legally, and that it's binding with my signature."

"You can't bind anything that has to do with me or with Elgin without our signatures."

Luke's smile froze. "You don't understand," he said.

"No, I don't. That's why I want to hear it from your own lips."

He seemed to stall by opening and closing the folder, then opening it again to peruse the document. He replaced it in the envelope. "Well, this is not easy for me to say," he began. "I wasn't very good about romantic stuff, even when I was married."

Romantic stuff? Miriam thought. She had not imagined she could become more uncomfortable.

"That was one of Lucy's complaints—I told you all about her, that I didn't know how to express my deepest feelings for her. But I told you once that I wouldn't even hold your hand unless...unless I, you know, unless I really cared for you."

"What you said was that you wouldn't even so much as hold my hand unless you were in love with me."

"Right, that's what I said."

"And you've since held my hand."

"Right."

He said nothing more.

"And so from that I should be able to assume something?"

"Right." He was smiling.

"Your late wife was right," she said coolly. "You don't express yourself well directly."

"I'm sorry," he said. "I'm trying. Don't make it more difficult for me."

She thought about apologizing and found that ironic. She remained silent.

"I held your hand because I realized that I was falling in love with you." He spoke quietly, haltingly, and she realized how she had longed to hear those words. Now she was not sure. They begged a response, one she thought she had been prepared to give.

"You let me hold your hand," he continued, "and at first I thought you meant the same by it that I did. But I had to be sure. I pulled back a little. Then at the shop you made it clear you...that you, uh, enjoyed at least shaking hands. At the game last night, you gave me your hand."

She waited, her face intentionally impassive.

"I thought maybe we felt the same about each other," he said. He seemed to wait for a response.

"Go on," she said, trying not to sound stiff or cold, just noncommittal.

"I didn't know where our relationship might lead," he said.

She nodded, agreeing that she faced the same uncertainties. She hated to make it so difficult for him, but if he was about to tell her that he had made some huge assumption about how Elgin's future would impact his, because they seemed to be getting serious about each other, she wasn't prepared to encourage him.

"The last thing I wanted was for you to think I was, what do they call it—an opportunist," Lucas said. "I mean, you and Mr. Thatcher are sure not."

"That's right. We're not. We hate that kind of a thing."

"I thought you might. No, I mean I *knew* you would. I know you at least that well."

"You should."

"Right, I sure should. Even though we really don't know each other all that well yet, do we?"

"No, we sure don't." How she longed for him to get to the point.

"So, anyway, I got to thinkin about that stupid little gift I gave you. I wasn't trying to mock you or be cheap. To tell you the truth, I just wanted you to know that I hear you when you talk. You said it was so ugly it was cute, and when I said it seemed like you liked it, you said you sorta did.

And then you said that about not ever seein me without my beard. I didn't want to seem weak or easy to lead, but I thought, hey, why not? Girl I'm in love with wants to see what she might be gettin herself into, then okay. I don't want you to have any surprises, not that I'm sayin we're gonna wind up spending the rest of our lives together."

"But when two available adults seem to start getting serious about each other, that's always a possibility."

"Right," he said.

"And so you didn't want me to be surprised by anything."

"Right again. And thus this legal thing here related to me and Elgin."

She took a deep, frustrated, irritated, just short of disgusted breath. "And so now are you ready to tell me exactly what it says, in language I can understand?"

⚾ ⚾ ⚾

Elgin didn't realize his legs were tight and cramped until the phone rang and he sprang to his feet.

"What's up, son?" Mr. Thatcher said, and Elgin had never heard a more welcome voice.

Half an hour later Elgin had left a note for his mother and was in Billy Ray's car.

"You did the right thing, son," the lawyer said. "Doesn't look like the ulna or the radius have been broken, but you've for sure got a deep bruise on either the tendon or the ligament."

"I wish I knew what you were talking about," Elgin said.

"Well, maybe a doctor can explain it to you. We'll get a picture of it and see if it's serious or just a nuisance."

"Nothing's gonna keep me out for long," Elgin said.

"Listen, does it hurt so bad that you don't want a preview of what I'm going to be telling your mother tonight?"

"A preview?"

"Yes. Do you want to know what's been happening today as it relates to your future?"

"Sure."

"You, my young friend, are about to meet the commissioner of baseball in person."

⚾ ⚾ ⚾

"Sure," Luke Harkness said. "I guess I was kind of hoping you'd get the drift of it from the paper, but it was a little hard for me to understand too. What that thing says, if Mr. Thatcher understood exactly what I wanted to say, is that no matter what happens between you and me—whether we stay friends, or get engaged, or get married, or even live together— Now don't look at me like that. I just wanted to make that clear. I know we wouldn't. I wouldn't and you wouldn't, but even if we forgot our morals and somehow found ourselves in that situation, which we won't, this thing still stands."

"Which is?"

"Which is that I don't now, never have, and never will make any claim on any money your son or you get from anything having to do with his career."

Miriam held her breath. She was grateful he had more to say.

"I don't want anybody thinkin I would take advantage, even if you wanted me to. I have too much pride for that. I mean, if we got married someday and all I did was still run my store while Elgin was makin millions in the majors, that's the way I would want it. I mean, if he wants to give you or us something, that's his business, but I just wanted it legal and clear that I would never ask, never expect, never demand, never think I was entitled to anything. And like I say, if our relationship ever got that far and you were my wife, I would want us to make it on our own. As long as you and Mr. Thatcher wanted to make that clear about yourselves, I wanted to, too. In fact, I think I have more of a reason than you two. I could really look like a goldbricker."

Miriam couldn't speak.

"Mr. Thatcher told me I shouldn't worry about it, but the more I insisted, the more he liked the idea. He figured you'd appreciate it, but he said he didn't think you'd think it was necessary."

"It's not necessary, Lucas," she said, her voice thick. "In fact, I should be insulted that you felt you had to do it. But it's so you, so sweet." She reached for his hand.

"Um, you know what I'm sayin when I hold your hand, don't you?" he said.

"I do, but you're not going to get away with expressin yourself that way all the time. In honor of your Lucy, who sounds like a wonderful person, you're going to speak your mind from now on. You said you would only hold my hand if you loved me, and even though I didn't say it, I heard you, and I let you hold my hand because I'm acceptin your love. Would you like to know how I feel about you?"

He looked startled, as if she had been too bold. "Yes!"

"Then you know what it feels like to wonder. I would like you to tell me straight out."

"I love you, Miriam, and I've loved you since long before I held your hand."

"I love you too, Lucas."

He squeezed her hand. "You know you're the only person in my life, other than my mother, who calls me Lucas?"

"You want me to call you somethin else?"

"No!"

"What does your daddy call you?"

Luke laughed. "Don't ask!"

⚾ ⚾ ⚾

"I don't think it's a bone bruise," the doctor told Elgin and Billy Ray. "There's no break, but there is some subcutaneous hemorrhaging."

"Bleeding under the skin," Billy Ray translated for Elgin. "You're gonna be all right."

"It *is* going to hurt for a few days," the doctor said. "Maybe a few weeks."

"How about playing ball?" Elgin said.

The doctor stepped back and took a good look at his face. "It is you, isn't it? I wondered."

Elgin smiled. "Who?"

"You. You're the young baseball star, am I right?"

Elgin nodded.

"Ah, my first Chicago celebrity. Let me give you a prescription, and a wrap, and some counsel. Rest this wrist three days and you'll be good as new. You can then play ball and move it as much as you want. Let pain, or lack of it, be your guide."

"Three days?"

The doctor nodded.

"You can't make that two and a half days?"

"You have a game, I take it?"

"Yes, sir."

"If you can move it without undue pain, you may play."

On the way home, Mr. Thatcher told Elgin about Luke's legal commitment. Elgin asked a lot of questions to be sure he understood.

"So then that was pretty good of him to do that, right?" he said.

"It surely was," Billy Ray said. "It surely was. I like the man."

⚾ ⚾ ⚾

Miriam and Luke waited in chairs in the lobby when Elgin and Billy Ray arrived at the transient hotel.

"I've been worried sick," Miriam said, embracing the boy.

"You got my note then?"

She nodded and looked at his bandage. "What's this? What happened?"

"It's not that bad, Momma," Elgin said. "I'll tell you all about it, but wait till you hear Mr. Thatcher's news."

54

MIRIAM STOOD AMONG THE THREE MEN IN HER LIFE on the cramped, decaying elevator and suddenly felt tired. Too much was happening too soon in her life. Where had she been when her son was injured? And what might a more serious injury have meant to him, to all of them?

She was worried about her son, uncomfortable with all she was accepting and expecting from Mr. Thatcher, unable to keep track of how quickly things were moving. On top of all that, she was hopelessly, helplessly in love. She couldn't help but compare this compact, rock solid, gentle, mustachioed, self-sufficient soul with her late husband. Neal had been violent, yet weak, dependent, fatally flawed.

Miriam unlocked the flat and pushed the door open, but when she was inside she realized that Lucas had hung back and was waiting in the hall. He stood with his envelope in hand.

"I'm gonna head home," he said, when she peered out at him.

"I'll be right in," she told the others as she stepped out. "Lucas, what's wrong?"

"Nothing, really. I just don't want to presume that I have to be in on all this. I mean, I'm curious and interested and all that, but you can tell me about it tomorrow or sometime. It'll give us a reason to see each other again."

"Oh, I think we have reasons to see each other," she said, searching his eyes. Was he feeling left out, ignored, set aside?

"I know," he said. "But really, I'd feel better if I just got home, okay?"

"Whatever you say, Lucas. Just know that you're welcome."

"I know."

"Tonight was special for me," she said softly.

He reached for her wrist with his free hand and gently pulled her toward him. As she drew close, he slipped his hand lightly around her waist and lowered his face to hers.

"May I?" he whispered.

"You may," she said.

His bristly mustache tickled her nose as he brushed his lips against hers. He held her, she felt, like a fragile china doll. They kissed only briefly, and she was determined not to scratch her face. But she couldn't help it. She wrinkled her nose and rubbed her hand over it.

"I'm sorry, Lucas. I didn't mean to spoil the moment, but that tickled."

He grinned. "My fault. See you tomorrow?"

She embraced him, realized she was bending his envelope, and pulled back. "I'm really a klutz tonight," she said.

"We'll get it right," he said, and she was sure he blushed.

"Good night, sweetheart," she said. "You'd better say your good-byes." She nodded toward the apartment.

Billy Ray began to protest when Luke said he was walking home, but Luke would not be dissuaded. When he was gone, Elgin piped up.

"Did you kiss him, Momma?"

"Elgin! Let me see that wrist, and then you get to bed."

"But I want to hear—"

"I thought you said you had already heard this," she said.

"I did, but I want to see your reaction. And—"

"No. Just let me see, and then get going."

There wasn't much to look at. The wrist had been bandaged tightly with a two-inch width of white tape over a spongy cushion.

"I can cover that with a wristband and no one will even know, Momma. But the way it feels right now, I'll favor it and they'll notice."

"If you're not ready, you shouldn't play."

"I can play. I wouldn't be able to hit from either side or throw, but the doctor says it'll only be a few days if I take it easy. I don't guess I can sweep Lucky's floors either, huh?"

"Bed," she said.

Billy Ray Thatcher, gentleman that he was, didn't sit until Miriam did. She flopped onto the couch and sighed aloud.

"I'm beat," she said.

"You don't look beat," he said, a smile forming as he sat across from her. "You know what you look like?"

"I can hardly wait."

"You look like a woman in love."

"It shows? That's flattering."

"I'm happy for you," Thatcher said. "He seems like a great guy."

They talked about the document Lucas had insisted upon drafting, then about Elgin's phone call and the trip to the emergency room.

"He's pretty good with adults, isn't he?" Billy Ray said.

She nodded. "I guess that's good. He's going to need to be."

Thatcher told her he had been on the phone most of the day. "I could fly in a team to start taking these calls, but I finally did hear from the commissioner's office. That allows me to legitimately put everyone else on hold. This is an unusual case, and until he decides what he's going to do about it, I can't really talk seriously to any organization. The fact is, every team in the big leagues is aware of Elgin and wants to protect its interests. I might have expected some would ignore him, as they would any exaggerated report, but apparently there's some magic in how long Elgin has been keeping this up."

"Tell me about the commissioner's office," Miriam said.

"Well, he had assigned someone to check Elgin out for him. He didn't want to make a media event out of this before he knew whether there was anything to Elgin. You'll never guess who was secretly at Elgin's last half-dozen games. Ronny Dressel."

"The great pitcher from when I was a kid?"

"One and the same. Hall of Fame."

"Wouldn't he be recognized by the press or at least the scouts?"

"He's been sick the last several years. He's better now, but he's lost his hair, his coloring has changed, and he's lost a lot of weight. He's got a bit of a limp, wears glasses, and with a hat and the right jacket or sweater, he's invisible. He stays away from the scouts and press and doesn't carry a stopwatch or a radar gun. He told me today that he figured there were enough guns and clocks at these games to start a specialty store."

"Sounds like an interesting man."

"Very. I could hardly believe it when I got the message. He's staying at the Holiday Inn in Glen Ellyn under his wife's maiden name. Said he figured if he stayed that far out, no one would notice. His message came in his own name but told me to ask for him under the alias. I don't return most calls. I figure if they want me, they can keep trying. As I told you, we're in the driver's seat."

"But you returned his."

"You betcha. I admit at first I thought it was some scout or agent trying anything to get to us, and I was fully prepared to hang up on him. But I recognized the voice, and his story made sense."

"So, what does he think?"

"He thinks Elgin could play in any rookie league right now, and he wants Rafer to see him somehow. He knows Rafer couldn't come to a game or meet Elgin anywhere where anyone knew such a meeting was taking place, but we're trying to work that out. We even thought of asking Luke if the meeting could take place at his apartment."

Miriam laughed. "Well, no one would ever suspect. Oh, my! Lucas would never forget somethin like that!"

"Well, it would be a lot of cloak-and-dagger stuff. One thing I got from Dressel was very interesting. You remember we heard that *Sports Illustrated* was planning a major piece? Dressel heard they got frustrated trying to get to Elgin and decided to do the story anyway. It's coming out Monday."

"Oh, no."

"Well, it could be good for us. I can't see how it can be negative, unless they say he's being protected too carefully or that his mercenary mother has already acquired an agent. But even if they do say that, it will be easy to set the record straight on how carefully we're managing this for Elgin's protection. I don't want to have to make public my arrangement with you, but I will if I have to."

"Does the magazine know about the commissioner or about Mr. Dressel?"

"No. No one does except the three of us. We'll have to let Luke know soon if we want to use his place. I assume he can keep a confidence. This could make or break us."

"Oh, he can. He will."

"We'll want to stall a meeting until Elgin's healthy and performing at his peak again. It's too bad he's got games Monday and Tuesday, because if that story hits, we're talking national media attention. You'd hate to see him have a bad game after that and make everyone think he'll fold under the spotlight."

"Elgin loves the spotlight. If he's healthy, he'll do better."

"If he's healthy."

⚾ ⚾ ⚾

A bigger than average crowd attended Monday night's game and seemed restless when Elgin took neither batting nor infield practice. He was placed eighth in the batting order and took his position at second in the top of the first.

He had not had one chance in the field when he came to the plate to lead off the bottom of the third. The game was scoreless. A buzz went through the crowd when he stepped in right-handed to face a righty pitcher.

What stunned opposing Park Ridge, however, was that he took the first two strikes, both over the outside corner.

Elgin hoped the pitcher, Charles Morley, would waste a pitch on oh-and-two, but he also knew that Morley might reach back for his best pitch ever, wanting to strike out the phenom. If he tried to bust one in on Elgin's fists, Elgin was ready.

"C'mon, Chuckie," the catcher bellowed. "Right past im, Chuckie baby!"

The pitch was tight and hard. At the last instant Elgin squared around but let the ball go. The infield didn't budge. No way a superstar switch-hitter was going to bunt from the right side with two strikes. But a pitch later, on an offering identical to the first two, he squared around again and pushed the ball up the first-base line. He exploded from the box, feeling and hearing the catcher right behind him. With every stride his wrist was pierced with pain.

Elgin caught up to the slow rolling ball and could see that the pitcher was in a good position to field it. The first baseman retreated to cover the bag.

As Morley reached for the ball, with the catcher also charging up the line, Elgin shouted, with as low a voice as he could muster, "My play, Chuckie! I've got it!"

Elgin was past the ball and couldn't tell if his ruse worked. His eyes were on the first baseman's eyes, and Elgin could tell a throw was coming. The first baseman was frantically backing up the line toward the bag, so he would have to tag Elgin for the out.

Elgin dove head first into foul territory, reaching for the bag with his left hand. He heard the catch and knew the first baseman was sweeping at him, but all he got was air. Safe.

Elgin wanted to clap as he brushed himself off, but the less he did with that right wrist, the better. Though he was stranded at first, Elgin felt he was off to a good start.

The Chicago shortstop was taking all the throws to second on steals, and once he even handled a double play himself, though it meant running a long way to tag the base. Elgin caught one short liner and underhanded it to the pitcher, but he knew it was unlikely he would go a whole game without a grounder at second.

Two came in the top of the sixth. The first was near first base, and he was able to underhand the ball again. The second was up the middle, and as planned before the game, Elgin shoveled the ball to the shortstop, who threw the runner out. Observant fans would have realized by then that Elgin was protecting a throwing arm or hand. The play was impressive, but Elgin would have otherwise handled the throw himself. He only hoped he was protecting his wrist enough. It hurt bad.

He finished the game with two bunt singles, a strikeout, and a walk. Ironically, his average dropped a point. Worse, Chicago lost the game to a team they hadn't lost to for three years.

The next night they would face their toughest opponent in the league, the only team they had lost to more than once that season. It was a team drawn from Mount Prospect and Des Plaines, called Mount Plaines. They played at a newly lighted field with about a thousand seats. Usually a hundred or so fans showed up. But with the release of the Elgin Woodell feature in *Sports Illustrated* that Monday, the ballpark was going to look very small Tuesday night.

55

EVERYONE AGREED IT WAS FORTUNATE that Elgin didn't have another game after Tuesday until Friday night. Coach Koenig approved Elgin's skipping the practices in between to let the tender bruise heal itself. Painkillers helped. Tuesday's game didn't.

Again there was a buzz in the crowd when Elgin didn't appear for batting or infield practice. This crowd, however, was incredible. The stands were filled twenty minutes before game time, and people kept pouring in even up to the fourth inning. Fans were lined up six deep behind the backstop and down both foul lines, continually having to be shooed out of play by the umpires.

No home run fences had been installed in the new park, so when even more people showed up, they were allowed to watch from beyond the light poles in the outfield. Elgin and his teammates normally liked fields with no fences because then the line drive hitters had chances for home runs too. On this field, anything that rolled anywhere but into the cornfield in left was still in play, and you could take all the bases you could get. Into the left-field corn, however, was a ground-rule double.

Elgin had spent a few hours in the basement during the day, seeing if he could hit one-handed. He decided he probably could, but it looked so strange and was so risky, he decided against it. He would rely on his bunting and his eye again.

That worked fine—two walks and a sacrifice bunt—until the top of the last inning when Elgin came to the plate with Chicago down by two with two out and the bases loaded. He clenched and released his right fist a dozen times, wincing every time. Any movement of that tendon aggravated the pain. The doctor had assured him he would do no permanent damage by merely using the arm and hand. What he had to avoid was any more contact on the injured area.

A right-handed reliever was on the mound with good speed but no movement. He had just come in for the starter, who had done well before allowing a bloop single and two straight walks after two were out. Elgin had nearly given up on the game with two out and none on, but most of the crowd had stayed, in the long-shot hope they might see Elgin hit again.

He knew it was crazy, but what he really wanted to do was to clear the bases. He stepped in righty again, looking to keep his front shoulder closed as long as possible and drive the ball to the gap in right center. He was as nervous as he had ever been at the plate, but it had nothing to do with the crowd or his future. He knew that somewhere in the count he was going to forget about his wrist and swing away for the first time since he had injured it. That was going to hurt like the devil.

The pitcher missed close on the first two pitches. The next was right down the middle. Elgin took it and shook his head slightly. How he would have loved to have seen that one with no handicaps.

The next pitch rode in just above his knee on the inside corner, and though Elgin did everything he could to make it appear the ball was inside and low, he knew it wasn't and he couldn't argue with the umpire. Strike two. Two-and-two.

The next pitch was a fastball in, and Elgin fouled it off. His wrist throbbed. He had not taken a full swing, but still the pain shot all the way up his arm.

Finally, he got his ball three. The pitch had come in straight and hard, the hardest he'd seen in days, but it was slightly high, not so high that Elgin could breathe until he heard the ump call it a ball, but high enough.

Elgin stepped out and watched the base coaches remind the runners to run with the pitch. He closed his eyes and told himself to forget his wrist, forget the pain that would come when he pushed the next reachable pitch into right. He was ready, dug in. He hoped this guy tried to shoot another one past him.

The ball headed for the center of the plate, belt high. Elgin stepped and began his magnificent swing, the one designed to push the ball into right, maybe right center. If he hit it solidly, he thought, it could roll a long way.

But he had been fooled, royally, classically fooled. The pitch was a change-up that seemed to die halfway to the plate, and as Elgin's stride and hip rotation began to whip his bat through the strike zone, the pitch was still hanging out there, dropping.

Elgin's only salvation was that he had planned to hit it to right. He was able to adjust enough to get the bat on the ball but was so far out in front that the ball shot past the heads of the third baseman and the runner at third, bounced fair once about two hundred feet out, and skipped hard toward the cornfield. Elgin yelled as he headed toward first, partly from the pain in his wrist, and partly out of frustration for what was surely going to be a ground rule double.

As Elgin rounded first, he saw the Mount Plaines left fielder make a colossal mistake. Rather than letting the ball go into the cornfield, the fielder dove and snared it, rising to hit the cutoff man.

The go-ahead runner came around third and was waved on. The previous two scorers waved at him to slide, and when he did, the relay hit him in the helmet and bounded past everyone. As the catcher raced back to get it and the pitcher hurried to cover the plate, Elgin rounded second and stopped halfway to third.

Koenig gestured wildly and screamed at him to come, but Elgin inexplicably stood still, like a deer caught in a hunter's headlights. When the catcher came up with the ball, the pitcher yelled, "Three!" Elgin hesitated, started, and hesitated again. Then he dove toward third. The throw was high and into left field, and he was up and speeding toward home. There was no play.

As soon as he crossed the plate, he ran back out to Coach Koenig, who was furious.

"I knew I had third easily no matter what, Coach. I figured if I could draw the throw we might catch a break. And we did."

"Yeah, we did," Koenig said. "But you also ignored me and showed me up, and I don't like it. Tell Doyle he's playing second in the bottom half."

Elgin ran red-faced to the dugout, wishing the crowd wouldn't cheer him after he'd gotten in trouble. He thought he had done the right thing. He wasn't unhappy about being taken out with a two-run lead in the ninth. His wrist needed the rest. And when the next hitter popped out, his daring move had been vindicated, at least in his mind.

Doyle ran eagerly to second for the bottom of the inning. Though he was normally an outfielder, he looked good and comfortable, and Elgin knew he could handle it. Though Mount Plaines scratched out a run and had a man at third with two outs, a pop-up to Doyle ended the game.

As his teammates celebrated, Elgin sat on the bench, awaiting the postgame team lecture, at which he assumed he would be singled out for reprimand. He deserved it, he knew. He had made a gutsy, heads-up play, and it had worked. It had not even been all that risky. But, he had done it independently, and that was one thing Coach Koenig would not tolerate. When Koenig had quieted everyone, Elgin raised his hand.

"Coach, I just want to apologize to you and to everyone for that play."

"What're you talkin about?" someone challenged. "That was great!"

Koenig stopped the chatter with a gesture. "I appreciate that, Woodell. You're right, you shouldn't have done that on your own. I confess it was brave and it gave us the win, and I congratulate you for that. I also know there are a lot of people in the ballpark tonight who are going to echo your teammates' comments, so who am I to tell you you shouldn't have done it? I guess I just wish I'd thought of it."

⚾ ⚾ ⚾

"Hey, Mr. Thatcher, could you please turn on the inside light?" Elgin had traveled to the game in a van with half the team, and now he was in the front seat of Mr. Thatcher's car for the ride home. He spun in his seat and stared at Luke. "Lucky! Your mustache is gone!"

"Yeah, I didn't like it," Luke said. "Too bristly. It tickled."

Miriam punched him.

"What're you gonna cut off next," Elgin said, "your eyebrows?"

"Elgin!"

"Sorry, Momma."

⚾ ⚾ ⚾

Elgin spent the next three days dodging the press and spending most of his time in the basement. There was little he could do since he still couldn't swing a bat as he liked, so he just stood in the box and watched the pitches, trying to guess where they'd go, how he'd hit them, and whether they were strikes.

He let the machine pitch his infield grounders and liners practice, and though he caught most everything, he threw nothing. For hours he crouched at the plate and caught pitch after pitch from different distances. He didn't know for sure, but he guessed all this would keep his eye and timing sharp. Through three buckets of balls he knelt just outside the batter's box and imagined himself swinging hard, swinging through the ball, driving it straight. He wanted that image burned into his brain, the way it had been for months and months. He could not let this injury slow him down.

The word had come from Mr. Thatcher: Rafer Williams was flying to Chicago late Sunday night. He would stay with Ronny Dressel in Glen Ellyn without registering, and he would have Ronny drive him into the city early the next morning. Once he was set up in Luke's apartment and had made contact with his office, he would send for Elgin.

"You'll be with me, right, Mr. Thatcher?"

"Of course he will, honey," Miriam said.

"Uh, no, I'm afraid not," Billy Ray said. "Ah, we're not exactly in the driver's seat in this situation. The commissioner has set a few conditions. If we had already filed suit against major league baseball to force them to allow Elgin into the June draft, then they couldn't talk to anybody but me. But in this case, he wants time with Elgin alone first."

"I don't think I like that," Miriam said.

"I don't think we have any choice," Billy Ray said. "This is the break we've been looking for, and we have to do it on his terms."

"Well, he won't get into details with Elgin, will he? I don't want Elgin having to wonder what's being said without you there to help him."

"Oh, I'll have some input. I'm sure I'll be seeing Rafer early. He has already assured me, through Ronny, that I'm next on his agenda. I assume he'll be trying to let me know how many hoops we have to jump through before we can even think about Elgin becoming eligible for the draft and then becoming the property of a professional organization."

"Ooh, I hate the sound of that," Miriam said.

"So do I," Thatcher said. "But that's where we hold the cards. Once the way is cleared—and I need to say that it may never be, except that the commissioner's willingness to come to us is very encouraging—then it's our decision. Then the conditions, terms, limitations, and dollar levels are ours to set. The club that wins this prize will earn it."

She smiled. "That sounds a little better."

⚾ ⚾ ⚾

Elgin found it easier and easier to flex his right hand. He began squeezing a golf ball in his palm, wishing he had a rubber ball, anything that would give a little more. He finally replaced the golf ball with a rag from his mother's sewing basket. He felt the tendon strengthening and become more elastic. By Friday morning, he was swinging a bat carefully, finding it equally painful from both sides, but not nearly as bad as it had been.

He was pretty sure he wouldn't blow his chances with the commissioner with three bad games, but he sure didn't want to risk it. He had a night game Friday and a home doubleheader Saturday. To go into that scary, once-in-a-lifetime meeting with Rafer Williams while still hitting over .700 more than twenty-five games into the regular season, had to be an advantage.

He spent hours poring over his statistics and realized just how precarious a hitter was while hitting that high. He was fifty-three for seventy-five for the season, hitting .7067. He could go seven for his next ten at-bats and see his average drop almost a point. But if he had one more at-bat than that, without a hit, his average would drop to .698.

Now even a thirteen-year-old, especially one as fundamentally sound as Elgin, knows that one hit or a few hundredths in a batting average doesn't amount to much. It wasn't as if he had a chance at the pros at .705 and not at .698, but in his mind, the .700 barrier was important. He liked and needed goals, and he'd been setting them his whole young life. His goal for the three weekend games was to keep his average over .700. His goal with Mr. Williams was to be honest. If the man wanted to know what Elgin wanted and expected, it was that he be given a chance to become not just the youngest professional baseball player ever, but the youngest big leaguer ever.

By Friday afternoon he had worked through the pain, rewrapped the tender wrist, and was hitting almost the way he had been before he had been struck by the golf ball. He didn't have the snap in his follow-through, and his liners had a bend in them he'd like to have straightened out, but he knew he could hit live pitching for base hits, even if they weren't all screamers to the gaps.

⚾ ⚾ ⚾

It was Sunday night. The three victories were in the bag. The Chicago team was almost assured a state berth. Adrenaline had made Elgin better than he hoped in the Friday night game. He had gone three-for-three including a home run, before being rested the last two innings, sitting on a skyrocketed batting average of a tick under .718. More than four thousand watched the game, which made Miriam nearly ill with nervousness.

Elgin was certain that without a disaster he could keep the average above .700 in the Saturday doubleheader. He was wrong. It plummeted to .682, yet he couldn't hang his head. Scouts from every major league team were there, media from all over the United States, and—he liked to speculate—maybe even the commissioner of baseball in disguise.

Though Elgin went one-for-three in the first game and one-for-four in the second, he hit the ball as well as he had all year. He also walked twice and hit a sacrifice fly so deep to center that two runners tagged up and scored.

His other outs, with the exception of one high hopper back to the mound, were prodigious shots. One was a liner that banged so hard off the second baseman's glove that it rolled all the way to the stretching first baseman who plucked it out of the dirt just before Elgin crossed the bag.

Another was a blast up the middle that made the pitcher duck, then it hit second and was caught on the bounce by the diving shortstop. He was lying across the bag with the ball in his glove when the runner at first steamed in, forced out.

The other two included a three-hundred-foot foul ball down the left field line that resulted in a career catch for the outfielder, and a line drive that appeared ten feet over the shortstop's head, but he leaped and snagged it.

"I feel like DiMaggio when his hitting streak ended," Elgin said. "He hit harder shots in the fifty-seventh game than he had in the five games before that, but none of them fell in."

"Yeah," Doyle commiserated, shaking his head. "I'd sure hate to be hitting in the high .600s. You must really be down."

"Shut up, Doyle."

"No, I figured out your problem, Woodell. You're actually hitting the ball too hard. You've got to lighten up."

The team roared.

⚾ ⚾ ⚾

Mr. Thatcher had gone to his hotel suite to await a call or any further instructions about the next morning's meeting. His parting words to Elgin: "Mr. Williams might try to bully you. He doesn't mean anything by it, but he might blame you for all the trouble he's been having over this matter. You just keep your future in mind and tell him you want to play pro ball. Talk baseball with him. He knows the game as well as anyone."

"I know all about him," Elgin said. "I remember a time in a playoff game when—"

Mr. Thatcher held up a hand. "Excuse me, Elgin, but I have to go. Tell that to him. He'll love it. Honest."

Elgin was jumpy. He wanted to tell the story, and Luke and his mother were the only available ears. "Bottom of the ninth, the Reds leading by one, Mets had runners at first and second with one out. Williams is catching for the Reds. Mets try a double steal. Williams sees he can't get the lead runner but that the tailing runner is dogging it. He guns down the guy at second; they hold the lead runner at third, two down. They go on to win. Gutsy, man. Gutsy play."

Luke smiled at him. "You're a little wired, boy."

"Am I ever." Elgin paced.

Miriam just sat, her eyes full, her face blotchy. "This is gonna drive me crazy, this waiting. How am I supposed to sleep? How am I supposed to work tomorrow, knowing my son is talking with the commissioner of baseball?"

Luke put his arm around her. "You just heard a sermon on worry."

She snorted. "It was pretty good too. It just didn't take, that's all."

"You think you've got worries," Luke said, trying to mimic her voice, "I've got scads of cleaning to do before my company comes tomorrow. Oh, I hope that gentleman from baseball doesn't mind drinking out of an old jelly glass!"

Miriam laughed. "Lucas, you do have some decent dishes and glasses, don't you?"

"Ha! Now I'm not good enough for the commish, is that it? I was gonna offer him toast and warm Coke. Sound good?"

"Lucas!"

"Oh, you know me, I'll take care of him. Sounds to me like all he needs is a phone, a chair, and somethin to munch."

"He's a fast-food guy," Elgin said, finally sitting.

"Really?"

"Yup. Fact, he's embarrassed about it, but he eats lots of burgers and stuff."

"This should be easy then," Luke said. "You guys go till late morning; I'll cater lunch in paper bags."

⚾ ⚾ ⚾

Elgin slept no better than his mother. He heard her sighing and tossing and turning all night. All while he was doing the same.

56

ELGIN MADE THE MISTAKE OF SHOWING UP too early at Lucky's Second-hand Shop the next morning. The place was locked and the street deserted except for the occasional apartment dweller hurrying off to work. Elgin thought about moseying over to Lucky's flat, but that was not part of the plan. Once Rafer Williams showed up and Luke spirited him to the apartment, Luke was to meet Elgin at the store and send him to the commissioner.

Elgin had whiled away the longest hour and a half of his life sitting on the pavement, looking in the window, lying on the pavement, hanging over the curb to watch the insects in the gutter, all the while rehearsing silently what he might say or not say to the commissioner of baseball. One thing he did not want to do was to ask for an autograph. Well, in fact he did. He had never been close enough to ask for one from anybody really famous. The only autographed picture on his wall at home was an eight-by-ten glossy of Bernie Pincham that read: "To Eglin, Best Wishes from your friend, Bernie Pincham."

Mr. Thatcher had gotten that for him, and Elgin appreciated his kindness more than a misspelled greeting from a player he had never seen from a sport he could take or leave. The uniform in the picture was out of date now, and so was Bernie's hair style. But the colors were neat and the glossy looked good on the wall, so Elgin kept it.

The boy rested his back against the short brick wall beneath the window of Lucky's and closed his eyes against the morning sun. It warmed him, but though his hands were folded in front of him, he was not relaxed. He was wound tight, wishing the clock would move, wishing Luke would show up, wishing he was already meeting with the commissioner, wishing he had already met with him.

Elgin scrambled to his feet when he heard Luke's boots on the sidewalk. "There's been a screwup," Luke said.

"Oh, no. He's not there?"

"Yeah, he's there, and he's a pretty impressive guy. But he's not happy. He thought everybody understood that he wanted to meet with your mother first. Nobody understood that. I called your place but that guy Bravado or whatever his name is said you'd left two hours ago and your mother an hour ago."

"I don't think she can get off work without telling them in advance," Elgin said. "I mean, if they knew what she was doing they'd let her, but she can't tell them."

"No, she can't. Well, he's working with his office to change his flight, and he said he'll see her at the end of the day if everything else goes okay. You'd better get goin. You know the place."

"Yeah. Is Mr. Dressel there with him?"

Luke nodded. "But not for long. He was going to head this way in a few minutes."

"So I'm meeting with Mr. Williams alone."

"You got it."

Elgin was almost past an old man with a cane when the man stopped and said, "Woodell!"

Elgin spun and stopped, startled. "Yes, sir?"

The old man reached out a huge and surprisingly strong hand. "Dressel. I been scoutin ya."

"Yes, sir. Nice to meet you, sir."

"Don't let that guy bully you now, hear? I told him the truth about your speed and your throwing and all that, but don't you let him compare you with big leaguers. All we're sayin is that physically you're ready for the minors. Whether you're ready in any of the other ways, who knows?"

Without another word, Ronny Dressel waved and moved on.

Elgin felt a tingle up his spine. Who would believe he had just met a Hall of Fame pitcher and was about to have a secret, private meeting with a Hall of Fame catcher who also happened to be the commissioner of baseball? He felt conscious of every step, even his arm swing. Would he be able to speak, or would he just melt all over the floor and have to be scooped up and poured back onto the street? He suddenly felt very young and alone and afraid.

When he reached Luke's apartment he thought of his dad and how proud of Elgin he would be right now. He knocked.

"It's unlocked," came the huge, bass voice that was neither unkind nor unpleasant.

Elgin turned the knob and pressed his knee against the door where it always stuck. It squeaked as it broke free of the frame. Standing a few feet from the door, facing Elgin head-on, was a chuckling giant of a black man. His feet were spread, his arms folded across his chest—which made his shirt cuffs and suit coat sleeves ride high off his wrists.

"You've been here before then?" Rafer Williams said, his voice too loud for the room. Elgin looked puzzled. "You knew just how to open the door!"

Elgin nodded, still trying to take in the vision. Mr. Williams was about six-four and had picked up at least forty pounds since his last playing day nearly ten years before. He had become a broadcaster, then—of all things for a born-and-bred National Leaguer—American League president, before becoming the surprise choice for commissioner. In the meantime he had become a first ballot Hall of Famer.

When he shook Elgin's hand, the boy felt as if his fingers would disappear into the meaty mass. Mr. Williams pointed to the couch, and Elgin was glad to have the chore of seating himself, just for something to do. How did one talk to such a person?

"Well, it's mighty nice to meet you finally," the commissioner said. He was shiny bald with a rim of long, curly hair. He removed his brown, pin-striped coat and draped it over the back of a kitchen chair. "I was gonna loosen my tie, but if you don't mind, I'm gonna get rid of it for now, huh?"

"I don't mind," Elgin said, wondering why his own voice sounded so far away.

Williams balled up the tie and stuffed it into the pocket of his coat. "Tell ya what, I'll put it back on when I meet with your attorney and your mom, how's that?"

"Fine," Elgin said, feeling foolish. He sat with his feet flat on the floor, knees together, fists on his thighs.

Williams pulled the coffee table away from Elgin's knees and settled right in the middle of it. Elgin had a fleeting image of the thing breaking and the man sprawling on the floor, but the table bowed without cracking.

Elgin felt more at ease as Rafer Williams made himself comfortable. There was a sparkle in his eye and excitement in every move. The man sat forward, elbows on his knees, not two feet from Elgin, and smiled. Then he raised each foot and pulled up his socks, still not taking his laughing eyes from Elgin's. He tugged at his pant legs until they rose a few inches above the tops of his socks. Elgin was intrigued that even with the morning sun streaming through the window, he could barely make out the different shades of black and brown between Mr. Williams's shoes, socks, shins, and pants.

The commissioner crossed his legs and held his ankle to his knee with both hands. He had a gold ring on each hand, a gold watch on his wrist. "You see that briefcase over there?" he asked.

Elgin looked. The satchel-style bag was stuffed to the limit, papers peeking out the top. He nodded.

"That's full of you. You're in there. I got video tapes, charts, graphs, radar gun printouts, timings of you to first, you to second, you from first to third, you all the way around the bases. If you can measure a ballplayer by the numbers, you've been measured, buddy."

"Uh-huh." Elgin didn't know what else to say.

"But you and me both know you don't measure a ballplayer like that, don't we? A ballplayer is measured by his head and his heart, am I right?"

Elgin nodded. "I do think you can tell a lot about a guy by his numbers though."

Williams stuck out his lower lip and nodded. "True enough. Like the numbers I've got on you show that you'd be about, oh, tenth or eleventh fastest runner on a big league club, maybe third or fourth on a rookie league team."

Elgin was stunned and he sensed Williams thought he would be. He had actually begun to think he might rank among the fastest big leaguers.

"Your arm is remarkable," the commissioner said. "You throw the ball like an eighteen-year-old. But I s'pose you know that most eighteen-year-olds would rank last on a big league team in throwing. For distance and for speed."

Elgin nodded.

"I thought maybe we'd talk some baseball today," the commissioner continued. "You know how rarely I get to do that?" Elgin shook his head. "Hardly ever. Seems all I talk about is other junk—legal stuff. Contracts, deals, negotiations. If I didn't insist on goin to a ballgame at least once a week I might as well be a banking executive or something! Let's talk baseball."

"Okay."

"Let me tell you what makes you such an unusual hitter and you tell me if I'm right. This won't be news to you if you know the game like they tell me you do. It's all bat speed, right?"

When Elgin paused before answering, the commissioner's face convinced him he had been led toward a too-easy answer to a trick question. "Well, I used to think bat speed was pretty much everything, sir," Elgin said. "But when I started facing faster pitchers, you know, those guys who throw in the low eighties, I had to start getting stronger. I don't know the scientific reasons and all that, but the faster a pitch is thrown, the harder it is for the bat to change its direction."

The commissioner looked as if he was about to laugh aloud. "You're right!" he said. "It's not just bat speed or all these little guys would be hitting home runs all the time! You think pitches in the low eighties make a bat hard to push through the strike zone, you ought to try to turn around one in the high nineties! That ball seems heavier, doesn't it? Huh? That ol bat seems to recoil in your hands. You ever hit offa one of those super fast pitching machines?" Elgin was grateful Williams did not wait for an answer. "Same feeling. You tend to hitch and move and get all ready to time the thing, then you stick your bat out and it bangs that stick right back at you. Then you have to tense up, toughen up, drive that sucker. And if you're gonna face that kind of pitching all the time, you've got to be built for it."

Elgin nodded.

"Are you built for it? Let me see your hands."

Elgin held them out. Williams took one in each of his.

"Resist me," he said.

He pulled Elgin's hands toward each other. Elgin resisted but not successfully. He was off balance, had no base. His rear end was mobile on the soft cushions. The more he fought, the more Williams was able to make him lean from side to side. Elgin planted his feet.

"Thatta boy!" Williams said. "Set yourself and hold steady."

Elgin squared his shoulders. He was no match against the big man, but he offered more resistance when he was braced.

"You *are* unusually strong for your age," Williams said. "It's truly phenomenal. You have the body and strength of a late teen, and the baseball knowledge—so they tell me—of an adult. No, better than that. The baseball knowledge of the expert adult. Your fielding and throwing are above average for summer collegiate ball, you hit like a double- or even triple-A player."

"Do you really think a double-A player would hit near .700 in college ball?"

Williams stopped and stared at the ceiling, cupping his neck in his hand. "Now that's a good question." His mind seemed to be cataloguing double-A players he was aware of. "I guess I should try to remember what these guys hit at that level before they were signed. I remember a couple of guys in the .550 range in the college playoffs, which means they probably hit close to that during their regular seasons against easier teams."

Elgin smiled slightly. He didn't want to appear cocky. He looked the commissioner in the eyes and mouthed the words silently. "Seven hundred?"

57

MIRIAM TOOK A CALL AT HER DESK FROM MR. THATCHER.

"Well, of course I want to meet with him," she said. "But not until after work." Billy Ray said he would pick her up at four o'clock. "How's it goin with Elgin? Do you know?"

"All I know is that Dressel and Luke are at the shop and that Elgin left for Luke's place more than an hour ago. I had talked to Williams by phone earlier, but I haven't seen him yet."

"Well," she said, "I don't mind tellin you, I should've taken the day off. I am worthless."

⚾ ⚾ ⚾

"Well now, you've got me there," Williams said, seeming to enjoy himself. "Can I think of a minor leaguer who would hit .700 in college ball? Hm. I remember a kid played for the Cubs some years back. Shortstop with a gun. Hit over .350 two years running in triple-A. Had trouble hitting his weight his first few years in the bigs. Wound up a pretty fair hitter. I believe he could have hit .700 in college ball. Maybe a couple of others."

"So I'm hitting like a high minor leaguer," Elgin tried. "Someone on his way to the majors."

"Could be. Course a lot more goes into making a professional ballplayer than a good bat."

"I'll do anything."

"You will?"

"Yes, sir."

"Really? Anything?"

"Anything you say."

"Would you stand in against the fastest pitcher in baseball and let him throw a hundred straight pitches past you?"

"No, sir."

"I thought you said you'd do anything."

Elgin smiled. "I'd do anything except let him throw them past me."

Williams howled. "You're somethin, kid! I gotta give you that. Would you work out with a trainer so you wouldn't overdo it, but build yourself up to where you can change the direction of a ninety-mile-per-hour fastball? Don't nod so quickly. I don't think you've faced that kind of speed yet. You know it takes eight thousand pounds of force to change the motion of a ball that weighs just over five ounces from coming at you at ninety miles an hour to going the other way at over one hundred ten?"

"I've heard that and read that," Elgin said, "but I don't understand it. I mean, how does even somebody your size, when you were playing I mean, get eight thousand pounds of force?"

The commissioner laughed loud. "I don't know. I always wondered that myself! I'm not a physics man, but I know it has to do with more than bat speed. It's got to be strength."

⚾ ⚾ ⚾

Billy Ray Thatcher was on the phone in the back room at Lucky's. He had called the general manager of the Houston Astros.

"Returning your calls of last week," Billy Ray said.

"It's about time, Mr. Thatcher. I'm calling about this kid who's getting all the attention. There's no hope of getting him into the June draft I suppose."

"You never know. If that happened, would Houston be interested?"

"You never know," the GM parroted. "I can't imagine being interested in a child."

"I hear you," Billy Ray said. "He's just a babe."

The man chuckled. "That with a capital B?"

Billy Ray smiled. "So you've been calling to tell me what? That you're interested or that you're not interested?"

"Just to ask about the June draft. If you can't get him into that, this is all academic, isn't it?"

"True. True. So, let's be academic. In fact, let's be hypothetical. Let's say you could be fairly certain that this boy would be the Wayne Gretzky of baseball. Dominate the game like no one ever has, lead the league in just about everything, win the MVP several years in a row, lead a team to the playoffs and Series year after year."

"Ha! Well, if the hockey boys had seen Gretzky coming, they would have all wanted him, wouldn't they?"

"Didn't they? He had a remarkable junior league career, got to meet Bobby Hull when he was a child, all that."

"Well, Mr. Thatcher, do all the major league teams have an interest in your client?"

"You'd say I was lying if I said I'd heard from every one of them, wouldn't you?"

There was silence on the other end.

"I was afraid you'd think that," Billy Ray said.

"Mr. Thatcher," the GM began slowly. "You have not represented baseball players in the past, have you?"

"No, sir, not big leaguers. Fact is, I represented the Woodell boy's father when he was in the Pirate system years ago. I did, however, represent Bernie—"

"Pardon me for interrupting, but I know you handled the basketball player. My point, I guess, is that you and I have not crossed paths. I don't know you, you don't know me. But, no sir, I would not call you a liar if you told me that every team in major league baseball is interested in Elgin Woodell. I've seen the numbers. I've seen the videos. This is a once in a lifetime opportunity for all of us. I know every team in baseball is interested, because we have first pick in the June draft and we've been contacted by all of them."

"Is that so?"

"Yes, sir. I realize that is no bargaining posture for me to take with you. Personally, I'm pessimistic that the boy will be allowed to be made available until he's of age. But if he is, I wouldn't trade his rights for anything I can think of."

"Not even millions?"

"Not even millions."

"We're not saying he's ready."

"Oh, I know. And he would never pay off until the majors. But if he keeps progressing, he could be one of the youngest big leaguers in history. He'd fill every stadium every game if he could simply compete with adults. He'd pay for a long-term deal within a half season."

Thatcher laughed. "Refresh me on which of us is on which side of the bargaining table, sir."

"Just let me congratulate you on the hottest property since the first Babe. Capital B. By the time he does become available, I assume we'll have rebuilt with some good picks and won't be in a position to be going after him. Protect him, Thatcher. For the good of the game and especially the good of the boy, protect him."

"You can count on that," Billy Ray said.

⚾ ⚾ ⚾

"You're not serious!" Rafer Williams thundered. "Not even to Wrigley?"

Elgin shook his head.

"Never to one big league game?"

"No, sir."

"Well, we're gonna have to see about that," Rafer said. He looked at his watch and stepped to the phone, dialing quickly. "Rafer Williams calling for Mr. Martin—Hey, Cliff! Rafer! Good! Listen, I need, uh, hang on." He turned to Elgin. "How many do you need? How many tickets?" Elgin held up four fingers. "Can you give me four tickets to, ah, hang on." He turned back to Elgin. "When can you go?" Elgin shrugged. "Saturday?" Rafer asked.

Elgin thought. He had a late morning game. "Is it a night game?"

"Cliff, is that a night game?" He nodded to Elgin who nodded back. "Yeah, give me four for that, box seats, best you've got—where you'd put me, hear? And then for the next day, you've got a mid-afternoon TV game, right?" He looked at Elgin again. Elgin nodded and held up four fingers again. "I want a sky box, lots of food and soft drinks, all on my office. Got it? Can do? Thanks, Cliff… No, don't send em to me. Leave em at the Will Call window for, uh—" The commissioner covered the phone and stifled a huge laugh. "I almost told him your name," he whispered. "Ha! The phone lines would have been burning! What's your friend's name here?"

Elgin told him.

"Leave em at Will Call for Luke Harkness. Thanks a million, Cliff. Good luck… June draft? I'm not prepared to deal with that yet. You'll know as soon as there's any news."

When the commissioner got off the phone, he rolled up his sleeves and sat back on the coffee table. "That guy wanted to know if you would be in the June draft, and when I tried to ignore him, he asked me have I seen you yet? Can you beat that? Wouldn't he love it if he knew where I called him from?"

Elgin smiled.

"Now, son, I want you to tell me about your daddy."

⚾ ⚾ ⚾

Billy Ray Thatcher apologized to Luke for tying up the phone at his shop. "I'd go back to the hotel, but I'd like to be here when Elgin gets back."

Luke assured him he was glad to be of service, so Billy Ray placed a call to the general manager of the Phillies.

"Give me some good news," the GM said.

"Just returning your call," Thatcher said. "What can I do for you?"

"Just tell me what it's going to take. What's the floor bid?"

"Congratulations," Billy Ray said. "You get to start the bidding."

"Ha! You know what the rumors are."

"Tell me."

"That the commissioner is going to have the kid scouted independently."

"That so?"

"That's what I hear. What do you hear?"

"I just hear offers," Billy Ray said.

"Cute. Listen, do you think Rafer will clear the kid for the June draft?"

"I couldn't tell you."

"But do you know?"

"Of course not. I would imagine there'd be a lot of hurdles."

"I'm not so sure," the Philadelphia man said. "There'll be do-gooders and social-worker types who'll cry bloody murder. But how can you keep a guy from doing what he wants to do and is capable of doing when he has parental consent? He can be tutored for school, can't he? I mean, he's going to make millions."

"How many millions?" Thatcher asked.

They both laughed and agreed to keep in touch.

⚾ ⚾ ⚾

Rafer Williams's voice was soft. "So there was no goin back for the funeral? That's rough. Uh-huh. That's a rough one. Made you a better player though, did it? Uh-huh. Wow. How's Momma doin now?"

Elgin smiled self-consciously. "Momma's in love with Luke Harkness."

"You don't say!"

"By the way, Luke said to just call him and he'd bring us some burgers."

"Burgers! Call him!"

But the line was busy.

⚾ ⚾ ⚾

Miriam skipped lunch and began to feel faint by early afternoon. There was little she wanted more than to talk with the commissioner and to be able to know something one way or the other. If this was all speculation, all futile, she wanted to know and be able to get out from under the pressure for a few years.

58

BASEBALL COMMISSIONER RAFER WILLIAMS tried to press a twenty dollar bill into Luke Harkness's hand when he delivered a sack of fast food no two people could eat, though one was a prodigy and the other a prodigious eater.

"No way," Luke said. "It's on me. I insist. Drink whatever you want from the fridge."

"Will you join us?" Williams asked.

"We're gettin a pizza, and it's probably there already, so I'd better get back."

As Luke left, the commissioner swept open the refrigerator to find it stocked with several different brands of soft drinks, diet and regular.

"What'll you have?" the big man said.

"Diet Coke."

"Good man. Stay away from the sugar. This is Monday, so I'll do the same." Williams howled at his own joke. Elgin smiled, not making the connection. They sat at the tiny kitchen table on vinyl-covered chairs. Elgin hadn't realized how hungry he was till he saw Williams take an enormous bite. The man made the stuff look delicious.

"I love this," Williams said. "I hardly ever get it, though. Usually it's some fancy hotel meal, banquet food. This is good, huh?"

Elgin nodded. Williams had a way of talking with his mouth full without being offensive or inarticulate.

"Elgin, if I compared you to Jackie Robinson, do you know what I'd be saying?"

"Sure. He was the first black ballplayer to play in the major leagues. Someday I'll be the first kid."

"Well, that about sums it up. The question is, do you bring to your job what he brought to his? First, he was a great, great player. That helped.

When he made an out, had an oh-for-four game, made an error, well, he was everybody's nigger. They told him to go back to the jungle. He even had a rough time with his teammates."

"Yeah, until he won Rookie of the Year."

"You do know your history, don't you?"

"I read a lot."

"But you see, Jackie Robinson was also a big enough man to not fight back. You know he had to get angry and you know he had to feel the injustice. If just one time he'd attacked somebody or treated them like they treated him, he'd have ruined it for all of us. Do you think I'd be commissioner of baseball today if it weren't for Jackie Robinson? Not on your life. But let me tell you this, doing as well as he did didn't protect Jackie from hatred and prejudice. It was still there. He won over a lot of people, but not everybody. Understand?"

Elgin nodded.

"Now tell me, son, what kind of heat you've taken? There had to be a lot of kids who lost jobs because you came along."

Elgin told him how he had suffered some, but that it didn't seem like much now that he was thinking about Jackie Robinson.

"Uh-huh. Other words, you've never been spit at."

Elgin shook his head.

"Called names?"

"Not really."

"Shunned?"

Elgin shook his head again. "I don't guess I'm a Jackie Robinson."

The commissioner finished off another burger and took a long pull on his Diet Coke. "Well, you see, there's where we have our problem. I don't know how much you know about the legal side of this thing, but to get you into the June draft I would have to make an exception to an old rule. Being that breaking old rules is part of my heritage, I'm not against that. I'm not even all that concerned if the worst that happens is that you're a paper tiger and you flounder in the minors and never see a major league inning. That makes us look bad, sure, for exploiting you, ruining your childhood, stuff like that. But the fact is, even if that happens, you and your mother will likely be pretty much set up for life. So there would be some give and take.

"My problem is if you're good. You're not going to have any trouble with the fans. They would eat you up. The difficulty will come with your teammates and your opponents. You see what I'm saying?"

"Jealousy?"

"Well, that's part of it. But let me put it to you this way. Think about this now. You're in summer collegiate ball and let's say you're hitting, oh, almost .700 halfway through the season. You're two hundred points ahead of everybody else and cruising toward a big league career, way ahead of schedule. Now in your next game, you're gonna face a prodigy. This is a baby. Can barely walk. He's still in diapers, get it?"

Elgin laughed.

"And this kid is a pitcher nobody can hit off. I mean, he's allowed four hits in five games and has an ERA of zero. Okay?" Elgin nodded, grinning.

"He walks your leadoff man, and now you're up. What're you thinking about?"

Elgin had been caught off guard. He shrugged and said nothing.

"Are you thinking about what pitch he might throw? Fastball, curve, slider, change? Or are you thinking about bunting, where to put the ball, what's the situation? What are you thinking about?"

Elgin's smile was gone. "I'm thinking how embarrassing it would be to strike out against a baby."

Rafer Williams slammed both palms on the table, crossed his arms and sat back, staring at Elgin. "There you go," he said. "Let me be the older guy now. I'm a catcher for the Reds. I've got a lifetime average of over .280 and I've hit over four hundred home runs. I'm gonna be a Hall of Famer, and everybody knows it. Now I'm catching and a child comes to the plate to hit. Do I want my pitcher to give up a hit, or even a walk, to a child? What am I thinking? I'm thinking, this kid wants to play with grownups, he's gonna have to face grownup pitches. This kid's gonna be on his butt the first three pitches. Then what?"

"Am I that kid?" Elgin said.

"Course. Now what?"

"I'm looking for the green light on three-and-oh."

Williams shook till he almost left the chair. He raised his head and shrieked. He clapped. "You're lookin for the green! Lookin for the green! I love it! I love you! You *are* Jackie Robinson. That's *just* what he woulda said!"

Elgin waited for the man to wipe his face and settle down. "I'm not saying I don't hear you, sir. I know what you mean. Nobody's going to want me to steal a base off them, get a hit, draw a walk, throw them out, tag them out. I figure I'll have to watch for hard slides, roll blocks, bean balls, pickoff attempts that are allowed to hit me. I s'pose people will bunt at me, rag on me, taunt me. It'll just make me more determined."

The commissioner had a hand over his mouth, studying the boy. "Let me ask you something. What happens if you make the majors and all of a sudden you're batting .100?"

"Then I get sent back down."

"Then you get sent back down."

"I don't think so," Elgin said.

"Oh, you'd get sent back down."

"If I was hitting .100 I'd expect to be sent back down. But I don't think I could be held to a .100 average. I know I haven't faced live, ninety-mile-an-hour pitching, but I believe I can put the ball where I want it at least half the time. And I have a good eye. I'll walk a lot."

Williams cleared away the trash and motioned to the other room where this time he sat on the couch and directed Elgin to the coffee table. "I like your confidence. It's naive, but it's confidence. Let me ask you this: Do you have any idea how noisy it would be if I allowed you into the draft?"

"Noisy?"

"Big. Newsworthy. I mean, I know you've already been drawing crowds and getting a lot of publicity, but I don't think you realize the magnitude of this. You'd be known all over the world. It wouldn't be long before you wouldn't be able to go out alone. You'd be on all the talk shows, there'd probably be T-shirt deals, shoe deals, you name it. But I've seen superstars come and go. I've seen kids pitch in the majors right out of high school, then never pitch in the bigs again. I saw a kid come up from A ball, fresh off a perfect game, only to be hit all over the yard in a third of an inning and never come back. That's the kind of a thing I need to think about when I consider this."

"I probably should tell you that I have no interest in the American League."

"What?"

"They'd make me a designated hitter, and I'd hate that."

"I hated that too. That's why I never thought they'd make me president of the AL. How strongly do you feel about it?"

"I wouldn't sign with an AL team unless they guaranteed in writing that I wouldn't be a DH."

"Hm. That could make a lot of people very angry. Make you look bad."

"Maybe just the American League teams would have to know."

"Elgin, if I allow you into the June draft, you won't have any more secrets as long as you live."

"Are you going to let me in?"

The commissioner's arms were spread on the back of the couch. His knees were spread. He looked as if he could use a nap.

"So, you come right out and ask me, do you?"

"Sorry."

"No, it's all right. I was kinda hopin you would, because if you didn't, I wasn't supposed to discuss it. But I'll tell you, in this day of agents and lawyers and spokesmen and all that, the guy who knows the least is always the guy we're all talking about—the player in question. That's not right, especially with someone like you, the Jackie Robinson of kids. So, just so you'll know from the beginning, here's where I am on this.

"A lot of people think that once we crack this door open, we'll have all manner of high school kids dropping out of school and running off to play baseball like they used to run off and join the circus. Well, I say we keep some limitations. Like a certain number of clubs have to express prior interest. Like more than half in the big leagues. Also, the kid has to be hitting at a certain level in the highest rank of amateur ball available to him. Or he has to have certain pitching statistics. And there has to be hardship. Most of all, the kid would have to agree to tutoring and would have to maintain a certain grade point average and graduate. If he fell behind at all, he'd be on the shelf until he was back on track."

Elgin nodded vigorously and smiled.

"Don't get ahead of me now, son. Just because you qualify on all those doesn't make it so easy. This gets kind of complicated, so stay with me. I couldn't make it appear I was doing this on behalf of baseball, even though you and I know that if you succeeded and made the majors at some ridiculously young age, it'd be the best thing that ever happened to the game. But see, if *we* came after *you*, rather than the other way around—all the clubs clamoring for you, offering you big money—and I allowed you in the draft because I thought you'd be exciting to watch grow, we'd look like zookeepers, or worse.

"What has to happen is that you push your way in. Now you've started that with your performance and your stats. And I know from talking with all the clubs that they'd jump at the chance to draft and sign you and see you develop. But if my hand was forced, you understand, we'd look better. Know what I mean?"

"No."

"Can you keep a secret, because this is going to be just between you and your people and me. It may not even get to the owners."

"I can keep a secret."

"I'm going to say no. No way I can let you into the draft. Now don't look at me that way. I'm going to take a position that this would not be in your best interests, even if it might be a good thing for baseball. Then I need you to force the issue. I need your attorney to threaten a lawsuit accusing us of discrimination on the basis of age, hammering away that you and your mother both want this, that she'll be with you all the way, that you'll be tutored, the whole bit. The public outcry will be incredible, and at some point I'll give in. I may throw out a few conditions of my own, but I'll concede that we really don't have a case and that we don't want the expense of a lawsuit we're sure to lose. Follow?"

"I think so. Then what happens?"

"Then your name goes into the June draft, the Astros take you, and you're off to the races."

Elgin felt emotion rising within him. Was he going to cry right here? "You mean it's up to me? If I tell Mr. Thatcher to make you let me in the draft, that's all there is to it?"

"Except this. I wish I could guarantee that you'll be the best thing that ever happened to baseball and that you'll make the majors in a few years. I doubt you'll make it while you're younger than Joe Nuxhall, but I hope you make it as a teenager. I will not be a happy man if it all falls apart for you. If you get hurt or disillusioned, or if we put you in over your head, I'll feel bad and only hope that the compensation has been worth it. Let me remind you that it's the baseball playing itself that's gotten you where you are now, and what you do on the field will always determine how everything else works. You quit playing at a top level, your money will dry up, your endorsements will be gone, your other-than-true friends, your popularity, everything else tumbles with your performance. But you conduct yourself like a pro, keep practicing and perfecting your skills, you will have no limits."

The commissioner reached to shake Elgin's hand. "I want to talk to your mother. I want to talk to Mr. Thatcher. And then I want to get back to my office. Between now and the draft, you and I are going to be busy people."

Elgin shook his hand and knew he couldn't speak. He wanted to thank Mr. Williams, but no words would come. His lips quivered, but all he could do was nod. The commissioner rose as Elgin stood. Williams embraced the boy as Elgin fought to keep from crying.

"You're welcome," Rafer Williams said with a smile. "Now give me Mr. Harkness's number at the store, and let's get this thing rolling."

59

WITHIN A WEEK, EVERYTHING RAFER WILLIAMS had predicted came true. The commissioner's office announced that it had been petitioned by the representative of an underage ballplayer to be allowed into the June draft. The commissioner denied the request, but soon anyone who had not heard of Elgin Woodell before was well aware of him because of his network television appearances, rallies in his behalf, call-in shows, letter-writing campaigns, and daily accounts of the lawsuit filed by Billy Ray Thatcher of Hattiesburg, Mississippi. Even Billy Ray took on Lincolnesque proportions in the articles and on television.

A meeting of Elgin and his summer coaches and teammates convinced him they would be thrilled if he was drafted and left them immediately. "Thanks a lot," he said with mock pain, but to a man they assured him they would be proud to say they had once played with him.

"We'll win the thing without you anyway," Doyle said. Everyone laughed, but that would prove true. Without Elgin's services the rest of the way, they would win the state and wind up third in the nationals.

Meanwhile, the commissioner held a news conference to announce what only Elgin, his mother, Luke, and Mr. Thatcher knew: that Williams was, "with great fear and trepidation, making this very unusual exception in the case of one very unusual young man."

The Astros, despite their earlier pledge to never give up Elgin's rights, traded the first pick to the Chicago Cubs. The Cub organization had been under tremendous public pressure, from the mayor to the populace, to make the local boy their own. Debate raged when the Cubs gave up two top triple-A prospects, along with three future draft picks and an undisclosed amount of cash, to the Astros.

Mr. Thatcher had made it clear that Elgin would not sign with a team that started him lower than double-A and that he was to be invited to spring training the following year—mother/tutor in tow—though his promotion to triple-A or higher could be determined solely by his performance.

The Cubs offered a million dollars, guaranteed, for three years. To some it sounded thin. Other clubs claimed they would have paid more. The Cubs maintained that despite all the publicity and Elgin's obvious potential, they were taking a tremendous and expensive risk.

Elgin proved a bargain. His arm and range and foot speed left him inadequate for any position in the field except first base, and though he was a small target for the infielders, he caught most everything and held his own defensively. He was thrown at, bunted at, run over, and taunted—sometimes even by his own teammates—but when it became clear that his bat had not suffered in the transition to professional ball, he changed a lot of minds.

He and Mr. Thatcher turned down flat the suggestion by the Cubs that they give him the uniform number 1/2.

"He's gonna have enough trouble fitting in without that silliness," Billy Ray said. "If he hits like a child, then give him a child's number. He's already going to look interesting in a real uniform at his size. I mean, he's big for thirteen, but he's still no adult."

Elgin offered to pay to have Luke visit his mother and him on the road, but Luke refused.

"I can't afford it just now," Luke said, but he borrowed a friend's car and saw several of Elgin's games in Illinois and Wisconsin. He and Miriam traded love letters and kept in touch by phone almost daily. She missed him terribly, but he seemed flat on the phone. His letters were simple but passionate, and they warmed her. Somehow, however, she felt more than the miles between them.

After a slow start, which Elgin attributed to nerves and getting used to a better brand of baseball, he caught fire.

Record crowds and media followed him as he ran his average up close to .320. Chicagoans began calling for his promotion to triple-A and even to the big club, which was in fifth place and floundering. The Cubs took a posture Thatcher thought was admirable. They announced that Elgin would not be moved up even to triple-A during that season. There was only a month or so to go, and then their impressive minor leaguers were added to the big league club. Elgin, they said, would not be one of them. He needed some normalcy in his life, and they wanted to bring him along slowly.

He finished with a flourish and garnered just enough at-bats to win the batting title by thirty points at .385.

"He could play in the big leagues today," his manager said. "I just don't know where they'd put him."

⚾ ⚾ ⚾

When the minor league season ended in late August, an exhausted Miriam returned with Elgin to their new address. They had purchased a condominium on the lake front and had one floor gutted without telling the workers what it was for. Elgin hid the machine there and spent hours every day smashing golf balls about the place.

Luke visited Miriam in her new place at the end of the season, and he seemed down.

"Elgin's hittin right now," she told him. "He'll be glad to see you."

"I'll be glad to see him too, but I really need to talk to you."

She led him to the spacious living room. He reminded her that he had seen the place while it was being decorated. "Are you happy with it?" he asked.

"You know me too well," she said. "Let's just say I'm happy for Elgin, because this is gonna be his place someday. When he comes of age or gets married, or whatever he's gonna do, I'm gonna live somewhere else."

"Doesn't he want you to live with him?"

"He thinks he does. But he won't. And I wouldn't. If I was a young wife, I wouldn't want that, no matter how charmin and wonderful my mother-in-law was. And you know I'm charmin and wonderful."

Miriam worried when Luke didn't smile. He just nodded.

"That's a long way off," he said. "Elgin will be gettin interested in girls here soon, but he won't be marryin anybody till he's at least twenty." She nodded. "You could get awful used to livin like this in the meantime," he added.

"Lucas, I will never get used to livin like this. To tell you the truth, I loved the road. I loved doin for Elgin and seein him succeed. I missed my job. I didn't miss some of the men. I missed my friends. I didn't miss the bus rides. In fact, we rode a lot of buses to games. I feel a little funny sittin around here without much to do, and I know that as Elgin does even better, I'll have even less reason to work, but this is not my idea of life, Lucas. Don't think I'm gonna be a woman of leisure."

"But Miriam, look at this stuff. It's gorgeous. I feel like I couldn't even invite you two to my place again. It's tacky, rundown, cheap. I mean, I do all right and I'm not in debt, but compared to this—"

"Why are you comparin it to this? They don't pay shop owners hundreds of thousands of dollars. It's not right and it's not fair, but there it is. I'm keepin close tabs on Elgin so he remembers where he came from. He starts gettin highfalutin on me, I can still deal with him, know what I mean?"

Luke nodded and stood to look out the window at Lake Michigan. "That's one beautiful view."

Miriam stepped behind him and slipped her arms around him. "Lucas, do you not like me anymore, now that I'm livin here?"

He didn't turn around. "Are you kiddin? Miriam, I love you more than ever. It's just that I feel like I'd be holding you back. You don't need me. Elgin can take care of you, and why should you be hangin with a guy like me when you can run in these circles?"

"What do you think, I'm going to meet some bachelor teammate of Elgin's, some veteran with millions of dollars, and he's gonna sweep me off my feet?"

Luke turned around, but still he did not embrace her. His hands were at his sides. "More likely, you'll sweep him off *his* feet."

"You really think that."

"I worry about it. Yeah. There's lots of guys our age in the baseball world, especially as Elgin moves up."

Miriam took his face in her hands. "I don't want guys. I want you."

"Why? What have I got to offer?"

"Who else would have shaved his beard and mustache off just for me?" He didn't smile. "And you've kept it off. Why?"

He shrugged. "For you."

"Then you do still care about me."

"Miriam, don't kid about this, okay?"

She couldn't get him to touch her so she backed away and sat down. He looked miserable and retreated to his chair.

"Lucas, this is not an attractive side of you, this self-pitying, poor-me, I'm-not-worthy-of-you thing. It almost sounds like you're beggin for some strokes. What do you want to hear?"

He sighed. "I want to hear that you still love me as much as I love you, Miriam." His voice was thick. "I want to hear that even though you could live like this, you realize that with me you probably never will."

"Have I ever said anything different?"

"No, but I worry."

"I don't want you to worry, Lucas. You know who I am. You know where I came from. You know how I lived just a few months ago. This is not my place, hon. This is Elgin's. He worked for it. He deserves it. I don't want it. I won't put it down, but I won't get used to it and call it mine. We're a little out of place here, you know. People look at us funny. Oh, they know who Elgin is, and they're proud to have him in the building. But we haven't learned to dress right for the place yet. And we still carry our own grocery bags up on the elevator."

Luke laughed. "Do you really? How tacky."

Now it was Miriam's turn to not smile. "Lucas, I want to tell you this once and for all and not hear another word about it, okay? I don't want you to doubt me. I never thought I'd get a second chance at love, and for it to be so much better than the first is just a gift. No matter where I am, no matter what I'm doing, no matter who I'm with, I'm not lookin for anyone but you. I'm lovin you. I don't know how else to say it."

Luke leaned forward and raised his eyebrows, as if pleased. She wondered if she had finally gotten through to him.

"I don't suppose you'd care to back up that statement?" he said.

"Sure I'll back it up," she said, rising. She went and sat on his lap, wrapping her arms around his neck. She lightly touched his lips with hers, then pressed her mouth to his as if she wanted to drink him in. She kissed him long enough to make her point, she hoped, then pulled her head back.

"I love you, Lucas. You got it?" He laughed. She stood quickly. "That was not intended to be funny, Lucas!" She turned to move away from him, but he caught her hand.

"I'm not laughing at you," he said.

"I'm the only one here."

"No, it's funny because when I asked you if you cared to back up your statement, that wasn't what I had in mind."

"Well, I'm sorry! What did you have in mind?"

"I was thinking more of something like this."

He reached in his pocket and pulled out a small box. Before she could even reach for it, he opened it and the diamond caught the sunlight from the window.

60

ELGIN CAME DOWN A TIGHT SPIRAL STAIRCASE, helmet on and fungo bat in hand. His mother and Luke stood in an amorous embrace, making the other kiss look like child's play.

"Hey, guys," he said, assuming they would compose themselves in embarrassment. For a few seconds they ignored him. "I just hit a hundred and five line drives, every one a solid shot."

Luke and Miriam pulled back and looked at each other, smiling. They looked at Elgin and spoke in unison. "Who cares?"

⚾ ⚾ ⚾

The ring had been the reason Luke could not afford to travel more with Miriam and Elgin. It was not a stone typical of Luke's station in life, though it wasn't gaudy either. Miriam had never worn a diamond, and she was thrilled.

They agreed to put off their wedding until just before spring training. They knew it would be hard on a new marriage for Miriam to be on the road much of the baseball season, especially not knowing where Elgin might land in the Cub organization. The only thing they knew for sure was that Elgin would be in Arizona for spring training, and that that would make a nice honeymoon trip. Meanwhile, Luke expanded his business and put away profits so he could invest in a home where the three of them would live during the off-seasons while Elgin was in the minors. Elgin would work out at his place on Lake Shore Drive and continue to furnish it for the day it would become his private home.

During the off-season, Elgin's time was taken with personal appearances, school (he was a full grade ahead already, having surged academically with all the free time he and his mother had during the season), and running through his three-hour-a-day workout. His mother had told him frequently how proud she was that he was not living on past achievements.

"Are you kidding, Momma? I haven't made it yet, and even when I do, I can't let up. The only way to be the best is to work the hardest, and the only practice that makes perfect—"

"Is perfect practice," she said. "Neal Woodell lives."

Elgin thought of his promise to his dad. The time had not yet come.

Luke purchased a brownstone in a nicer part of Chicago and did most of the refurbishing himself. Miriam helped as she was able. During one of those sweaty, late fall sessions with drywall dust in their hair and paint on their hands, Miriam grew melancholy and told Luke one of her life's secrets.

"You know what I've always wanted to do, Lucas? Ever since I lost my baby girl?"

Luke was drilling. He spoke between punches on the trigger. "Tell me. Just don't tell me that beatin story again. I hate that story. Makes me want to kill a guy who's already dead."

"I shouldn't do that to Neal, speak of him now that he's gone. And I did forgive him."

Luke took a break, setting the drill on the floor and settling himself against a studded wall. "Tell me your dream, love."

"I'd like to open a home for girls."

He slowly looked up at her. "I can't believe you've never told me that."

"Me either. It's always been in my heart. I wanted a daughter. I had a daughter. I've never even discussed this with Elgin."

"This is too unbelievable," Luke said.

"Oh, honey, I don't expect to still do it. I know my life is going to be too hectic for a lot of years, especially if Elgin becomes a big leaguer and we're married and all."

"No," he said, "it's unbelievable because ever since I was in the military I've had a soft spot in my heart for orphans. Lucy and I had decided to wait to have kids till I got back because we were afraid somethin might happen to me over there. Then I come back to bury her. Now it's too late for me to be a father. I think that's one of the reasons I like Elgin so much."

"I thought it was just because he was mine."

"He's yours, all right. You guys are like this." He held up two fingers.

"So what are you tellin me, second-hand man?"

He smiled. "Keep dreamin, that's all. You never know. My store is sure not as much fun as watchin that kid play ball, and you're so antsy not workin, you might as well have somethin to do that's so big it would never get done."

"You mean takin in a bunch of girls or finishin this monstrosity?"

"I thought you liked this place!"

"Nope. I'm only humoring you."

"I *had* to buy this place! I'm marryin this rich woman who's impossible to please."

⚾ ⚾ ⚾

By spring, Elgin had grown another inch and had bulked up. He had turned down an opportunity to play winter ball because his mother and Mr. Thatcher thought it would be better for him to be in school and live at home. He was on a diet and weight program developed for him by the Cub trainer. It was working.

He arrived in Arizona with his mother and her new husband, and the media made them stars. Few would believe the strapping young first baseman was not yet fourteen. His birthday a few days later made newscasts around the country.

"You think I'm ready for second base?" he asked his minor league manager.

"Uh, no."

Elgin shrugged and took the field. If there was a surprise at spring training, it was the sheer number of ballplayers who showed up from various levels throughout the organization. He was most impressed to see the guys he had watched on television since he moved to Chicago. He didn't know whether to ask for autographs or make himself scarce. Some of them treated him like a batboy. Others scowled at him and left him alone.

Three of the big league Cub starters were great. Bob Henson, the left fielder, Ken Clark, the catcher, and Luis Sanchéz, the shortstop, asked his mother if they could take him to dinner one night.

"We'll baby-sit," Luis told Miriam. Elgin had a pleading look in his eye.

"I'm inclined to allow this," Miriam said, realizing these were all family men. "Come here a moment, Mr. Sanchéz." Luis giggled as he tried to mimic her accent in spite of his own and winked at his friends as she dragged him off to the side. “This is the type of thing I think will be good for Elgin,” she said. “But you understand I don’t want him at any bars. I don’t even want you guys drinkin when he’s with you. No funny stuff. You’re responsible, and I want him home by nine.”

“Oh, man!” Luis complained. “You sound like my father-in-law, before he was my father-in-law!”

“Any funny stuff, Luis, and you’re in deep weeds with me. And you don’t want that.”

“You’re right, I don’t. We’ll just go to dinner and bring him home. We’re goin to a movie, but I just realized it’s probably one you wouldn’t want him to see.”

“What is it?”

“Let’s just say we’re not takin our wives, so don’t ask.”

“You’re right. Bring him home first.”

“You got it.”

Miriam was a nervous wreck from the time Ken Clark raced out of the parking lot in his BMW until she heard him pull into the driveway at their condo just after eight-thirty. Elgin had had a wonderful time.

“Man, it’s going to be great growing up on this team.”

“If you make it,” Luke said.

“C’mon, Lucky!” Elgin said. “You’re the one who’s always telling me to keep believing in myself.”

“I just don’t want to see you getting overconfident.”

“I won’t. Man, those guys gossip. It’s fun.”

“It’s also wrong,” Miriam said. “What’d they say?”

Luke roared.

“There’s a guy on this club with drug problems,” Elgin said. “Cocaine, I think.”

“Who?”

“Gerry Snyder.”

“The first baseman?” Luke said. “He’s been in rehab before. He’s hitting good right now.”

“Yeah, but these guys think he’s still in trouble with drugs.”

“They shouldn’t be sayin that,” Miriam said. “Especially not to you.”

“Oh Momma, it makes me feel like part of the team.”

Maybe so, Miriam thought, but that was the end of going out with the guys.

⚾ ⚾ ⚾

Despite all the media attention, the Cubs wisely kept Elgin on a B team in spring training, playing him sparingly against the regulars and keeping the pressure off him. When he played, he played first base, and there was no harassing him because the coaches protected him. When the team left Arizona for the regular season, Elgin had hit a shade over .300 but with fewer at-bats than most other players. He was assigned to triple-A where he played backup first base to an overweight twenty-four-year-old named Biff Barnett who hit towering home runs to the opposite field when he wasn't striking out. He had hit .229 the previous season and showed a decent glove for a big man. The Cubs had high hopes for him as a run-producer. Until Elgin Woodell showed up.

Elgin went five-for-seven in a blowout first game of a doubleheader, and when the coaches approached Biff about letting Elgin play the second game too, just to see how many hits he could get in one day, Biff jumped the club and never came back.

By the time Elgin had his first hitless game, seven weeks later, Biff Barnett was pumping gas at the family franchise station in Burns Flat, Oklahoma. Elgin was hitting well over .300 and the country was following him in *The Sporting News* and clamoring for his graduation to the bigs.

The problem was Gerry Snyder. The Cub first baseman was leading the team in RBIs and batting .310 himself. He was one of the best glove men in the majors, a left-hander who had the ability to almost always cut down the lead runner.

The Cubs contended for the Eastern division lead during the first three months of the season, then hit a slump and found themselves ten games out of first and slipping toward fourth. Banners appeared in the stands:

"It's Time for Elgin!"

"Bring Up Woodell, Woodja?"

Had it not been for Snyder's drug problem resurfacing, the Cubs had planned to quietly bring Elgin up. They told Mr. Thatcher that they hoped to have him in Chicago and in uniform before the media found out. It wasn't that they didn't want to capitalize on his newsworthiness; they just didn't want to appear to be doing that. They had planned to sneak him into the last three innings of a makeup game, and then start him in the annual Cubs-Sox game at Comiskey Park.

But two weeks before that, Gerry Snyder turned himself in. He was back on drugs and in trouble financially. He said he put off asking for help again because he feared his job would not be there when he got back, "and everybody in this city knows why. I played with the kid in spring training."

61

BILLY RAY THATCHER FLEW INTO CHICAGO early on a July Wednesday morning and headed straight for Wrigley Field. After an hour meeting with the brass and stopping by the clubhouse to pick up a package, he drove to Lucky's Second-hand Shop.

"Ready?" he asked Luke, shaking the smiling man's hand.

"You don't even have to ask." Luke was in a new suit with a tie and new shoes. He turned the sign around and locked up, checking his watch and patting his back pocket for his wallet. "We gonna make it?"

"Plenty of time," Thatcher said. "Plane hits the ground at eleven."

Miriam and Elgin had booked flights in their own names to O'Hare, at Thatcher's instruction, then received at their hotel an Express Mail package with tickets to Midway Airport under aliases.

"Elgin doesn't need a big welcome at the airport," Billy Ray had explained. The secret arrival worked. The press showed up at O'Hare.

"How'd you do last night?" Billy Ray asked on the way to the Lake Shore condo.

"It was only my worst game this year," Elgin said. "I think that was the first time I ever struck out twice in a game."

"And in such a long career," Thatcher said. "Any hits?"

"Nope. Hit one pretty good to center, but I'm still only gettin em out there about three hundred feet. Grounded into a double play. Made an error."

"Humph," Thatcher said. "I don't think I'd start you tonight. Leverance is on the mound."

"Nobody told me that. He's gonna win the Cy Young this year, you know. That'll be the second year in a row the Dodgers have had a guy win it. How do they always come up with that pitching? They've been doing it for decades."

Elgin tapped his foot and drummed his knee with his thumb. "Need to spend an hour or so with the machine this afternoon. How we doin on time?"

"Relax," Billy Ray said. "Just treat this like any other game."

They all laughed and Miriam dissolved into tears. "Right, El," she said, smiling and crying at the same time. "It's just another game for a fourteen-year-old starting for the Cubs."

"I have to be there for the press conference at four, remember."

"I still don't know why they're doing that to you, Elgin," Miriam said. "You don't need that today."

"Mom, if I can't handle a press conference I sure can't handle Leverance." He shook his head. "Didn't mean to bring up his name again."

As they entered the condo, Billy Ray trailing with his wrapped bundle, Elgin said he could just as well use a nap as batting practice.

"But could you sleep?" Luke asked.

"Like a baby," Elgin said, smiling.

"You're not gonna get me with that old joke," Luke said. He put his arm around Elgin and drew him close, whispering. "I couldn't be prouder if I was your own dad."

Elgin hugged him in thanks.

"We bout ready to head to the ballpark?" Elgin asked Billy Ray.

Thatcher ignored the question and asked Elgin to sit down. "First," he said, "you need to know that no one in this room, yourself included, is more interested than I am in getting you to Wrigley on time. So please, quit worrying about that. You want to work out, fine. Don't overdo it. Get yourself sharp, work off a little nervousness, whatever. Now, before you get all hot and sweaty, and before you have to dress in the coat and slacks your mother has selected for the press conference, I want to give you a slightly belated birthday present."

"You already got me a birthday present, Mr. Thatcher. What's this?"

"Well, it's not really from me," Thatcher said, handing him the package. "It's from your employers."

No one spoke as Elgin removed the strings and tore away the brown paper, revealing the new home and away Cub uniforms. There is nothing, Elgin decided, like the real thing. He had worn leftover, football-numbered, hand-me-down jerseys in the minors that sometimes didn't even match the pants. Here were beautiful whites and grays with shiny blue numbers and letters, red piping, logos in place.

"Turn that one over, honey," Miriam said. "The away jersey should have your name on it."

Elgin turned the gray Chicago jersey over and fought to keep his composure. He bit his lip hard but lost the battle. Under the crisp, perfect lettering that read WOODELL were two huge and beautiful digits: 16.

Elgin's face contorted and the tears came. "Daddy's number. How did they know?"

Mr. Thatcher put a hand on his shoulder. "I wonder. Somebody told me you and your daddy had the same agent."

⚾ ⚾ ⚾

Miriam was still dabbing her eyes when Elgin emerged with the away uniform on. He padded around in stocking feet, looking in the mirror and tugging at the cap. She still couldn't believe it. Elgin looked like a long, lanky teenager, maybe four years older than he was, but he sure looked small in that uniform. Had it been that long ago that he begged to play on a team that had both shirts and pants?

"Sure beats that old T-shirt, doesn't it, El?"

"I can't believe this," he said, turning to show her the back again. "I'll always think of that name on there as Dad's, not mine."

She knew his emotion had as much to do with nervousness as it did sentiment for his father, but she had to admit it was sad that Neal wasn't here to see this.

Elgin tried on the uniform he would wear that night. Somehow, in the pure white with the blue pinstripes, he looked even smaller. He's a child, a baby, Miriam told herself, playing a man's game for all the right reasons. If people ever wondered what they came to the ballpark for, they'd know after they saw her son play that night.

She knew he would hustle on and off the field, would run out every grounder, encourage every teammate, know every situation. He played baseball the way it was meant to be played, and he enjoyed it as no one ever had or ever would again.

If anybody deserved this, she decided, Elgin did. He had taken no shortcuts, never got discouraged, always bounced back. What other kid on the face of the earth would have spent as much time with that crazy machine that flung those rock-like balls at him from so many different directions at blinding speed? Gifted? Sure he was, but he had begun honing his gifts from the first day.

She and Luke and Mr. Thatcher would be in a private box with Cub executives when Elgin was introduced to the standing-room-only crowd for the first time. Miriam knew she would be good for nothing, probably not even able to clap for him. She stuffed two packets of tissue in her purse and dressed in a way she hoped would make Elgin, and Lucas, proud of her.

She would have less and less influence on Elgin as the season went by and as his years in the majors continued, but she felt good about that. She would stay close enough to keep him humble, to remind him who he was and who he wasn't. But tonight he would become a baseball legend, and she wouldn't get in the way of that for anything.

Miriam stood at the rim of the crowd of reporters and cameramen at the late afternoon press conference. If she could have been invisible, she would have been. This was Elgin's moment. She didn't need or want the spotlight. Let him have it. She couldn't have imagined Elgin looking smaller or younger, with the manager on one side of him, the GM on the other, and the president and owner's representative behind.

"Gentlemen," the GM intoned, "I know this is a historic day, but we'll have to move it along, because this young man has to be on the field soon. He has a job."

There were the usual photos of handshakes and holding up uniforms. Then Elgin asked for the away jersey. "This is the one I'm proudest of," he said. "My dad's number was sixteen, and of course his name was Woodell. I've learned a lot from all the coaches I've had, but I'm really here because of my dad. He's gone now, but he was the one who really taught me the game and made me love it and work at it. Thank you, Daddy."

62

ELGIN RECEIVED A WARM OVATION from the standing-room-only crowd at Wrigley that night when he jogged out for infield practice at first base. His dream had been to play before a crowd of substance, of real numbers. Now, with at least four times the people who had ever seen him play riveting their eyes on him alone, he felt embarrassed, self-conscious. He had heard of butterflies in the stomach. His were moths.

Every grounder or pop or throw to him seemed strange. It was as if he were aware of every move. Nothing was natural. Did he, he wondered, look as tight and awkward and out of place as he felt? In batting practice he fouled off several pitches and chuckled to himself that no one would believe it, but he had always hated batting practice. If the real pitches thrown in live games by men whose livelihoods depended on getting hitters out seemed slow compared to the machine, BP pitches looked like beach balls hanging in the air. They were more of a detriment than a help to Elgin's eye.

The scoreboard flashed the news that the youngest player in the history of baseball would be starting that night, as if it was news to anyone. He ran out for the top of the first inning, having been announced as batting eighth and playing first. How strange it felt, throwing grounders to infielders like Luis Sanchéz, the shortstop he'd idolized on television and had met only in spring training.

Elgin felt that same nervousness he'd had in the pregame workout, but it began to subside when the Cub starter threw his last warm-up toss and Ken Clark rifled the ball to second. Elgin tossed his ball toward the dugout and watched the others throw the game ball around before delivering it back to the mound.

Clark had reminded Elgin that he should care as much about the signal as the pitcher, "because you'll start to learn where the ball is going off the bat if you know what we're trying to throw the guy."

Elgin found himself hoping for a routine grounder to second so he could receive a nice, easy, early throw. He knew that was the wrong attitude. He should hope for a big league line drive right at his feet, and he should be prepared to go on automatic pilot and prove he belonged here.

But did he? The stadium was so huge and green and bright. He felt like a pretender. Am I a fake? Get ready. What if I make a fool of myself? Where did all that confidence go? He knew his belief in his ability had been as responsible as the pitching machine for his miraculous rise.

The big, bearded Roger Densing was on the mound. He was the oldes Cub, a veteran of eleven years. He'd won a Cy Young, and though his fast ball had slowed into the high eighties, he was still an intimidating force.

Ken Clark called for a fastball in, and the leadoff hitter skied a high pop to third. Elgin was relieved he had not been in on the play but wished the Cubs used a throw-around routine after the out that included the first baseman. He needed something to do to get his mind off himself and into the game. He almost didn't notice that Clark had jogged to the mound and was motioning Elgin to join him.

It wasn't cool, he knew, but he nearly sprinted to the mound. He was embarrassed, knowing he looked like a Little Leaguer doing that. Elgin arrived and looked expectantly at Clark. He was honored to have been invited and had always wondered what these guys talked about. But Clark wasn't looking at him. He was looking at Densing, who turned and glared at Elgin. He wasn't making it obvious for the crowd or even the TV cameras, but when he spoke softly in a gravelly voice, Elgin heard him well.

"Who was coverin first on that play?" he said.

"Well, I—"

"Runner was doggin it to first base. That ball drops, we still get him if our first baseman's covering. You were five feet away and watchin the play. He drops it, you try to get back, you're a small target anyway, he throws it away, and they'd have a guy in scoring position."

The ump started toward them, and Clark backed away. Densing continued. "I don't care if you're three years old and the best thing that's come along since quiche on a stick. Don't miss a trick. Do the little things right. We're throwin this guy low and away four straight times if we have to. He hates to walk so he's gonna put one of these in play and it's probably gonna come to the right side. You're gonna be in on a play, Rookie, so get your butt in the game. Okay?"

Elgin's face burned as he hurried back into position. He found himself too close to the grass and Clark was waving him back. But what if there was a bunt? He didn't care. For now he would just obey.

First pitch, hard and down, off the outside corner. Batter swings. Ball is between first and second. Elgin breaks to his right on the swing. He bends and reaches, still on the dead run, and backhands the ball. Densing is all arms and belly, angling to cover first. Elgin plants and fires as he pivots, leading Densing by a step. The big pitcher catches up to the throw as he draws parallel to the line and beats the runner to the bag.

Elgin is smacked hard on the seat by the second baseman and is suddenly aware of the cheering crowd. This was a play they had seen the left-handed Gerry Snyder make in his sleep. But who knew the rookie would be up to it?

Ken Clark had followed the runner down the line and as he took the ball from Densing before throwing it around the infield, they both stopped and jabbed index fingers at Elgin and made gunshot noises, as if to say, "That play was *yours*, buddy, and it was big league!" Elgin could have done a cartwheel. Best of all, he had made the play without thinking.

With two outs the third hitter sent a grounder to Sanchéz at short. Luis looked the ball into his glove, then came up searching not for Elgin's glove but his eyes. It was as if the shortstop were saying, "Look how easy we make it for you here," before Elgin knew the joy of taking a long, hard throw straight to the glove. Elgin had enough presence of mind to turn and toss the ball to the first base umpire, who said, "Nice inning, Rook."

The Cubs didn't fare much better against Leverance, so Elgin didn't come up until he led off the bottom of the third. The self-conscious nervousness returned in the on-deck circle as he watched the heavy, hard strikes popping the catcher's glove. As his name was announced he heard the thunderous applause, but when he stepped in left-handed against the Cy Young candidate, he was suddenly on automatic again.

Leverance's first pitch was a straight fastball that he should have jumped on. Strike one. Would this guy dare another fastball, just like that one? Of course he would. He wouldn't suspect a kid could hit his best pitch.

It was on the outside corner, and Elgin sent his third base coach diving out of the way of a screaming foul. The crowd laughed, then cheered. Was that the lucky swing of a child, late on a big league fastball? They could think that only until the next one came inside and Elgin did the same to his first base coach.

Regardless how impressive he was, Elgin was still down oh-and-two and would not likely see another hittable fastball. He waited, patient, reaching out to foul off pitches that were close enough to be called strikes but not fat enough to hit hard. Eventually he ran the count full. When Leverance lost him on a pitch at chin level, the crowd was merciless to the pitcher.

Densing pushed Elgin to second on a sacrifice bunt, and Leverance nearly threw the ball into center on a pickoff play that might have otherwise caught Elgin. Leadoff man Mike Martinez followed with a double in the gap, and Elgin ran so hard and fast that he nearly stumbled twice. How sweet to feel his spikes dig into that plate and score his first big league run.

When he got to the dugout, no one looked at him. Elgin looked hopefully into the eyes of the reserves and coaches. It was as if they hadn't realized he was back.

"Well," he said, sitting and clapping his thighs with his palms. "One to nothing, huh?"

"Yup," someone said on his way to the water cooler.

"Yeah?" someone else said. "How'd we score?"

"How'd we score?" Elgin said. "Well, I just did when Martin—" but he stopped when he realized what was going on and before he had made a fool of himself. Only then did the guys on the bench takes turns congratulating him.

Elgin popped out in the fifth, again to a huge ovation. When he came to the plate batting righty against a fireballing lefty reliever in the seventh, he was welcomed by the crowd as a new friend. He felt as if he had done little so far.

"All heat," the previous hitter told him as he trudged to the bench after a strikeout. "Just try to get wood on it."

It had been years since Elgin had simply tried to get his bat on a ball. He wasn't going to reach out and hope for the best. He was going up there to drive the ball. The first pitch was hard and tight, just off the inside corner. Ball one.

The next one should be the fastball on the outside corner, Elgin guessed. If he was wrong, he might get plunked. If he was right, he would take the pitch to the opposite field...

As Elgin slid into second, well ahead of the throw from the right center-field ivy, he couldn't remember having rounded first or looking to the third base coach. All he knew was that he had his first major league hit, and the crowd was up and roaring. Roger Densing stood silently a couple of feet from the box, leaning on his bat and letting Elgin have his moment.

That one was for you, Dad, Elgin thought, and he knew his dad would be telling him to keep his head in the game. The Cubs were up by three, but it was time to try to put this thing away.

Densing called to the pitcher and asked for the ball. He gave it to the batboy, who was older than Elgin, and the kid ran it to the dugout.

Densing sacrificed Elgin to third, and Elgin scored when the second baseman erred on Martinez's grounder. The Cubs knocked the reliever out of the box, and Elgin batted again in the eighth, forcing a runner at second to finish one-for-three plus a walk and two runs scored.

When he got to his locker, he found the ball Roger Densing had removed from the game. The big pitcher had dated it and written: "The first of many."

That, above all, Elgin realized as he dressed hurriedly and prepared to face the press, was his ultimate goal: that this was simply the beginning. He had found a level of competition that would challenge him, and he wanted it to last forever.

Miriam stood in the bowels of the stadium at the players' exit, waiting with Luke while Mr. Thatcher went in to be at Elgin's side for the crush of the press. She looked at her husband, her lips pressed to hold back a torrent of emotion. She was grateful that Luke seemed to know there were no words worthy of the occasion.

She was as proud as a mother could be, and while she was not naive enough to believe it would be all smooth sailing, she looked forward to the ride. Her man-child had already achieved his dream.